Traumatic Divorce and Separation

Traumatic Divorce and Separation

THE IMPACT OF DOMESTIC VIOLENCE AND SUBSTANCE ABUSE IN CUSTODY AND DIVORCE

Lisa Fischel-Wolovick

OXFORD
UNIVERSITY PRESS

OXFORD
UNIVERSITY PRESS

Oxford University Press is a department of the University of Oxford. It furthers
the University's objective of excellence in research, scholarship, and education
by publishing worldwide. Oxford is a registered trade mark of Oxford University
Press in the UK and certain other countries.

Published in the United States of America by Oxford University Press
198 Madison Avenue, New York, NY 10016, United States of America.

© Oxford University Press 2018

CIP data is on file at the Library of Congress
ISBN 978–0–19–027598–3

9 8 7 6 5 4 3 2 1

Printed by WebCom, Inc., Canada

CONTENTS

PREFACE

In 1980, while working as a hospital social worker, a severely injured battered woman was admitted to my service. X-rays revealed that she had old fractures that were poorly healed. This time her husband had beaten her with a chain when she spoke to a neighbor in the hallway of their apartment building.

My client was a soft-spoken mother of two children who was anxious to make sure that her children were safe. After an incident in which her husband attempted to visit her at the hospital, we began safety planning to find a place where she could stay with her children. While my client had family, staying with them was not a viable option as her husband knew where they lived. The police had been called to her home on numerous occasions, but, until the night when she was brought to the hospital emergency room, he had never been arrested. It was apparent that the batterer's abuse had escalated to lethal levels, and her doctors did not believe that she could survive another beating; her ribs had been broken, puncturing her lung.

With my client's permission, I began to investigate how best to protect her, calling the prosecutor assigned to her case. I learned that the judge had released the defendant without bail because he was employed. He had been charged with attempted assault in the third degree, a misdemeanor. Advocating for my client with the prosecutor, I argued that if she had been attacked by a stranger the charges would have included felony assault and advocated that more serious charges were necessary. However, the prosecutor was not optimistic, believing that my client would not cooperate; he reluctantly agreed to investigate further. Finally, supported by the hospital records, the prosecutor informed me that if my client would testify before the Grand Jury, the State would bring felony charges. Without her testimony, the case would be dismissed.

Entering the citywide shelter system did not ensure anonymity, and so I began to investigate where my client could safely live with her children after being discharged from the hospital. I learned that, in 1980, there was one domestic violence shelter in New York City—with a total of four beds—and all were filled. I continued to call this shelter daily without success.

Later that week, I received a panicked message from my client: her husband had removed the children from her mother's apartment. When children's protective services were notified, we were informed that the fact that he had beaten my client did not mean that he was not a good father. Over the next forty years, I have continued to hear these same comments about abusive fathers from many judges, attorneys for the children, and mental health professionals regardless of the extent of the injuries or the risks involved in continued unsupervised contact.

I spoke to my client daily, assuring her that I would continue to try to find her a safe place to live, and, if that failed, her testimony before the Grand Jury might ensure that his parole would be revoked. But one morning I found her hospital bed empty and was informed that she had left a few hours earlier to find her children, without leaving an address. She did not testify before the Grand Jury, and the charges were dismissed. I never heard from her again.

This was the moment when I first recognized how we make assumptions about survivors of domestic violence while failing to provide them with the means to protect their children. Since the 1980s, law enforcement and the criminal justice system have made considerable progress in combating domestic violence. Federal and state funding has resulted in increased services for battered women that include domestic violence shelters, treatment, and civil legal services. Federal laws have provided for funding for necessary training of law enforcement and the judiciary, which has improved the criminal justice system's response. The development of model courts to address the problems of families impacted by domestic violence, substance abuse, and mental illness has enhanced the criminal justice response by ensuring increased resources and attention to these problems. Finally, prosecutions are enhanced by expert testimony on the impact of domestic violence and the admission of medical records when women are afraid to testify.

However, battered women today are still hampered by their inability to protect their children from further abuse. Many women fear that if they leave the abusive relationship they could lose custody of their children or that their children will have significant unsupervised contact with their fathers. Theories have developed that minimize the risks of separation and veracity of such allegations, and, as a result, battered women and their children continue to be exposed to life-threatening trauma, threats, stalking, and abuse. Many mothers who stay in such relationships have been treated punitively by child protective services, even as they seek to protect their children.

After completing law school, I began to work in the field of domestic violence, clerking for a judge and helping to organize the first New York State model criminal court that handled only cases of domestic violence. I began the enormous task of researching and learning about domestic violence and trauma. Later, after leaving the court system, I went on to represent battered women in custody and divorce litigation, something that I have continued to do to this day. My interdisciplinary perspective provided the context for my work and research on abuse and trauma, confirming my understanding that my clients and their children frequently displayed symptoms of such exposure. Often such exposure is intensified during litigation, or "traumatic divorce," when clients are forced to have ongoing contact with batterers in ways that have endangered their safety and that of their children.

The history of the treatment of domestic violence survivors in the courts is part of what Evan Stark refers to as the "long march" for justice. During the seven years that I worked on this book, theories have been updated and new research made available. Advances in our understanding of trauma, public health, and the legal responses to domestic violence are often followed by missteps and losses. Even the terminology has changed as we have shifted from a discussion of domestic violence to intimate partner violence, which can include the elderly and LGBT community.

Today, the family court's failure to address trauma and the safety concerns of battered women and their children is a costly one. The research on the medical and mental health consequences of long-term exposure to abuse has indicated that the impact of domestic violence on women and children during traumatic divorce and separation will haunt us for many years. There are many myths and misconceptions about domestic violence and human behavior that are all too common in the family courts and that prevent the development of trauma-informed custody and divorce jurisprudence. It is my hope that this book will help to change the conversation in the family courts to protect public health and safety.

Finally, it has been my privilege to represent women who refused to be defined by the abuse they experienced, who possessed great courage, and, even when terrified, endured traumatic divorce and separation to confront their abusers. It is through this body of work and study that I have had the insight to write about traumatic divorce.

ACKNOWLEDGMENTS

There have been many people who have offered their help and support while I wrote this book, and if I have inadvertently omitted anyone accept my sincere thanks. First and foremost, this book would not be possible without the help and vision of my editor Dana Bliss and all the staff at Oxford University Press: thank you.

It would be impossible not to acknowledge my father, Daniel Fischel, a writer and editor who empowered many writers, including myself, to find our individual voice. As my first reader, my father was instrumental in encouraging my work and quietly prodding me to continue this effort. It is an enduring loss that my father died just two weeks after I finished the final chapters of this book, but comforting to know that he realized that this long undertaking was finally completed.

There have been many people who have provided help and encouragement through the years, whom I acknowledge and thank: my friend and colleague Nancy Erickson for her insights, willingness to read sample chapters, and answer questions at all hours of the day and night; colleagues, Dorchen Leidholdt; Chitra Raghavan of the City University of New York, at John Jay College; and Stephanie Brandt. Jennifer Collins and Jenna Taono provided essential research assistance, and my thanks to Laura Cheatham, my teaching assistant. My friends Emily Kelman-Bravo and Sue Ellen Dodell were enthusiastic supporters of this effort, to name a few. The engagement of my forensic psychology students at the City University of New York at John Jay College during this time provided an enlivened environment for the discussion of the "marketplace of ideas" so necessary for research.

I have been blessed with brilliant teachers and colleagues: Phyllis Caroff, at the Hunter College School of Social Work who, along with the late Florence Lieberman, demonstrated that learning is a lifelong task. My special thanks to Evan Stark who has been unfailingly generous with his time and whose knowledge and insight into domestic violence is unsurpassed and breathtakingly precise. I also thank Marjory Fields, my first teacher in domestic violence and child abuse, for her willingness to share her library, her experiences, and answer questions. I thank them all for their assistance and acknowledge that any deficiencies are mine. While my work with my clients has enhanced my understanding of domestic violence, I have changed their names and identifying information to protect their privacy.

My thanks to my parents Daniel and Maxine Fischel. All my children have contributed to this effort in their own unique ways as, over the years, I have learned from having been their parent and stepparent. Michael Wolovick provided his invaluable research support at all hours, and Sara Wolovick contributed her updated knowledge of legal research. Finally, my husband David Wolovick never stopped supporting this effort every day, in more ways than I can enumerate here; expressing gratitude and thanks does not begin to describe my feelings.

Lisa Fischel-Wolovick
April 29, 2017

Traumatic Divorce and Separation

1

Identifying the Problem
TRAUMATIC DIVORCE AND SEPARATION

Over the years, I have represented women and children in custody and divorce litigation and have come to understand the hidden nature of the harmful policies that impact vulnerable families. This book attempts to focus on separating families, married or unmarried, impacted by domestic violence, trauma, and the related problems of mental illness and substance abuse. The problems of these families, during what I have called traumatic divorce and separation, are not readily identified by the legal system. These at-risk families challenge the legal system and mental health professionals. Their problems are not readily ameliorated as the legal system's approach to such vulnerable families during litigation frequently fails to recognize the traumatic nature of their problems and is unable to protect them from the long-term impact of abuse. Such families are at risk.

At-risk families without children also have safety and financial concerns that typically cannot be resolved without prolonged litigation. What distinguishes them is the inability of one family member to negotiate. Rather, one person will respond to even mild disagreements with an arsenal of controlling behaviors that is well known to the other family members. In traumatic divorce and separation, although physical violence should not be minimized, the use of financial control, threats to wrest custody of the children, to bankrupt the other spouse, and similar coercive measures also have long-term consequences and are an inherent part of their lives.

The legal system is unable to accurately identify these troubled families without a conceptual understanding of abuse, defined by Stark as coercive control.[1] Without such an empirical understanding, the courts frequently fail to recognize the patterns of domestic violence that can include not only physical abuse, but also harassment and sexual, economic, and legal abuse. Identifying the high-risk implications of domestic violence, mental illness, and substance abuse is a complex process.

It is in the integrated context of divorce and trauma theory that traumatic divorce and separation can be more clearly identified so that women and children can receive the structure and support they need, as domestic violence is frequently a source of trauma. Families with high-risk factors are frequently difficult to identify at the onset as the family members may have impressive work histories and strong community roles. Their legal concerns—custody, support, parenting access, decision-making, and the allocation of financial resources—are no different from those of any other family, yet they remain engaged in traumatic conflict for years, whether in litigation, mediation, or in new forms of alternative dispute resolution, such as parenting coordination.

Researchers agree that most separating families resolve their differences without the assistance of the courts.[2] For those less-distressed families, children experience multiple transitions that typically include relocation, economic difficulties, and the addition of new family members.[3] Hetherington and Stanley-Hagan also found that children from these families frequently experienced anxiety, depression, anger, and antisocial behavior in the months following divorce. These early researchers additionally concluded that adults experienced isolation and significant stress in the first year following their divorce and that women experienced financial difficulties as well.[4] They noted that children who experienced divorce may demonstrate difficulties in their relationships, including problems with parents, siblings, peers, and teachers. However, Hetherington and Stanley-Hagan concluded that many children and adults from divorced families go on to lead healthy and productive lives.

It is important to understand that even when there is an absence of abuse many parents experience grief and anger during separation and divorce, and these emotions will be evident to their children, and parents and adults may need mental health services. Johnston et al. indicated that many children have difficulty understanding the reasons behind their parents' divorce depending on their ability to comprehend interpersonal interactions, which may be limited by their stage of development.[5] Informed treatment can help with their adjustment to these life changes. In comparison, separating families, whether married or unmarried, that have been impacted by domestic violence, substance abuse, or untreated mental illness frequently suffer from exposure to trauma and have difficulty resolving their problems without the help of the courts.

While intimate partner violence among the elderly and the LGBT community in nontraditional households are problems that should not be minimized, these are beyond the scope of this book, which will focus primarily on domestic violence in custody, divorce, and separation. Given the widespread literature on domestic violence as a gendered crime against women, the differential impact of male violence, and the fact that, over the years, my practice has consisted primarily of the representation of battered women, I will be referring to batterers as men and discussing the systemic impact of abuse on women during custody, separation, and divorce.

The Study of Divorce

The early research on divorce attempted to determine whether children were harmed by their parents' separation and concluded that children had a range of responses to divorce. Social scientists developed a body of research on divorce as an emerging social phenomenon in which more-troubled families were classified as "high-conflict" and less-distressed families were considered "low-conflict." Amato et al. concluded that the well-being of children from the more conflicted families frequently improved after separation, when they transitioned to more stable family life, but the children who experienced the most distress were from the more troubled intact households.[6] It can be inferred from a review of this research that it was the conflict and not the separation that had the most impact on the children's functioning. Significantly, these researchers observed that the more conflicted families reported a history of domestic violence.[7] While these researchers acknowledged the potential impact of such abuse, the prevalence and extent to which the children were affected by the domestic violence was not fully explored in their research. They concluded that, in the more troubled families, the children's problems may have predated the divorce and stemmed largely from what was termed the "marital conflict." However, domestic violence is much more than conflict. Many of these troubled families were taken from a clinical population and also struggled with their history of mental health and substance abuse problems.

The Study of Trauma and Abuse

Herman, the seminal researcher on trauma, found that the experience of horrifying events and victimization, which included a range of experiences including domestic violence, resulted in significant psychological harm.[8] This researcher stressed the importance of treatment in which the therapist can ally with the patients' need to develop their sense of empowerment. Safety, refuge from harm, and a growing sense of control were identified by Herman as essential elements of recovery.

The Impact of Traumatic Exposure

There is an extensive body of empirical research on the cumulative impact of adverse childhood experiences (ACEs) that result in long-term physical and mental health problems for survivors of abuse, as indicated in the research of Kendall-Tackett.[9] For battered women, the research by Jones et al. estimated that between 31% and 84% of domestic violence survivors had symptoms that were consistent with a diagnosis of post-traumatic stress disorder (PTSD).[10] In their study of battered women in domestic violence shelters, they also found that significant numbers had experienced PTSD. While women in domestic violence shelters may not be typical, traumatic experiences are not limited to this population and have been found in veterans and victims of war and domestic violence, regardless of race or social class. Significantly, many trauma victims have been found to respond to treatment. Griffing et al. emphasized the need for treatment for women who have developed symptoms of PTSD because of their exposure to abuse to provide them with appropriate education about possible symptomatology to help them to normalize their experiences.[11]

Some battered women experience significant trauma because of their abuse. However, while researchers disagree about the rates of PTSD, Jones et al. concluded that only 5% of women who were never assaulted displayed symptoms of PTSD, and the experience of being abused by an intimate partner may even intensify affected women's responses. These researchers noted that PTSD symptoms included persistent reexperiencing of the trauma, insomnia, irritability, difficulty concentrating, hypervigilance, fearfulness, anxiety, and psychic numbing.[12] Herman noted the impact of disassociation, as the recollection of the traumatic memory is disconnected from the emotions experienced.[13]

In my practice, I have frequently seen clients devoid of affect recount events that are terrifying, humiliating, and even life-threatening. Sometimes, judges and mental health professionals fail to recognize this lack of affect for what it is—disassociation, a symptom of traumatic exposure—and are unwilling to believe my clients' allegations of abuse. After all, she doesn't seem upset. One of my clients recounted a terrifying event in which her spouse held a gun to her head while her children slept and described this experience as one in which she felt that she was watching a movie that had happened to someone else. Suffering from the impact of trauma, she testified in a tearless, flat, and unemotional voice. An understanding of trauma and the related symptoms of exposure would have enabled the judge to understand why she was not teary and emotional during her testimony and could have allowed for the provision of supervised visitation and an order of protection for herself and the children.

There is some disagreement as to whether there are gender differences in symptoms experienced as a result of trauma. Hourani et al.'s study of gender differences among military men and women found that male and female veterans of combat experienced similar rates and symptoms of PTSD: as they were distressed by reminders of the initial trauma and experienced intrusive thoughts, nightmares, flashbacks, emotional numbing, and hyperarousal.[14] Men were found to experience higher levels of numbing, hypervigilance, and alcohol abuse; women experienced greater distress related to the more violent aspects of war.[15] Herman also found that symptoms such as depression and constriction of affect are persistent and even chronic, lasting for many years, and may be confused with underlying personality traits.[16]

It is well-documented that children exposed to domestic violence frequently experience somatic and psychological complaints that can impact their functioning in many ways. Volpe found that children can experience problems with concentration, confusion, self-blame, flashbacks, or intrusive thoughts about the traumatic experience, as well as social withdrawal, interpersonal stress, decreased intimacy, and later substance abuse.[17] In children, exposure to abuse and childhood maltreatment can also lead to PTSD. In this vein, the fifth edition of the *Diagnostic and Statistical Manual of Mental Disorders* has indicated that infants and toddlers can be diagnosed with PTSD.[18] Alisic and Kleber have noted the difficulty in validly measuring children's symptoms of PTSD, recommending more research, and that children's symptoms of traumatic exposure are frequently different from those of adults; this will be discussed in Chapter 4.[19] In fact, much of the research has observed that the experience of multiple victimizations increases the likelihood of the development of PTSD and trauma-related symptoms. Griffing et al. also noted that women who experience domestic violence often reported exposure to other forms of interpersonal violence, including childhood physical abuse, sexual abuse, and witnessing maternal abuse.[20] However, much more is needed, beyond a listing of the symptoms of traumatic exposure, to understand the impact of custody and visitation decisions on traumatized children. Custody jurisprudence that understands that children who have been exposed to domestic violence are more vulnerable to the impact of other traumatic exposures and that cumulative exposure can result in more serious symptoms, requires that the courts impose long-term solutions to provide safety and promote recovery.

Significantly, the research on divorce did not integrate the emerging research on trauma, traumatic exposure, and PTSD. The literature on high-conflict separations also failed to take into consideration the complex patterns of domestic violence and the need to identify the many ways in which such abuse is manifested. When batterers utilize multiple forms of abuse, Stark has noted that their sole purpose is to create and maintain a power imbalance to control their spouses.[21] However, despite the extensive body of medical and psychiatric research in trauma and PTSD in adults—and even in very young children—trauma is not readily identified or understood by the legal system. Furthermore if such abuse is acknowledged by the courts, there is a profound belief in the importance of fathers in children's lives, even when such fathers have been abusive. Meier has indicated that this belief has created a climate in which battered mothers' allegations of abuse have been treated with suspicion and distrust.[22] This atmosphere is significant for children as exposure to multiple forms of abuse heightens the risks of increased mental health problems in adulthood. For family courts charged with determining the best interest of the children in custody litigation, facilitating recovery during what I have called traumatic divorce means providing children with safety and a sense of control, which can only happen when their mothers are empowered. Women who have been economically abused over a long-term relationship require spousal support, relief from coerced debt, and an acknowledgment that their economic opportunities were impaired because of their abuse. Adams et al. have found that the presence of economic abuse is frequently overlooked, yet most women who have suffered this also experienced physical abuse.[23]

The Court's Response to Domestic Violence

In this subjective environment, it is incumbent upon the legal system to look for ways to minimize biases against mothers in custody and visitation cases. While fathers are more involved than in the past, women continue to remain responsible for the bulk of child-rearing tasks. This trend continues even in families where women work. Parker and Wang have indicated that many working women remain primarily responsible for the management of their households and children, including the selection of schools and child care providers, and they rearrange their schedules when child care arrangements fall through.[24] In some separated families, the parents may have a relationship with minimal conflict and a balanced view of the other. In other families, over time, the children may be able to comfortably live in two households. However, this is not always the case. Imposition of a "one size fits all" visitation schedule does not take into consideration the individual needs of the children.

Despite the enormous impact of trauma, many of my clients have faced their abusers in court, terrified but implacable in their efforts to protect their children's safety and their own. It has been my privilege to represent many such courageous women. However, without the help of the family courts and mental health professionals, their task is daunting, and the likelihood of further abuse is heightened. The courts are a forum in which there are expectations of justice. It is essential that we hold abusive fathers to the standards imposed on mothers, reject exploitation of battered women, and envision a solution in which the long-term implications of such abuses are recognized. The solutions do not lie in stop-gap, short-term measures but require long-term safety measures. These include extended orders of protection, long-term judicial monitoring of supervised visitation and substance abuse programs for offenders, and, finally, a model court system that has sufficient resources to provide structure and support to families. This can only happen when a dramatic effort is made to prevent further harm and to integrate the study of trauma into custody and divorce jurisprudence. This effort must include a discussion of the impact of traumatic exposure, enhancement of resilience through protective measures, and a hard look at the gender-biased theories that can exacerbate the effects of abuse.

Many battered women are highly capable individuals, as mothers, co-workers, and friends. Their children can display enormous resilience to exposure to domestic violence, substance abuse, or mental illness. However, if the family courts are unable or unwilling to recognize such abuse, and thus fail to take the steps necessary to minimize unsupervised exposure, the research supports that long-term medical and psychological problems may develop.[25]

Mental health problems during custody and divorce remain a concern: Juodis et al. found that such problems may be indicators of batterers' future violence and risks.[26] The research on whether batterers have a defined psychiatric diagnosis is inconclusive. However, batterers share common personality traits, exhibiting a significant degree of manipulation and sense of entitlement. In addition, while batterers are not a homogenous group, those who demonstrate significant mental health symptoms and suicidal tendencies should raise "red flags" for the courts and mental health professionals because of the associated risks of increased violence. Furthermore, mental health professionals, including custody evaluators who are often not trained in domestic violence, may not recognize the common traits and risk factors of batterers. However, the family courts see many troubled families who have experienced abuse and child maltreatment, and they must have the understanding and resources to help them.

The family courts' response to these families experiencing traumatic divorce is hampered by inadequate resources, conflicting theories regarding domestic violence and its impact on children, and the intractable nature of domestic violence and substance abuse. The mental health problems associated with some batterers must also be addressed as an additional risk factor. Misconceptions about domestic violence, gender, and the prevalence of domestic violence have created an environment in which the courts minimize the impact of such abuse to the detriment of battered women and their children.

Notably, Stark's research has identified domestic violence as coercive control, in which batterers engage in a pattern of abusive behaviors to exert dominance over women's lives, and described this abuse as a gendered crime against women.[27] Stark later noted that the impact of exposure to domestic violence is well-documented, but also concluded that the batterers' chronic abuse is accompanied by many tactics that are intended to denigrate the batterer's partner and that impact parenting and children's well-being.[28] In addition, economic abuse in the form of coerced debt or identity theft, stalking, harassment, and physical violence are crimes that warrant criminal prosecution and thus should not be minimized during divorce and separation.

Gender Bias in the Courts

The family courts' growing trend of minimizing allegations of domestic violence whether in custody or divorce proceedings has troubled many domestic violence advocates and researchers. Notably, this trend has been reported in several of the more recent gender bias studies which documented the concerns of battered women in New York, Massachusetts, and Arizona.[29] Despite clear advances in the laws requiring judges to consider domestic violence in their custody decisions, such bias persists. Rejection of the existence of abuse, or minimization of it as situational violence, has been used to justify batterers having unsupervised visitation, joint custody, or custody. This can be partially explained by the growing development of psychological theories that assume that women fabricate such charges. This theory has gained widespread acceptance in the family courts despite the lack of empirical data to support it. In addition, extensive research by Trocmé and Bala has demonstrated that false allegations are rare.[30]

However, the underlying gender biases in custody and divorce litigation have created an atmosphere in which such theories can thrive. Meier has indicated that legal standards in custody litigation that adhere to gender neutrality, together with the underlying belief that the fathers' involvement is always desirable, has created a legal environment in which the courts do not adhere to the laws regarding custody and domestic violence. The legal standard to determine custody—the best interests of the child—implies a gender-neutral approach in which either parent can be the preferred custodial parent.[31] However, in families that have experienced domestic violence, gender roles are typically not equal. Also, even in families in which there is an absence of abuse, many mothers work outside the home, and they typically juggle the bulk of child care responsibilities. This pattern is even more exaggerated in families in which there is domestic violence. During custody litigation, the concept of gender neutrality has failed to address the gender inequities that exist in such families because the defining principle of coercive control negates the possibility of gender equality. Thus, application of the best interests of the child standard in determining custody, by its very gender neutrality, fails to address the existence and impact of domestic violence which may be exacerbated by substance abuse. In fact, Dragiewicz has found that the courts frequently hold battered mothers responsible for the impaired relationships between such fathers and their children.[32] Normalization of such abuse and the court's refusal to hold fathers responsible have continued to expose battered mothers and their children to continued risks of physical and psychological harm.

Children remain vulnerable to their abusive fathers' parenting deficits, which are not limited to the risks of abuse, but also includes exposure to their fathers' contemptuous behavior toward their mothers. Bancroft et al. have indicated that such behaviors resonate throughout the family.[33] Changing the current course of practice and adjudication of family law cases requires an understanding of the symptoms of traumatic exposure and the need to provide long-term monitoring of families in traumatic divorce. The family courts have the responsibility, albeit with scarce resources, to help battered women establish safety for themselves and their children. In this, the family courts have not kept pace with the systemic changes in the criminal courts, in which long-term monitoring is available for perpetrators of domestic violence.

Interdisciplinary Collaboration in Divorce and Custody

Many mental health professionals who provide recommendations to the courts regarding custody do not have expertise in the conflicting theories and identification of domestic violence, substance abuse, or child maltreatment. Often, mental health professionals who provide custody evaluations have difficulty understanding the symptoms of traumatic exposure or the validity of children's disclosures. Children's memories and symptoms of sexual abuse are frequently discounted because many mental health professionals lack specialized training in this area. Traumatic memories are vivid, searing, and may have life-long implications. Despite this, when children recount incidents of abuse, the mental health profession and the legal system have enormous difficulty in acknowledging and validating their experiences.

Frequently, mental health professionals avoid working with families already engaged in custody litigation. These families are enormously challenging, and it can be a thankless task for the mental health professional to be subpoenaed for testimony at trial. The result is that a small group of mental health professionals provide custody evaluations and parenting coordination. During custody litigation, it is rare to find a diversity of professional opinions or researchers who have spent considerable time in graduate programs that emphasize domestic violence, child maltreatment, and substance abuse. The courts, relying on such evaluators, have been unable to develop consistent child-centered custody decisions that recognize that families with high-risk factors of abuse require safety and boundaries. Thus, the courts are unable to provide safety and financial security to women struggling to separate from their abusive partners. In such cases, court rulings also fail to empower the protective capacities of nonabusive parents or promote necessary resilience in children.[34]

It is reasonable to assume that, when the courts fail to support battered mothers, their children's ability to rebound from their exposure to trauma will be jeopardized. Sadly, the need to support protective parents, or what has been referred to as the non-offending parents, during custody disputes is not widely understood or encouraged. Prolonged litigation of family law issues, without definitive results that protect children, presents significant public health and safety concerns. Frequently, these high-risk families repeatedly return to court as abusive fathers pursue custody or visitation or attempt to avoid payment of their child support obligations.

Early identification of the high-risk factors of abuse and traumatic divorce can allow the courts to apportion resources to provide fast-tracking for these cases. When necessary, expedited hearings should be held and rulings made that allow for the implementation of orders of protection, supervised visitation, and immediate provision of orders of support.

This book will address the legal standards and practices for the admission of expert evidence as it pertains to custody litigation and the need for training in trauma theory on the part of forensic experts. Lack of training and bias in forensic custody evaluators in domestic violence have also been recognized by Saunders et al. as significant issues that should be addressed.[35] Although the medical profession has made enormous progress in understanding the impact of trauma on memories and the brain, mental health and legal professionals have failed to keep pace with these advances.

Courts are beginning to use mediation and conflict resolution to address the concerns of families, referring to those families engaged in traumatic divorce as experiencing high-conflict divorce. These families are better served when their high-risk factors are assessed and identified appropriately, or they will exhaust such conflict resolution resources. Families engaged in traumatic divorce will later require litigation, often over a period of years, to address— but not resolve—each individual situation they encounter.

The Model Standards of Conduct for Family and Divorce Mediation (Model Standards) indicated that mediating couples must be screened for domestic violence, that such abuse requires specialized training on the part of the mediator, and that, in some instances, these couples were not appropriate for mediation, particularly when there were threats of bodily harm.[36] Concerns about safety, intimidation, and the misuse of the process by the abusive partner have raised significant concerns about the appropriateness of mediation. Ver Steegh noted that, in many instances, domestic violence involves an imbalance of power, making mediation unworkable.[37] Bancroft et al. noted that batterers can be highly manipulative in negotiations by initially taking an extreme position in their negotiations, later making some concessions that may still present problems, and causing battered women to appear inflexible.[38] In my practice, women have reported numerous concerns about the process of mediation, including the mediators' failure to identify or consider the history of abuse and, as a result, being pressured to accept overnight visitation and similar extended access schedules despite their safety concerns. In one instance in my practice, the male mediator shouted at my client, mirroring the batterers' behavior and effectively attempting to browbeat her into accepting a schedule that was not in her children's best interests. In another instance in my practice, the judge shouted at an abused client, directing that she enter mediation despite her concerns. A judicial response that incorporates the model court approach used primarily in the criminal courts can be adapted for use in the civil courts to address high-risk families during custody litigation and divorce. Such courts can provide referrals and monitoring of drug treatment and supervised visitation to minimize safety risks. While a significant group of mental health professionals have begun to provide parenting coordination to these families, it is my position that a controlling or abusive parent is incapable of co-parenting, and thus this form of dispute resolution is not appropriate.

While the importance of physical abuse should not be minimized, it is also essential that we develop court interventions which identify not just current physical abuse, but also recognize the effects of financial and psychological abuse. Screening for these issues will make it easier to address high-risk factors earlier in the divorce process as these underlying concerns contribute to the difficulties involved in resolving traumatic divorces and separations. In my practice, I have also seen many cases in which my clients have also been sexually abused, which has been largely ignored by the courts during custody and divorce litigation. This book acknowledges the significance of other forms of controlling and abusive behaviors and the need to identify these risk factors in assessing the appropriate legal and mental health interventions. Finally, this book will address the need for systemic changes that include specialized graduate training, development of custody and divorce model courts that address the needs of families in traumatic divorce, and independent court monitoring to provide transparency and equal protection.

2

The Impact of Divorce and Separation on Adults, Children, and Adolescents

Social scientists have struggled to understand the rising trend of divorce and the impact on adults and children to differentiate the more troubled families that have a history of domestic violence and substance abuse from those without such concerns. The early research on divorce reflected the commonly held belief that children were better off in two-parent, heterosexual families, even as our understanding of families expanded to include two-income parents, stepfamilies, single-parent families, and same-sex couples. The question of whether children can thrive in other forms of families has haunted our early understanding of divorce. Focusing on conflict and the impact on children, early researchers noted that not all separations impacted families in the same way. In some instances, children and adults gradually adjusted to their changing lives, while, in other families, more serious concerns arose. This might occur whether children lived in homes with a single parent or in intact families. Some of the early researchers noted that more-troubled families experienced domestic violence and referred to them as high-conflict. While these researchers understood that such exposure could be harmful to children's development, they viewed domestic violence as a form of conflict. Researchers concurred that children fared better when the "conflict" stopped, without distinguishing such conflict from abuse. This chapter will discuss the research on divorce and separation, the impact on families and children, and the view of conflict without integration of the research on abuse and trauma that has permeated this field.

Divorcing Families and the Courts

Social scientists originally focused primarily on the difficulties of married couples experiencing divorce. However, the number of unmarried couples has also risen as epidemiologists agree that, following World War II, marriage rates have dropped.[1] Unmarried parents must also resolve issues about custody, visitation, and financial support, and they may engage in prolonged litigation. Thus, my discussion of divorce includes married and unmarried families during separation.

Our understanding of divorce and separation has profound implications for how the courts and mental health professionals respond to the needs of separating families. Divorce in less-distressed families is a crisis in which adults and children may need mental health services and financial support. However, such families are seen less frequently by the family courts and are typically able to resolve their differences without court intervention. In comparison, families with a history of domestic violence, untreated serious mental illness, or substance abuse during separation frequently have safety concerns that must be addressed. Furthermore, abuse can create a toxic environment in which the resulting harm may cause trauma, as clinically defined in the fifth edition of the *Diagnostic and Statistical Manual of Mental Disorders* (DSM-5).[2]

Separating families without a history of trauma and abuse may experience grief, loss, anger, or even relief. While many experience their divorce as a life crisis, not all divorces are traumatic. Our understanding of divorce and separation should include a greater awareness of our own attitudes about gender, culture, class, and abuse to avoid misconceptions and to ensure a sound institutional response. Ahrons noted the influence of personal biases on the part of researchers and the impact these attitudes have had on our understanding of divorce.[3] In families that have a history of intimate partner violence, substance abuse, or untreated serious mental illness, the prevailing beliefs about high-conflict divorce are problematic. Johnston et al. viewed those families as being locked in mutual conflict, involving the court in their prolonged litigation in a highly toxic environment of allegations and distrust.[4] Their position is at odds with that of researchers in domestic violence who advocate for the courts to be protective rather than remedial, providing clear boundaries and orders that protect women and children from further abuse.

Amato et al., some of the earliest researchers on divorce, noted that less-distressed families typically resolved their problems without litigation.[5] Specifically, Haselschwerdt et al. estimated that only between 10% and 20% of separating families are involved in the legal system during divorce.[6] Patel and Choate also noted that only 10% of separating families seek assistance from the courts to resolve their differences.[7] The American Academy of Child and Adolescent Psychiatry (AACAP 1997) and the American Psychological Association (APA 2010) have concurred with these findings on the numbers of families seeking judicial intervention.[8] Regarding unmarried families, the U.S. Census Bureau (2011) reported that 46% of children were not living with both of their biological parents, regardless of whether the parents had ever been married.[9] While much of the research on separating families grew out of the study of divorcing families, we can hypothesize that there are commonalities in how adults and children in unmarried families adjust to separation and

that these families have similar experiences in response to the impact of intimate partner violence and substance abuse. Further research would be useful to
determine whether there are any distinctions between married and unmarried
families in regards to their separations. Finally, it is helpful to note that the
percentage of families that need assistance from the courts is relatively stable
at approximately 10–20%. For those families that do need the assistance of the
courts, it is important that we understand their needs.

Adults and Divorce

During the 1970s and 1980s, early researchers on divorce analyzed adults
and children's adjustment to the growing social phenomena of divorce as the
divorce rate increased. At roughly the same time, over the past four decades,
Herman researched the phenomenon of trauma, recognizing that exposure to
horrifying events such as war, a natural disaster, domestic violence, or abuse
can cause profound psychological and physical changes.[10] The study of trauma
has continued to have an enormous impact on our understanding of neuropsy-
chology, memory, adaptation, and treatment.

In early research, Hetherington et al. found that adults in the year following divorce reported considerable stress and isolation, with those who had not
married after two years experiencing significant loneliness.[11] Fathers reported
that they frequently buried themselves in their work and experienced social isolation. These researchers found that mothers were often overwhelmed and also
felt socially isolated living in a couple's world. Furthermore, Hetherington's longitudinal study of divorced families in Virginia noted that parents in divorced
and remarried families had more life stresses in the first two years following
separation and that female-headed single-parent families experienced significant financial problems.[12] Many divorced women lived with their parents in the
period following the separation for financial reasons, and Hetherington concluded that many women were overloaded, juggling multiple tasks, experiencing child-rearing problems, loneliness, and financial pressures.[13] It is not clear
whether the reforms in divorce laws—specifically in the laws that governed the
equitable distribution of the marital property and payment of child support—
had any impact on the income disparities for divorced women. Hetherington
et al. noted that less-distressed families restabilized and became less disorgan-
ized within the two-year period following separation.[14] Furthermore, when parents remarried, they reported that their new relationships were more egalitarian,
household tasks were shared in their new relationships, and they experienced
more marital satisfaction although less sense of family cohesiveness. This lack
of family cohesiveness may be a result of the adjustment to new stepparents,
sibling relationships, and the challenges of child-rearing in such families. These
researchers also noted that women experienced significant health complaints

and depression following divorce, which may be related to the higher levels of stress they nevertheless experienced. Despite this, 75% of women reported that they were happier in their new situations than in the year prior to their separations. Finally, Hetherington concluded that, within two years following divorce, both men and women reported that their problems were lessening, and, within six years, most of the subjects expressed satisfaction with their lives.[15] Divorce clearly continues to represent a challenge, elevating financial and child-rearing stresses and requiring complex adjustments to multiple new relationships. However, it is important that researchers separately identify families impacted by domestic violence, mental illness, and substance abuse because of the long-term nature of these problems and resulting safety and public health concerns.

Children and Divorce

Significantly, Hetherington and Stanley-Hagan noted that the original studies on divorce were entitled "father absence studies" and assumed that children, particularly boys, were best reared in two-parent, presumably heterosexual families.[16] Social scientists were concerned that children had fewer problems when placed with a parent of the same sex, and Hetherington et al. initially questioned whether boys might fare better upon their mothers' remarriage.[17] From that vantage point, earlier researchers assumed that children without fathers were at a significant disadvantage, regardless of the quality of the parental relationship with their mothers. However, it is interesting to note that Bornstein found that children could thrive in a variety of families.[18] Furthermore, Amato and Gilbreth's review of the research on father involvement and children's well-being found that it was the quality of the relationship and not the frequency of contact that was more important.[19] These researchers also found that payment of child support, authoritative parenting, and feelings of closeness were associated with better child well-being and relationships between fathers and children. In other words, responsible parenting is helpful to children. From this vantage point, the field of divorce can be enhanced by an understanding of the strengths of extended families, same-sex households, and those families that differ from the prototype of a two-parent heterosexual family.

Hetherington and Stanley-Hagan found that children specifically experienced problems in the two-year period following divorce, displaying anxiety, depression, anger, and anti-social behavior.[20] These researchers also found that children who have experienced divorce may demonstrate difficulties in their relationships, including problems with parents, siblings, peers, and teachers, and they noted the long-term effects in children of divorced parents as compared to children in nondivorced families.

The longitudinal study by Hetherington et al. concluded that there were some differences between boys' and girls' adjustment to their parents' divorce, with boys having more difficulties in response to divorce and girls being more affected by their parents' remarriage.[21] However, they concluded that children in separated households with low levels of conflict fared better than children in intact but conflicted families. Again, this distinction between levels of conflict does not distinguish conflict, or arguments, from abuse.

In comparison, Wallerstein and Kelly began a study of divorcing families in 1971, known as the Marin County Project, which found that very few divorced fathers had close relationships with their adult children.[22] The later research of Wallerstein et al. of these same sixty families twenty-five years later concluded that the children of divorce had anxiety about forming and maintaining long-term relationships that persisted into adulthood and were more likely to have experienced their own divorces.[23] Finally, Wallerstein et al. argued that the impact of divorce should not be minimized, criticizing the "trickle down" concept that argues that children's well-being is linked to their parents. These researchers concluded that the difficulty children of divorce have in committing to long-term intimate relationships is related to their lack of experience in successfully resolving conflicts with their own partners.[24]

Lansford noted the complexity and difficulty in assessing the adjustment of children to divorce because multiple factors, including the level of parental conflict, age at time of divorce and research, the impact of stepfamilies, and, finally, genetic factors, contribute to their functioning.[25] This researcher also noted that, while children of divorce have higher levels initially of externalized behaviors, internalizing difficulties, lower academic achievement, and more initial problems with social relationships, we cannot determine whether they have long-term difficulties. Amato's later review of the relevant research acknowledged that parental divorce is a risk factor for psychological problems in young adulthood and attempted to reconcile the different views regarding resilience versus vulnerability.[26] However, Amato disagreed with several key points in the research. Specifically, Amato's later research found that only 10% of children of divorce suffered psychological problems, not one-third, as Wallerstein et al. concluded.[27] Amato also concluded that more research on young adults from divorced families was needed, with studies that utilized a control group before conclusions could be made about these children's ability to maintain long-term relationships.[28] Finally, Johnston found that children's reaction to divorce was limited by their developmental understanding at the time of the crisis, finding that children attribute blame and explanations that are consistent with their current cognitive and emotional development.[29]

Parenting and Divorce

While acknowledging that the well-being of children and adults are not necessarily intertwined, it is interesting to note that there have been many studies on the impact of divorce on children. Lansford acknowledged that parents' adjustment impacts children. Hetherington et al. described the problems divorced parents experience, including depression, anxiety, health problems, and disruptions in identity, which was also noted in the earlier research of Kiecolt-Glaser.[30] Many researchers concur that divorce compromises parents' ability to care for their children's needs.[31] Hetherington also noted that, given that parents had more difficulties in the first two years following separation, these disruptions in their ability to parent may occur at a time when children most need warm, consistent support.[32] This researcher found that stepparenting in remarried families was challenging because a close marital relationship in the first two years of remarriage was linked to more negative behavior on the part of the children, although this subsequently improved.

In my practice, many of my clients experience multiple difficulties during the divorce process, including loss of employment. They frequently attribute their loss of employment to time missed from work for illness, court appearances, anxiety, depression, increased difficulty with co-workers, or difficulty concentrating, causing a reduction in their productivity. During litigation, many of my clients express great concern about their children and state emphatically that they do not want the divorce to "hurt the children." Some of my clients are themselves the adult children of divorce and do not "want their children to go through what they went through."

While my clients are aware of their children's anxiety, many attempt to make up for this by providing them with emotional support on their own. The ability of such parents to support their children may be hindered by the legal system or by their financial situations. Most parents experience the legal system as hostile and intrusive. My clients often fear the legal process and delay separation until the situation is untenable. They are particularly appalled at the possibility of a custody evaluation and find this process intrusive. Contrary to the widely held belief that divorcing parents fail to place their children's needs above their own, most of my clients are deeply aware of their children's distress. While the judgment of divorcing parents may be affected by the stress of the termination of their marriage, the parents I represent uniformly express concern about their children and a desire to shield them from the impact of the parental conflict.

My clients' concerns raise questions regarding how we help adults and children during the legal process of divorce. Without a proper clinical theoretical formulation of divorce that takes into consideration trauma theory and grief, divorcing couples often seem to be treated with contempt by the legal system. Divorcing parents are widely viewed as lacking in maturity and unable to place their children's needs ahead of their own by engaging in conflict rather than co-parenting.

It is true that divorcing parents may not function at their best, whether at work, home, or in their intimate relationships. Divorce is a loss. A parent grieving the loss of a marriage may be judged, blame is placed, and the parent found to be the responsible party may be treated punitively by the legal system. Economic concerns frequently have an impact on the levels of household stress experienced. Families reorganize and new relationships are formed, creating tensions in the new marital relationship and between parents and children. An informed mental health professional can offer appropriate treatment and support, provided they can distinguish between less-distressed families and those experiencing the traumatic impact of domestic violence, substance abuse, or mental illness.

Divorce and Separation as Transitions

Hetherington and Stanley-Hagan began to view divorce for many families as a series of transitions in which new relationships are developed within a changing family structure, impacting relationships and children's adjustments.[33] These researchers also noted the resilience of many children who experience divorce and that, while initially these children experienced difficulties, over time their problems diminished as their families restabilized.[34] Hetherington and Stanley-Hagan noted that girls seemed less vulnerable than boys, demonstrating independence and the ability to handle new responsibilities. They espoused a view of the life course that emphasized a risk and resiliency perspective, indicating that events that occur after the divorce contribute to stress and the children's initial difficulties. For children, Hetherington and Stanley-Hagan indicated the additional impact of the accompanying transitions of relocation, changing schools, parental remarriage, and new siblings and stepparents that were found to frequently accompany the separation and divorce.[35]

Differentiation of less-distressed families from those with more severe problems is an essential part of helping these families reorganize and adapt. It is instructive that many researchers have agreed that, when divorce was the result of a transition from a conflicted family life to a less stressful situation, children in these divorced families were found to have rates of adjustment similar to those in intact, less-distressed families.[36] Hetherington and Stanley-Hagan found that these same children of divorce scored higher in social responsibility and cognitive agency and lower in externalizing and internalizing than did those of high-conflict distressed marriages.[37]

Co-Parenting and Children's Adjustment

Amato's later research found that divorce has an impact on the father–child relationship and that 35% of young adults from families of divorce had weaker ties to their fathers than those in the study's control group.[38] However, this finding fails to delineate the reasons behind the strained father–child relationships and whether these tensions could have stemmed from exposure to domestic violence, substance abuse, or untreated mental illness in the fathers. In fact, earlier researchers frequently assumed that single mothers had significant difficulties in establishing limits with their children, and Simons et al. argued that children fared better with fathers who could establish discipline and control.[39] However, Forgatch and DeGarmo, in a study of mothers and their sons, found that the impact of divorce on adolescents could be ameliorated by effective parenting.[40] Contemporaneously with this theory, the research of Maccoby et al. in the Stanford Custody Project analyzed whether children have an easier adjustment to divorce if they continued to have contact with both parents in an atmosphere in which parents communicate frequently and co-parent.[41]

These researchers conducted the Stanford Custody Project during the mid-1980s, two studies that attempted to measure parent involvement and the impact on children following changes in California's divorce laws.[42] In one aspect of the study, they compared parental satisfaction in homes where one parent had sole custody while the other had overnight visitation with those in which children had dual residences in split-custody arrangements. They found that, in two-thirds of the families, the children resided primarily with their mothers, and, of this group, one-half of the children had overnight visitation with their fathers. In approximately one-sixth of the families, the children had dual residences, residing equally with each parent; one-tenth of the children resided primarily with their fathers; and, in a few instances, the siblings resided separately from each other. Under the assumption that children would benefit from continued contact with both parents and that parental communication was an important part of child-rearing, these researchers studied the frequency and patterns of parental communication between the parents. This study found that noncustodial fathers reported the least satisfaction with the custodial arrangement. In a later review of the research, Neilsen argued that fathers in shared custody arrangements are less stressed than those in sole custody arrangements, which will allow them to have more meaningful relationships with their children.[43] Significantly, this researcher did not address considerations regarding exposure to domestic violence, mental illness, and substance abuse and the appropriateness of such shared custody arrangements in these instances. However, Maccoby et al. concluded that mothers with physical custody and noncustodial fathers were the most satisfied when the parents were not engaged in active conflict, while mothers with custody were the least satisfied with the parenting arrangements when there were elevated levels of conflict.[44] It is interesting to note that the researchers found that, even in low-conflict families, many of the parents avoided direct communication with each other and confined their interactions to discussions of the logistics of visitation. Raising the question of whether the amount of communication between parents impacted the adjustment of children, Maccoby et al. noted that parents with higher levels of initial hostility had difficulty communicating with each other during the latter half of the study.[45]

The research of Maccoby et al. studied the adjustment of adolescents in father-resident children, mother-resident children, and dual-resident children.[46] These researchers noted some of the limitations in their study, notably that their research was limited to telephone interviews, and did not include observations of parent–child interactions and classrooms. Limited comparative information was available regarding young children as their sample population was restricted to children aged 10–18 years. Notably, these researchers did not evaluate young children's adjustment to divorce. This study noted differences in levels of the fathers' financial support and that many women had more economic difficulties after separation and were reentering the work force. The researchers concluded that children in dual residences functioned somewhat better than children in mother-residences, while those in father-residences had the most difficulty. The reason for this increased rate of difficulty was not clear.

While this study noted that in some households the other parent worried about the children's safety because of violence or alcohol abuse, these researchers did not specifically evaluate the impact of such exposure or adolescent adjustment in families with a history of intimate partner violence, substance abuse, or untreated mental illness. Finally, these researchers did not address whether in more-troubled families, extensive communication was appropriate for children. Notably, the research on divorce is also divided as to whether parents' well-being following divorce ensures that children will also have a favorable adjustment.[47]

Visitation with Infants and Preschool Children

Less-distressed families need an informed legal and mental health response that provides for young children's sound emotional development even when the children have not been exposed to abuse. However, most visitation and parenting schedules do not vary substantially between children who are toddlers, preschoolers, elementary school-aged children, or adolescents. The impact of unsupervised visitation on young children in families with a history of violence will be discussed in Chapter 9.

Children under the age of two experience significant distress if they are rushed into visitation schedules that fail to consider their needs. McIntosh stressed the importance of a continuous and stable attachment with the primary caretaker as a basis for the child's development of the ability to regulate stress and emotional arousal.[48] This researcher noted that such young children needed continuity, a predictable routine, and caregivers who provide support and protection.[49]

McIntosh goes further and argues that overnight visitation for infants is inherently harmful to development and is not necessary for establishment of a warm relationship with the noncustodial parent.[50] It is notable that her research did not consider children who had been exposed to domestic violence, substance abuse, or other forms of traumatic exposure. She noted the damage of repeated separations in the form of shared parenting time as being normatively stressful for young children. To summarize, infants from zero to twenty-four months who spent one or more overnights a week with the noncustodial parent were found to demonstrate difficulty in regulating stress as compared with other infants without such visitation schedules. Children two to three years of age, who spent more than one night a week with the noncustodial parent have been repeatedly found to show greater separation anxiety, eating problems, and poor persistence in accomplishing tasks.[51] It is important for young children to have stable and consistent day visits with their noncustodial parent until they are old enough to feel comfortable with overnight visitation. Even within these guidelines, young children should not have overnights until they are ready, and their schedules should be established with flexibility.

The imposition of overnight visitation and shared parenting custody schedules for such young children represents a disruption in their relationship with the primary caretaker—typically the mother—that impacts their ability to withstand stress. In fact, much of the research on attachment discusses the developmental vulnerability of children under the age of four who are undergoing rapid changes physically, cognitively, linguistically, and emotionally.[52] Van Ijendoorn and Kroonenberg cite the enormous neurological changes that occur during these years.[53] Often the circumstances are hostile and uncertain. My clients with children under the age of four have reported the most significant problems, including regression, increased thumb sucking, clinginess, tearfulness, and dramatic incidents in which children retreat into fetal position.

In my practice, mothers of children who are under the age of seven have reported that their children experience significant anxiety after extended overnight visits, also becoming clingy, teary, and fearful. Although opposing counsel frequently argue that it is the mother who is anxious and communicating this to the children, visitation schedules should be implemented that are respectful of the children's neurological and emotional development. There is also a dearth of available research on the impact of children under the age of seven who spend virtually half of their time commuting between two households. Many of my clients have children under the age of seven who have been rushed into overnight visitation with little preparation or who have extended weekend visitation scheduled from Thursday through Monday mornings, when children are dropped off at school.

Children benefit from a positive relationship with their fathers when there is a nurturing, healthy relationship. However, this paternal–child relationship must be built around the child's developmental need for stability and sense of security. We also cannot assume that all parents want to impose visitation schedules on their children. Without an understanding of the long-term impact on their children, many parents are confused about the conflicting information and theories available from professionals. Frequently, despite their children's reluctance, parents are told that such early overnight schedules are best for their children without regard for their children's developmental stage. Young children in homes without abuse, in which their developmental needs are accommodated, may fare better in terms of lessened anxiety and attachments without such extensive overnight access. Children in less-distressed families may benefit from therapists and educators who understand that their families are experiencing a life crisis that need not be traumatic. Clinical work with such children and their families can assist them in adjusting to the loss and reorganization of their families. Parents of such children require the advice and support of informed mental health professionals who can empower them to meet their family's needs.

Adolescence and Divorce

Assisting adolescents during divorce is one of the most challenging areas of practice for attorneys and mental health professionals. Hetherington's longitudinal research noted that stresses and conflicts between parents and children were particularly difficult during parental remarriage if such a transition occurred after the child was nine years old.[54] Her later research in collaboration with Stanley-Hagan has noted the vulnerability of adolescents because of divorce, even with children who had initially displayed better adjustment.[55] In my legal practice, I have observed adolescents display extraordinary maturity as they demonstrate glimpses of the adults they will become. The ability of these adolescents to express themselves can be breathtaking, and yet their ability to make sound decisions may be dramatically flawed—all in the span of one interview. Despite these inconsistencies, their opinions about where and with whom they will live with are given enormous weight in custody disputes.

Buchanan et al. observed that adolescents typically exhibit problems in measurable ways, such as decreased school performance, deviant behavior, and depression.[56] These researchers concluded that girls living primarily with their fathers had the most difficulties following the divorce.[57] Wallerstein et al. also noted that some adolescents may become caregivers for their parents, while others may act out in school or home.[58] Others seek comfort from teachers, peers, and mental health providers and display more resilience. In my practice, I have noted that those adolescents with a history of developmental, educational, or psychological problems that predated the separation have the most problems during the divorce or in later custody disputes. It is these children who are most at risk during this time.

In the context of a divorce, many researchers have found that adolescents have a challenging time. Simons et al. found that adolescents' difficulty immediately following the divorce is demonstrated by internalized and externalized behaviors.[59] The problems of children and adolescents in traumatized families will be discussed in greater depth in Chapter 4.

However, while we know an enormous amount about adolescents and children exposed to domestic violence, there needs to be further research to differentiate between the responses of adolescents from high-risk homes and those from less-distressed families. More research is needed to assess whether adolescents with special needs from high-risk families have more adjustment problems during traumatic divorce than those adolescents with preexisting vulnerabilities from less-distressed families.

While there is some research that indicates that involvement of the noncustodial father reduced acting-out behavior in adolescents, Simons et al. cautioned against accepting these findings without further testing, as some adolescents may act out more immediately following the divorce.[60] These researchers puzzled over why more contact with a father did not necessarily mean that the children fared better and hypothesized that it was the quality of the relationship, not the quantity of the time together, that was significant. Simons et al. acknowledged that high involvement on the part of fathers might foster conflict between spouses, that this could create problems for children, and that there was no evidence that frequent contact with fathers influenced children's adjustment. However, Buchanan et al. noted that adolescents with more contact with the nonresidential parent had better relationships with their noncustodial parents than those who did not.[61] This finding may reflect the fact that adolescents from less-distressed families have more input into their visitation schedules with their parents. Such input is appropriate for such adolescents, given their need to balance conflicting and emerging responsibilities of school, extracurricular activities, and employment. Additionally, more visitation with the noncustodial parent may reflect mutual shared interests with that parent and the quality of their relationship.

Adolescents with a history of developmental delays or learning or psychological difficulties have special needs requiring support and consistent parenting. Karaaslan concluded that social engagement with caretakers has a significant impact on children's development and that this is particularly important for children with disabilities.[62] In comparison, in my practice, I have noticed that abusive fathers may minimize or deny the impact of their children's special needs, although Karaaslan found slight differences in intact families between mothers' and fathers' ability to parent such children.

In my practice, I have found that, in the context of custody litigation, adolescents with special needs are particularly vulnerable to pressure or coercion from an abusive parent. It is essential that their vulnerabilities be considered separately in the context of divorce, litigation, and custody arrangements by the legal system and the mental health professionals they encounter.

However, I have found that the legal system may minimize or discount the mothers' concerns about adolescents with a history of learning, physical, or psychological disabilities. It is essential for attorneys and custody evaluators to have the appropriate medical or psychological documentation early in the litigation, to provide guidance to the courts so that they do not assume that the mothers are overprotective. The prevailing view—that these children have outgrown their earlier difficulties—is widespread and often misleading. Because of positive parenting and support, these adolescents are often in the process of developing positive coping strategies to overcome their earlier difficulties.

Unfortunately, the process of divorce and litigation typically impairs the ability of the more vulnerable adolescents to continue such positive development. Such children may minimize the impact of their history when speaking with their attorneys or court-appointed custody evaluators. For judges, attorneys for the adolescent, and custody evaluators, it is essential that these preexisting problems be considered when a child requests a change in custody. This can be difficult as teens may be embarrassed to acknowledge prior difficulties and set forth impressive reasons why they can decide for themselves where they should live. Currently, an adolescent who expresses strong desires to live with an abusive or manipulative parent will be heard, and frequently their wishes will be followed, regardless of whether this is in their best interests.

An abrupt change of custody, school, and friends is rarely in the teenager's best interests. However, such adolescents are particularly susceptible to pressure from an abusive or manipulative parent and need protection. In my practice, I have seen older adolescents leave their schools and friends to live with an abusive parent only to become suicidal after they move. Rather than plan for their higher education, these children become immobilized, depressed, and are unable to focus on obtaining the life skills they need.

Adolescents need to be helped so that they can continue to thrive. Typically, this means that they need to continue to reside with their primary caregiver, generally the mother. A father who entices an adolescent to change residences by offering lavish gifts or more freedom may be undermining his child's ability to achieve academic success and, ultimately, independence. In some instances, adolescents may willingly want to live with their noncustodial parent, and such changes should include continued contact and an ongoing relationship with their other parent. We expect older adolescents to become independent, to become career-focused, and to develop educational goals. However, without stability in the form of continued support from their primary caregiver, this becomes more difficult, even if the adolescent vigorously objects to such support. Rather than promoting abrupt and confrontational modifications of residential custody arrangements, the mental health and legal systems should find ways to support the primary caregiver. Referrals for counseling for a beleaguered primary caregiver, clear limits, and deference to a parenting style that has been effective should be the preferred response, even if the teen is clamoring to leave. It is helpful to assess the history of the family. Abusive fathers may file for custody for a myriad of reasons, such as the avoidance of their child support obligations, and often may have been the less involved parent. In such cases, the vulnerable adolescent may long for a father who has been unavailable and express willingness to accept a less stable and supportive environment for fear of rejection. Sadly, in my practice, the more supportive parent is sometimes the rejected parent because the children know that their mother will always be there for them.

In families without high-risk factors of domestic violence, mental illness, or substance abuse, divorce and separation are still a challenge. For elementary school-aged children, visitation and parenting schedules are generally confusing. For adolescents, changes in their living arrangements that conflict with time with their peers may feel catastrophic. Their participation in the reorganization of their family is important in helping them develop the ability to form intimate relationships. For an adolescent to learn that relationships can change, that new family members can be absorbed, and that they will continue to thrive is a vital component of their own ability to develop and maintain intimate relationships later in life.

The impact of divorce and litigation on adolescents should not be minimized as they struggle to navigate their family conflicts, separation, and their own need to establish a separate identity from their parents. McIntosh indicated that some may find support or protection from their relationships with siblings.[63] Johnston and Campbell observed that the only child may be particularly vulnerable to problems during divorce or custody disputes.[64] Adolescents who have a network of support from teachers, guidance counselors, friends, and therapists who understand their conflicted but healthy relationships with their primary caregivers can be more resilient.

In a Canadian study of more than 3,000 adolescents from grades 6 through 12 from divorced families, Ehrenberg et al. found that the participants had an optimistic and active attitude toward seeking help, although teens typically sought help first from their peers.[65] These researchers hypothesized that such willingness to seek help could enhance resilience and adjustment. Research on effective treatment modalities, including the use of groups with adolescents who value relationships with their peers, may be appropriate. It is also important that the more vulnerable adolescents, including those with disabilities, have assistance in developing appropriate coping strategies and support systems.

In families without substantial risk factors, Buchanan et al. noted that adolescents may have moved from one parent's residence to another, in contradiction to the existing legal custodial arrangements.[66] Despite legal agreements or orders that direct joint physical custody or custody with one parent, by the time these children enter adolescence, the arrangements had frequently changed. Adolescents may make these decisions impulsively and without understanding their long-term consequences. Enhancing their resilience will require the support of mental health professionals who can be flexible in their use of treatment modalities to help them understand the long-term implications of their decisions on their schooling, social life, and adult plans. Teenagers often consult with their parents about their summer arrangements, college choices, and the like, yet here they are alone and without adult guidance. Whether they can safely make such decisions, are susceptible to manipulation, and how much weight their opinions should be given are sources of confusion in the courts.

Wallerstein et al. noted the devastating effects that occur when adolescents at eighteen are not provided with financial support and are unable to attend college.[67] This analysis overlooks the fact that a father's failure to pay child support is typically part of a pattern of abuse. Failure to separate families impacted by domestic violence, mental illness, or substance abuse from the general population of less-distressed divorcing families makes it difficult to find appropriate remedies. By emphasizing high-conflict divorce rather than traumatic divorce, we overlook the intractable nature of the problems of families in the latter group and fail to provide swift and effective legal remedies. Court mandates that are properly enforced regarding the financial support of the children are essential in supporting these families. However, in the absence of real family wealth, children of divorce from less-distressed families have less financial stability as the household incomes must stretch to cover the cost of two households. Post-divorce or separation, families that receive adequate child support will be households in which there is less stress. Resilience of parent and child will be enhanced if they are less worried about the realities of having enough money to pay for housing, food, clothing, and the things that children need. In the past two decades, the federal government has encouraged the states to establish minimum child support guidelines, with enforcement procedures available, such as wage garnishment, that will be discussed further in Chapter 7. These efforts have helped considerably to provide financial stability to single parents.

In my practice, I have seen vulnerable adolescents, typically a young teen who has struggled with developmental concerns, argue for a change in residence to reside with an abusive father out of fear of losing this parent. Even where such a move involved leaving friends and her school in which she was performing well academically, she was willing to give this up at the request of an abusive parent who promised a less structured home life and material possessions. In some cases, a single mother who rarely gets child support and is struggling financially may be confronted with a custody battle in which the abusive parent offers lavish gifts and promises.

Children and adolescents have a range of responses to growing up in homes where there are high-risk factors of domestic violence, mental illness, or substance abuse. However, it is important that we develop an informed response to adolescents that differentiates those who come from less-distressed families from those with high-risk factors.

In the more extreme cases of severely abused adolescents, they may demonstrate significant and sudden improvement after being removed from the source of the traumatic exposure. In less-distressed families, children may demonstrate a need to protect or care for one parent or to align themselves with one or the other. In the best cases, parents continue to work together to prevent such splitting. In the context of the legal system and a custody dispute, the stories that these teens recount to their attorneys may be edited, coerced, or, conversely, be an accurate portrayal of their own family situations.

The Concept of High-Conflict Divorce

There were early assumptions made about the impact of divorce on children: that children's well-being suffered because of divorce, academically, socially, and economically, and that children had less time with their parents and suffered economic strains.[68] However, these researches noted that as divorce has become more acceptable, the stigma and problems associated with many families have lessened. Cherlin et al. conducted a comparison study of children from Great Britain and the United States, finding that, while there were behavioral differences in children of divorced parents, many of these problems were the result of conditions that existed prior to separation.[69] Amato and Keith's meta-analysis of the research on divorce concluded that children from less-distressed intact families had the least difficulties, followed by children from divorced, low-conflict families, with children from conflicted divorced families having less difficulties than those children from intact conflicted families.[70] Amato et al. obtained data from a longitudinal study of 11,000 families with children between the ages of 7 and 11, over a twelve-year period. Looking at adults who grew up in families of divorce, they found that long-term outcomes for children who grew up in high-conflict families of divorce showed better adjustments than children from intact conflicted families, while children from less-distressed intact families fared better than children from less-conflicted divorced families.[71] Many members of the more-conflicted families reported incidents of pushing, kicking, hitting, and throwing things, although the level of the severity of the injuries was not reported. The impact of domestic violence as a possible trigger of traumatic exposure was beyond the scope of this research. Amato and Keith also observed that many of the earlier studies on divorce were taken from a clinical population in which there were also problems of parental mental illness, alcoholism, and domestic violence, which may have compounded the problems of children of divorce. Finally, Amato et al. concluded that continuous exposure to parental conflict was a risk factor that might cause children to experience their own psychological and marital difficulties later in life.[72]

Helpful as this research is on children of divorce, it failed to integrate an understanding of domestic violence that is much more than conflict. In such a large study, it would have been helpful to have an accurate assessment of the extent of domestic violence in these families that could determine whether other forms of abuse existed, including harassment, threats, and financial or sexual abuse. However, social scientists have continued to rely on Amato et al.'s classification of high-conflict, separating families without isolating those that experienced domestic violence and substance abuse. More recently, Amato and Hohmann-Marriott have begun to quantify such separations as high- and low-distress divorces.[73]

Johnston and Campbell's early research observed that 75% of families enmeshed in high-conflict custody disputes had a history of domestic violence.[74] Subsequently, Johnston's writings noted the lack of clarity in defining high-conflict divorce and sought to resolve these ambiguities surrounding this theory by analyzing the types of difficulties that occur in divorcing families.[75] This researcher identified several forms of conflict, including the domain, tactics, and attitudinal areas, and posited that, in conflicts of domain, couples argue over support, property, custody, and the children. Johnston's analysis of the tactics dimension described the methods used in such families to resolve disagreements including avoidance, discussions, and, finally, aggression.[76] Notably, this researcher divided aggression into verbal assaults, physical assaults, and, last, physical coercion. While acknowledging the harm to many battered women, this researcher argued that higher levels of conflict were to be expected during divorce, but viewed post-divorce conflicts as more serious in nature and a symptom of individual and family dysfunction that could be reflected in financial disagreements and related child-rearing issues.[77] It should be noted that Johnston and Campbell's early work found that parents in these families typically had a history of personality disorders and other mental health concerns and that these parents channeled their feelings about the divorce into arguments over their children. Notably, these authors concluded that this could result in children feeling tension and pressure to take sides in these custody disputes. Jaffe and Crooks discussed the confusion in distinguishing high conflict from cases of domestic violence and indicated that these terms can be used interchangeably despite their differences.[78]

More recently, Johnston and Goldman have also spoken about estrangement of children toward one parent, arguing that this is different from parental alienation.[79] These researchers acknowledged that the estrangement may have stemmed from the children's concerns about their parents' violence, alcoholic, or abusive behavior, and they noted the impact of that parent's manipulations, controlling behavior, and lack of empathy. While it is positive that these authors advise against reunification therapy, a subject that is beyond the scope of this book, they have not accounted for the impact of trauma on the custodial parent. Johnston and Goldman continue to hold both parents responsible for one parent's abusive behavior while not acknowledging that removing the abusive behavior and providing services to the protective parent may enhance their ability to parent capably.

A review of the research on high-conflict divorce indicates that this theory rests on two assumptions about divorcing families. The first assumption is that many allegations of abuse are falsified in an atmosphere of blame and anger. The second assumption is that when the history of abuse has been substantiated, in many cases, this behavior was a result of the parents' poor conflict resolution skills. The danger inherent in this approach is that abuse may be understood as transitory, separation-related, and irrelevant to the well-being of the children. Johnston et al. repeatedly describe what they view as high-conflict families litigating custody in an atmosphere fraught with distrustfulness, blame, and an inability to work together to raise their children.[80] As stated previously, domestic violence should not be viewed as conflict. Without enforced barriers and protections for battered mothers, the family courts compel them to have frequent communications with their batterers so that they are unable to resolve ordinary concerns about their children. Efforts to make day-to-day decisions about the children are frequently highjacked by the batterers' efforts to undermine the mothers' parenting. The emphasis on high-conflict divorce theory has made it easier to view both parents as responsible for the abuse. Subsequently, it is also simpler for some legal and mental health professionals to see the mothers' accusations of abuse as evidence of dysfunction and not address concerns about the impact of chronic traumatic exposure. Finally, at present, there is no reliable way to predict the escalation of violence. In Chapter 6, I will review the literature on batterers' psychopathology and common traits and the research by Joudis et al. showing that perpetrators of lethal violence are not a homogenous group, a fact that can make it difficult to predict future violence.[81]

The empirical weakness of the high-conflict model of divorce has been noted by several researchers. Walker et al. noted the empirical weakness of this high-conflict classification.[82] In Bancroft and Silverman's critique of high-conflict divorce theory, they noted that Johnston and Campbell recognized that many families in this category had a history of domestic violence yet failed to consider the dynamics of such abuse.[83] These researchers observed that the high-conflict theory assumed that the violence was the result of inappropriate behavior on the part of both parents and noted their own observations of batterers' heightened sense of entitlement and lack of responsibility. A number of researchers have concluded that there was insufficient data to support the classification of high-conflict divorce.[84] Finally, one of the major obstacles to helping families impacted by domestic violence, substance abuse, and mental illness is that the family courts frequently mislabel these families as high-conflict.

Allegations of Abuse During Divorce or Separation

Research on the validity of allegations of abuse has called into doubt the prevailing distrust of mental health and legal professionals when such abuse arises in the context of divorce. Johnston et al. reviewed concerns about the past histories of domestic violence and allegations of abuse, neglect, substance abuse, and sexual abuse in high-conflict families and whether such allegations have merit.[85] These researchers studied a group of 120 families whom they deemed to be high-conflict to determine the rate of unsubstantiated allegations of abuse and neglect. Johnston et al. concluded that women were no more likely to have made unsubstantiated allegations than men.

As discussed in more depth in Chapter 4, Trocmé and Bala also reviewed the rate of false allegations of abuse in a Canadian study of reported child abuse and neglect on a much larger scale, finding that only 4% of these allegations were considered intentionally false.[86] This small percentage of deliberately or maliciously false allegations brings into question the empirical underpinnings for the theory of high-conflict divorce. Without a common and accepted definition of abuse, it is possible to overlook significant red flags. Thus, the concept of high-conflict divorce has frequently been used to minimize the traumatic impact of intimate partner violence, substance abuse, and untreated mental illness on women and children.

Domestic Violence, Trauma, and Divorce or Separation

Significantly, the studies of divorce did not integrate the emerging research on trauma, traumatic exposure, posttraumatic stress disorder (PTSD), and the impact of such long-term exposure on children and adults. The literature on high-conflict divorce is steeped in family systems theory, which views abusive behavior as the outgrowth of poor conflict resolution skills in a manner that ascribes choice and mutual responsibility for the conflict. Such reasoning fails to recognize the inherent power imbalance, where one person, typically the father, finds multiple ways to abuse the other family members. Family researchers have acknowledged the validity of the earlier findings of Amato et al. regarding preexisting conflicts that included domestic violence and alcohol abuse.[87] Researchers even disagree about how to define domestic violence, making it difficult to establish consistent public policy and a unified legal response. The complexity of the field of domestic violence and the controversy over the different definitions will be discussed in Chapter 3.

Johnston and Straus acknowledged that many of the children in the high-conflict families in their research were traumatized by violence in their families. These researchers described in detail the symptoms of traumatic exposure displayed by these children, including hypervigilance, a distrust of the outside world, and emotional constriction that were not seen in their control group.[88] These researchers also agreed that traumatized children require more than supervised visitation and that guidelines are needed to determine if children should be forced to have ongoing contact with a dysfunctional parent. These concerns highlight the need for an informed response to divorce and separation that integrates our understanding of intimate partner violence and the related risks of child abuse.

While divorce is often referred to as a traumatic experience, the term "trauma" has a specific clinical meaning, as will be discussed in Chapter 4. Thus, not all separations involve exposure to traumatic events. As indicated previously, the fifth edition of the DSM-5 (2013) enumerates the kinds of traumatic events that can trigger PTSD, including war, childhood neglect or abuse, natural disaster, genocide, or interpersonal violence.[89] Such experiences are so overwhelming to the human psyche that they can cause profound psychological and neurological responses in adults and children.[90] While early research on PTSD studied the impact of trauma on combat veterans, this research has been expanded to include victims of intimate partner violence, including child maltreatment, domestic violence, and sexual assault. The DSM-5 expanded the category of this disorder to include small children who have witnessed an attack on their primary caregiver or faced a life-threatening situation. Jones et al. found that women in domestic violence shelters who have been subjected to abuse have higher rates of PTSD than the population at large.[91]

The research and writing of Herman on trauma describes a spectrum of traumatic disorders, noting the differences between a single exposure to a horrifying event to the impact of prolonged and continuous exposure.[92] Her research on the treatment of women with PTSD emphasizes repeatedly that it is essential to establish their safety before recovery can begin. In contrast, battered women in family court are expected to have frequent communication with their batterers. In this environment, their recovery is challenged. Sadly, by neglecting the importance of establishing safety for battered women and their children, the legal system has inadvertently exacerbated the problem.

It is therefore of concern that in custody and divorce litigation the allegations of battered women are frequently minimized or discounted entirely. In my practice, I have observed cases in open court where women who have alleged sexual or physical assaults were humiliated when their allegations were treated with disbelief. I have also frequently observed how, without physical evidence of injuries, the allegations of battered women during litigation are often initially treated with disbelief. During custody litigation, a higher level of proof is necessary before such allegations are taken seriously.

Similarly, in my practice, women who allege physical abuse are often disparaged by opposing counsel as having fabricated the charges, particularly where they are coming forward with this problem for the first time. Battered women may take a long time to come forward about being abused. They hope that the batterer will learn better ways to resolve their problems. They fear retaliation in the form of custody litigation or extensive litigation that will bankrupt them. They are ashamed and blame themselves. The circus-like atmosphere in family court can only increase battered women's experiences of shame and guilt and may be retraumatizing. When battered women experience validation from mental health and legal professionals and are treated with respect and care, they can begin to heal.

Notably, abusive fathers frequently demand communication over every detail of their children's lives, with no respect for scheduling or the daily routines that children need. In many instances, the children are aware of the continued efforts by the father to control their lives, although these efforts are couched as fathers' attempts to co-parent their children. Clearly, this type of continued harassment generates an atmosphere in which children cannot trust their own perceptions or their mothers as their primary caretakers. In this environment, children are frequently manipulated and confused, alternately seeing evidence of their fathers' use of intimidation and abuse and being misled by their fathers' assurances. Johnston and Straus movingly described how children will blame their mothers for the fathers' abuse in their effort to maintain their attachment to him.[93] Given the atmosphere of fear and intimidation in which many of the children in my practice were raised, continued unsupervised access is problematic. The courts' failure to provide firm boundaries between households and clear decision-making authority for protective mothers may create an environment in which children are more vulnerable to PTSD and obstructs mental health treatment for women and children.

More research is needed to determine the prevalence of psychological harm caused by shared decision-making and unsupervised contact. In traumatic divorces, mothers should not be hamstrung by the need to confer over every bit of minutia concerning their children's lives. It is essential that the mental health and legal professions develop an approach to divorcing and separating families that incorporates our understanding of trauma and abuse so we can provide long-term solutions that address the need to establish a safe zone for recovery and allows women and children to rebuild their lives.

Most states have now enacted laws that allow the courts to consider the existence of domestic violence when determining custody and visitation. In the criminal courts, passage of mandatory arrest laws in cases of domestic violence created a backlash against women. Dual arrests of both parties because of batterers' false allegations soared. As a result, most states have passed Primary Aggressor Laws that require law enforcement to consider the prior history of domestic violence, the relative size of the parties, prior orders of protection, and threats before a dual arrest could be made.[94] Law enforcement training on dual and retaliatory arrests and the passage of Primary Aggressor Laws helped to ensure that women were not revictimized by false arrests. We must now consider whether the same backlash against women is taking place in the family courts and whether the use of high-conflict divorce theory and its failure to integrate the research on trauma endangers public health and safety.

Conclusion

In many families, divorce is a crisis. Separated families may experience financial stresses, relocation, and the changes in the family structure with the addition of stepparents and siblings. However, these families experience less stress within 2 to 6 years following divorce. Many parents experience more well-being after separation, and their new relationships are often more egalitarian than their earlier marriages. However, without a therapeutic understanding informed by careful research into the impact of divorce, trauma, separation, and domestic violence and the identification of the symptoms of trauma sometimes associated with these problems, the legal and mental health response may be intrusive and inappropriate. Understanding divorce and separation in less-distressed families as a series of transitions will also enable a more informed response from the courts and mental health professionals. Questions remain whether children from less-distressed families will fare better if their parents receive the support they need during this time. In families with a history of traumatic exposure, it is important to build a legal response that provides structure and safety. It is further indicative of this lack of therapeutic understanding that, in large part, many graduate mental health training programs do not provide programs of study on divorce or separation and their impacts on adults and children. Furthermore, there is little agreement in defining the problems of more-distressed divorced or separating families

Currently, in less-distressed families, many visitation schedules and custody agreements fail to take into consideration the developmental needs of children. Similarly, without research and training on trauma and divorce to inform legal practices, court personnel may fill in the gaps of their knowledge with subjective and unsubstantiated theories of divorce. The lack of resources and confusion regarding the needs of less distressed families and those engaged in traumatic divorce have encouraged a "one-size-fits-all" approach to visitation schedules, vacations, and decision-making, regardless of the children's age, vulnerabilities, and history of abuse.

3

The Struggle to Define Domestic Violence

The family court's response to intimate partner violence has been hampered by a lack of agreement concerning the definition, prevalence, and context of such abuse. Questions remain in the legal and mental health professions as to whether men and women are violent at the same rate or whether some forms of abusive behavior are less dangerous. Raghavan and Cohen acknowledged that the social sciences are deeply divided in their understanding of domestic violence.[1] These fundamental disagreements about the nature, prevalence, and gendered impact of domestic violence have contributed to the current unpredictable quality of the family courts' response. This chapter will address the conflicting arguments about the definition of domestic violence, the controversy over how abuse is measured, whether men and women are violent at the same rate, and, finally, the disparate impact such behavior has on women when men are abusive.

Domestic Violence: The Definition of the Problem

Our understanding of family violence began with an attempt to determine its prevalence. The original research on domestic violence by Gelles and Straus defined it as physical acts of aggression against another family member.[2] A decade later, Gelles noted the difficulties in quantifying the problem of domestic violence and child abuse because of the secrecy surrounding these issues and the potential to stigmatize those who have been abused.[3] Burge et al. described the development of our understanding of domestic violence.[4] Early researchers spoke about competing theories, including Walker's cycle of violence; Giles-Sims' family systems theory; and the Duluth model by Pence and Paymar, in which survivors of domestic violence identified multiple forms of abuse as control.[5] Over the years, our understanding of such abuse has broadened to encompass many other types of behavior that extend into multiple areas of personal life. A more expansive definition of abuse is essential to our understanding of families entering the courts during custody and divorce litigation in which there may not be a history of prior criminal prosecutions.

Domestic Violence as Coercive Control

Stark noted that an understanding of domestic violence as physical assault overlooked a crucial reality: that the most frequent and devastating context in which such abuse occurs is in an atmosphere of coercive control in which batterers engage in patterns of behaviors that include threats, stalking, and other forms of intimidation as well as physical abuse in the home.[6] This researcher further observed that coercive control shares common elements with a number of crimes that include stalking and harassment along with ongoing humiliation and exploitation.[7] Notably, physical abuse is only one form of such coercion, and other methods of control should not be overlooked. Finally, this seminal researcher observed that domestic violence is entirely personal in nature and that the impact is heightened because of women's vulnerability. Batterers employ strategies of abuse and coercion to obtain privileges they feel entitled to and not simply because they lose control. To think of this another way, the motivation behind batterers' abuse is to control their victims, and such control is in no small measure possible because of women's unequal status and can take many forms, some may include minimal physical abuse. Thus, we can understand that domestic violence is typically a gendered crime against women. In the context of custody litigation, the family courts frequently are unable to recognize that abusive behavior is a pattern that takes multiple forms and that its impact is compounded by the vulnerable status of women and children in these families who cannot get away.

This understanding of domestic violence as coercive control has been adopted in Britain, which incorporated Stark's model of coercive control into its "cross-governmental" definition of partner abuse that recognized that such abuse was not limited to one incident but could also include patterns of "controlling, coercive, or threatening behavior."[8] The British government noted the importance of the early identification and recognition of all forms of abuse and not simply physical assaults, stressing that this could prevent the escalation of violence. More recently, the British government went further, to criminalize those behaviors utilized to exercise coercive control over intimate partners.[9] Evans noted that the government criminalized nonphysical forms of abuse including financial, sexual, psychological, and emotional abuse.[10] The elements of this criminal behavior included coercion, which encompassed psychological, physical, sexual, financial, and emotional abuse.[11] Controlling behaviors critically encompassed acts that made the other subordinate, dependent, or isolated and caused economic exploitation for the personal use of batterers to regulate their victim's lives and continue their abuse.[12]

Similarly, the Council of Europe's Convention on Preventing and Combating Violence Against Women and Domestic Violence, known as the Istanbul Convention (2011), adopted a broad definition of domestic violence.[13] The Istanbul Convention defined violence against women to mean "all acts of gender-based violence that result in . . . physical, psychological or economic harm or suffering to women, including threats of such acts, coercion or arbitrary deprivation of liberty."[14]

It is essential that mental health and legal professionals in the United States become part of this broader, international dialogue about the gendered aggression against women that is the result of battered women's particularly vulnerable status. In the family courts, our failure to recognize these patterns of behavior has caused significant harm to battered women and children. In custody disputes, failure to recognize these patterns of abusive behavior frequently leads to stalking, increased risks of post-separation violence, and legal abuse which further entrap women.

In custody determinations, Stark noted the widespread belief in family court that children are best served by having a relationship with both parents, despite the research that indicates children can thrive with only one significant caretaker. While children may long for a relationship with both parents, an informed judicial response requires the courts to weigh their emotional bond against their safety. Looking to the future, the courts must weigh the long-term impact of allowing an abusive parent to undermine the parenting of the nonoffending partner. Many studies have demonstrated that the risk of violence in abusive relationships is greatest during the period just preceding and following separation, particularly during visitation, largely due to the abuser's experience of loss of control over his partner. It is at these times that it is essential that the family courts proceed with caution and provide long-term monitoring. Understanding the risks of domestic violence during and after the relationship has ended is at odds with the current values frequently expressed in the family courts: that it is best for parents to communicate frequently about the children despite the courts' obligation to protect mothers and children.

Libal and Parekh observed the dichotomy between public and private rights and the family courts' difficulty in changing private behavior.[15] These researchers argued that it is difficult to modify private behavior and that increased public awareness and education on the nature of intimate partner violence as a human rights violation is necessary to overcome this distinction.[16] In the context of the public institution of the family courts, the judge must make decisions over private child custody disputes, the settlement of property, and support. When there are allegations of domestic violence or child maltreatment, the judicial response to such problems can either be helpful or damaging. In my practice, I have noticed that many well-meaning judges have taken an activist approach to allegations of abuse or neglect, using the custody litigation to attempt to improve the relationship between abusive or neglectful fathers and their children. Without an empirically based understanding of domestic violence and the other red flags of substance abuse and untreated mental illness, the courts fail to prevent chronic exposure to such abuse.

Are There Classifications or Typologies of Domestic Violence?

In comparison to Stark's theory of coercive control, there have been other attempts made to categorize domestic violence. Johnston and Campbell initially studied two groups of separating families utilizing the Conflict Tactics Scale and individual interviews and identifying four different forms of violence.[17] Acknowledging the difficulty in distinguishing these families and that some households could not be classified, they concluded that there were four subsets of domestic violence including episodic or chronic male battering, female-initiated violence, male-controlled interactive violence, and separation and post-divorce violence. It is notable that Johnston and Kelly classified incidents in which women used self-defense as mutual acts of violence while also acknowledging that men sometimes initiated the abuse and that such abuse could be life-threatening. However, the family court's use of such typologies of domestic violence must be balanced against the difficulty in predicting pre- and post-separation abuse.

Exposure to coercive controlling behaviors damages not only the parent–child attachment but the mother's parenting role. Batterers' efforts to control their spouses are subtle and may seem minimal when taken out of the context of pervasive coercive control, but they are nonetheless toxic. Stark's critique of the growing body of research on the different typologies of domestic violence cautioned that such study required a stronger empirical basis and reiterated that coercive control remained the most pervasive form of abuse in which women were the primary targets.[18]

To reconcile the debate about domestic violence, Johnson argued that researchers on each side were describing different forms of abuse.[19] These included, among other forms of abuse, "situational couple violence" and intimate partner terrorism.[20] Johnson noted that the research on the shelter population reviewed coercive control while the national incidence studies were capturing situational couple violence.[21] Johnson and Kelly's review of the literature argued that intimate partner terrorism was widely identified by the police, hospitals, and shelters. The abusers' behaviors mirrored that of those identified in the Duluth Power and Control Wheel, including threats and economic, emotional, and physical abuse and was believed to raise more significant safety concerns and risks of fatalities.[22] Kelly and Johnson argued that, unlike Stark's theory, situational couple violence was the most common, perpetrated by men and women, and that these incidents can be classified as resulting from conflicts in which violence erupts.[23] This has been used in the family courts to assume that, once the parties separate, everything will settle down.

Meier noted that while Johnson attempted to reconcile differing theories of abuse and made a significant contribution to our understanding of coercive control, she raised concerns about the widespread acceptance of "situational couple violence."[24] She noted the inconsistencies in Kelly and Johnson's argument that "situational couple violence" was less frequent and unlikely to escalate, although they acknowledged that, at times, this violence could have serious implications and could instill fear. Kelly and Johnson also considered two other scenarios: "violent resistance," where victims respond defensively with violence, and "mutually violent control."[25] Some critics have pointed out there is little empirical data to support the concept of mutual violent control, which is thought to be violence between two coercively controlling partners. These researchers concluded that situational couple violence is less likely to escalate, may be sporadic, and may even stop over time and that intimate partner terrorism presented risks that this would continue after separation. However, notably, Johnson indicated that situational couple violence can result in abuse that is severe and, at times, homicidal.[26] A critique of Johnson's research by Stark noted there are different forms of abuse but that this emphasis on discrete acts of abuse overlooked incidents in which women reported that the abuse was chronic because of the many other ways their lives were controlled.[27] Coercive control involves a level of intrusion into women's lives that, along with threats of abuse or physical aggression, induces fear and entrapment that can continue long after the violence has stopped.

It is true that not all cases of domestic violence are the same. In some instances, alcohol or other forms of misused drugs can exacerbate the abuse.[28] In some families, batterers rarely use physical violence, resorting to less public methods that can include isolation and financial and sexual abuse. Much of the research on domestic violence has concentrated on the shelter population. Large-scale efforts to study domestic violence in the general population may be hampered by the need to use telephone interviews and the difficulty of interviewing both members of the household to examine the validity of the reported abuse. Given the research that supports men's minimization of their behavior[29] and manipulation, this is no small matter and remains a challenge for researchers in this field. However, abusive men may be aware of the risks of arrest and the criminalization of such behavior and therefore refrain from physical abuse. They may only rarely use violence to establish control and will only assert such control through violence when all other methods of abuse have failed. Sometimes desperate women defend themselves, requiring law enforcement to begin a primary aggressor analysis to ensure that justice is done.[30] For these reasons, Kimmel has indicated that the separation and post-separation periods are particularly unpredictable, unstable, and dangerous.[31] Finally, there is an inherent contradiction in the applicability of "situational couple violence" in custody cases. There is no foolproof way of predicting whether future violence will escalate or whether children will be hurt. National studies may not provide data on all the subtler forms of domestic violence that accompany coercive control. Furthermore, many of my clients need time to integrate their experiences and only gradually will their stories emerge.

In my practice, I routinely speak with women who relate a minimal history of physical abuse but speak of the accompanying history of economic, sexual, and emotional abuse. These women describe situations in which their lives have been structured around accommodating their spouse's whims and needs, to the detriment of other family members. They speak of being pressured to have sex but do not classify this as rape. Sometimes they have difficulty recalling events that were particularly humiliating. At other times, family and close friends are a better source of information about the abuse to confirm such incidents. Yet, at the time that these women turn to the courts in custody or divorce litigation, the batterer may retaliate with violence, threats to obtain custody, and economic and legal abuse. Many threats to take custody of the children are long-standing and emerge whenever a woman seeks to extricate herself from the situation. When the courts, in collaboration with mental health professionals, classify such abuse as short-term, situational couple violence, they have frequently overlooked the other forms of coercive control that inflict a pervasive level of debilitating harm in which women are the primary targets.

Significantly, Kelly and Johnson have applied this typology to classify the abuse seen during custody litigation in the family courts, and many custody evaluators have adopted this classification to help judges determine whether the parent who instigated the violence should have unrestricted access and decision-making authority about his children. In other instances, such classifications are designed to help select couples for mediation.[32] Given the acknowledged uncertainty concerning these classifications, this is a risky enterprise. Further, such classifications overlook the coercive aspect of any violence, as Dutton and Goodman have indicated that many battered women respond with terror to physical abuse or the threat of such violence.[33]

Frieze and McHugh's early research on the distribution of power in abusive marriages is instructive.[34] These researchers found that women with violent husbands made fewer decisions in the marriage, that decision-making in nonviolent families was more equally shared, and, finally, that marital happiness was lower in homes where husbands were abusive. Thus, they reached an important conclusion: that even one incident of violence permanently changes the balance of power in the marriage.[35] In this context, we can conclude that even one incident of physical violence is a form of coercive control. Such incidents of physical abuse warrant inquiry into whether there are other red flags in the form of a history of economic, emotional, or sexual abuse. Meier correctly notes that the application of Johnson's typology of domestic violence during custody and visitation litigation is at direct odds with the statutory changes to the laws that direct the courts to take the existence of domestic violence into consideration when formulating parenting plans or determining custody.[36] Further, concerns were raised by Johnson as he acknowledged that women experiencing common couple situational violence can be physically injured and that such injuries can be severe. In the family courts, reliance on the concept of situational couple violence is unwise, particularly when it is used to justify custody determinations that require continued contact between the parents without a sound empirical understanding of the pre- and post-separation risks.

Measuring the Prevalence of Domestic Violence

Straus and Gelles developed some of the earliest definitions and research on family violence, focusing primarily on physical abuse, from minor slaps to life-threatening assaults.[37] Their First National Violence Survey was conducted using in-person and telephone interviews on an unprecedented scale to determine the extent of domestic violence in the United States. This study and their development of the Conflict Tactics Scale (CTS) was significant as it tracked the prevalence of domestic violence in the United States. Since its first use, the CTS has been modified and used internationally. However, as our understanding of domestic violence has grown, so, too, have concerns about the validity of the CTS as a comprehensive measurement of family violence. The conclusions reached in studies that utilize this instrument raise concerns about whether we are capturing the correct data: Are we measuring incidents over a lifetime or limiting our inquiry to incidents that occur during conflicts or before separation?

Straus et al. also conducted later studies that sought to quantify the prevalence of domestic violence and, following the development of the CTS1, developed the later version, the Conflict Scales 2 (CTS-2).[38] The CTS originally only measured physical aggression prior to separation that had occurred within the past twelve months. Later revisions have included additional categories to measure stalking incidents and sexual coercion.[39]

The CTS-2 continues to be limited to recent incidents of abuse and has been criticized for a variety of factors, including the test's focus on behaviors that are the result of conflict. Zorza has also criticized the CTS as being overinclusive, as incidents of self-defense and simple accidents are not differentiated, and has questioned its use of telephone interviews when women are still living with their abusers and may be fearful of answering questions.[40] She also noted that the CTS-1 and -2 do not measure post-separation violence. This researcher further argued that men surveyed in such telephone interviews regarding their spouses' abuse may be underestimating their own violence and underemphasizing any physical contact that they initiated.

In my practice as a family law attorney, such minimization is a common occurrence. In defense of the CTS-2, Straus has argued that this instrument can be easily modified to obtain information beyond the one-year period. Kelly and Johnson acknowledged that the CTS has been modified to include behaviors such as cursing, threats, stalking, and controlling finances, but that its primary purpose was to record physical abuse.[41] Finally, while the CTS has been useful in quantifying the extent of domestic violence, its failure to denote the severity of the individual incidents raises concerns, particularly in the ways in which it is used to compare male and female behaviors.

Analysis of the Gender Symmetry Theory

The results of the CTS-2 are frequently cited to support the theory of "gender symmetry": that is, that men and women are violent in roughly the same proportion. Using the CTS Straus has concluded that women initiate physical abuse at approximately the same rate as men.[42] In the family courts where women's allegations of abuse are typically met with counter-allegations, use of this theory is problematic. Critics of the CTS also argue that this methodology fails to control for the context in which domestic violence occurs and that such abuse does not occur only during arguments.

However, the concept of "gender symmetry" is completely at odds with the premise of the Convention on the Elimination of All Forms of Discrimination Against Women (CEDAW 1979), which specifically strove to prevent discrimination and abuse of women.[43] To date, the United States remains one of a handful of countries in the United Nations that has not ratified this important treaty. Kimmel noted the body of research that supported claims of gender symmetry and its reliance on the CTS to determine the rate of such mutual violence and the public policy confusion that has resulted.[44] This researcher observed that domestic violence occurs in context and that this is not always measured by the CTS. By way of example, researchers using the CTS will record the act of a woman defending herself from an assault in the same way that they quantify actions of the male abuser. This researcher also questioned the assumption of gender symmetry, noting that men are more violent than women in other areas of life and questioned why this finding would vary to such a degree in intimate relationships.[45] This researcher also noted that while the CTS found that there was gender symmetry, national crime victimization studies found that violence escalated over time and that men were more violent than women in intimate relationships. Finally, Kimmel also noted the United Nations statistics that estimated that 20–50% of women worldwide have been subjected to abuse, that the clear majority of residents in domestic violence shelters are women, and that emergency room documentation revealed that women are the primary victims seeking help for their injuries.[46] Additional research would also be helpful to understand the prevalence and different forms that abuse takes with same-sex couples and the elderly. Stark has warned of using an "incident-specific violence" definition as not all abuse is physical rather than subordination.[47] It is also significant that Tjaden and Thoennes, seminal researchers who conducted the National Violence Against Women Survey (2000), utilized a modified version of the CTS, but also noted the weakness in their data collection methods because they relied on telephone calls rather than face-to-face interviews of their subjects.[48] Tjaden and Thoennes acknowledged the limitations of such telephone surveys in this national study of domestic violence in the United States.[49] Gelles, a seminal researcher in domestic violence, also noted the weaknesses of conducting telephone interviews.[50] Tjaden and Thoennes found it necessary to modify the CTS to include questions about violence experienced over a lifetime, including stalking and sexual assault. Using this approach, these researchers found that, in the United States, those women physically assaulted by an intimate partner within the past twelve months prior to the survey were subjected to 3.4 physical assaults, resulting in an annual victimization rate of 44.2% of intimate partner physical assaults per 1,000 women aged 18 and older. Finally, these researchers found that women were more likely to experience physical assaults in the context of intimate partner violence, and 22.1% of surveyed women, as compared to 7.4% of surveyed men, said they were assaulted by an intimate partner at some time in their life.[51] Researchers should also consider at what age these incidents occurred and the context.

Tjaden and Thoennes's findings reveal a significant discrepancy between men and women and the use of violence in intimate relationships and the disparate impact of such abuse on women who are more likely to seek medical treatment following assaults than men, which does not support the theory of gender symmetry. Finally, allegations of mutual violence are not new. In criminal court, the national backlash against mandatory arrest led to a wave of dual arrests as batterers made allegations against their victims. To combat this alarming trend in which women were terrified to ask for help for fear of being arrested or traumatized by the criminal justice experience, reform domestic violence legislation was initiated to train law enforcement in assessing the claims of mutual violence.[52] The dual arrest rate has dropped, and women can now safely call the police when assaulted. Many social scientists acknowledge that women are more severely injured in assaults and sometimes respond to aggression in self-defense.

The research of Dobash and Dobash utilized qualitative face-to-face interviews of men and women to measure the relationship to gender and abusive behavior among couples with a history of domestic violence.[53] They determined that many men perpetrated acts of severe violence or threatening behavior, such as choking, property damage, and threats to hit, while both men and women reported that it was rare for women to engage in such behaviors. While noting the lack of clarity about self-defense, these researchers found that many women reported using violence in self-defense, while men did not. Men did not indicate that their partners' violence upset or frightened them and indicated that these physical acts were typically limited to slaps or throwing things. Men appeared to underreport their abusive behavior while women overreported their own acts of aggression. Kimmel also noted this tendency of men to underreport their aggression and for women to overreport their own behavior.[54] Finally, these researchers concluded that the rarity of women's threats of abuse indicated an absence of the patterns or constellation of abusive behaviors that is the hallmark of male violence.

In Canada, Dobash and Dobash summarized the Violence Against Women Survey of 1995 and found that 12,300 women surveyed were at greater risk of violence from intimate partners than from strangers.[55] This research took pains to modify the typical telephone method of surveying battered women by asking if it was safe to talk, providing a toll-free number for their subjects to call back, and offering to talk at a more convenient time. The study also found that 29% of women who have been married or lived in a common-law relationship with a man had experienced at least one incident of physical assault by their intimate partner.[56] For women still living with an abusive man, two-thirds experienced more than one assault, and one-tenth had suffered ten or more attacks. These researchers confirmed that the rate of violence increased following separation. They noted that 41% of such women experienced more than ten assaults, 45% of the women were physically injured, 40% saw a doctor at least once because of their injuries, and 85% reported experiencing depression, anxiety, or related mental health problems because of the abuse.[57]

Dobash and Dobash have also cited the extensive body of research that indicates that when women are surveyed for abuse over their lifetimes, they reported a minimum of two to four times more violence than men and are more likely to report living with chronic abuse.[58] Dobash and Dobash further noted that while the CTS has been found to have some validity, critics argue that these instruments are "act-based" assessment tools, equating the acts of a small woman with those of a large, physically fit man. Such behavior could include throwing a pillow, as opposed to a lamp or a similarly heavy object, with very different results. These researchers noted that questions that simply measure whether someone committed, or attempted to commit, an act, without regard to the size discrepancies between the parties or the results are not accurate measurements of domestic violence. Zorza argues that acts of self-defense by women should not be included in surveys about domestic violence.[59] Stark noted that batterers' threats may be veiled and only recognized by the battered woman, and she may be viewed as hysterical or unstable when she responds with terror to such references.[60]

Finally, Dobash and Dobash concluded that further research on domestic violence is needed to include qualitative and quantitative data. In other words, domestic violence occurs in situations where the playing field is not level, where one partner—typically the man—uses many forms of abuse, including his economic position, to exert control and threats. Evaluating all actions as capable of having an equal impact means that we are failing to comprehend the inequality of male–female violence that permeates such abuse. It is essential that the mental health profession and family courts look at the whole picture to assess whether there is a history of domestic violence. Have both parties contributed equally and freely to the family finances? Has one party experienced threats, sexual abuse, or psychological abuse? These factors are important indicators of the context in which domestic violence takes place.

Lehmann et al. developed the Checklist of Controlling Behaviors (CCB), which is a useful measurement.[61] Their research is based on Dutton and Goodman's analysis of intimate partner violence and the use of coercion, rather than simply acts of physical aggression.[62] These researchers noted that such abuse is best understood in the "context of the relationship and the cultural, social, and institutional systems within which the perpetrator and victim live."[63] Following this model, Lehmann et al. conducted research with 2,135 women seeking battered women's shelters. The study measured such variables as economic, sexual, physical, and emotional isolation; intimidation; blaming; threats; assertions of male privilege; and minimization. These researchers found that the CCB was an important instrument for measuring and understanding the subtleties of battered women's experiences. They noted that use of this instrument can help others to understand the depth of the coercive control experienced by women in the context of intimate partner violence, even where the battered woman herself is unaware of the full extent of her abuse. This is important to consider as many battered women do not understand the full extent of their abuse and need help to understand that what seems normal to them is, in fact, abuse. Mental health professionals who can listen for coercive elements in our clients' relationships can provide essential help to the courts and policy-makers. This is critical as, in many instances in my practice while actively listening to my clients, I have been able to identify the existence of abuse and help them understand that their freedom has been compromised.

Conclusion

In my practice, I represented a woman who was thrown across the room by her husband during the divorce proceedings. She was badly bruised and required ongoing treatment for her injuries. During the hearing, the husband admitted to hurting my client and excused his behavior, indicating that he was extremely upset because of the divorce, and he apologized to the judge, but not to my client. The husband's testimony demonstrated his extreme sense of entitlement, in which he believed that he was justified in his use of violence to control my client because of her growing independence after she filed for divorce although they still lived together. While previously the husband had not resorted to physical assaults, he considered himself entitled to have sex with his wife regardless of her willingness, failed to contribute to the household expenses, and constantly belittled his wife in the presence of their son.

The judge concluded that this incident was situational couple violence in the context of a high-conflict divorce. This finding had consequences in the related custody and visitation case. While the judge was aware that he would have to take into consideration the proven existence of domestic violence in custody litigation, by reframing this incident as situational couple's violence, he did not have to confront the husband's unfitness as a custodial parent.

The application of the theories of situational violence and gender symmetry in the context of custody and divorce litigation in the family courts has been used to justify arrangements that present significant safety risks for battered women and children. There is a significant body of research that indicates that women continue to be at risk of abuse for many years after separation. Severe physical abuse and threatening behavior has been more widely attributed to men as part of the constellation or pattern of abusive behaviors. Women have been found to overreport their own aggression, while men underreport their behavior. Research has indicated that women are more severely injured during incidents of abuse, requiring emergency room treatment or relocation to battered women's shelters. Large-scale research of domestic violence over the lifetime may require the use of telephone interviews. However, it is important to understand the limitations of such interviews and, when possible, to include comparative in-person interviews of the participants to more fully understand the context of such abuse, including the significance of threats and the severity of any injuries.

There are also concerns about the reliability of data obtained in telephone interviews. In my practice, I have found that abused women may be ashamed to admit that they have been abused or may have difficulty recalling incidents of abuse because of the traumatic nature of their experiences. Problems with memory are frequent, as many traumatized survivors have difficulty distinguishing one incident from another, particularly where the abusive incidents are so numerous that they merge into each other. Interviewing a client about her history of abuse takes time to establish trust and to allow her to process the difficult memories of abuse. It would be difficult to obtain this information in a single telephone call, without face-to-face contact, and requires considerable skill on the part of the interviewer. Difficulty in recalling and relating abuse is symptomatic of trauma but is frequently misunderstood in the context of custody and divorce litigation where, without supporting evidence, her allegations may be perceived as exaggerated or fabricated.

There is considerable confusion in the family courts because of the different conceptual definitions of domestic violence, the context of physical aggression which may be linked to self-defense, the problems in self-reporting, and the failure to identify the significance of threats of future violence or abuse. Many of the earlier studies of domestic violence used telephone interviews to gather information for the first time on an unprecedentedly large scale, providing important data about the extent of domestic violence. This has influenced our discussion of gender and violence. Notably, more recently, social scientists have argued that while women were more severely injured during incidents of abuse than men, women were violent at roughly the same rate. However, the use of in-depth personal interviews—albeit on a smaller scale—to study patterns of gender violence reveals much more about the context, severity, and reporting patterns of men and women. Notably, research that includes in-person interviews and an analysis of the ability of the aggressor to instill fear reveals that domestic violence is a gendered crime against women, with significant physical consequences. Allegations of mutual violence were found to be less credible in the criminal court arena. Many states have now enacted criminal laws that require law enforcement to conduct a primary aggressor analysis to determine the full history of abuse, the relative size of the parties, and the presence of any threats.[64] The application in the family courts of a typology of domestic violence that includes mutual and situational violence has been used to justify orders of unsupervised visitation, overnights, and joint and sole orders of custody to fathers who have been abusive.

Understanding domestic violence as a form of coercion and manipulation, in which batterers utilize a range of behaviors that are not limited to physical abuse, allows us to return to the important work of protecting women and children. A careful understanding and identification of families with such histories can provide the family court with a broader understanding of abuse that will allow the family courts to develop visitation and custody arrangements that avoid retraumatizing women and children.

4

The Effects of Trauma on Children

It is widely recognized that exposure to domestic violence, substance abuse, and untreated serious mental illness has harmful consequences for children. This exposure can be traumatic and has profound implications for children during custody and divorce litigation. When these children have additional vulnerabilities, such as physical or developmental disabilities, they are even more at risk for harm. This chapter will discuss the importance of identifying the symptoms associated with exposure to traumatic events, including domestic violence and sexual abuse, and the impact of substance abuse on parenting and attachment. Finally, this chapter will discuss the theories of parental alienation that have thrived in the courts and created a culture in which the needs of children and their public health concerns are not addressed.

To recognize potentially traumatized children, it is important to review the research in this area and the cognitive and developmental impact of trauma on children because their development is affected by complex environmental and biological influences. When children experience trauma, their development is profoundly affected and they may display symptoms in many areas. As discussed in Chapter 2, trauma has been recognized as the experience of an overwhelming and terrifying experience, frequently accompanied by a profound sense of helplessness; traumatic events may be so devastating that they bring about neurological and psychological changes. Traumatic exposure can cause posttraumatic stress disorder (PTSD) in children and adolescents of all ages. Herman also identified complex PTSD, occurring when there is exposure to severe repetitive traumatic experiences.[1] Such experiences can include exposure to a wide range of environmental factors including natural disasters, war, childhood victimization, exposure to domestic violence, physical or sexual abuse, or neglect.[2]

Children's Exposure to Trauma

Traumatized children frequently present with symptoms that can include physical, psychological, educational, and behavioral difficulties. There is an extensive body of research on the neurological impact of trauma on children and adults. PTSD in children, adolescents, and adults has been widely recognized in the *Diagnostic and Statistical Manual of Mental Disorders* (DSM-5) in the category of trauma- and stressor-related disorders.[3] It is now recognized that children as young as one year may develop PTSD if they are directly exposed to threats of violence or life-threatening abuse, witnessed the threat or attack on a parent or primary caregiver, or learned that this incident occurred. Individuals six years of age or older, including children, adolescents, and adults, can also be traumatized by subsequent repeated exposures to details related to the initial traumatic incident, and the threats or abuse may be directed at a close friend or relative.[4]

Similarly, children are also affected by their mothers' traumatic exposure. Pat-Horenczyk et al., in a study of Israeli mothers exposed to traumatic events such as war and bombing, found that there was a connection between the mothers' difficulties in regulating emotions and their children's deficit in such regulation.[5] The research on preschool-aged children by Chemtob et al. following the attacks of September 11, 2001, found that although children were affected by the impact of direct exposure to that attack, they may also have been affected by their mothers' responses.[6]

Bremner has also found that exposure to life-threatening situations can cause a broad range of "trauma spectrum" disorders that include depression, PTSD, dissociative disorders, substance abuse, and borderline personality disorder in adults.[7] The problem of the comorbidity of trauma and substance abuse if clients self-medicate can be addressed by therapists and attorneys with referrals to appropriate counseling and services.

The Public Health Impact of Childhood Exposure to Trauma

While exposure to trauma is troubling for all ages, children are vulnerable developmentally to its cumulative effects if they are not removed from the source of their exposure. Childhood trauma has a dramatic impact on children's neurological development, one that is complex and impacts their functioning in myriad ways. Finkelhor noted that the study of child victims had been largely ignored by the academic field of criminology, allowing myths about childhood victimization to thrive.[8] This oversight on the part of criminology is also reflected in the family courts' response to traumatized children.

The link to childhood victimization and public health was clarified in the Centers for Disease Control (CDC) study (1998) conducted by Felitti et al., which analyzed the relationship of childhood abuse to long-term health effects.[9] These researchers' large study of 9,508 adults enrolled in an health maintenance organization (HMO) found that adults who had experienced four or more forms of abuse as children had increased risks of alcoholism, drug abuse, depression, and suicide attempts. Felitti et al. conceptualized these as adverse childhood experiences (ACEs) or abusive experiences that included psychological, physical, and sexual abuse; living in homes where there was domestic violence directed at their mothers; or living in homes where a family member had a substance abuse problem, was mentally ill, or suicidal. These researchers raised the important question of whether exposure to more than one adverse experience in childhood could have cumulative and long-lasting effects. They asked participants to provide retrospective reports about their exposure to ACEs and found that 23.5% of participants grew up with an adult who abused alcohol, and 28% of women and 16% of men had been sexually abused. Participants who had experienced multiple ACEs suffered from increased risks of using illegal drugs, including the injection of illegal substances, alcoholism, and sexually transmitted diseases. Alarmingly, Felitti et al. concluded that multiple exposures to abuse or household dysfunction were linked to increased risk factors for the development of life-threatening diseases, including ischemic heart disease, cancer, chronic lung disease, fractures, and liver disease.

There is also a significant body of research about the neurological impact of childhood stresses. The epidemiological study by Anda et al. of exposure to ACEs and its neurological impact found considerable evidence of the relationship between health and social problems over the lifespan.[10] Their research covered 18,175 adults exposed to ACEs that included exposure to child abuse, sexual abuse, domestic violence, substance abuse, criminal behavior, and parental separation. They also found considerable evidence of the impact of childhood stress on the brain and other physical systems. Bremner's review of the research on PTSD and the brain found a significant body of research on the impact of trauma on the brain in adults and children resulting in changes in the structure of the hippocampus, an area of the brain related to memory.[11] This researcher concluded that adults and children with PTSD suffered from memory deficits and that children exposed to ACEs had deficits in their verbal declarative memory and difficulty in storing memories and in mood regulation. However, despite the differences found in the hippocampus of individuals exposed to trauma, traumatic memories endure. There is considerable research that supports the concept that traumatic memories are processed differently, causing them to be inaccessible from time to time.[12] However, McPherson-Sexton concluded that, despite differences in the hippocampus of individuals exposed to trauma, traumatic memories remain well preserved in what has been called *implicit memories*, in which the abuse is recalled in flashes of vivid images, a rush of feelings, and sensations associated with the recall of traumatic incidents.[13]

Anda et al. also found that traumatic exposure can lead to the development of hallucinations, poor anger control, and the risk of becoming a perpetrator of intimate partner violence. This finding is not far-fetched. In my practice, I have seen very extreme symptomatology in some of the preschool-aged children whose mothers had been abused. Some of these children had active hallucinations following a prolonged period in which they had unsupervised overnight visits with their abusive fathers.

Widom et al. faulted studies that focused on retrospective reports of child maltreatment while acknowledging that child maltreatment had an impact on children, causing symptoms of anxiety, depression, or PTSD.[14] However, these researchers acknowledged the ways in which such exposure to child maltreatment could cause disruptions in child development and the ability to complete age-appropriate tasks. Despite these concerns, the vast body of neurobiological research has demonstrated the complex and decades-long mind–body impact of toxic stress and ACEs.

Kendall-Tackett conceptualized five ways in which trauma impacts the body through physiological, behavioral, cognitive, social, and emotional pathways that result in enormous personal and public health costs.[15] This researcher found that physiological changes included a lower pain threshold and a higher risk of developing chronic pain syndrome, somatic complaints, irritable bowel syndrome, rheumatoid diseases, lupus, and scleroderma. Behavioral pathways of toxic stress are evidenced in increased risks of substance abuse, obesity, and eating disorders—to name a few—and higher risks of suicide and risky sexual behavior. Cognitive pathways included learning problems, while social problems are seen in the increased risk of homelessness among traumatized persons; finally, emotional pathways include increased risks of symptoms of depression and other mental health problems.

In conceptualizing the impact on cognitive pathways, Kendall-Tackett noted that the experiences of shame, embarrassment, and humiliation were frequently associated with the experience of abuse and development of a negative self-image. This finding is consistent with research that indicates that while PTSD was initially viewed as a fear-based disorder, Beck et al.,[16] in a small study of battered women, noted that they experienced elevated levels of shame and guilt related to the abuse.[17] Feiring et al. studied the attributional styles of abused children and adolescents who had been sexually abused under the assumption that survivors of abuse frequently blame themselves for the abuse, rather than external factors, causing them to experience shame and significant psychological distress.[18] These researchers concluded that such feelings of shame are a significant part of the experience of victimization, along with the victims' negative feelings about their own culpability in the abuse.[19] These researchers found that adolescents were particularly vulnerable to experiencing elevated levels of depressive symptoms and lower levels of self-esteem following sexual abuse. Pico-Alfonso also found that battered women are more traumatized by psychological abuse than physical abuse.[20] This is consistent anecdotally with many women in my practice who have been abused; they frequently blame themselves and experience low self-esteem, shame, and more serious psychological distress. It may be that this is a result of the degradation that accompanies psychological abuse.

Biomedical research has found that the experience of childhood abuse creates toxic levels of stress that can lead to a wide range of medical problems. In adulthood, Kendall-Tackett has indicated that these individuals are at risk of developing chronic pain syndrome, somatic complaints, joint pain, insomnia, fatigue, abdominal pain, severe headaches, diarrhea, constipation, shortness of breath, facial pain, dizziness, nausea, and chest pain.[21] This researcher also found that adults abused as children are at greater risk of being hospitalized with autoimmune diseases, including diabetes, irritable bowel syndrome, rheumatoid diseases, lupus, and scleroderma. A number of researchers have indicated that their increased risks for hospitalizations for such autoimmune diseases persist for decades.[22] Adult survivors of childhood abuse have a significantly higher rate of mental health concerns, including PTSD and depression. Finally, the research indicates that adult survivors of childhood sexual abuse will incur greater health care costs and increased hospitalizations.[23] We can infer from the overwhelming body of research on the biomedical impact of toxic stress caused by exposure to abuse and trauma that allowing such exposure to continue has significant public health consequences. For children, continued traumatic exposure may make it impossible for them to have a normal life. Therefore, it is essential that the legal system develops an informed approach of trauma prevention for children and battered mothers.

Trauma in Infants and Preschool Children

There has been considerable research on the impact of trauma and development of PTSD in infants and toddlers. Lieberman observed that children in the first five years of life can be profoundly affected by exposure to domestic violence, child abuse, community violence, and war.[24] She concluded that maternal well-being had a key role in building resilience in children and that when mothers suffered from depression, anxiety, and PTSD, they were less sensitive to their children's distress. It is important that these findings inform the services we give battered mothers because, with more social supports, they will be better able to facilitate resilience in their children.

Feldman and Vengrober conducted a study of 232 children aged 1.5 to 5 years of age, 148 of whom had been exposed to life-threatening bombing and war, sometimes daily.[25] Many of the children recreated the trauma in their play, displayed increased interest in objects while demonstrating withdrawal from social interactions, and had difficulties in sleep, regulation of their moods, and self-soothing. Children who were exposed to more war-related trauma were more likely to develop PTSD. Finally, these researchers concluded that the children's attachment to their mothers empowered them to be more resilient. Feldman and Vengrober also found that their findings on resilience were consistent with Bowlby's research on attachment and the role of mothers who displayed sensitivity to their children's feelings.[26]

Additionally, Alisic and Kleber noted the need for developmentally appropriate ways to measure children's stress responses to trauma. These researchers found that while children may demonstrate many of the symptoms experienced by adults, there are also symptoms that are found only in this age group. Thus, traumatized children may demonstrate regressive behaviors, separation anxiety, somatic complaints, and recklessness.[27] In a review of the research by Pynoos et al., these researchers noted that the severity of the symptoms is linked to the level of their exposure and that these symptoms may also consist of specific new fears and sleep disturbances.[28]

In my practice, clients have reported that their children experienced sudden nightmares, regression in toilet training, increased aggression toward adults and other children, and even sexualized behavior. In one instance, a five-year-old boy experienced hallucinations after unsupervised overnight visitation with a father who had been suspected of sexual abuse. In each case, the symptoms were verified by treating medical personnel and mental health providers. These instances should be viewed as red flags indicating possible exposure to ACEs that may include domestic violence, child maltreatment, and abuse. Too often during custody litigation, these symptoms are dismissed as a reaction to a high-conflict divorce. The integration of trauma theory into our understanding of divorce and custody will enable the legal and mental health systems to identify and address the problems of traumatic exposure to abuse.

Traumatic Exposure to Domestic Violence in Children

Bair-Merritt et al., noting the impact of exposure to domestic violence in children, spoke compellingly about these "silent victims" and noted the link between their high-stress home environment, their neuroendocrine stress responses, and the development of multiple physical and mental health problems, which was confirmed by other researchers.[29] Bair-Merritt et al. found that such elevated levels of stress accompanying exposure to domestic violence and the constant "fight-or-flight" response generated have debilitating long-term effects on children. These medical researchers agreed that it was essential for the medical profession to utilize safe screening mechanisms to protect their patients and that such screening should be part of our public health response to this problem. Herman, a seminal researcher in the field of trauma and recovery, also observed that exposure to trauma in children influences the fundamental development of their personality structure.[30] Thus, early studies of preschool children of battered mothers by Pagelow found that they were excessively fearful, suffered from sleep disorders, and associated nighttime with the occurrence of violence.[31]

Researchers have agreed that children in homes where there is domestic violence are at significant risk of being abused, with some researchers finding that this risk is as high as 50%.[32] It is also widely acknowledged that exposure to domestic violence is harmful to children and can result in a range of physical and psychological problems.

Critics of the initial studies argued that the sample research population was taken from the shelter system and represented the most extreme levels of intimate partner violence.[33] However, there is a body of more recent research that has confirmed the relationship between the symptoms observed and the abuse of women and children.[34] Studies have also confirmed the harm to children exposed to domestic violence, and Holt et al. concluded that witnessing the violence can take many forms, including overhearing their father abuse their mother or viewing the aftermath of a beating.[35]

For the legal system, it is essential that we begin to acknowledge the dramatic impact on all family members of abuse, even if the batterer only targets one person in the family. Further, intimate partner violence is not limited to poorer families. In my practice, I have noticed the impact of abuse on children from affluent professional families where their mothers were doctors, lawyers, accountants, teachers, and nurses. The Recommendations of the National Council of Juvenile and Family Court Judges (1999) also noted the co-existence of domestic violence and child maltreatment in such high-risk families, indicating that children in such households were particularly vulnerable.[36] Learning that there is domestic violence in a family should be the beginning of inquiry into the potential harm to children and resulting vulnerabilities.

McCord has indicated that boys exposed to domestic violence as children may have a greater risk of becoming violent adults.[37] This researcher's fortyyear longitudinal study found that close to one-half of the men raised in homes with an aggressive father had themselves been convicted of a violent crime. This researcher concluded that witnessing aggression reduces the child's ability to experience empathy or to respond to others' pain.[38] Foshee et al. found that adolescents exposed to domestic violence have been found to have a higher incidence of engaging in physical dating violence, bullying, and sexual harassment.[39] Finally, these researchers concluded that such aggression coincided with low maternal monitoring, depression, and anger reactivity and noted that domestic violence interfered with parenting.[40]

Preschool children may have emotional bonds to parents who are abusive. Stover et al. noted that attachment and emotional bonding are a normal part of development, and small children may not exhibit fear or resistance to seeing a parent who has been abusive.[41] In the context of custody or divorce litigation, the protective parent can provide the history of the children's symptoms. This process may be complicated by children delaying disclosure or by the difficulty traumatized mothers have in recalling or discussing events and the dates when incidents occurred.

The Prevalence of Childhood Sexual Abuse

Sexual abuse has long been viewed as a taboo topic. Although studies have concluded that a considerable number of sexual abuse offenses are committed by someone other than a family member, this discussion centers on intrafamilial abuse.[42] Sexual abuse may also not involve direct physical contact or penetration, but may include sexualized touching of a child or incidents in which the abuser exposed himself.[43]

The U.S. Fourth National Incidence Study of Child Abuse and Neglect (2010) conducted by Sedlak et al. provided a wealth of data regarding the prevalence and characteristics of sexual abuse that can assist the legal system in identifying the numbers of children who have been abused.[44] This national study reviewed the child welfare case records of 2.35 million children who have been maltreated in the United States and found that almost one-quarter had been the victims of sexual abuse.[45] Follow-up research by Putnam found that girls were the target of sexual abuse more than boys, and children between six and eight years of age were found to be the most frequent victims, although earlier studies had concluded that there was a significantly higher rate among children aged twelve years and older.[46]

Putnam identified various risk factors that increased the likelihood that children could be sexually abused; these include the presence of a stepfather in the home and a child's physical disability, with disabled boys having a higher level of risk than disabled girls.[47] Bolen has indicated that there is consensus that sexual abuse continues to be an underreported crime.[48] A retrospective small study of sexual abuse in female college students by Arroyo et al. found that only 27% of these students had ever disclosed their abuse to anyone.[49]

There is some controversy as to whether sexually abused children display symptoms of psychological harm as children. Putnam's research indicated that many adult psychiatric conditions have been clinically associated with childhood sexual abuse, including major depression, borderline personality disorders, somatization, substance abuse, PTSD, dissociative disorder, and eating disorders.[50] Boys have been found to experience more symptoms than girls.[51]

More recently, the Mayo Clinic as well as the Center for Disease Control (CDC) identified the following psychological problems as symptoms of sexual abuse: sexualized behaviors that are age-inappropriate, statements that the child has made displaying an age-inappropriate understanding of sexual behavior, and sexually aggressive behavior toward other children.[52] Other symptoms frequently observed in sexually abused children include nightmares, bedwetting, regression, sexually acting-out behavior, and sudden fears of one person. Putnam agreed that sexualized behaviors in children are closely linked to sexual abuse and found that younger children display more significant symptoms than older children.[53] Researchers agree that sexually abused adolescents are at greater risk for earlier pregnancy and that the risks associated with teenage pregnancy include delivery complications and infants with low birth weights.[54]

Finally, research has indicated that 10–20% of the children who have been sexually abused do not immediately display symptoms. However, these children may deteriorate over the next twelve to eighteen months. Putnam found that those children with such delayed symptomatology experienced significantly more problems than the other children.[55] These delays could be a result of their internalization of their reactions and depression. Depressed children may also not demonstrate behavior problems, thus falling through the cracks and failing to come to the attention of their teachers and caretakers.

As published by the Mayo Clinic, physical symptoms of abuse include changes in the genitals, anus, or mouth; persistent pain while urinating or during bowel movements; soiling or wetting unrelated to a toilet-training accident; and difficulty walking.[56] However, it is important to understand that when there are delayed disclosures, physical injuries may have already healed. Psychologically, it is important to remember that children who are sexually abused may recant, or disavow, their earlier statements, and recantation should be viewed as an additional symptom of sexual abuse. Children who are facing widespread hostility from their family for disclosing the abuse will simply decide to deny that the problem existed to avoid further ostracism.

Childhood sexual abuse has also been linked to neurobiological manifestations that are like those displayed by adult survivors of combat PTSD. Putnam and Trickett found that sexually abused girls developed increased neurological manifestations within six months of disclosure of the abuse.[57] There is some controversy as to whether adult survivors of child sexual abuse or survivors of physical abuse are more prone to symptoms of PTSD. Pico-Alfonso has indicated that the combination of both physical and sexual abuse causes the highest levels of PTSD and related symptomatology in adults and is a risk factor for later victimization.[58] Finally, childhood sexual abuse and exposure to domestic violence cause significant physical and psychological problems for many years and should be of significant concern to the family courts entrusted with the protection of children.

Identification of Sexual Abuse

McBride noted the need for training in sexual abuse dynamics and the persistence of many myths regarding sexual abuse, including the notion that children are highly suggestible to what has been termed "implanting false memories."[59] However, McBride noted that while children may be suggestible regarding the peripheral details of the incidents, their ability to recall and describe the actual abuse is reliable.[60]

Concerns about the process of investigating child sexual abuse remain. There is a wide disparity in how medical and mental health professionals are trained to identify sexual abuse and the physical symptoms that should trigger an investigation. When children have experienced physical sexual abuse, they may have medical symptoms such as sexually transmitted diseases. The existence of sexually transmitted diseases should be treated with utmost seriousness. The CDC noted that infants can contract such sexually transmitted diseases as neonates and that symptoms may persist until the child is a toddler. However, it is wrong to assume that infected children are not at risk. The CDC specifically recommends that physicians report evidence of sexually transmitted diseases, including genital herpes, chlamydia, syphilis, gonorrhea, and HIV to the child protective services (CPS), noting that physicians are mandated reporters of abuse.[61]

While there may be confusion as to whether such sexually transmitted diseases are the result of sexual abuse, these children require treatment and careful investigation. Rather than quickly discounting the presence of physical symptoms such as vaginal discharge, tearing, redness, or difficulty urinating, the child should be seen by a physician trained to detect sexual abuse. A hearing should be held in which evidence can be presented and the child protected.

Plummer and Eastin's study about the experience of nonoffending mothers during the criminal and CPS investigation found that the mothers were dismayed at the treatment of their concerns.[62] In this study of fifty-nine mothers aged twenty-one through fifty-five years, whose suspicions that their child had been sexually abused had been confirmed by at least one professional, reported that they were treated as if they were guilty or crazy and that they felt helpless and unable to prevent their children from being treated insensitively. Many women felt that they were viewed as unsupportive of their children and not "good mothers." They reported that they experienced isolation and financial harm when they notified the authorities, that many were rejected by relatives when the perpetrator was another family member, and that they had to spend thousands of dollars to protect their children in custody proceedings. Corcoran's review of the research has found that nonsupportive maternal responses to children's disclosure of sexual abuse have a negative effect on child victims of sexual abuse. Similarly, this researcher found that the non-offending parent's support after a disclosure of sexual abuse is positively associated with children's short- and long-term adjustments.[63] However, during custody litigation, women who make allegations of sexual abuse against fathers are frequently treated with suspicion and risk losing custody of their children. Significantly, Plummer and Eastin spoke about the importance of supporting mothers through this process as they can help provide necessary information about changes in children's behaviors. The child protective system, law enforcement, and the family courts cannot investigate these cases in a vacuum and fail to gain access to valuable information that would aid in the investigations when they treat protective mothers like criminals. Finally, children need to know that they are not to blame for the abuse. Their non-offending parent can be a helpful presence if they acknowledge the abuse and seek help for the child.

Furthermore, when allegations of sexual abuse are rejected during the CPS investigation, it is difficult for protective mothers to refute these findings in a custody proceeding. Access to the records of the investigations is limited. Protecting children in a meaningful way requires transparency. The full report and any recordings should be available to the family court, to be reviewed by the attorneys with their clients to determine how they arrived at their findings. The notes and identity of the professionals involved should be available. The questions that need to be asked include how much time was spent on information gathering, what inquiries were made, if the children were interviewed more than once, what statements were made, who reviewed the findings, and if were there any disagreements. Finally, all the investigators should be available to testify as witnesses.

Most of the centers that interview children remove them from their parents to interview them alone. Faller refers to the Child Interview Model as the model preferred by CPS at children's advocacy centers unless a criminal investigation is ongoing, in which case professionals use the joint investigation approach.[64] There are legitimate concerns that children will be pressured by parents to say things that are not true and may be intimidated by the presence of the offender. It is essential that the investigative process allows children sufficient time in a child-friendly place. Interviewing of children must be done in a way that is culturally competent. Not only must the interviewer speak the same language as the child, but they should also be familiar with culturally specific terms the child may use for genitals or body parts.

In my practice, a bilingual, preschool-aged child disclosed an incident of sexual abuse in his primary language, which was not English. When asked to repeat his story multiple times, he switched to English to make sure that he was correctly understood. Unfortunately, this was interpreted by the investigator as if the child had changed his story and the allegations were discredited. In this case, we can assume that the investigator did not understand the cultural and developmental nuances of interviewing a very bright bilingual child who was questioned repeatedly about his memories.

Faller indicated that children may need to be interviewed multiple times to establish sufficient trust to disclose that they were abused, and noted that some children are embarrassed to discuss their body parts and that they may omit highly personal events. However, this is not the same as questioning a child repeatedly to challenge their assertions. This researcher also noted that the typical budget for CPS is sufficient for one interview and not for the extended series of interviews that may be necessary.[65]

Finally, after a review of the literature, we can conclude that children who have been sexually abused have been subjected to trauma and are more likely than not to eventually display symptoms of neurological, psychological, and educational difficulties. Knowledge of the dynamics of children's response to abuse and symptoms of traumatic exposure and PTSD in children must inform investigations of childhood sexual abuse. Such investigations require more than interviewing the child and should include interviewing teachers, physicians, day care providers, therapists, mandated reporters, and family members. A thorough investigation should review whether the child has developed sudden fears, difficulty sleeping, nightmares, age-inappropriate sexualized behavior, and increased problems in school. Law enforcement and the mental health profession should be highly skilled in identifying such symptoms of traumatic exposure.

Substance Abuse and Attachment

In cases of parental drug or alcohol misuse and dependency, many researchers have indicated that parenting skills and attachment can be affected.[66] Kroll and Taylor have indicated that parenting may be chaotic or neglectful as parents become more focused on maintaining their drug abuse, and parenting behavior can become inconsistent and even neglectful. Kroll and Taylor's review of the research indicated that children's attachment to their substance-abusing parent can be impacted because the parent may be less reliable and responsive to their children's needs. Fortunately, several researchers have concluded in a study of at-risk female adolescents that the presence of a secure attachment with their primary caregiver has been found to lessen the possibilities of substance abuse in adulthood.[67] Schindler and Broning also concluded after a review of the research that insecure attachments were also a risk factor for substance abuse in adolescents. While the courts view adolescents as independent, it is important to remember that adolescents continue to need a secure attachment with their parents to provide the basis for their transition to independent lives.[68] Without such an attachment, adolescents are more vulnerable to experimentation and drug or alcohol abuse, engaging in such behaviors to cope with their own exposure to trauma or to regulate their emotions. Thus, Cihan et al. recommended that treatment should focus on helping clients develop more secure attachments, which can help to minimize their psychological and physiological needs for chemical substances.[69] The role of attachment and the responsibility of the family courts to support this relationship are clear, as Bancroft et al. indicated that batterers frequently engage in denigration of mothers, thus undermining their parenting.[70] Furthermore, battered women may have co-occurring trauma-related symptoms and could benefit from treatment that fosters, not impinges, their parent–child relationships. Such an approach requires an informed treatment approach that identifies battered women's support systems and levels of isolation, to support the children's primary attachment figure who may be suffering from the effects of trauma.

Fatherhood, Children, and the Impact of Abuse

While this book will not address the vast academic study of fatherhood in detail, it is important to note that this area of research developed alongside the study of divorce. Marsiglio et al. noted that many of the male-led social movements, including the Promise Keepers, the Million Man March on Washington, and the fathers' rights movement, have influenced our understanding of fatherhood.[71] In their critique of the literature, these researchers emphasized the need for further study that included fathers from diverse backgrounds to determine the influence of cultural variables, interviewing children to confirm the quality of their relationships, the impact of cohabiting partners, and whether children received support. Finally, Marsiglio et al. concluded that a politicized agenda may continue to shape research agendas on whether men have gender-specific parenting behaviors that make a unique contribution to children's development. While fathers can be very important in children's lives, positive treatment of their children's mothers and ability to negotiate family life without violence and abuse are essential in providing their children with positive role models.

In the context of custody litigation, children from households in which fathers have been abusive have complex relationships with their fathers that many mental health professionals find confusing. Their ambivalence and intense emotions about their fathers are frequently the reasons for allowing unsupervised or overnight visitation. Typically, my client's children do not display fear when seeing their fathers. Stover et al. indicated that children have attachments to their fathers regardless of the level of violence toward their mothers.[72] Finally, children from homes in which there has been abuse need mental health treatment to help them with their very real inability to understand their own ambivalence about their connection to a parent who violated their trust and the boundaries of family life by engaging in violence.

Decisions about visitation are complicated by the level and intensity of the feelings of the children involved. Lieberman and Van Horn[73] found that preschool children who have been separated from their violent fathers yearn for reunification, while Stover et al. noted the intensely ambivalent feelings such children feel toward their fathers that include fear, longing, and identification. Typically, during custody evaluations, children will not appear fearful with their fathers and may express enjoyment in supervised visits, particularly if there has been an extended absence.

In my practice, fathers typically bring gifts to these visits and the children respond positively to such treats. This is particularly true of very young children and should not be misconstrued. It is important to remember that the supervised visitation setting is unique and is not typical of interactions that take place without supervision.

Attachment and emotional bonds are a normal part of development despite a parent's flaws and behavior. The issue of whether abusive parents should have unsupervised access cannot be decided by children, but must be made by mental health professionals in collaboration with the legal system. Yet frequently in my practice, I have read reports from supervised visitation supervisors in which they ask very young children whether they feel safe in unsupervised visits with their father and whether they want such supervision to continue. Such questioning is developmentally inappropriate for young children. Young children are unable to grasp the concept of safety in that context and are unable to make clinical decisions about parenting arrangements. This is an adult decision, and we should not burden children with this task. We need to further consider that women are at a higher risk of elevated violence after separation and that this violence tends to occur around visitation with the children.[74]

Of concern is a recent trend in which some court evaluators or visitation supervisors have attempted to evaluate the parent–child relationship first as a means of determining whether child abuse or exposure to domestic violence has taken place. Meier noted that only if this relationship is impaired do they consider the possibility that the child could have been abused.[75] Too often, they have credited "parental alienation" rather than the impact of traumatic exposure to an abusive parent as the source of the strained relationship between fathers and children.

Children in such abusive families have a distorted sense of family life and may have impaired relationships with the nonabusive parent. Their relationship with their father, particularly when they have been separated because of domestic violence, is complex and ambivalent and causes them pain, disappointment, and confusion.[76] In families in which the father is abusive, it is troubling that the batterer will frequently devalue the role of the mother. Bancroft et al. observed that batterers frequently display contemptuous behavior, using ridicule, name-calling, verbal abuse, or insulting behavior toward the mothers in the presence of the children.[77] These researchers observed that children who observed such contemptuous attitudes toward their mothers may find this behavior acceptable. Mothers of traumatized children in households where they have been taught not to love and respect her will have difficulty parenting their children after the separation. Children with such impaired parenting and devalued role models may have difficulty with their teachers, advisors, and other adults whom they encounter. In this context, it is important to note that Bancroft et al. specifically distinguished the impact on children witnessing domestic violence from the additional problems caused by exposure to the batterer's parenting.[78] This is a significant distinction as batterers are not harmful to children simply when they are physically abusive, but display a toxic form of parenting in which they undermine their children's relationship with their mother, who is frequently the primary caretaker.

A small study by Stover et al. of children who had visitation with fathers who had been found to be abusive, included a clinical sample of fifty preschool children, twenty-two girls and twenty-eight boys, aged thirty-six to seventy-one months.[79] Each child in the study had witnessed at least one episode of severe marital violence, as reported by the police, their mothers, or CPS. Their mothers were no longer involved in the relationship with the fathers, and there was no other father figure or stepparent living with the child. Building on prior research indicating that, in violent families, the child's behaviors begins to stabilize approximately six months after separation, this research studied families who had been separated from five to forty-eight months.[80] Stover et al. observed that there were links between the fathers' level of violence and the children's behavioral problems and that those children displayed more aggression and antisocial behaviors, while children who did not see their fathers displayed more internalized feelings.[81] These researchers acknowledged that their research did not evaluate whether visitation was supervised or unsupervised and that it would be important to have more research to determine if the detrimental effects of such visitation could be minimized with supervision.

The research by Shepard of children who had court-ordered supervised visitation with fathers from families with a history of domestic violence, while small, demonstrates the harm to children from continued exposure to domestic violence.[82] Of these families, 40% of the mothers reported that the fathers had been arrested for incidents of domestic violence, none of the fathers reported that their former partners had ever been arrested, while 92% of the mothers and 45% of the fathers reported being abused. More than one-third of the mothers reported incidents of threats, harassment, failure to pay child support, abuse within the past six months, and alcohol abuse. Finally, Shepard noted that 29% of the mothers reported being sexually assaulted. Significantly, these mothers rated the children higher on conduct disorder, psychosomatic, impulsive-hyperactive, anxiety, and hyperactivity scales using the Conner's' Parent Rating Scale-48.[83] As a result, this researcher concluded that not only had the children been impacted by exposure to the domestic violence, but that maternal stress played a significant role in the children's adaptation, and, finally, that the mothers needed extensive support and protection.[84] Much more research, on a larger scale, is necessary to inform our understanding of the impact of visitation on children with abusive fathers.

Johnston and Straus discussed the children's needs for safety—both physically and emotionally—in the supervised visitation setting.[85] These researchers agreed that supervised visitation programs should minimize the risk of retraumatizing children and that such contact should take place in child-friendly settings to enhance the children's need for psychological safety. Finally, it may be that some children need to have contact with their abusive fathers in a safe supervised setting on a long-term basis to avoid idealizing this parent, although much more research is needed on the quality and safety of such supervised visitation programs.

Parental Alienation

The most controversial subject in the family courts has stemmed from parental alienation claims that have been the subject of considerable discussion in the legal and mental health fields. Most of the public believes that the phrase "parental alienation" refers to parents who speak badly of the other in the presence of the children during divorce or separation. In divorces in which there is no history of domestic violence, substance abuse, or untreated mental illness, couples may experience anger and grief immediately following their separation and not behave at their best. Johnston and Straus have indicated that children may be aware of their parents' complex feelings toward each other and may align themselves with one parent over another, ascribing blame for the breakup of their family.[86] This behavior is not pathological and is part of the anger and grief related to the separation. Rather than stigmatize parents who are not functioning at their best during separation, the delivery of informed, bias-free mental health treatment can be helpful as families meet the challenges of multiple transitions.

However, Gardner's theory of a parental alienation syndrome (PAS) argued that one parent, typically the mother, alienates the children from the other parent, typically the father, by making false allegations of abuse to gain an advantage in litigation.[87] His theory specifically indicated that false allegations of sexual abuse may be the result of such alienation and argued that the cluster of symptoms he described rose to the level of a psychological syndrome.[88] This theory clearly targeted women as alienators and goes even further to argue that such mothers can implant false memories, or delusions, of abuse in their children. It is highly problematic that use of this theory has created a climate in which children's allegations are treated with suspicion and that mothers of abused children risk losing custody of their children.

Gardner agreed that sexual abuse existed, that 95% of all cases of sexual abuse are true, and that children might reject the abusive parent in those cases, but he also articulated a profound distrust of mothers who claimed intrafamilial abuse. Notably, his work did not integrate the research on intrafamilial sexual abuse or domestic violence and thus was able to reach the flawed conclusion that this phenomenon was rare. Unfortunately, the prevalence of sexual abuse of children is well established by many researchers.[89]

Notably, Faller has also called for more research to determine the relationship between separation and sexual abuse allegations, positing that the nonoffending parent might make allegations upon learning of the abuse.[90] However, Gardner blamed a myriad of factors for such allegations during divorce, including the influence of sexual abuse prevention programs, lawyers, no-fault divorce laws, gender-neutral custody standards, and economic interests, to name a few.[91]

In my practice, battered women frequently must combat allegations of parental alienation whenever they raise issues of domestic violence, child maltreatment, mental illness, or substance abuse. This theory is also used whenever clients are reluctant to agree to extensive overnights with fathers or a schedule in which young children will reside with the other parent 50% of the time, even when there are no such allegations of abuse. Furthermore, many courts require mental health professionals to determine whether parental alienation exists whenever there are allegations of domestic violence or orders of protection during custody evaluations.

It is important to note that Gardner's theory was based on his anecdotal observations of his own practice in several of his self-published books.[92] Currently, most mental health professionals acknowledge that while his concept of parental alienation as a syndrome is invalid, they accept the underlying premise of this theory (although parental alienation is not recognized in the DSM-5, the most recent edition of this manual). However, in custody litigation, assumptions about the validity of parental alienation are so commonplace that even if allegations of domestic violence are substantiated, mothers may be accused of parental alienation if they object to unsupervised visitation, extensive access, or joint custody. Furthermore, when allegations of child or sexual abuse are not substantiated, mothers are accused of engaging in parental alienation and may lose custody of the children.

Alarmingly, the confusion over identification of the related symptomatology of sexual abuse has been exacerbated by Gardner's attempt to refute several findings regarding it. Referencing Freud's concept of children's sexuality, he argued that they were polymorphous perverse and capable of behavior that adults consider inappropriate; Gardiner claimed that age-inappropriate sexualized behavior was not symptomatic of sexual abuse.[93] While young children may have an uninhibited sense of their bodies, this can be distinguished from age-inappropriate sexualized behavior that displays knowledge of sexuality that is developmentally inappropriate, and a symptom of sexual abuse. Gardner argued instead that such symptoms could be a symptom of other psychological disturbances, or even normal behavior.[94] Age-inappropriate sexualized behavior in children could be a result of other psychological disturbances; however, it is misguided for mental health and medical professionals to overlook the empirical significance of such symptoms when investigating sexual abuse. Given the potential for trauma to abused children, when professionals are confronted with such symptoms, sexual abuse must be ruled out before proceeding to other possible diagnoses or theories.

Gardner originally developed the Sexual Abuse Legitimacy Scale (SALS) to evaluate the legitimacy of such allegations in which he utilized eighty-four factors to measure such abuse.[95] Faller has reviewed the empirical problems with SALS in depth, noting that it has been widely criticized and is no longer in use.[96] Questions that asked therapists to report whether a child had been subjected to direct programming, if an attorney or mental health professional had been hired to act as a hired gun, and whether there was a history of vengeful acts suggests an outcome.[97] Wood noted that this scale has been rejected by the courts and is no longer in use by mental health professionals to determine the validity of abuse.[98] This researcher also found that this instrument was not recognized among scientific and medical experts in this field, and criticized Gardner's interviewing methods as well.[99]

Trocmé and Bala noted that many of the scales utilized to assess whether a child has been sexually abused continue to articulate the commonly held belief that separating mothers fabricate claims of sexual abuse—despite the research to the contrary.[100] This is in part based on Gardner's early writings in which he stated that 90% of disputed custody cases include parental alienation, that 90% of allegations are made by mothers, and that the vast majority of these allegations are false—all of which remain at odds with the U.S. and Canadian national studies.[101]

Faller also found that, for many mothers, learning that their child had been sexually abused by the other parent could be the catalyst for the divorce or separation.[102] In fact, when mothers do not leave, the courts hold them responsible for failing to protect their children. It is disturbing that the backlash against protective parents, typically mothers, is so severe that many women are terrified about raising sexual abuse allegations during litigation or are warned by their lawyers not to bring this up for fear of losing custody.

Hans et al. also noted that a lack of training in the field of sexual abuse identification has contributed to the commonly held belief in the courts that mothers make false allegations of domestic violence.[103] The theory of parental alienation has influenced the climate surrounding the investigation of sexual abuse, causing investigators to be suspicious of such allegations made during custody litigation. Today, while the American Psychological Association (APA) 1996 Presidential Task Force on Violence noted the empirical weakness of parental alienation syndrome, they take no position on the validity of this theory.[104] In my practice, I have repeatedly heard professionals refer to the notion that 90% of mothers fabricate charges of sexual abuse during divorce—without an awareness of the fragile basis for such claims.

The research of Clemente and Padilla-Racero studied 296 children ranging from the first to the sixth grade in high-pressure situations and determined that it was rare for these children to lie under pressure about aggression, criticizing the underlying empirical basis for the theory of parental alienation.[105] Their research was criticized by Bernet et al. who argued that the authors' blamed

PAS and parental alienation (PA) for the errors of the legal system and that mental health professionals who evaluate for such alienation first consider whether the abuse occurred before finding that this disorder exists, sparking a response by the original authors.[106]

However, while Gardner's work may be viewed as a response to the confusion in the growing field of sexual abuse investigation, this does not mean that children's disclosures of abuse during custody and divorce litigation should be rejected or that they are as suggestible as frequently claimed. Furthermore, there is significant concern that the symptomatology described in parental alienation can also be attributed to exposure to abuse or trauma. Stark has also described the significant pressure that has taken place to discredit critics of the theory of parental alienation.[107]

In contrast, Cheit's exhaustive review of studies on children's suggestibility found that such research was inconclusive.[108] While children should not be asked leading questions, this should not preclude investigators from asking essential follow-up questions to determine the meaning of the original statements. If investigators do not clarify what children mean by their statements, it is impossible to obtain an understanding of the facts and circumstances of the incidents alleged. While not all sexualized behaviors are symptomatic of abuse, such behavior should raise significant concerns and warrant investigation into the context in which such behaviors have occurred.

In New York, the Court of Appeals upheld admission of the child's therapist's statements that the child had reported that the "respondent had 'put white paste' from his genital area in her mouth and all over her" along with other symptoms of abuse. *Matter of Nicole V*.[109] The Court found that this statement, exemplifying age-inappropriate knowledge of sexuality to the child's therapist, along with other physical symptoms of abuse and depression, was corroboration of the child's sexual abuse *Matter of Nicole V*.[110]

Finally, there needs to be improved education and training of mental health, medical, and law enforcement personnel on the investigation and substantiation of sexual abuse allegations. However, such training and investigations must begin with data and theories that are empirically supported and unbiased.

The Rate of False Allegations

Trocmé and Bala's review of the Canadian Incidence Study of Reported Child Abuse and Neglect addressed the rate of substantiated allegations of child abuse or neglect.[111] These researchers studied 135,574 child neglect and abuse cases, finding that there were an average 21.58 investigations of maltreatment per 1,000 children. They found that 42% of these total investigations were substantiated, 23% of cases were suggestive of maltreatment but required more information, and the remaining 35%of the investigations were unsubstanti-ated. Critically, Trocmé and Bala concluded that, of the unsubstantiated cases, the overall rate for intentionally false allegations was only 4%.[112] Significantly, this study determined that the rate of substantiation was significantly lower where families were involved in custody or visitation litigation.[113] Furthermore, Trocmé and Bala noted that, because most investigations of abuse are con-ducted by child welfare workers who typically do not possess a graduate degree, this may result in the underreporting of such incidents of abuse.[114] Similarly, in the United States, most first-responding caseworkers do not have a graduate education and may have limited clinical training in the identification of phys-ical and sexual abuse. Stark has observed that false allegations of abuse occur with less frequency than false denials in custody disputes.[115]

These research findings raise the critical issue of whether child protection caseworkers, the medical, legal, and mental health professionals who investi-gate such allegations during custody, are influenced by the psychological theo-ries that treat with suspicion intrafamilial allegations during separation. This raises significant public health and safety concerns that must be addressed.

More recently, McBride has indicated that most child sexual abuse investi-gations are conducted at child advocacy centers that utilize a multidisciplinary approach with law enforcement and mental health professionals in a child-friendly environment.[116] However, many misconceptions about sexual abuse, the perpetrators, and children remain. Hetherton and Beardsall's study found that half of the physicians interviewed believed that most sexual abuse allega-tions made during divorce proceedings were false.[117] This is a persistent miscon-ception that has been incorporated into some of the formalized trainings about investigating sexual abuse.

When custody evaluators do not have sufficient background and exper-tise to determine the veracity of allegations of sexual abuse, it is disturbing that many such allegations are discounted. Haselschwerdt et al. concluded that the notion that women falsify such allegations, either to obtain custody of the children or to alienate these children from their fathers, continues to be a com-monly held belief among custody evaluators.[118]

Allegations of Mothers as Gatekeepers

More recently, claims that mothers, as the custodial parents, act as gatekeepers to restrict fathers' access have grown. Austin et al. argued that custody liti-gation should be referred to as gatekeeping disputes in which mothers may assume a gatekeeping role to restrict the fathers' access.[119] These researchers describe various forms of gatekeeping including facilitative, where one parent actively supports the children's relationship with the other parent.[120] Austin et al. indicated that facilitative gatekeepers resolve their issues outside of court and are not seen in litigation. Facilitative gatekeepers were defined as parents who are flexible about scheduling, encouraging phone and Skype calls to the other parent, supporting the other parent's exercise of discipline, and, finally, keeping the other parent fully informed of all aspects of a child's life.[121] Austin et al. identified restrictive gate keepers as those who may engage in parental alienation.

In my practice, abusive fathers frequently demand a rigid daily schedule of telephone conversations to take place at specific times for a predetermined duration. In other cases, these fathers may complain if they are not provided with daily reports of the child's activities. Efforts to discipline a child, to make decisions about bedtime or homework, can result in interrogations and threats to return to court, thinly disguised as co-parenting communications. No parent should deny a child the right to talk to their other parent when requested or refuse to provide the other parent with school or medical records, if this does not jeopardize safety. However, the formalization of such demands with abusive fathers should not be confused with their desire to remain involved in their children's lives, but rather should be recognized as an effort to assert control and undermine the mothers' parenting. In my practice, my clients are constantly made to feel on the defensive and threatened with continued litigation if they do not give a daily report to the batterer of all details in their children's lives. Significantly, in less-distressed families without domestic violence, mental illness, or substance abuse, many parents in my practice have refused to establish a telephone schedule and have only a minimal formalized visitation schedule. Such parents argue that they have the flexibility to resolve such issues together and do not want these things included in a formal agreement. When faced with a formal visitation schedule, they renegotiate this together, considering their children's wishes.

In comparison, Austin et al. advocates that forensic mental health custody evaluators measure whether parents are facilitative, restrictive, or protective gatekeepers, finding that the more restrictive are engaging in severe parental alienation.[122] In my practice, a battered mother with a very sick young child had to withstand allegations of parental alienation and gatekeeping as opposing counsel argued that her efforts to keep the child safe in supervised visitation reflected her need to be in constant control. When the court learned that the child had a significant life-threatening medical problem, opposing counsel alleged that my client was overly anxious and controlling, engaging in restrictive gatekeeping. These allegations had the potential to obfuscate the real parenting difficulties the batterer had in caring for his child with special needs. Finally, it is essential that the mental health and legal professionals have training on trauma, the evidence of physical injuries, and symptomatology of sexual abuse that is grounded in empirical research.

Resilience in Children

Herman has indicated that the impact of domestic violence or child abuse is frequently affected by the severity and frequency of the traumatic exposure.[123] Children's resilience can be enhanced if they receive help and support in the aftermath of these incidents. It is in this area that the legal system plays an essential role in either promoting or hindering children's treatment and potential recovery. Bancroft and Silverman cite several factors that influence resilience in children exposed to domestic violence, including involvement in activities that they enjoy, peer support, access to a relationship with an adult they can trust, and their ability to escape self-blame.[124] These are relatively benign factors, but they cannot be made available if the family life continues to be permeated by violence and abuse. In the context of family life, when one parent has been abusive, access to these ameliorating factors can be enhanced by providing support to the nonabusive parent. Along these lines, Margolin has noted the importance of the nonabusive parent, typically the mother, in the lives of children who have been exposed to domestic violence.[125] We can conclude that supporting battered mothers is a critical factor in strengthening the resilience of traumatized children and that the family courts can play an essential role in helping such children recover.

Conclusion

The family courts were established to address the legal needs of families. While the individual family members may have competing interests and our definition of a family has grown, the primary focus in the twenty-first century must be to protect children. In this context, the family courts must provide due process protections for the parents in recognition of their fundamental right to raise their children. However, the history of custody jurisprudence and gender bias against single mothers created an atmosphere in the family courts in which arguments are heard that have little empirical support and endanger the safety of children. Given all that we know about trauma and its life-long effects, it is essential that the courts provide for the safety of children. First and foremost, we must credit what we know about symptoms of traumatic exposure in children and the causal links with domestic violence, maltreatment, and trauma.

Recognition of traumatic exposure in children begins with an understanding of the symptomatology of exposure to domestic violence, child maltreatment, and sexual abuse. These are areas of practice that require intensive training in interviewing children, public funding, and a clinical education that is informed by an understanding of trauma and the public health consequences of its impact. Considering the research about the importance of the nonabusive parent in the adjustment of abused children and the need to support attachment between children and the nonabusive parent, it is essential that the legal system affirmatively support this relationship. Battered women may not be perfect parents, but, critically, they have not engaged in criminal behavior in the home, and, with help, they can provide the support their children need to recover from their traumatic exposure to abuse.

5

Gender Bias in the Family Courts

All states have established courts that are given statutory authority to hear a broad range of family problems related to children, safety, and support. Families may need orders regarding child support, spousal support, custody, visitation, and restraining orders. In cases where families are at-risk, the State may intervene in child protective proceedings, or there may be prosecutions for acts of juvenile delinquency. For the purposes of simplicity, this book will be referring to such courts as "family courts."

The families seen are typically in crisis; some are present voluntarily, while others are compelled to be there. The family courts' mandate when hearing such problems is to provide legal rulings that administer the law in a neutral, fair, and unbiased manner. Much of the public never knows what goes on behind the doors of this courthouse as the family courts are generally not open to the public and they can be closed at the discretion of court administration. Thus, the family courts are largely immune from public oversight. Many of the litigants are poor and lack the funds to appeal. Protection of these families' fundamental rights as provided in the Constitution, within reasonable limits, to raise their children without interference and to live in safety, requires that this judicial forum be free from gender, racial, and cultural biases. This chapter will discuss the history of the family courts, the research on gender bias in the courts, and how this has influenced legislation and public policy.

The family court system is frequently the first point of contact for troubled families as they seek help managing their financial and familial concerns. Following incidents of domestic violence, they may be referred to the family courts by the police to obtain orders of protection, child support, orders of custody, and access to their children. Many families confront problems of domestic violence, untreated mental illness, and substance abuse. Stark has indicated that the abuse may range from extreme acts of violence—kidnapping of children and sexual abuse—to other forms of coercive control including threats of serious bodily injury and economic abuse.[1] Should the batterer have fled the home prior to law enforcement arriving on the scene so that an arrest cannot immediately be made, victims are frequently referred to the family court. Not all the history of the family may be available to law enforcement when they make such referrals, so their failure to arrest should not be the final word in assessing the dangerousness of the abusive behavior. While newer models of integrated criminal and family courts have developed and will be discussed in Chapter 9, many cases in which mothers seek protection for their children in the form of custody orders, support, or restriction of the father's access to the children are heard in the family courts.

The Family Courts' History

The tension between the family court's stated mission and the biases of the court's supporting professionals is reflected in the history of these courts and the attitudes of our times. The history of the family court and child welfare system is fraught with class, gender, and racial biases. These biases are a part of the court's history, from the unequal treatment of juveniles to the current theory of parental alienation used to discredit abused women in custody litigation.

Thus, a number of landmark cases have been brought over the years. From the process of appellate review, there were substantial modifications of the procedures and practices of the family court system. The legal issues presented in such cases provide a shocking history of human rights violations that impacted women and children. While poorer women were more frequent victims of such abuses, middle- and upper-class women are not immune from the pattern of gender discrimination that has pervaded the atmosphere of the family courts.

Bernstein reviewed the family court's disparate treatment of African-American children who were placed in the foster care system.[2] However, the family courts also hear cases involving juvenile delinquency and domestic violence, including orders of protection and custody, and the resulting class actions and appellate practice reveal the widespread biases that helped formulate the judicial response to social problems and public policy.

Much of the history of family court and the child welfare system goes far beyond the purview of this book. However, it is only by understanding this courts' problematic history that we can fully understand the current dilemmas and competing financial forces at work for at-risk families. It is also important to remember that the changes in the family courts were not accomplished voluntarily. Constitutional challenges to the treatment of juveniles resulted in significant due process protections for children facing charges of delinquency. Similarly, in termination of parental rights cases in which legal bonds between parent and child can be severed permanently, the United States Supreme Court required the trial courts to provide free legal representation to those parents who are unable to afford representation. *Lassister v. Dept. of Social Services of Durham County North Carolina.*[3]

In 1966, *in re Gault*, the United States Supreme Court case ruled that due process protections should be extended to juveniles accused of crimes. Here, the Court confronted an appeal of an Arizona trial court's decision that shockingly sentenced a fifteen-year-old boy to six years in a juvenile detention center for making a harassing telephone call.[4] This youngster never received formal notice of the charges against him and did not have legal representation. The Court noted that there was no transcript, and the victim of the crime failed to appear. *In re Gault*.[5] The youngster's sentence was significantly longer than that of the average adult who would typically receive several months' incarceration for what was normally considered a violation and not a crime in Arizona. The Supreme Court's ruling extended many of the due process protections in criminal proceedings provided to adults to juveniles, except for the Eighth Amendment right to bail. Now, adolescents charged with juvenile delinquency in family court have the due process protections of the Fourth, Fifth, and Sixth Amendments that include, among others, the right to counsel, to confront witnesses who will testify against them, and to be free of unreasonable search and seizures or to be compelled to testify in their own defense.

In 1973, Marcia Lowry, in *Wilder v. Sugarman*, on behalf of the New York Civil Liberties Union, challenged the methods used to place minority children with foster care agencies that "matched" their religious affiliation.[6] Historically, New York State provided funding to child welfare agencies that were responsible for the placement of children in foster or institutional care. Many of these agencies had religious affiliations, and thus the State matched foster children with those agencies with the same religious affiliation, in adherence to the Establishment and Free Exercise Clause of the First Amendment.[7] The resulting class action challenged these placements as being in violation of the Equal Protection Clause of the Fourteenth Amendment, as children requiring foster care who were black and Protestant were singled out to receive unequal treatment.[8] Bernstein described in stark detail the harsh and punitive conditions in which black children were housed in large congregant care facilities without access to the more prestigious and better foster care facilities.[9] Only through this class action in federal court were the foster care placements administered fairly for children in the child welfare system. Now a system has been enacted in which black children can have the same access to proper foster care services as white children. The child welfare agencies that provided foster care placement for white children were willing to spend significant financial resources to continue their practices of religious and racial exclusion. Today, the larger congregate care facilities—known as training schools or orphanages—have been dismantled. Similarly, today, custody battles are frequently fought between fathers with significant financial assets against mothers who struggle to afford their attorneys or who may be forced to continue without representation.

In 1977, New York's landmark class action litigation, *Bruno v. Codd,* paved the way for domestic violence legislation.[10] This class action was brought to challenge law enforcement's policy of not arresting batterers and the family court's refusal to provide same-day access to battered women seeking emergency orders of protection.[11] As a result, the courts were directed to hear applications for orders of protection on the same day in which these abused women filed their requests. The previous practice of the New York City Family Courts was to refer these battered women to the Department of Probation, where the counselors would attempt to mediate a solution. Despite the possible availability of civil orders of protection, battered women were rarely given such restraining orders and were left unprotected. The New York City Police Department and the Department of Probation were also parties to this class action, as orders of protection were meaningless unless the police were directed to make arrests.

In 2000, *Nicholson v. Scoppetta*, a class action of battered mothers, addressed the growing problem of gender discrimination in child protection proceedings as women who had failed to leave their abusive partners were charged with neglect in family court.[12] While it was acknowledged by the courts that the fathers had perpetrated the abuse, battered mothers were also charged with neglect and the failure to protect these children, who were frequently placed in foster care. During the trial, the caseworkers and mental health experts testified to the arbitrary and punitive way in which children were removed from their mothers. The traumatic impact of such removals was clear from the testimony. Because of extensive federal and state litigation, *Nicholson* was essential in preventing further abuse of battered mothers by mandating training of child protection workers and granting money damages to the members of this class action. *Nicholson* acknowledged that children were traumatized by separation from their caregivers and that mothers in abusive situations were frequently protective of their children. Finally, the New York State Court of Appeals held that exposure to domestic violence did not mandate removal of the children nor was it per se evidence of the mothers' neglect.[13]

Gender Bias and Domestic Violence

Today, in response to increased public awareness of the harm caused by domestic violence, all the states have enacted legislation directing judges to consider domestic violence in custody rulings, and this topic will be discussed in greater depth in Chapter 8. Many states have enacted rebuttable presumptions in which it is assumed that abusive parents should not have custody of the children, while other states require the courts to weigh the existence of domestic violence in their custody and visitation determinations. Despite this progress nationally, judges in custody disputes have resisted restricting abusive fathers' access to their children. This problem is not merely an absence of training on the new laws. As Meier noted, while judges may have received training in domestic violence, they have difficulty acknowledging this abuse when they must make difficult decisions about custody and visitation.[14] In my practice, I have observed that judges may provide the mothers with orders of protection in which children are not included as protected parties, while allowing the father to have unsupervised visitation and even decision-making authority or custody. It is unsettling that these results are widespread and acknowledged in the research.[15]

In many instances, judges overlook significant episodes of abuse so long as they are not directly in view of the children. If there are allegations of child abuse and neglect, the courts are given wide discretion by the appellate courts to determine the credibility of the witnesses. It is in these determinations of credibility where gender bias is frequently an unrecognized factor. Frequently, the abuse allegations are so horrific that the judges and attorneys simply cannot accept that they could be true. Rather than struggle with their own biases that form the basis of their resistance to the reality of an abusive parent's power in the family, they reject, minimize, or discredit the protective parent.

Meier noted that in the field of criminal justice and even in the litigation of civil orders of protection, there is an increased awareness of the harm caused by domestic violence to women and children.[16] However, Bancroft et al. observed that even judges who provide women with orders of protection will continue to balk at restricting fathers' access to their children and are reluctant to include children permanently on these orders, despite the long-term impact of their actions.[17]

Thus, judges who determine custody and visitation have gone to great lengths to distinguish whether children were present to witness the abuse or whether it occurred while they were asleep, despite the impact on children of living in a household with the dangers associated with domestic violence. Many judges refuse to acknowledge that domestic violence continues in its myriad forms after separation and may include physical, harassment, stalking, and financial or legal abuse. Such behavior can continue for years after the separation. The court's reluctance is particularly significant as state laws require them to consider domestic violence in custody and visitation litigation. Thus, it is important to review the efforts taken to remediate the unequal treatment of women in the courts to provide the context for the current discussion regarding the discrimination battered women experience today during custody litigation.

The Gender Bias Task Force Movement

It is essential that we understand the history of the gender bias task force movement to understand the context of many of the current problems in the family courts today and to enable us to build on past achievements. Gender bias is defined by the National Judicial Education Program (NJEP) for Women and Men in the Courts as (1) stereotypical thinking about the nature and roles of women, (2) how society values women and what's perceived as women's work, and (3) myths and misconceptions about the social and economic realities of women's and men's lives.[18] In the 1980s, because of concerns regarding unequal treatment of women in the courts, a movement to establish gender bias task forces developed. Hecht Schafran and Wikler observed that, as a result of this advocacy, over a ten-year period, a total of forty-three states conducted studies on gender bias in the courts.[19] Resnick noted the contributions of the National Organization for Women's Legal Defense and Education Fund now called Legal Momentum, which advocates for women's rights, in contributing to the gender bias task force movement.[20] As a result, NOW established the National Judicial Education Program to Promote Equality of Women and Men in the Courts (NJEP).[21] Swent also noted the increase in women in the legal profession, as women became judges and law professors at a time when the court system began to address the need for organized judicial education.[22] Hecht Schafran and Wikler prepared a manual for the Foundation of Women Judges in which they noted New Jersey's research on gender bias in the courts and research to inform judicial education and training. In arguing for recognition of the problem of gender bias against women in the courts they stated the following:

> Legislative reform alone will never be enough. As long as judges adhere to gender based myths, biases and stereotypes, the intent of the laws can be compromised or subverted through the exercise of judicial discretion. Equal treatment of women and men in the courts cannot be achieved unless all judges become educated about sex based discrimination in the law, in court procedures and in their own belief systems.[23]

The resulting early studies in forty-three states were sponsored by the courts and bar associations and included members of the judiciary, law professors, and sociologists. Over the past three and a half decades, the resulting study of gender bias in the courts has continued, whether in court-based research or in the participatory activist research of the past decade. Again and again, advocates and researchers have addressed the pervasive and insidious problems experienced by women in the courts.

Today, these problems are particularly acute when battered women seek relief from domestic violence and find that many members of the judiciary have biases or misconceptions about gender and abuse. Resnick correctly noted that gender bias is not the only form of bias in the court system because race and ethnicity remain areas in which the laws may be unequally applied.[24] While this book has focused primarily on the problems of women during divorce and custody litigation, immigrant and minority women have a particularly difficult time in the courts. These resulting gender, class, and racial biases can create an atmosphere in which the laws that are intended to protect women are subverted if women are not believed or their claims are minimized.

The research of the Gender Bias Study Committee of the Commonwealth of Massachusetts Supreme Judicial Court is an example of the kind of resources and attention marshalled to address the problem of the inequities experienced by women during litigation.[25] While the Massachusetts' Gender Bias Study addressed many issues of unfairness, in particular there was concern that, while there had been changes in the laws regarding the division of marital property, the standard of living for divorced women remained low. There were also concerns about the treatment of women during custody litigation. This Gender Bias Study raised questions about whether the courts were fairly determining the division of property, child support, and spousal maintenance in divorce. To that end, the Gender Bias Study held public hearings, conducted a survey of family law and general practice attorneys, surveyed judges and court personnel, and held regional meetings and focus groups. The focus groups consisted of separate meetings with male and female attorneys, litigants, and court personnel.[26] The Gender Bias Study collected data through surveys of family law attorneys, general practice lawyers, and judges. Focus groups were held throughout the state. The public hearings gathered testimony and written documentation. Researchers assisted the Gender Bias Study in evaluating the data collected on the income levels of women pre- and post-divorce.

The Gender Bias Study concluded that women consistently experienced a drop in their standard of living after divorce and that the same was not true for men. In fact, despite the complaints of individual male litigants, many men experienced a rise in their standard of living following divorce. Further, while there were new child support guidelines to standardize such orders of support, alimony or spousal support was ordered less frequently. The evidence of the Gender Bias Study's research indicated that judges were reluctant to direct fathers to provide both child support and spousal support, and attorneys concurred that judges did not want to enforce these laws. The study concluded that this judicial response reflected a bias against women and discriminated against women who had postponed their careers, and such bias could be particularly harmful to such women when their children reached adulthood as then they would have no other provisions for their financial support. Enforcement of existing orders of alimony or spousal support also remained a problem. The Gender Bias Study noted that compliance with such orders was very low, with only 43% of the women awarded alimony receiving such support, as indicated in the 1989 US Census Bureau Report.[27] In terms of the division of retirement savings and pensions, the Gender Bias Study found that these assets were frequently overlooked and not divided during litigation. Finally, this study concluded that, despite the stated purpose of the Massachusetts Legislature regarding the equitable division of marital property during divorce, these goals were typically not met. In the past decade, there have been states that have made orders of spousal maintenance mandatory when there is a discrepancy in the parties' incomes, and this will be discussed in greater depth in Chapter 7. This study finally concluded that the judges' attempt to treat men and women equally by applying principles of gender neutrality overlooked the fact that men and women were not equal in terms of their earnings, retirement savings, and assets. The laws regarding the equitable distribution of property were intended to be remedial; that is, to adjust for women earning less in the work force or their absence from the workforce to raise children. Imposition of gender neutrality in their court rulings ignored the purpose of Massachusetts' legislative reforms: to remediate the financial conditions of women following divorce. While there has been some improvement in terms of awards of equitable distribution and distribution of pensions, women's earnings still lag behind men's, creating income disparities at the time of the divorce or separation.

The Gender Bias Study of Massachusetts also addressed the treatment of women during custody litigation. Significantly, the proven existence of domestic violence was not yet recognized as an important consideration in custody determinations. While the Gender Bias Study determined that in most cases women received custody of the children, they concluded that this was primarily by consent in cases in which women had been the primary caretakers. The Committee concluded that this did not reflect gender bias against men on the part of judges but a presumption that children fared better with their primary caretaker. Given that the Gender Bias Study found that women received custody more often than men, this is reflected in the standards and child-rearing practices of the time. However, the Gender Bias Study noted the body of research that found that men who litigated were more likely to obtain custody.

However, subsequent research on gender bias in the courts in cases of domestic violence in custody and visitation cases reflected the disparate treatment of women. In California, Danforth and Welling indicated in their final report that the family court was an arena in which the problems of gender bias were particularly problematic.[28] Additionally, Czapansky and O'Neill noted that the 1989 gender bias report in Maryland concluded "that the most pervasive and difficult problems facing victims of domestic violence are attitudes and lack of understanding of many judges and court employees about the nature of domestic violence."[29] In New York, the Task Force on Women in the Courts concluded that gender bias against women is a pervasive problem with "grave consequences" and that women endured a climate of "condescension, indifference, and hostility."[30]

The Gender Bias Study in Massachusetts concluded that the public perception that women were at a disadvantage in custody disputes was contradicted by the fact that the courts manifested a double standard, requiring much more of mothers than of fathers. Finally, this study determined that the courts placed "the needs of noncustodial fathers above those of custodial mothers and children."[31]

Gender Bias in the Federal Courts

Federal courts are also venues in which women can experience gender bias, whether as litigants, attorneys, or court employees. Resnick noted that while federal courts are not traditional forums for family issues, laws that address federal pensions, equal opportunities in employment, and bankruptcy court are subjects that are litigated in the federal courts.[32] Thus, gender bias in the federal courts is also important and worthy of research. Significantly, Cortina's review of a study of 4,605 attorneys engaged in federal court litigation found that incidents of rudeness, gender disparagement, and sexual overtones were common and primarily impacted women.[33] While Cortina noted that the judges did not overtly intend to discriminate against women, however, by not recognizing that some behaviors were gendered and discriminatory against women, they failed to address the problem.

Gender bias studies of the federal courts found additional evidence. Resnick noted that in 1996, 90% of the male judges were white men, although the rate of female bankruptcy and magistrate judges had increased to 15–18%. In comparison, Resnick found that 98% of the legal secretaries in the federal courts were women.

In the Eighth Circuit, Lonsway et al. indicated that several states, including Missouri, Iowa, and Minnesota, enacted rules of professional conduct prohibiting attorneys from engaging in conduct that reflected gender bias.[34] These authors noted that judges have a role in discouraging incivility; in other words, the tone is set at the top.[35] In 1990, the American Bar Association's Model Code for Judicial Conduct was revised to require judges to perform their duties without bias or prejudice and to require lawyers practicing before them to refrain from demonstrating such bias against witnesses or opposing counsel.[36] Today, the ABA Model Code (2011), as amended, continues to uphold these principles.

It is particularly important that judges are held to this standard as the Massachusetts Gender Bias Study found that only 4% of the attorney participants in this study reported having ever seen a judge intervene to prevent such behavior.[37] Lonsway et al. further noted the findings of the Minnesota Supreme Court Task Force, in which 51% of male attorneys, as compared to 13% of female attorneys, found that judges frequently intervened to prevent biased conduct.[38] Gender provides a unique perspective. Some judges may lack awareness as to the subtle—or not so subtle—ways in which such biases are manifested.

The problems of incivility and diversity in the courts are not insignificant. They create a climate in which women feel diminished and unheard. A study of federal judges in the Eighth Circuit by Lonsway et al. found that these judges identified a minimal number of gender-biased incidents. In fact, most male judges surveyed indicated that they had rarely intervened to prevent incidents of gender-based incivility.[39] It is significant that the female judges more frequently identified women as the primary targets of such gender-biased incidents. With the help of judicial education, some judges were willing to intervene in such incidents. It is not surprising that these researchers concluded that, when judges themselves engage in such biased behavior and share attitudes that are demeaning to women, they are unlikely to recognize gender bias incidents. Today, there are more women employed in the federal court system as attorneys or judges, yet, anecdotally, while the presence of women attorneys and support staff has greatly increased, instances of bias remain.

Women are not the only victims of incivility. However, many of the behaviors I have witnessed or experienced in my practice today are intended to diminish women. For example, a judge who had behaved contemptuously toward women in his courtroom created a climate in which a male attorney and adversary felt entitled to refer to a female attorney by her first name during a hearing, in clear violation of the rules on attorney conduct in which all persons are formally addressed. Dragiewicz's review of the statewide gender bias reports found that many female attorneys reported that court personnel used terms of endearment to address them without their title, that they were not acknowledged as attorneys, and that they were the recipient of sexual comments and advances.[40] This practice of discriminatory behavior may be even more widespread in terms of racial bias as I have observed some of my African-American colleagues, with their briefcases in hand, being questioned at the door of the courtroom by court personnel to determine if they were lawyers.

Gender Bias, Custody, and Visitation

Earlier studies on gender bias in the courts were possible because they were funded and conducted by the courts in forty-three states. Funds were appropriated to ensure that men and women were heard on this issue, records and documentation were obtained, and judges, lawyers, and litigants provided testimony. Thus, these state task forces could recommend broader changes in legislation based on their investigations to ensure that women were not disadvantaged financially during divorce. During the 1990s, statewide child support guidelines were established to limit judicial discretion, and judicial trainings were implemented.

The Model Code on Domestic and Family Violence National Council of Juvenile and Family Court Judges (Model Code 1994) was established to develop legislation for family and criminal court. The Model Code recommended that:

> In every proceeding where there is at issue a dispute as to the custody of a child, a determination by the court that domestic or family violence has occurred raises a rebuttable presumption that it is detrimental to the child and not in the best interest of the child to be placed in sole custody, joint

legal custody, or joint physical custody with the perpetrator of family violence.[41]

Davidson's report for the American Bar Association's Committee on Children and the Law also advocated for a presumption that abusers should not receive custody of their children.[42] However, while many states have enacted laws that direct the courts to consider the proven existence of domestic violence when determining custody or visitation, Morrill et al. noted that, as of 2000, only fifteen states had enacted laws that included a presumption that sole or joint legal custody with the abusive parent was not in the children's best interests because of domestic violence.[43] Further, this researcher also indicated that other legislative amendments that established statutory presumptions regarding custody were in direct conflict with the laws regarding domestic violence. Specifically, many states had enacted laws that provided for presumptions that favored joint legal custody and "friendly parent" laws that indicated that custodial parents had an obligation to encourage the relationship between the noncustodial parent and child. Additionally, while the Model Code also recommended education on domestic violence for judges and other court personnel, six years later, in 2000, Morrill et al. found that only sixteen states had such legislation and that funding was not included for this training.

Morrill et al. studied custody determinations in families in six states in which an order of protection had been issued within three years and included the review of court documents and records in 393 cases involving sixty judges. These researchers found that in those states with only a statutory presumption against perpetrators of domestic violence in custody cases, orders granting joint legal custody were less common than orders giving custody to the mothers. In states without a presumption, judges were twice as likely to grant joint legal custody than sole legal custody to the battered mothers. Finally, in states with competing statutes, judges were four times as likely to grant joint legal custody than sole custody to the mothers. This research highlights the weakness of domestic violence laws if there are also competing laws on the books that direct judges to favor joint legal custody and "friendly parent" laws. Significantly, while Morrill et al. found that statutory presumptions against custody to batterers reduced awards of sole legal custody, they also concluded that 40% of the fathers received joint custody even though they had abused the mothers. These researchers noted the risks involved in joint legal custody, an arrangement that requires consultation and communication. Morrill et al. also concluded that statutory presumptions against batterers receiving custody were undermined by the other competing laws and found that the friendly parent statutory provisions unfairly penalized abused parents.[44]

O'Sullivan reviewed 1,692 families, with a total of 2,421 children litigating custody and visitation between 1990 and 1997.[45] This researcher found that fathers petitioned for custody in visitation in 74% of the cases, while mothers petitioned for custody in 38% and visitation in only 8% of the cases. O'Sullivan concluded that there was no difference in outcomes between mothers and fathers, that fathers were more likely to petition the court for custody and visitation, and they were equally successful. In cases in which there was an order of protection that documented a history of domestic violence, the courts were less likely to grant the enjoined party custody, and in only a small percentage of cases were fathers granted custody when the mothers had an order of protection. However, when mothers were granted an order of protection, fathers who filed petitions received visitation in 53% of the cases. O'Sullivan concluded that the fathers' chances of having visitation were improved when mothers received orders of protection. This research is consistent with many battered mothers' concerns about separation in households in which there is a history of domestic violence. In my practice, this is frequently the reason why battered mothers remain in abusive relationships. This study did not determine whether the final orders of visitation for fathers had required that the visitation be supervised, although it should be noted that publicly funded long-term programs are virtually unavailable in New York City.

Concerns about gender bias have also been raised about custody evaluations. Saunders et al. noted that the extent of the impact of gender bias in custody determinations has been noted in the research, but the prevalence is difficult to assess because data is not readily available.[46] The common practice is for the family courts to rely on court-appointed mental health professionals, or custody evaluators, to assist in determining the validity of allegations of mental illness, child maltreatment, domestic violence, or substance abuse. If these mental health professionals are unaware of their own biases, this can profoundly impact whether they believe allegations of abuse made by women. Briefly, a national study of custody evaluators in 2011 by Saunders et al. evaluated their training and beliefs in the context of domestic abuse allegations and noted the impact of training and gender bias.[47] Further, this study found that those evaluators who believed that mothers made false allegations of domestic violence also believed that domestic violence survivors alienated the children and that domestic violence was not important in custody cases. Many of these same evaluators also believed that those mothers refused to co-parent and, finally, that domestic violence victims frequently make false allegations of child abuse.[48] These results starkly reveal the harm caused by forensic custody evaluators viewed as experts who have little or no training in domestic violence, its impact on children, and the heightened risk of child abuse. Practice development and training of court-appointed custody evaluators will be discussed in greater depth in Chapter 10.

Meier noted that while decisions about custody and visitation are generally made along gender-neutral lines that utilize the "best interests of the child" standard, gender bias has been observed to have an insidious impact on custody determinations.[49] This standard has been found to be highly subjective, often reflecting the prevailing biases of the individual judges regarding class, race, and gender. From its inception, the "best interest" standard has been criticized because it is subjective and can result in battered women losing custody of their children. Children can be manipulated and may express the desire to live with the abusive parent. Depending on their age, their feelings may be the determining factor in the judge's decisions as older children are given more say than young children. There are inherent risks in this process because children may not be cognizant of the safety risks involved in their decisions.

However, Dragiewicz observed that women are typically the primary child care provider for the family and thus received physical custody of the children in earlier custody decisions. This may be true even when women work and should be reflected in custody determinations that seek to award custody of the children to the primary caretaker. Thus, Morrill et al. observed that complaints of gender bias among men may reflect their concerns about challenges to their status and power.[50]

Dragiewicz, in summarizing the reports on gender bias, noted their significance in custody decisions.[51] The problem may be compounded in the legal system when mental health and legal professionals view intimate partner violence as a gender-neutral offense despite the research suggesting that this is not the case. Stark referred to domestic violence as a gendered crime, and there is voluminous evidence that typically men, rather than women, are the primary physical aggressors. Nor should such abuse be minimized as situational in the context of divorce or custody litigation, as discussed in Chapter 3. Stark's view that such abuse consists of a constellation of coercively controlling behaviors is a more accurate description.[52]

The question of whether judges should impose more restrictions on the fathers' contact with the children against their stated wishes is just one of many challenges for the mental health and legal professions. Attorneys for the children, sometimes called *guardians ad litem*, must make complex decisions when advocating for their clients. In my practice, I have worked on cases where the attorney for the child may advocate for their client's wishes rather than for their safety. Judges frequently defer to the position of the attorney for the child. In some jurisdictions, the attorneys for the children can substitute their own judgment when children are unable to articulate a position or if their position raises significant concerns. At such times, these attorneys for the children may advocate for unsupervised overnight visitation or joint custody, particularly if they lack sufficient training on abuse.

Current efforts to overcome the problems of gender bias in the courts have resulted in efforts to provide judicial education on gender bias, racial bias, and domestic violence.[53] As will be discussed in Chapter 7, many recommended changes were implemented in the courts, including the implementation of spousal support, child support guidelines, and laws that required the courts to consider the impact of domestic violence in custody cases, and judicial training.

However, Dragiewicz noted in a review of the statewide gender bias reports that the respondents repeatedly stated that gender bias was not a problem in the courts—even while describing such incidents.[54] In my practice, I continue to observe that changes in attitudes expressed in the courts are slow. Further, as a panelist in New York State's judicial and court personnel training on the changes in the criminal and family courts response to domestic violence, I have noted that some of the judges and court personnel who attended these mandatory trainings were openly resistant to being directed to give women any special consideration in custody and domestic violence litigation.

Human Rights Research on Battered Women

Continued concerns about the treatment of battered women in the family courts resulted in a movement of battered mothers working with advocates to document the courts' failure to adequately respond to the risks to their children. These studies utilized narratives from battered women, their advocates, and, in some instances, judges and other state actors. A report by the Battered Mothers' Testimony Project at the Wellesley Centers for Women entitled "Battered Mothers Speak Out" documented continued human rights violations against battered mothers in the Massachusetts family courts.[55] Although the results of this project were initially criticized as being primarily composed of interviews with disgruntled litigants and not empirically sound, Goodmark has noted the importance of obtaining narratives from women who had been silenced.

The design of Battered Mothers Speak Out's qualitative, narrative human rights study was quite complex. It included many interviews and focus groups with other key players, the review of supporting documentation in sample cases, interviews with victim advocates, and focus groups for attorneys for battered women from various demographics including immigrants and members of the LGBT community.[56] Additionally, this research included interviews with forty battered women from eleven of the fourteen counties, ranging in age from twenty-four to fifty-eight, and with incomes between less than $15,000 to $105,000. In other words, the participants fairly represented the diversity of the women affected, including affluent professionals, women with scarce financial resources, and advocates of the LGBT and immigrant community. Significantly, Slote et al. noted the limitations of their research while also calling for further documentation of the continuing problem of gender bias against women.

Gentile describes a study by the Voices of Women (VOW) Organizing Project of the experience of battered women in the New York City Family Courts, in which they found that 30% of the women felt unsafe in the courtroom and 40% felt unsafe in the waiting areas.[57] This report, entitled "Justice Denied: How Family Courts in NYC Endanger Battered Women and Children," indicated that half of the cases in family court involve allegations of domestic violence—regardless of whether they involved petitions for child support, custody, visitation, or child protective cases.[58] Many of the women were not aware that they could obtain assistance from agencies that provided services to battered women in the courthouse. This report called for funding of an independent court-watch program, limiting judicial appointments to five years rather than ten, and that at least once a year the judge should see the children again to determine if the decision is in their best interests.[59]

The Arizona Coalition Against Domestic Violence in 2003 also developed the Battered Mothers' Testimony Project (BMTP) utilizing methodology that was similar to the Massachusetts study, interviewing women who had engaged in custody litigation in cases of domestic violence following the passage of state legislation that mandated consideration of domestic violence in custody cases.[60] It is troubling that this research indicated that in 74% of the cases in Maricopa County, Arizona and in 56% of the other counties included in this study, the courts ordered sole or joint legal custody to men who had been abusive, and in 63% of the cases the women had provided documentation of this abuse.

As an attorney for battered women practicing in New York City for many decades, the experiences described in the VOW report are all too familiar. There have been many times when my clients and I felt unsafe in the courthouse or waiting rooms. Safety has been a concern at the end of the business day for my clients when battered women still waiting for their protective orders to be made available must wait in public waiting rooms because those areas designated for the safety of victims of domestic violence close after 5 p.m. It is not uncommon to find battered women forced to wait with minimal court personnel supervision in public waiting rooms just a few yards away from their abusers late in the afternoon and into the early evening. Sometimes their abusers use these opportunities to harass, stalk, or photograph the women, creating an atmosphere that is unsafe and volatile. Although many women live in confidential locations, appearing in family court provides batterers with the opportunity to locate their new residences by stalking them after court appearances, thus undermining their safety. It is also not uncommon for advocates for battered women to feel afraid in the courthouse's waiting rooms. Brinig et al. also noted the heightened risk to battered mothers in joint custody arrangements as this situation gives the abusive parent the opportunity to continue the emotional abuse through threats and harassment and increases the likelihood of further physical abuse.[61]

The results of the research in New York, Arizona, and Massachusetts, are particularly chilling. Earlier government-sanctioned studies recommended specific legislative reforms, including greater access to the court in petitions for orders of protection, statutory guidelines for child support, temporary orders of child support, and awards of counsel fees for the spouse with less income.[62] However, a review of the initial report of the Battered Mothers' Speak Out

Project in Massachusetts and a subsequent testimonial project by the Arizona Coalition Against Domestic Violence indicates the urgent need for further documentation, public hearings, and reforms to protect battered mothers and their children.[63]

International Law Protections

The Wellesley Massachusetts Battered Mothers' Testimony Project particularly noted that the treatment of women and children in the Massachusetts Probate/Family Courts was in violation of the Convention of the Rights of the Child; and the Convention on the Elimination of All Forms of Discrimination Against Women (CEDAW Convention).[64] The authors argued that, although these treaties are not ratified, the fact that they have been signed binds the government—and by inference the states—to refrain from engaging in governmental action contrary to the intent of these agreements.[65] The authors noted that, in particular, the Convention on the Rights of the Child has been ratified by almost all the members of the United Nations—but not the United States.[66] As a result of the United States' failure to ratify these treaties, many domestic violence attorneys are particularly isolated and unable to access all of the tools they need to defend their clients in custody and divorce cases.[67]

Celorio noted that the protections for women articulated in the CEDAW Convention are prevention, protection, and eradication of violence against women.[68] In the past, the use of the CEDAW Convention allowed the Inter-American Court of Human Rights to review the ruling of a Chilean Court in which a woman with a same-sex partner lost custody of her children. The Commission and Court specifically faulted the State of Chile and charged it with violations of the mother's right to equality and privacy, finding that this ruling demonstrated discrimination based on the mother's sexual orientation. The use of this treaty allows for a review of court proceedings, which is particularly important in a custody case. Thus, the Commission concluded that the Court's stated goals of protecting children had little relationship to the harshness of the Court's ruling, which separated the children from their primary caretaker simply because of her sexual orientation.[69]

Here, application of these treaties could be utilized by attorneys who represent women in divorce and custody cases. The question we should ask is whether the family courts' stated mission of preserving the best interests of the children can be met if abusive fathers obtain custody, joint custody, or unsupervised visitation with their children. Battered mothers are frequently their children's primary caregivers. Forcible separation of these children from their mothers may cause considerable emotional distress and presents significant public health and safety concerns. Use of the commissions employed through the CEDAW Convention would provide for observers in the family courts and the independent review of cases. However, in the United States, these protections are not available to advocates for women. While ratification of the treaties would be helpful for battered women, there are other steps, including the presence of objective, neutral court observers, that could dramatically improve conditions.

Gender bias in the courts is evidenced in multiple ways. Expectations for men and women as parents vary enormously. The following case is illustrative: in my practice, I represented a battered mother in a custody case in which the child had a serious physical disability. The father had become increasingly abusive toward the mother, was persistently neglectful of the child, and denied the severity of the child's medical problems, refusing to follow medical advice. The father refused to diaper, bathe, supervise, or give the child his medication. The court initially ordered supervised visitation, and thereafter we appeared periodically for monthly reports that reviewed the progress of the visits. During the visits, the supervisor noted that the father was volatile, easily frustrated, and had difficulty comprehending the child's needs. The father, who clearly loved his son, was nevertheless oblivious to the needs of the toddler: at best, he was neglectful, and, at worst, easily angered and resistant to accepting the supervisor's advice. Given the severity of the child's condition, these were significant lapses in judgment. Yet the attorney for the child clearly empathized with the father, who was highly manipulative. Despite the father's deficits, the supervisor recommended gradual unsupervised visitation—which was ordered by the judge and supported by the child's attorney. In comparison, lawyers for women who have such problems expect swift, judicial punishments with little hope for ever obtaining unsupervised visitation.

A review of the transcripts of this court proceeding indicated that, like the findings of the Wellesley Battered Mothers Study, I was frequently silenced and my many objections to violations of the evidentiary rules were ignored. This contributes to an atmosphere in which my client's concerns could not be heard and in which she lacked confidence in the courts' ability to ensure her safety and her right to a fair and impartial hearing.

Custody and the Fathers' Rights Movement

Dinner's discussion of the fathers' rights movement noted that many of the men involved opposed the equal distribution of child care within marriage, which kept women subordinate, while demanding gender equality in the laws surrounding divorce and custody.[70] Thus, Dinner observed that formal equality in divorce laws without equal division of labor in marriages makes women more economically insecure. The growing fathers' rights movement represents a backlash against feminism and, as such, has recruited men during separation and divorce. Flood found that separating men experienced loneliness and loss and were vulnerable to recruitment from this movement.[71] Crowley argued that the fathers' rights movement in the United States was an outgrowth of three political and religious movements: divorce reform, antifeminists, and religious conservative groups.[72]

The fathers' rights movement is a well-funded group that has promoted the concept of the "friendly parent" in custody litigation and joint legal custody, which is at odds with the principle of protecting battered women and their children from further abuse. Additionally, there are many beliefs, or myths, embedded in the family courts that have limited acceptance in the modern academic world. By way of example, while the courts have posited a gender-neutral approach to custody so that either sex can be the custodial parent, judges continue to apply very different standards for men and women as parents. True gender neutrality means that both the mother and father must live up to the same standards of parenting. Theorists differ on whether the courts in civil proceedings are motivated by gender bias or by a misguided sense that the proceedings must be gender neutral. Currently, Meier indicates that the courts idealize the concept of co-parenting, in which parents put aside their animosity for the good of the children.[73] This researcher also noted the idealization of the "friendly parent." Consequently, this emphasis has placed battered women at risk of claims of parental alienation or having her allegations of abuse discredited or minimized. As a result, battered mothers seeking to minimize the traumatic contact between their children and the abusive parent are viewed negatively by the courts and supporting mental health professionals, while fathers who are arguing for joint parenting are seen as inherently virtuous.[74]

The theory of parental alienation, whether as a syndrome or disorder, is the current manifestation of gender bias against women in the courts, arguing that many women make false allegations of abuse. While I have discussed the unreliability of parental alienation theory in Chapter 4, it is essential that we understand why this theory has become so commonly accepted in family court. Given the reforms implemented in the state legislatures, judges have discretion to restrict an abusive parent's access to his children and may deny his applications for custody. However, the strong public sentiment against restrictions on fathers' "rights," competing legislative presumptions that undermine the protections of battered women, and use of such theories allows the courts to discredit the allegations and thus circumvent the mandates of the law. When such theories are finally dismissed, some other theory equally toxic to women and children may be in vogue if we do not address the underlying gender bias against women and the punitive measures used against them.

The family courts were quick to adopt the widespread casual use of parental alienation theory to discredit battered mothers. Faller has provided a thorough analysis of the literature on false allegations of sexual abuse, rebutting the concept that mothers in custody disputes frequently make false allegations of such abuse.[75] Trocmé and Bala have studied the actual rate of false allegations of abuse and neglect and found that the rate of intentionally or maliciously false allegations is low.[76] Unfortunately, our history of custody jurisprudence in which children were considered the property of the father and the belief that women are not reliable or valuable, combined with the closed doors of the family courts, has not leveled the playing field for women.

Today, despite the increased awareness of the impact of domestic violence as traumatic for children, custody litigation is fraught with misconceptions and outmoded gender stereotypes.[77] Meier aptly described domestic violence allegations as being "gender charged" and noted the differing treatment of male and female litigants and their attorneys.[78] As a practicing family law attorney, I can attest to the not-so-subtle gender-based disparagement or bullying that is part of the practice in this court system. Some matrimonial and family law attorneys utilize bullying as a strategy, rather than the reasoned practice of law, adopting tactics and exploiting biases in ways that are considered unacceptable in most workplaces. Family law attorneys who allow gender bias to permeate their actions in the form of bullying, disrespectful, and aggressive behavior do a profound disservice to the legal profession. For most of the public, their only contact with attorneys during their lifetimes will be during their divorce, separation, or custody dispute. A gender-influenced practice of law in which women are disparaged and treated with contempt has certainly contributed to the public's perceptions of this profession.

In terms of openness and transparency during custody litigation, Slote has indicated that the Battered Mothers Speak Out project also noted that reports by the *guardian ad litem*—who typically represents the children—were not made available to the litigants although read by the judges.[79] Sometimes, mothers could read the reports in their attorneys' offices, but they never received a copy. This made it difficult for them to challenge the factual allegations in the reports and the findings that could be detrimental to the safety of their children. Access to their file, albeit with restrictions and penalties in place if privacy is violated, is a significant necessary step.

In New York, forensic reports prepared by mental health professionals that substantiate or discredit the allegations of abuse and make recommendations for custody are also typically not distributed to the litigants. In some counties, litigants are never allowed to read the reports, and in others, they can only read them but are not permitted to have a copy. Under the guise of privacy protection, this practice is a serious due process violation. In the criminal context, the Sixth Amendment right to confrontation of witnesses and the right to review charges would never permit this kind of practice. In family court, parents who are facing the State's interference with their fundamental right to parent their child are unable to read significant reports about the disposition of their children's custody.

A bias-free courthouse requires more transparency. We can still protect the privacy of the litigants. The courts can bar cameras, filming, and distribution of the victim's names and identifying information, mirroring the procedures in the public criminal court that have been highly effective in sensitive rape cases. Judges are also empowered to issue restraining orders in which litigants face significant penalties and even incarceration if they speak to the press or disseminate confidential reports.

Furthermore, gender bias is rarely exhibited on the record. It is demonstrated in body language, tone of voice, facial expressions, and gestures of court personnel that are not captured in the transcripts. At best, judges may appear skeptical about the allegations or exert herculean reasoning to minimize the impact of the traumatic exposure of the abusers' high-risk behavior that may include domestic violence, untreated mental illness, or substance abuse. At worst, judges who are openly dismissive of the litigants before them may instill fear. Such behavior may result in women feeling pressured to enter into stipulations regarding custody and visitation that do not sufficiently protect their children.

Stipulations can rarely be appealed and are difficult to modify, making substantive change elusive. However, appeals of judicial decisions after trial may result in appellate decisions that require judges to apply the laws regarding custody and domestic violence. Appeals of gender-biased decisions in which these abusive behaviors were underestimated will mean the development of a body of law that recognizes that harm to children can be caused in a variety of ways. Exposure to trauma may mean that the children will have significant physical and mental health needs for decades.[80] It is clear that women will continue to be intimidated into entering into harmful agreements until we open the doors of the family courts. Substantive due process requires that these proceedings be open to observers to prevent violation of the fundamental rights of battered women to parent their children in safety.

Understanding domestic violence means understanding all the forms of abuse that the abusive parent, typically the father, is willing to use to exercise control. Such efforts can involve an enormous amount of manipulative behavior. As an attorney representing battered women, I have reviewed fathers' emails containing accusations of being excluded from their children's lives and of parental alienation. These are frequently attempts to build a written record for the court of their allegations of parental alienation in order to overturn existing custody arrangements. Frequently, they are accompanied by threats to return to court. Joint decision-making is productive and supportive of children when parents have made positive efforts to raise their children together in the past. In families without high-risk factors of domestic violence, untreated mental illness, or substance abuse, joint legal custody can be helpful for children. However, these less-distressed families do not need the courts to ensure that they will put their children's needs above their own. They already have a history of cooperation.

In my practice, I am frequently called upon to review emails and communications from abusive fathers, rife with accusations and threats to return to court to obtain custody of the children. When mothers are obligated to co-parent with such abusers, they cannot make even minor decisions about their children's lives without interference and are prevented from acting in their children's best interests. While communicating with the other parent after the separation is important for children in families without abuse, this typically occurs without the need for judicial oversight.

Imposition of co-parenting in high-risk families is inappropriate in families with a history of abuse. Bancroft and Silverman noted that a father who is abusive to his children's mother is not capable of good parenting.[81] Meier concluded that, if the courts impose or promote co-parenting and joint custody, they assume that harming the mother is separate and distinct from harming the child and that the domestic violence ends when the parties are separated.[82] Brinig et al. also noted that abusive parents may model poor methods of conflict resolution and interfamilial relations in which they frequently devalue the other parent. Abusive fathers are incapable of negotiating. I have seen my clients continue to struggle to support their children's development long after the divorce is finalized only to find that their former spouse will turn each decision about the children into a war zone. Sadly, decisions about schooling, travel, summer camp, extracurricular activities, and even selection of the children's college can be derailed by the fathers' efforts to coercively control the family. Allowing abusive fathers to "co-parent" provides them with the ability to inflict years of trauma on the children and their mothers. These problems are particularly acute when life decisions must be made. For example, even after many years, abusive fathers may refuse to pay college expenses arguing that they were not consulted or provided with sufficient information. In other instances, the mothers risk returning to court when fathers balk at paying for college or other agreed upon expenses. Even in very wealthy families, fathers may refuse to pay for the college of their children's choice as they argue that the mother did not make the required efforts to consult with them before decisions were made. Negotiation and joint decision-making require that parents can relinquish individual control before any mutual decision can be made. It is essential that the legislation regarding custody and decision-making be amended to reflect the reality of coercively controlling parenting.[83]

We know that abusive fathers use these opportunities to preserve control. If we want children to recover from their traumatic exposure, we can support their mothers by allowing them the freedom to parent their children in ways that support growth. Firm and consistent orders of child support will also prevent abusive fathers from holding their children hostage to their attempts to seize control of each aspect of their lives by withholding financial support.

What is clear is that we should allow children to be safely cared for by their primary caretaker. Despite women's entry into the workplace in large numbers and an increase in fathers' contributing to household tasks, many mothers continue to be the primary caretakers of their children while juggling the demands of work. Even when they are not there, they are primarily the ones who organize the household and ensure that their children's needs are met. A careful history of the family is necessary. Who takes the children to the doctor, who attends parent–teacher conferences, and who cares for a sick child in the middle of the night? Such actions reveal the primary caretaker.

The reluctance of judges to follow the law and apply known research that is recognized in the legislation is highly suggestive of the underlying biases inherent in their reasoning and decisions. The anxiety many judges feel about ensuring that fathers have access to their children is harmful if it means that they are separating the children from their primary caretaker for extended periods of time. If there are allegations of abuse, untreated mental illness, or substance abuse, there are also concerns about the impact on parenting. Meier observed that the rationale behind the courts' resistance to existing laws has been justified by gender-neutral perspectives that assume that either parent can be abusive.

Stark noted the importance of viewing domestic violence as a gendered crime in which women are understood to need institutional protection.[84] All fifty states have passed legislation that provides that the family court judge must take into consideration the history of abuse in determining custody and visitation, and, in some states, there is a presumption that this parent is unfit. Despite this, women in custody disputes where there has been abuse, mental illness, or substance abuse face an uphill battle to protect their children.

As the study of domestic violence continues, we now understand that abuse means more than physical violence and that it also covers a constellation of behaviors that enable the abusive parent, typically the father, to exert coercive control over the family.[85] There is increasing awareness that domestic violence is not an isolated incident or a situational response: Stark has indicated that this is part of a pattern of behavior in which batterers assert control through verbal harassment and financial, sexual, and in my opinion, legal abuse.[86] Thus, the incidence of physical violence may be less extreme, but the other forms of coercive control may be devastatingly effective. In this category, threats to kidnap the children, to remove them from the jurisdiction or country, to kill the children, or to obtain custody are all of such effectiveness that it may not be necessary for the batterers to use physical force.

However, this pattern is less understood and recognized in the context of a custody case. In my practice, women have recounted how their abusive spouse punched holes in walls inches from where they stood during an argument or threatened to kidnap the children or to have the mother deported while the children remain with him. These behaviors are intended to assert control through coercive means. They are highly effective. A thorough history of the abuse requires an understanding of the motivation behind the other forms of abuse. Once the batterer has exerted coercive control, there is no further need for violence.

Unfortunately, these forms of abuse are more commonly seen in the family courts and do not rise to the level of criminal behavior, or they are largely unreported to law enforcement. In the context of a custody dispute, however, it is essential that family court personnel understand abuse as a dynamic method of control. This dynamic also underscores the difficulty and risks involved in leaving the abusive partner. Stark concluded that the family courts' refusal to acknowledge the gender-based abuse of women in the context of custody disputes, and the vehemence with which forensic evaluators and other members of the legal system hold on to arguments that are rejected in the criminal courts, speaks volumes about the concerns at stake in the family courts.[87]

Conclusion

Family court is an arena in which racial, class, cultural, and gender biases have had an insidious influence on the proceedings. Given our expectation that the legal system will be embodied with fairness, the levels of gender bias in divorce and custody cases and the ways in which allegations of domestic violence, mental illness, and substance abuse are often minimized is particularly harmful. It is axiomatic that the best way to help children traumatized by witnessing abusive behavior is to protect their primary caretakers. This is consistent with our understanding of traumatic exposure, that before women and children can heal they must be removed from the source of the traumatic exposure.

The gender bias research of the 1980s and 1990s provided clear documentation to support the unequal treatment of women during divorce and separation and their lower standards of living that resulted. The gender bias task forces' recommendations paved the way for reforms of the laws that governed child support and the equitable distribution of marital property. Statutory presumptions that directed judges to consider domestic violence when making determinations regarding custody and visitation were passed in most states. However, more research is needed to determine whether joint legal custody presumptions and the "friendly parent" requirements have circumvented judges' obligations to protect women and children and safeguard against post-separation abuse. The research of the participatory action research movements provides essential information about battered women's experiences in the courts through narratives and interviews with advocates and judges. However, the public resources brought in the first gender bias research reports are needed again to provide objective proof through a review of court documents, decisions, and observations to determine whether battered women are disadvantaged in custody cases. Furthermore, the family courts lack sufficient resources in terms of judges and administrative support, resulting in extensive delays and the need for judges to make split-second decisions with very little information to guide them.

Women are often perceived as being primarily responsible for everything having to do with family life, including the raising of their children. Thus, their very presence in family court may denote failure. They are judged as having failed in their obligations to their children even before they speak. Had they done a better job as a wife and mother, their children would not be facing charges of juvenile delinquency. Had they been better mothers, their children's fathers would not be demanding custody and access. But the real questions— whether the fathers have been abusive, and what protective measures should be put in place—should be paramount.

The courts are an adversarial system, and significant fundamental rights attach to both parents in custody disputes. Fathers should receive zealous representation, and, notably, many nurturing fathers endeavor to resolve their parenting issues without litigation. However, family court must have the means to identify domestic violence and the other high-risk factors and the traumatic impact of such abuse on women and children through a lens that is not clouded with gender bias or undermined by competing legal standards.

The continuing problem with gender bias in the courts has been widely studied in almost every state and some federal courts for more than thirty years. It is helpful that ongoing task forces and increased training have been established to address these problems. However, we cannot expect the family courts to reform themselves. The problems in family court cannot be resolved with piecemeal legislative reform or training that—while important—fails to address the pervasive gender bias against women. It is in this subjective field of custody jurisprudence that gender bias against women, and specifically mothers, has the most devastating impact. Meier's (2003) research noted the pronounced disparity in the harshness of treatment of women compared to that of men who are neglectful and abusive.[88]

A simple look at the numbers of people in the waiting rooms and lobbies of the family courts indicates that these are places where vulnerable families are seen without sufficient resources to care for them. Only recently has training on domestic violence for forensic custody evaluators become mandatory in some jurisdictions. Not all states have funding to adequately provide training for judges and court personnel on domestic violence. Judges, lawyers, and mental health professionals have the power to protect children by minimizing the impact of their trauma and decreasing the risks to children and public safety. Court monitoring and public hearings are necessary to combat the problems of custody and gender bias against women. Properly trained mental health professionals can lead the way in their ability to examine their own attitudes and beliefs so that the legal system can begin to change. Finally, legal advocates in collaboration with informed mental health professionals can challenge the inequities that result when gender bias continues.

6

Intimate Partner Abuse, Mental Health, and Substance Abuse

This chapter will discuss the impact of substance abuse and mental illness on domestic violence, the traits associated with abusive men, the factors that increase risks, and the impact of domestic violence on the mental health of battered women. The issues of intimate partner abuse, mental health problems, and substance abuse in the context of parenting and custody disputes are frequently complex and intertwined. In some instances, the risks associated with mental illness and abuse are significant indicators of future violence.

The literature on batterers, mental health, and substance abuse reveals a correlation between the levels of violence and risks in such households—before and after separation. Styron has indicated that much of the research on mental illness and parenting has focused on mothers and not fathers.[1] Even when mothers have obtained mental health treatment during custody litigation, there is little reliance on the research outcomes regarding the effectiveness of such care. Furthermore, Risser et al. have indicated that many mothers with mental health issues remain legitimately concerned that disclosure of their problems can result in a loss of custody.[2] In some instances, batterers threaten disclosure of their problems to co-workers and friends. Some of my clients have expressed reluctance to enter counseling during custody litigation for fear that this will jeopardize the outcomes. It is important for the courts to understand the importance of such mental health treatment to enhance parenting.

Recognition of the increased risks of physical injury and homicide following separation should be an integral part of the court's response during divorce and custody litigation. Campbell et al. developed the Danger Assessments (DA), a tool used to identify the high-risk factors for femicides—the murder of women by intimate partners.[3] Significantly, these researchers noted that mental illness, substance abuse, prior criminal involvement, and the presence of guns in the homes are factors that independently increase the risk of murder of women in their homes by intimate partners.[4] Although not all abuse carries the risk of femicide, it is essential to understand the complex mental health and substance abuse problems that are present for some abusers involved in custody or divorce litigation. The risk of post-separation violence and the escalation of these risks should be given thoughtful consideration in the development of custody, visitation, and parenting plans when there is a history of abuse. Laing has indicated that parenting plans that require women to have frequent and ongoing contact with batterers continues to expose them to post-separation abuse.[5] Even when the parties do not have children, safety and public health concerns remain and may be exacerbated when battered women seek spousal support or division of the marital property during divorce. Laing, in a study of Australian women, noted the escalation of physical abuse—sometimes becoming lethal—following separation or a sudden change in the tactics the abusers employ.[6]

In the context of custody litigation, a legal response that provides support, structure, and skills-building for parents with mental health and substance abuse problems can also allow for the enhancement of battered mothers' parenting abilities. We also need a clinical understanding of batterers that can ensure that custody and visitation decisions promote public health and safety. Finally, battered women may have been impacted by the abuse they experienced. Bancroft et al. have indicated that battered mothers may suffer from the effects of abuse that include PTSD and that more research is needed on the impact of battering on the functioning and emotional atmosphere in families traumatized by abuse.[7] It is also important for the mental health and legal professions to make nuanced assessments of battered mothers' ability to parent that considers such impact.

Mental Health Questions Regarding Batterers

Not all cases of domestic violence are the same. The issue of predicting violence and lethality has been discussed extensively. Juodis et al.'s study of perpetrators of domestic violence homicides found that approximately 30% of the batterers had threatened or made suicide attempts before murdering their victims, stressing the need for appropriate identification, assessment, and treatment for perpetrators.[8] Many of these batterers display a high degree of obsessiveness as well. In such high-risk situations, these researchers emphasized that traditional treatment programs for batterers are not appropriate, are ineffective, and present significant safety concerns. In such cases, incarceration or confinement is necessary.

In the context of divorce and custody litigation, the mental health and legal professions need the tools to recognize the pathological behaviors demonstrated by batterers. However, there is no consensus among researchers that batterers uniformly fall into any existing psychiatric diagnosis.[9] On an individual basis, many mental health professionals have found that such batterers meet the criteria for a range of other categories of mental illnesses or have no diagnosis at all.

Common Personality Traits in Batterers

However, batterers share commons traits. Bancroft et al. noted that an exaggerated sense of entitlement is the single most defining characteristic of a batterer. This sense of entitlement is a significant impediment to effective parenting as batterers display self-centeredness and the inability to place their children's needs above their own in family life. These researchers define this sense of entitlement as an inherent belief that the individual should receive special benefits and privileges without similar responsibilities.[10] Dutton and Golant also described the batterers' sense of entitlement, patriarchal beliefs, a lack of empathy, and an inability to place their children's needs above their own as just some of the characteristics noted in the research on abusive men.[11] Anecdotally, the presence of these traits is borne out in my observations in my practice, when clients repeatedly report that their spouses want custody but then display little interest in their children's lives and consistently fail to take care of their children's needs. While many fathers who have not been abusive improve their parenting skills after the divorce, batterers continue to have significant difficulties because of their profound sense of entitlement.

Furthermore, Bancroft et al. have indicated that batterers do not necessarily use violence in an impulsive manner but as a tool to control their spouses.[12] In court, they are frequently relentless and spend enormous resources, time, and planning to retaliate against their spouses' perceived transgressions. Anecdotally in my practice, I have observed that batterers plan how best to undermine and abuse many of my clients. Bancroft et al. also noted this same phenomenon in their most recent research.[13]

Echeburua and Fernandez-Montalvo found in a study of incarcerated batterers that only one out of eight men fit the profile of a psychopathic batterer who had no prior mental health history but engaged in a criminal offense that displayed cruelty and a lack of empathy.[14] This study of Spanish incarcerated batterers found that most of these men were not psychopaths but displayed hostile feelings against women and had unstable affect, substance abuse problems, and poor impulse control. These researchers did not rule out whether these participants could be considered to have impulse control disorders or intermittent explosive disorders.[15]

Battering and Parenting

In the context of custody disputes, the batterers' parenting has significant consequences for children. Bancroft et al. noted that the batterers' abuse and criticism of their spouse is damaging to the children's relationship with their primary caretaker.[16] This factor is particularly important in custody determinations, when each parent is expected to support the children's relationship with the other parent.

At the same time, Bancroft et al. observed that abusive fathers may demonstrate characteristics like those found in narcissistic disorders, although such narcissists do not typically use violence in their interactions with other family members.[17] These researchers noted that it is frequently difficult to distinguish batterers from narcissists as they share similar traits of entitlement and grandiosity. They found instead that the batterer's grandiose tendencies stem from his sense of entitlement, whereas in narcissistic personalities, the sense of entitlement seems to evolve from damaging early childhood experiences that impact their developing sense of self. Furthermore, narcissists frequently experience conflict in other areas of their lives, resulting in troubled work histories and social conflicts. In comparison, Bancroft et al. found that the batterers' sense of entitlement, inability to place others' needs above their own, possessiveness, and control is predominantly limited to their family interactions.[18] These researchers also noted the extreme contempt that batterers express toward their spouses that, along with their need to control by any means, allows them to abuse her. Their contempt should not be confused with anger, and, in fact, their behavior can be cold and extremely calculated to inflict the maximum level of harm.

Gondolf's research on batterers noted that many, though not all, of these individuals also had a diagnosis of narcissism.[19] Significantly, Beasley and Stoltenberg found in a comparison study of men from batterer and nonbatterer programs that the batterers were more likely to display narcissism and antisocial, aggressive, and borderline traits.[20] Anecdotally, I have found that batterers repeatedly express their sense of entitlement during custody and divorce litigation in very pathological ways.

In one instance in my practice, a batterer admitted to beating my client, although he minimized the impact of his behavior and even displayed some remorse to the judge. He repeatedly excused his behavior because she was telling him what to do with "*my* children" in "*my* home." In these statements, we can see the sense of entitlement and resulting belief that no matter how dangerous his behavior, he was justified and entitled to his children, his wife, and his home. Nor are batterers accurate reporters of the level of their abusive behavior. In my practice, batterers will admit to some form of low-level abuse and justify their conduct with allegations about their spouses' behavior or the provocations they experienced. What we can observe is that the batterer cannot empathize with their spouse's fears or the hurt experienced. It is only about him.

Finally, batterers are manipulative and can evoke significant levels of sympathy for their perceived plight. Judges, court personnel, mental health experts, and attorneys for the children may see the batterer in a positive light, in which their behavior is excusable. Most batterers minimize and excuse their violent behavior, and acceptance of these beliefs does not promote their ability to change. An effective interdisciplinary response to batterers that protects children must focus on training of mental health and legal professionals to identify the common traits of batterers, including their sense of entitlement, lack of empathy, narcissism, and contempt for their spouses. An understanding of male partner abuse and the range of behaviors associated with battering can help the court system recognize the batterers' ability to manipulate others so they can consistently respond to efforts to circumvent court rules, visitation orders, and orders of protection. Abusive men frequently evoke sympathy from the courts and mental health professionals. How abusive men successfully manipulate the courts and the mental health profession should not be ignored.

By way of example, while working for a judge in a criminal court that handled cases of domestic violence, a young attractive man in his twenties was produced in court, having spent several days in prison after his arrest for beating his wife. His new girlfriend waited for him in the courtroom. When he appeared, he sobbed—telling the judge he did not know how this had happened and that he needed help and would do whatever it took to get help. The judge quickly released him on his own recognizance, telling him not to worry: he was going to get him out, and directed him to an anger management program. His new girlfriend sobbed along with him. Everyone in the courtroom was deeply concerned with this attractive young man's well-being and anxious to see him freed from prison.

Puzzled, I looked through the defendant's court file and noticed the photograph of the defendant's current wife taken at the time of his arrest at the precinct. In contrast to the handsome young defendant before the judge, her face was unrecognizable. She had a badly cut lip that was swollen and bruised. Her eye was blackened. The defendant had beaten his wife savagely around the face and body. Yet those in the courtroom were moved by the defendant's tears and had suddenly forgotten all about his victim. The question we needed to ask ourselves—who was the defendant crying for—was never addressed. However, when we ask ourselves this very important question, we are unable to avoid the answer: the defendant's tears were solely motivated out of a concern for himself.

This defendant was being held accountable criminally for the harm he had committed. He was not crying for his wife whom he had severely injured. His apology was directed only to the judge and not to the wife whom he had brutalized. No one asked the defendant how he would make this situation right for his victim. The assumption was that the wife had somehow provoked the defendant, that he needed to learn better responses to her harmful behavior, and that he needed to remove himself from this very toxic relationship.

Is There a Diagnosis?

In analyzing the mental health of batterers, the issue of whether there is an abusive personality has not been fully resolved in the mental health field. Brasfield argued that while partner violence is recognized as a public health and human rights concern, without a supporting diagnosis there is no effective treatment available for this population.[21] Domestic violence advocates conversely argue that abusive behavior is criminal and that sentences that include treatment options may undermine the safety of victims. Both arguments have merit. The work of the domestic violence movement has largely focused on criminalizing and prosecuting abusive behavior. This remains an essential part of the judicial response to domestic violence, but, unfortunately, many incidents of abuse are still not prosecuted, are undetected, or are minimized. The problem with this approach is that we fail to develop an understanding of abusers and their many strategies during custody and divorce. For example, there may be some abusive men who are extremely successful and do not fit the definition of someone who easily loses control. Moreover, the human cost of their behavior toward their children and spouses is a well-kept secret. During custody litigation, judges and mental health professionals have difficulty assessing the mental health of batterers and their parental fitness.

Dutton questioned whether male partner abuse could be the result of a combination of factors, including modeling of a parent's abusive behavior and the perpetrators own struggle with post-traumatic stress disorder (PTSD).[22] There is a significant body of literature that demonstrates the harm caused by fathers' abuse and its impact on future generations. Furthermore, the impact on the development of boys who may have been traumatized by their fathers' abuse has been discussed at length in the literature. In response to these concerns, Dutton proposed a model of the "abusive personality" which he argued could be a response to childhood trauma.[23]

Conversely, Gondolf's study of 840 men, most of whom were enrolled in court-ordered batterers' treatment programs, utilized the Millon Clinical Multiaxial Inventory (MCMI-III) and found no support for the concept of an "abusive personality."[24] However, Gondolf's research found that 90% of their sample demonstrated higher levels in areas intended to measure clinical personality patterns frequently associated with personality disorders. These included elevated levels of narcissistic, passive-aggressive, antisocial, and depressive tendencies, ranging from 19% to 25%.[25] In response, Dutton has criticized Gondolf's earlier research, arguing that this research tested primarily for personality disorders and not the traits he associated with the abusive personality.[26] Dutton has continued to write extensively about batterers' early experience of being shamed by their parent and insecurely attached to form what later becomes what he refers to as the "adult abusive personality."[27] His research also described batterers' psychological defensiveness and underreporting of their violence, anger, parental maltreatment, and trauma symptoms.[28] These factors may be reflected in the data gathered in many of the national incidence reports because batterers may underreport their own abusive behavior and express a profound sense of being victimized. Finally, while acknowledging that more research is needed in this field, Brasfield argued for inclusion of the abusive personality as a mental disorder in cases of chronically abusive behavior.[29]

The judicial response to intimate partner abuse in the context of divorce and custody litigation must focus on the harm caused by the person who is abusive and not be swayed by manipulation and minimization. When confronted by tears and manipulation, we must ask ourselves the hard questions: Why are we compelled to comfort and forgive these men, and what purpose does their contrition serve? Has the abuser made amends to his wife and children, or are his apologies directed at the person who might punish him? Does this sudden apology serve to minimize the consequences of his own behavior? These are the questions that all mental health evaluators, visitation supervisors, attorneys for the children, and, finally, judges must ask themselves whenever they feel moved by the batterer's tears.

It is impossible to ignore many of the traits that batterers share and the impact of their behavior on their children. The question of whether some batterers experience the hypervigilance and hyperaggression that often accompany PTSD should be the subject of more research. Similarly, our understanding that boys are more susceptible to modeling their own fathers' abusive behaviors should inform our child custody laws and decisions to prevent such exposure. If batterers are themselves traumatized, the courts must fashion treatment programs that include supervision, confinement, and protection of their victims.

While to date there is no diagnosis for batterers, we must be able to identify the traits and behaviors that endanger their families, including a sense of entitlement, narcissism, and the ability to manipulate those in authority. All graduate mental health training on domestic violence should focus on identification of the manipulative strategies employed by many batterers and seek to label our responses correctly as countertransference. For reasons that I do not fully understand, when men cry, many individuals feel a strong urge to help them and excuse their behavior, which may have something to do with the profound sense of victimhood batterers display despite the harm they have caused their family. This tendency to protect the batterer distracts from the essential task at hand; protecting women and children from their abuse. In divorce and custody proceedings, identification of abusive behavior is critical. Finally, it is important to identify those situations where batterers display suicidal and obsessive tendencies and have other risk factors, such as substance abuse problems and a criminal justice history, that increase the risks for some femicides.

Assessing Dangerousness

While not all batterers have a diagnosis that can be found in the *Diagnostic and Statistical Manual of Mental Disorders* (DSM-5),[30] researchers have noted that a significant percentage of the most physically abusive perpetrators of domestic violence display substantial mental health symptoms. Juodis et al. found that approximately 30% of perpetrators of domestic violence homicides in their study had threatened or attempted suicide before committing these murders and displayed obsessive behaviors.[31] These researchers indicated the need for safety planning and contact with the victims to provide for their protection.[32] During this dangerous time when the perpetrator is free, it is important to provide safety planning for the victim who may not fully understand her own vulnerability. These researches also stressed the need for intensive follow-up with such perpetrators, that included frequent contacts with social service, mental health, medical, and court personnel.[33] With these high-risk perpetrators, Hart stressed the use of home and work visits, electronic surveillance, drug testing, and even the reading of emails and letters to monitor the levels of danger.[34] Such safety risks mean that some form of confinement is necessary, although medication and treatment can be part of this program provided the victims are kept safe. Significantly, Juodis et al. noted that high-risk abusers are resistant to batterers' intervention programs and thus such programs should not be part of outpatient treatment.[35]

For battered women murdered in their homes, Campbell et al. have indicated that the majority were murdered by former or current intimate partners.[36] These researchers found that mental illness, substance abuse, and prior involvement in the criminal justice system were significant factors that, in many instances, were also associated with drug use. Juodis et al. hypothesized that men who engaged in the most violent behavior were a subset of the violent and antisocial batterers believed to be psychopaths and noted that perpetrators were a heterogeneous group.[37] Their research identified important triggers for the lethal level of violence that included separation and starting a new relationship.[38] Joudis et al. found that in 70.3% of the cases in their study of correctional inmates, the homicides were triggered by separation, and perpetrators who were psychopathic were less likely to appear suicidal or distressed before killing, indicating the need for more research on the potential risks to intimate partners and children.[39] The Ontario Domestic Violence Death Review Committee (2005) found that informal or formal custody disputes were also a triggering factor in lethal domestic violence.[40] Lethality risk assessments have been developed, including the DA developed by Campbell et al.[41] More research is needed to help us understand the level of risks to families with the most serious cases of homicidal and suicidal batterers.

There are times in custody and divorce litigation when the system is confronted with very dangerous and suicidal litigants. In such situations, it is essential that mental health professionals take a careful history that gathers information about any threats, the presence of weapons, or suicidal ideation. In my practice, during custody and divorce litigation, a seriously mentally ill father who had been referred to a supervised visitation program demanded unsupervised contact with the children the night before the court date. It seemed likely that the visitation program was going to recommend the same the following day. Fortunately, my client called me to ask what she should do. During my contact with her, she had recounted a history of the father's violence, threats, and erratic behavior. That night, I advised her not to allow him access to the children. Fleeing before the police arrived, the father went home and killed himself using an unlicensed weapon. Thankfully, the children were not with him. While not all batterers are seriously mentally ill, and not all mentally ill parents are violent, it is essential that the courts and mental health professionals be trained in risk assessments to avert the tragedy of femicides and the murder of children.

When judges and mental health professionals are aware of the batterer's level of abuse, we must also ask ourselves whether these professionals are minimizing the consequences of abuse because they fear retaliation. This is a significant issue that must be addressed. It is essential that we consider the impact of judicial elections, the lack of court monitoring, licensing complaints, and public awareness on divorce and custody decisions. Judges and mental health professionals sometimes do realize in a visceral way that the batterer is dangerous but fail to connect their own concerns with the safety of the children.

In one case in my practice where I had made an emergency motion to suspend an abusive father's unsupervised visitation, the court personnel routinely called for security back-up in the form of additional court security during the father's court appearances because of his volatile and threatening behavior. Court personnel rightly called for extra safety precautions to protect the judge, yet, at the same time, my client was pressured to consider unsupervised visitation. Pointing out that this particular child could not call for the type of emergency help needed to protect court personnel caused the judge to stop and reflect about the dangers to this vulnerable three-year-old; to her credit, she responded thoughtfully thereafter to the child's need for safety and supervised visits.

Many litigants in custody disputes in family court have not been prosecuted or even arrested for their abusive behavior. Sometimes, the physical abuse was a single incident followed by years of coercively controlling behavior to keep the mother in line. Sometimes, the abuse consists only of sexual abuse, which, although criminal, was never reported. These batterers display similar traits and evidence narcissistic behavior and a sense of entitlement. Some may be psychopaths. The visitation supervisors and mental health evaluators are frequently not unaware of the extent of the batterer's need to hurt the mother of their children. Their fears of retaliation if they stand their ground must lead to protective strategies for women and children.

Significantly, Stark argues that we have failed to protect battered women when we overemphasize the issue of physical violence and instead points out that abuse is intended to deprive women of their liberty and takes many forms.[42] This researcher correctly cites many studies that have measured the extent of verbally abusive relationships in which coercive control is an integral aspect.[43] In the context of custody or divorce litigation, we should examine the purpose of the batterer's behavior and ask whether this an attempt to deprive someone of their ability to be financially independent or to undermine the relationship of the children to their primary caretaker. Goel and Goodmark criticized the emphasis on physical violence in identifying intimate partner violence.[44] These advocates argue further that mandatory arrest and criminalization is not effective. However, while mandatory arrest and the use of the criminal justice system do not prevent legal abuse or ensure justice in custody and divorce cases, the New York City Domestic Violence Fatality Review Committee noted that this has been shown to dramatically reduce homicides.[45] Similarly, Lapp and Watson found that, in New York, passage of mandatory arrest laws that promote criminal sanctions has reduced recidivism even if the penalties are relatively light.[46] Given that 80% of the victims of homicides in New York are female, the importance of reducing homicides and recidivism should not be minimized.[47]

However, in the context of divorce and custody disputes, physical abuse is only one aspect of the problem, which arrest and criminalization alone cannot alleviate. The World Health Organization has not only included physical, sexual, economic, and psychological abuse, but has also added unspecified controlling behavior to its definition of abuse.[48] While we should never underestimate the risk of physical violence or minimize the harm that results, it is also important to understand that there are many ways to exert coercive control. I am always amazed at the level of deceit, planning, and manipulation that batterers engage in to punish and control their partners, before or after separation. Jaffe et al. cautions that judges should recognize and protect abused women from legal abuse, and we can assume that utilization of a model that minimizes some forms of abuse has allowed abusers to exert their prodigious manipulation skills to harm women.[49]

Maternal and Paternal Mental Health Concerns

My students have focused on the stigma of mental illness and substance abuse in custody litigation. They note that the research has focused on mothers and mental illness and largely ignored the role of fathers who may struggle with mental illness as well. The overemphasis on the impact of mental illness in mothers can reinforce negative stereotypes while leaving open the question of the impact of the father's psychological difficulties. Furthermore, the emphasis on diagnosis alone does not answer questions about the parties' strengths and weaknesses in their parenting. A mother with a diagnosis of anxiety, depression, or bipolar disorder may be very aware of the importance of timely mental health treatment and have good self-awareness. The stigma of mental illness can make women afraid that if they seek help, they will lose custody of their children, and therefore they may postpone treatment. Styron et al. have found that severe mental illness, including schizophrenia, major affective disorders, and personality disorders, may be associated with more specific and measurable problems in parenting, including difficulties with parent–child communication and with providing emotional and physical care and discipline.[50] Risser et al. have indicated that other problems with less-disturbed parents may include a lack of understanding of age-appropriate behavior and situations in which the children must care for the parent.[51] These problems may be mitigated by providing social support, education, and treatment to reduce the isolation experienced by parents with mental health problems.

Lee's analysis of the Fragile Families and Child Well-Being Study reviewed the impact of paternal mental illness on child neglect or abuse. This researcher noted that fathers were more frequently found to be the perpetrators of child maltreatment, thus making it important to identify the risks associated with this phenomenon to increase prevention. This study reviewed 1,134 fathers who resided in the home. Utilizing the revised Parent-Child Conflict Tactics Scales (CTS-PC), the study found that paternal depression, higher levels of paternal stress, and alcohol use significantly increased the risk of child maltreatment.[52]

In custody litigation, rather than stigmatize the parent struggling with mental illness or substance abuse, it is important for the mental health and legal professions to have criteria, regardless of diagnosis, to assess the impact of such mental health problems on parenting skills. A parent with a mental health diagnosis is not necessarily someone with extensive parenting problems but may have significant ego strengths and self-awareness. In my social work practice, many mothers had various kinds of mental health, physical, or substance abuse problems but were often desperate for social support from families and their community. Parent education or group experiences with other parents and appropriate professionals can enhance parenting and reduce isolation. In custody litigation, while it is important to understand the mental health diagnosis, it is also essential that the courts have thorough assessments from mental health professionals that focus on parenting skills and functioning.

Mental Health, Domestic Violence, and Symptoms of PTSD

The impact of trauma on adults is widely recognized in the research on Adverse Childhood Experiences (ACEs), PTSD, and the burgeoning discussion of complex PTSD. Herman discussed the spectrum of responses to trauma ranging from a minimal reaction to a single traumatic incident for which the individual does not need treatment to recover to the more severe responses described in her analysis of complex PTSD.[53] In Herman's research and treatment, she observed that many in the mentally ill population had been exposed to trauma.

She noted that many of her patients diagnosed with borderline personality disorder were those suffering from complex PTSD because of the impact of cumulative exposure to trauma.[54] This is an area that requires more research as the diagnosis of complex PTSD has not been accepted in the DSM-5 as of the writing of this chapter. However, in a study of 582 women in which the majority had experienced childhood trauma, including physical, sexual, or emotional abuse, Cloitre et al. found that those adults who had been exposed to greater levels of trauma similarly experienced more complex symptoms that resembled multiple psychiatric disorders.[55]

Griffing et al. has observed that symptoms following traumatic exposure fit into three categories: intrusion, in which there is persistent reexperiencing of the traumatic incidence; avoidance, that includes psychic numbing; and hyper-arousal.[56] Noting that there is also a link between past traumatization and PTSD, these researchers have called for additional research to determine the relationship between past traumatic exposure and these particular categories of symptoms to inform the research and treatment methodology.

It is also important to view PTSD not as a form of mental illness but as a response to exposure to trauma that takes many forms. Thus, even if the battered woman suffers from some form of mental illness, it is essential for the mental health profession and the legal system to first consider her motivation to parent effectively and her receptiveness to treatment, including her ability to gain insight. In this context, mental health professionals who are trained to view the impact of the environment and abuse on ego functioning and parenting skills are best qualified to provide custody evaluations. Infrequently, I have encountered instances in which battered women may self-medicate using alcohol or prescription medication. In my experience, referrals to trauma-informed mental health treatment can prevent further misuse of such substances, particularly when there are also sufficient social supports.

Nonetheless, there may be a small minority of battered women with significant mental health concerns. Significantly, we must still consider whether her response is due to the abuse she experienced. In those instances, the courts should not reward batterers by treating them as good parents. In some instances, their mental health or substance abuse issues are extremely challenging for domestic violence advocates. This should not be confused with clients who have legitimate disagreements about strategy with their attorneys. As advocates, it is important to explain our point of view, quietly hear their concerns, and finally reach a consensus with our clients in a way that enhances their growing autonomy and keeps them out of harm's way. For mental health professionals, the challenge is to provide an assessment of parenting and appropriate referrals to trauma-informed treatment.

The medical model stresses the toxic level of stress created when there is abuse. Toxic stress and its impact have been widely recognized by the medical profession in terms of adverse childhood experiences (ACEs) as discussed in

Chapter 4.[57] It is essential that we consider not only the physical risks such behavior engenders but also the psychological impact on children and mothers. Narcissism, a lack of empathy, and a sense of entitlement—frequently exhibited by batterers—are traits that do not make for good parenting. Recognition of the toxicity of such abusive behaviors in the context of a divorce or custody dispute is essential before we can protect children from exposure to continued trauma.

During divorce and custody litigation, battered women may display a wide range of reactions and symptoms. These may include disassociation, hyper-vigilance, intrusive thoughts, depression, and chronic anxiety.[58] Anxious, and hyper-vigilant clients may worry constantly about legal strategy or whether we will be successful. This is not an unreasonable response given the stress involved in litigation. They may report having difficulty sleeping before and after court dates, asking endless questions and questioning strategy. Battered women may testify without emotion, their disassociation making it difficult for them to link their fear and vulnerability to the recollection of traumatic events. When the batterer's coercive control is acknowledged, most of the women I have represented accept guidance and advice from their therapists and attorneys as they navigate a very difficult legal process. With informed representation and mental health treatment, these women can display enormous resilience.

Pico-Alfonso et al. found that exposure to intimate partner violence had a negative impact on women's mental health that included depressive symptoms, anxiety, and, in some instances, suicidal ideation.[59] Depression, anxiety, and interpersonal problems are also associated with PTSD.[60] I have seen the most significant mental health issues, albeit anecdotally, when the fathers are more manipulative and the abuse takes multiple forms that may include a high level of verbal abuse. In the context of a custody dispute when batterers are highly manipulative, judges, attorneys, and mental health professionals often display excessive sympathy for them, excusing and minimizing their behavior. In one instance in my practice, the father had displayed profound disrespect for the judge, accusing him of being biased, shouting insults at my client, and disobeying court orders repeatedly. After a long and contentious trial, he apologized to the judge for his behavior. In the custody decision in which the father was awarded extensive unsupervised visitation, the judge remarked that the father's apology was a sign of significant growth. This decision completely ignored the fact that the father's apology displayed no remorse for his treatment of the mother or their children, but was intended to curry favor with the judge. Because of this kind of manipulation, mothers and children are forced into situations that are unsafe and are continually retraumatized.

For battered mothers, their inability to protect their children from abuse has the potential to be traumatic, and, in my practice, I have seen many women become hypervigilant, anxious, and highly distrustful of the legal system. In those instances, when clients are particularly distrustful and anxious because of their history of abuse, they may trigger negative responses from judicial personnel, custody evaluators, and even their attorneys. At those times, it is essential that their advocates be aware of the countertransference responses generated by such clients and to consider their levels of trauma to rebuild their trust. This does not mean that such clients can make endless demands on our time or resources. Limit-setting that is transparent but not rigid is important to establish the necessary attorney–client or patient–client relationships. Furthermore, when judges, custody evaluators, and attorneys respond with anger or hostility, we must consider whether they have had adequate training and are not overwhelmed by excessive caseloads.

More research is needed to compare the psychological well-being of women and children who have experienced a more protective response from the legal system in the form of protective orders, clear control over parenting decisions, and limited visitation for the fathers, with those abused women and children who had unsupervised contact. In comparison, it is important to determine whether those abused women and children who had to negotiate continued communication, extensive visitation, and joint custody arrangements have more difficulties. It would be interesting to determine whether protected women are more effective parents and whether their children have better mental health outcomes when there are appropriate boundaries in place.

Substance Abuse and Domestic Violence

Substance abuse, particularly alcohol abuse, was originally thought to be the root cause of domestic violence and was one of the driving motivations for Prohibition. However, while it is widely recognized that alcohol abuse frequently exacerbates the incidence of domestic violence, the research on causation and violence among alcohol-abusing men is more difficult to establish.[61] In short, a batterer with a drinking problem has two problems: his abuse and his drinking. Conversely, while not all who struggle with addiction are abusive, Juodis et al. noted the importance of abstinence for perpetrators of domestic violence because alcohol abuse is one of the risk factors in danger assessments.[62] For battered women, Risser et al. have indicated that it is also widely believed that the stresses of parenting are exacerbated when the primary caretaker is struggling with her own substance abuse and mental health concerns.[63]

The relationship among substance abuse, aggression, and domestic violence is a significant factor that should be considered in custody and divorce litigation. Corvo and Carpenter conducted a retrospective study of the intergenerational impact in families known to be violent and to also have a history of substance abuse. Their research found that if the abuser had a father who was violent and engaged in substance abuse, the paternal substance abuse had an independent and powerful impact.[64] They concluded that domestic violence could develop in the children of abusive men who were also substance abusers but that further study was needed to determine if these behaviors were learned intergenerational responses. Thus, it is important for judges and mental health professionals in custody cases to consider the profound and long-reaching impact of both substance abuse and domestic violence. Significantly, Corvo and Carpenter observed that the treatment methods for substance abuse and domestic violence are currently in conflict because domestic abuse is a voluntary act while substance abuse is viewed as a disease.[65] Researchers who study alcoholism and domestic violence suggest that these problems have a shared etiology.[66] However, this research does not suggest that treating the substance abuse will prevent further domestic violence.

It is important for judges and mental health professionals to understand that substance abuse has a dramatic impact on the level of domestic violence in families. There is a significant body of research that indicates that the more severe violence occurs in households where there is substance abuse and that substance abuse also increases the rate of domestic violence in families.[67] Finally, Martin and Bachman concluded that the percentage of women who were injured in domestic violence incidents increased when their intimate partner had abused alcohol.[68]

These considerations are important as substance abuse increases the risks to other family members if there is a history of domestic violence. Furthermore, treating the substance abuse problem does not prevent further incidents of domestic violence. The legal system should recognize that mandating substance abuse treatment programs, whether in the criminal or family court context, does not address the underlying issue of domestic violence in the family and requires separate legal interventions that include penalties, restrictions, and limitations on the batterer's access to women and children.

Severity of Aggression and Alcohol Abuse

Graham et al. have indicated that the abuse of alcohol appears to fuel aggression and domestic violence, whether as part of episodic or chronic heavy drinking, and often occurs before incidents of abuse.[69] Graham et al. also found that there were differences between male and female aggression during incidents of alcohol abuse, finding that females reported that males exhibited more severe aggression in incidents of domestic violence, whereas males did not report that women demonstrated the same level of violence.[70] The later research of alcohol abuse in thirteen countries by Graham et al. concluded that such abuse was associated with the most severe incidents of physical aggression and that male aggression was perceived as the more violent.[71] Male violence also has a greater tendency to spill over into the public arena when complicated by alcohol abuse, whereas women's aggression is typically limited to the family.[72] Most significantly, a retroactive study found that 60% of violent incidents by males occurred two hours after drinking, and 20% occurred between two and four hours after drinking.[73] Finally, the amount of alcohol consumed had a direct impact on aggression, as both the frequency of alcohol use and the level of consumption increased the likelihood of domestic violence.[74] Male aggression was also associated with incidents in which women were more likely to be injured.[75] Testa et al. also found that men were more abusive in incidents in which they had been drinking as compared to incidents of violence when they were not drinking.[76] It is clear that alcohol abuse increases the levels, rates, and risk of injuries for women from abusive men and is a significant risk to public health and safety.

The Impact of Parental Substance Abuse on Children

A study by Risser et al. of 492 children enrolled in a community-based treatment program for children who had been exposed to domestic violence and in which the majority were cared for by their mothers noted whether the primary caretaker suffered from depression, anxiety, or bipolar disorder.[77] Service providers were asked to reveal whether either parent had been hospitalized psychiatrically or had a substance abuse problem. This study utilized the Child Behavior Checklist (CBCL) to measure psychosocial functioning of children exposed to domestic violence who had parents with mental health or substance abuse problems. As was expected, children from families with this added layer of difficulty initially displayed more problems than those in the control group. However, the more troubled children from homes where parents suffered from substance abuse or mental health problems significantly improved after treatment for domestic violence exposure. This study only focused on the short-term effects of such domestic violence–related treatment and recommended further research on the long-term impact of treatment in families exposed to domestic violence as well as substance abuse and mental health problems.[78] It also noted that various other factors have a positive impact on parenting capacity, including exiting an abusive relationship, mental health or substance abuse treatment, and education about the impact of parental risk factors on child functioning. Safety planning and case management can contribute to improvement in parental function and have an impact on children's functioning as well.[79] This study acknowledges the impact of mental health and substance abuse problems on parenting but indicates that treatment for domestic violence exposure may have a positive impact on other adverse childhood experiences.

Significantly, children who have been exposed to domestic violence respond better to treatment if the caretakers receive treatment for substance abuse.[80] Keiley et al. found that treatment of caretakers who struggle with substance abuse alone also has a significant impact on the adjustment of children.[81] These researchers' longitudinal study of adolescents concluded that alcohol use and aggression have a reciprocal impact on each other, as greater aggression leads to greater drinking, which again leads to greater aggression.[82] Alcohol use is also closely linked to problems with anxiety and depression in men and women. However, in men, there is also a significant correlation among depression, alcohol abuse, and aggression.[83]

Thus, the interrelationships among mental health, substance abuse, and aggression are complex. Households in which there is substance abuse and domestic violence are more at-risk of severe and frequent incidents of domestic violence. While mandating treatment programs for substance abuse is important, this does not guarantee the safety of other family members.

Mothering, Domestic Violence, Substance Abuse, and Mental Health

Many of the women seen in custody and divorce litigation do not display significant mental health issues.[84] However, there are also times when the courts must balance the mothers' symptoms of traumatic exposure against the risks of their children's exposure to their fathers' violence. Herman found that exposure to intimate partner violence or other adverse childhood experiences may be the underlying cause of some mental health conditions. In other instances, these traumatic experiences may exacerbate existing vulnerabilities in the non-abusive parent.[85]

Researchers have also studied whether childhood sexual abuse by a parent or significant caretaker is linked to the development of borderline personality disorder.[86] At this time, the DSM-5 does not recognize complex PTSD as a diagnosis, and more research is needed to determine whether individuals correctly categorized as borderline are in fact simply part of the spectrum of PTSD and complex PTSD. It remains an open question whether such individuals who develop borderline personality disorder were simply more vulnerable than others and more severely impacted by their traumatic exposure. Nor can we definitively say that all mental illness is simply the result of exposure to trauma.

Most of the research on parenting and mental illness focuses on mothering and serious mental illness. Oyserman et al. conducted an exhaustive review of the literature on mothers with serious mental illness and parenting, focusing on those with long-term, serious mental illness, which included schizophrenia, bipolar affective disorders, and depression.[87] These researchers did not include women with simple postpartum depression, which they estimated impacted between 5% and 8.8% of women who give birth.[88] Significantly, Oyserman et al. noted that while the impact of mothers' serious mental illness and depression impacts children, there is little research on the impact of serious mental illness and fathering, but they hypothesized that these effects may be similar if fathers are involved with their children.[89]

Oyserman et al. noted that good parenting includes the ability to provide supervision that is balanced with an understanding of the child's need for developing independence in an age-appropriate manner.[90] Thus, parenting requires constant juggling and flexibility while providing needed structure.[91] These researchers found that women with mental illness may experience problems with parenting because of their symptoms, lack of social supports, and knowledge about parenting issues, and they may need help in coping with their own mental health and the demands of parenting.[92] Gelkopf and Jabotaro also observed that a mother's lack of confidence in her capacity to parent has a negative impact on her ability and that such mothers with serious mental illness are frequently isolated.[93]

Gelkopf and Jabotaro also have noted that mothers with serious mental illness are a diverse group, that not all have deficits in parenting, and that not all children will be affected by their caretakers' difficulties.[94] While this was a small research study, these researchers concluded that there is a need for programs that reduce maternal isolation and increase social supports, as their research suggests that this will increase maternal confidence and, ultimately, maternal competence.[95] Lacey et al.'s 2015 study of mothers and fathers with serious mental illness noted that mothers were more likely than fathers to perceive stigmatization and were more critical of themselves and lacked confidence in their own parenting abilities.[96] In comparison, fathers were more likely to report stigmatization because of their gender. These researchers concluded that these mothers were more self-critical of their own parenting, which might be a result of their internalization of the elevated expectations we have for mothers' parenting as opposed to fathers. This double standard often internalized by mothers is also evidenced in the family courts during custody litigation. Not surprisingly, mothers without custody experienced the highest levels of self-stigmatization. Oyserman et al. also noted the importance of being a parent to mothers with serious mental illnesses and that this may be a motivating factor in their obtaining treatment.[97] However, many of the research participants reported receiving discriminatory treatment from mental health, legal, and child welfare services. Finally, Lacey et al. stressed the importance of programs that reduce social isolation among parents with mental illness. Enhancing social supports for battered women, whether they have mental health problems or not, also means that we must provide services to those family members who are their support system. Peled et al. also observed that mothers of daughters who have been abused experienced social isolation and self-blame and felt stress as a result of the ongoing burden of helping their daughters after separation.[98]

The impact of mothering and depression has also received attention.[99] In a review of the research, Gelfand and Teti noted the ways that maternal depression and related lack of responsiveness can interfere with children's attachments and ability to master language and developmental goals.[100] Bowlby articulated that stable attachments are a critical factor in competent parenting and provide the base from which children and adolescents can explore the outside world.[101] While Oyserman et al. observed that mothers with serious mental illnesses may have difficulties establishing secure attachments with their children, they also noted that the underlying problems are complex.[102] These researchers indicated that the reasons for this are not always clear but may be the result of a combination of factors that include the impact of the mothers' insecure attachments with their own parents, their isolation, and lack of social support.[103] Despite this, Green et al. noted that there were no current studies that tested the impact of social support, attachment, and changes in parenting behavior.[104] However, consistent with Bowlby's theory of attachment as malleable and capable of change, Green et al. concluded that when parents had an anxious and ambivalent attachment with their children, they benefited from social supports that decreased their anxiety.[105] We can assume that, in the context of custody litigation, the better approach to maternal mental health problems would be to provide support to enhance their parenting. Too often, women are stigmatized for the impact of domestic violence rather than helped to become more competent parents.

Laing's 2016 small research study of survivors of abuse referred by domestic violence service providers involved in custody litigation in the Australian family court system is instructive.[106] This researcher noted the impact of secondary victimization when battered women are treated harshly after exposure to abuse.[107] In this environment, these researchers concluded that the women were revictimized by the family court system, experienced the litigation as exacerbating the traumatic impact of living with domestic violence, and also were subjected to continued post-separation violence.[108] The women were afraid to disclose the history of domestic violence, and some women were warned by their lawyers not to raise these issues and were even threatened by the judge if they disclosed false allegations.[109]

We can hypothesize that, in custody litigation, the legal system can also help to enhance the effectiveness of battered mothers' parenting by providing them with support from the judiciary and from mental health professionals. Furthermore, Graham-Bermann et al. conducted a study of 120 mother–child pairs who had been exposed to intimate partner violence within the past two years.[110] Children of mothers who had received services and completed treatment that intended to enhance their social supports and emotional adjustment demonstrated better adjustment. Thus, a commitment to the eradication of domestic violence means that we must provide support to even the most vulnerable mothers who suffer from substance abuse or depression after leaving abusive relationships. It also means that the judiciary must recognize that mothers and children display more resilience when they are protected from further abuse. We can assess the treatment strategies that facilitate coping to provide help to battered women who may have trauma-related symptoms or depression. The mental health profession and the legal system can assist battered women to obtain services that will enhance resilience. Enhancing competent parenting does not occur in a vacuum: it requires financial stability and access to sufficient medical and mental health services in the form of consistent court orders and referrals to domestic violence service agencies. The provision of services from victims' advocates groups that provide mentoring, counseling, and support groups and early referrals to substance abuse programs after careful assessment can all enhance resilience.

Nor is it acceptable to diminish responsibility for violence and abuse. Even if some mothers are psychologically vulnerable, absent a clear inability to parent, we need to support the abused parent and invest in treatment with mental health professionals who understand the importance of trauma and enhancing social supports. As a family law attorney who represented battered women, I was always amazed at how quickly women responded to support and safety after leaving their batterers.

Conclusion

To summarize, the question of how well men parent if they suffer from mental illness has not been widely researched, and additional research is needed in this area. We do have significant research about the additional impact of abusive behavior and substance abuse on children. As the impact of adverse childhood experiences has long-lasting and chronic effects, care should be taken to avoid retraumatizing children with orders of unsupervised visitation or custody. On a positive note, treatment programs for children exposed to domestic violence has also been found to be effective in treating the impact of substance abuse and mental health problems. Mothers with mental health concerns should be able to obtain access to services without fear of losing custody. The courts should hesitate before giving credence to fathers' claims that their spouse is mentally ill or has a substance abuse problem in the context of domestic violence. These are complex situations where the information given to the courts should include an understanding of the research on the mental health and safety implications for fathers with abusive behavior.

Helping mothers with trauma-related mental health problems caused by exposure to domestic violence will demonstrate to their children the importance of living a violence-free life. Additionally, the literature suggests that mothers are capable of better parenting with social services and mental health support. This can be enhanced by the courts in terms of orders of protection and custody and visitation decisions that provide consistent protection and boundaries for women and children. Given the harm caused by exposure to abusive behavior in children for decades, it is essential that the focus of the legal and mental health professions shift to firmly establish safety for children and mothers.

7

Economic and Legal Abuse

Economic abuse is not readily identified during divorce or separation for what it is—a symptom of long-standing abuse—in what I have termed traumatic divorce. For many women, the batterers' myriad forms of economic abuse remain invisible throughout the litigation. Even when there is an absence of abuse, researchers have found that the standard of living for divorced women declined dramatically following divorce.[1] Economic abuse is frequently part of a pattern of coercive control and is an integral part of the constellation of abusive behaviors employed by batterers over many years. It is difficult for women to leave abusive relationships without their economic deprivation becoming particularly frightening. This deprivation often deters women from leaving these relationships. This chapter will discuss the research on economic abuse that includes coercive debt, the impact of domestic violence on employment, and the legislative responses to the financial disparities between men and women during divorce or separation.

As stated in earlier chapters, Stark noted that coercively controlling behavior takes many forms, including physical abuse, verbal threats, harassment, and economic abuse.[2] Pollett described economic abuse as the unseen side of intimate partner violence that can also inflict long-term harm.[3] Many women have reported that economic and verbal abuse are particularly painful aspects of intimate partner violence because of the long-lasting impact.[4]

Identification of Economic Abuse

Researchers have also observed that economic abuse frequently went hand in hand with other forms of domestic violence. It is important to understand the prevalence and forms of economic abuse experienced by battered women so that their efforts to leave the abusive relationship will not be jeopardized and their economic independence can be maximized. Furthermore, the impact of economic abuse may linger for years as women struggle to pay off debts or reenter the work force while earning less than men.

Evaluations of intimate partner violence have focused on the impact of physical abuse, which, while significant, is not the whole picture. More recently, Outlaw's research has focused on other forms of abuse, including social, economic, and psychological abuse, to determine whether there were any connections between these different patterns of behavior.[5] Although this researcher found a slight correlation between economic and physical abuse, she did not measure coerced credit card debt or other forms of financial abuse and called for more research in this area.

Adams et al. also concluded that, although the rate and impact of physical, psychological, and sexual abuse had been studied extensively, economic abuse has received far less attention.[6] These researchers studied 103 women from shelter and nonshelter populations, ranging in age from eighteen to eighty-five years of age, of whom 63% were unemployed, 21% held full-time employment, and 16% were employed part-time. These women described abusive experiences that included physical incidents of pushing, shoving, and grabbing, and psychological abuse that included yelling, screaming, and name-calling. Of these women, 57% had been sexually abused, and 65% of the assaults included attempted strangulation. Finally, Adams et al. indicated that an overwhelming 99% of these women indicated that they had also suffered economic abuse.[7]

Their research utilized the Scale of Economic Abuse (SEA), developed with input from survivors, practitioners, and the literature on domestic violence to identify the frequency and impact of such behaviors.[8] This study identified 120 behaviors while also allowing the participants to describe additional forms of abuse to clarify their individual situations. These researchers elicited information about how the women had fared economically since the onset of the relationship and how their partners' abuse had diminished their ability to achieve economic independence. Alarmingly, participants in this research indicated that many of their abusers had damaged their credit, spent household money intended for the payment of the bills, and forced the women to give their partners money and ATM or credit cards. Significantly, many of the women reported that they had no knowledge of their spouses' finances or income although they shared a household residence. In these situations, Adams et al. indicated that these women reported that their economic stability was threatened and that they were exploited economically.[9]

The behaviors that comprise economic abuse are varied; frequently, they are unrecognized in the context of divorce litigation and are often accompanied by verbal, physical, and sexual abuse. The research of Adams et al. has endeavored to identify a broader range of economically abusive behaviors. Identification of these "red flags," or patterns of behaviors that constitute economic abuse, can help the mental health and legal professions to understand the history of coercively controlling behavior in families. Battered women may not self-identify as victims; they may experience embarrassment or shame regarding the abuse, and sometimes only by their accidental admissions of financial abuse can we learn about the history of domestic violence.

In the legal system during divorce litigation, many judges focus on the very real harm caused by physical violence in families. However, an informed judicial response also includes an awareness that there are other behaviors that are symptomatic of domestic violence. The presence of economic abuse is significant, as well as the other myriad ways in which coercive control is manifested. Only with proper identification and a careful history of the family and its finances can we begin to take steps to prevent economic and legal abuse of women during divorce and separation.

Erickson's discussion of economic abuse in New York noted a recent state Appellate decision on child custody that recognized the harm caused by the husband's failure to pay child support and his termination of the household's utilities *Wissink v. Wissink*.[10] Clearly, the husband in this case did not care whether the children had such necessities as food, shelter, electricity, heat, or hot water. Thus, the Appellate Division noted that the husband's actions failed to consider the children's needs and remanded the case back to the trial court for a hearing to review whether his behavior warranted a change of custody. Erickson noted that although the court failed to expand the concept of economic maltreatment as a form of domestic violence, it signaled its awareness that such behavior was harmful to the children and, as such, should be a consideration in determining custody.[11] In divorce and separation, it is essential that the courts be made aware of all forms of domestic abuse, including economic, so they can correctly determine custody, visitation, the distribution of property, and support.

In my practice, when men refuse employment, hide their finances, encumber their spouses with enormous debt, or are underemployed despite professional qualifications, they do serious long-term harm to their spouses. Nor is economic abuse a problem confined to married women because unmarried women may also be victimized by these patterns of behavior. Unfortunately, unmarried women frequently do not have the same access to the courts as married women to address their economic concerns beyond child support, and they often find themselves in untenable financial circumstances.

Employment and Domestic Violence

While employment discrimination of battered women is beyond the scope of this discussion, interference with their ability to work is an integral aspect of economic abuse. Sometimes loss of employment is the result of direct interference with the battered woman's ability to work, or it may indirectly occur when women lose their jobs because of the domestic violence. Sanders discussed the very complicated relationship between employment and spousal abuse and noted that the research indicates that when women obtained equal employment status with their spouses they experienced fewer incidents of abuse.[12] In other words, employment can be an equalizing factor that provides independence and power. In a small study of thirty women ranging in age from twenty-three to forty-five years, Sanders found that these women identified a connection between spousal abuse and financial independence. These women also noted the importance of economic independence as an essential factor that enabled them to leave their abusers, identifying the impact of economic abuse on their employment, education, debt, and ability to obtain credit.[13] This is a small study but one that should be replicated on a larger scale.

When women are not financially independent, it is easier for batterers to maintain control or to exploit their partners.[14] For some women, the experiences of economic abuse can lead to the loss of employment opportunities and depleted assets because of the batterer's active interference with their ability to work. Park has indicated that many women may be employed at jobs alongside their batterers and are unable to continue this employment following their separations.[15] In a study of 842 women in Chicago, many of whom were abused, Lloyd and Taluc found that one in ten reported that their male partner prevented them from going to work, thus threatening their job security.[16] Following separation, Warrener et al. found that battered women are still not secure because they may lose their jobs due to missed work for the court appearances necessary in related criminal cases or when they sought civil orders of protection.[17]

Battered women's lack of job security is complex and remains an important concern that has begun to receive more attention. The US General Accounting Office (1998) reported that between one-fourth and one-half of domestic violence victims lost their jobs because of their abuse, indicating that employment instability is a significant concern for battered women.[18] Because of these factors, employment policies and laws that protect battered women from economic discrimination are critical in helping to establish their financial stability. The American Bar Association's Commission on Domestic Violence (ABA 2009) noted the growing number of federal and state laws that prohibit employment discrimination against employees victimized by domestic violence.[19] Hayes found that an increasing number of states now provide time off for battered women to obtain medical care, counseling services, domestic violence–related services, and legal assistance and to attend court appearances, with varying provisions made for leave.[20] Despite these reforms, problems have continued for battered women. Many of my clients have reported being terminated for what their employers referred to as "productivity concerns" that are primarily the result of their employer's reluctance to have battered women in the workplace either because of safety concerns or their absences from work.

Batterers may harass their victims on the job. Because of these safety concerns, Park has found that some employers are reluctant to continue to employ battered women.

Conversely, I have also seen large-scale employers make significant accommodations for employees that are models for human resource policies. Such accommodations include redirecting employee's telephone calls to prevent harassment, relocating battered women to a different office for their safety, or assigning security guards to escort battered women to their cars or public transportation after work. These are exemplary efforts that help to maintain a productive, stable work force.

Adams et al. labeled interference with employment as another form of economic abuse, describing the harm caused by the batterers' interference with their spouse's ability to obtain and hold employment through employing such tactics as harassing phone calls to co-workers.[21] Researchers have noted that abusers' efforts to restrict their wives' employment included damaging the car so that she could not go to work, physical threats, sleep deprivation, and even damaging her clothing.[22] In my practice, clients have reported being followed after leaving work, embarrassing calls to co-workers or supervisors, stalking of co-workers when batterers believed them to be involved with their spouse, and incidents in which their cars were damaged in the employee parking lots by their abusers.

For women, the ability to take advantage of advancement opportunities means having the time to attend conferences, training programs, and the like. Anderson et al. also noted the frequency with which batterers interfered with their spouses' attempts to engage in such educational pursuits.[23] Withholding funds for food, clothing, and other necessities are additional forms of economic abuse that may permeate the relationship and are another way to keep women financially and emotionally dependent. Again, the importance of detecting economic abuse cannot be minimized as multiple researchers concur that women are more likely to leave an abusive relationship when they know they can be financially independent.[24]

Finally, the Adams et al. study for the first time noted the existence of credit card abuse, with batterers stealing or pressuring the women to give them their credit or debit cards. This is a frequently used tactic in which extensive debt is incurred in the women's name, thus damaging her credit rating and saddling her with excessive debt. Women confronting the choice of leaving the batterer realize that achieving economic independence may be difficult if not impossible.

Employment also provides essential social support for working women from their co-workers, and this has positive implications for health (unless such jobs have occupational hazards or heavy and unrealistic job demands).[25] Staggs et al. have emphasized the importance of these findings because battered women are frequently isolated, and, while such social support does not prevent violence, the presence of such support can lower the duration of such abuse.[26] In my practice, I have had many women referred by their co-workers. Clients describe seeking help after a colleague noticed a bruise, refused to accept the explanation that "they fell," and offered invaluable support. Some women have been referred to my office by their female supervisors who even provided them with a place to stay following their separation. Others have taken advantage of Employee Assistance Programs to obtain referrals, safety planning, and crisis intervention services. The importance of employment for battered women cannot be overemphasized.

Bankruptcy, Debt, and Domestic Violence

A later study by Littwin of battered women participants in the Consumer Bankruptcy Project (CBP) is revealing.[27] This researcher formulated the term "coerced debt" to define damage to the woman's consumer credit that included nonconsensual, credit-related transactions that can include taking out credit cards in the spouses' name without her knowledge.[28] Significantly, this study of bankruptcy filers screened for domestic violence and found that the rate of domestic violence for women filing for bankruptcy within the past year was almost 18%. However, this study did not screen for women who had been abused within the context of their entire relationship, suggesting that the rate of domestic violence for female bankruptcy filers could be much higher.

Coerced debt may also be identity theft. I have always advised my clients to obtain a credit report following their separation to determine whether the batterer has obtained credit cards in their name. Batterers have access to their partners' address, dates of birth, social security numbers, and other personal information that makes it easy to obtain credit cards or loans in their spouses' names. In my practice, many of my clients have found themselves overwhelmed with debt after their spouses manipulated them into taking out second mortgages or credit card advances to pay for their husband's business ventures. My clients frequently reported that they never benefited from these investments, that their spouses never contributed to the household expenses, and, finally, that they were left paying the bills when their husbands left, trying to salvage whatever they could from the financial wreckage of their marriages. This type of exploitation is frequently seen as criminal when it occurs between strangers.

Furthermore, Littwin correctly noted that coerced debt may not depend on the immediate threat of force. Sometimes even a single incident of physical abuse is sufficient to generate fear, and the threat of further abuse continues to permeate the relationship so that less violent methods of abuse are sufficient to establish control. In the context of a coercively controlling relationship in which there is constant intimidation, economic abuse takes many forms. It can take the form of women "allowing" men to use their credit cards to borrow excessively on their homes or retirement savings to accommodate the batterers' demands.

Furthermore, the use of credit ratings and reporting has economic consequences for battered women because Littwin has indicated that they may be unable to find safe and affordable housing and jobs after separation. Much of the battle to help battered women depends on our ability to help them win economic independence and be free from excessive debt.

Littwin concluded that consumer protection laws and matrimonial laws are frequently not in sync so that battered women saddled with coerced debt may not obtain needed financial relief during the process of divorce. During divorce litigation, debt is generally presumed to be marital, so that, regardless of whose name is used, the battered woman may find that she is liable for part or all her spouse's excesses. Even when responsibility for consumer debt is assigned to the batterer, outside creditors may continue to hound her for payment. In New York, only very severe forms of domestic violence are considered when responsibility for marital debts is determined.[29] After years in an abusive relationship, many women find that their assets are depleted by crushing debt.

Legal Abuse

We think of economically abusive behaviors as including efforts to prevent women from working, restricting their movements, and not providing them with financial support even when they live together. However, when battered women are forced to have continuous contact with their abusers through the very expensive process of litigation, this becomes legal abuse. Miller and Smolter described legal abuse or "paper abuse" as another form of stalking, in which batterers use the court proceedings to force the victim to have continued contact with them.[30] Researchers have noted that when battered women are involved in litigation they are required to have contact with their abusers, and they further noted the difficulty in classifying this behavior as a form of stalking because of the legitimate nature of the court proceedings.[31] However, the economic abuse seen in divorce and custody battles has developed into something subtler, as in many instances batterers capitalize on the financial disparities between the parties by filing frivolous demands and motions in the form of emails, letters, and legal briefs. This practice wastes precious financial resources as women are forced to respond and serves to obscure the issues before the court. In this environment, it is easy for an overwhelmed court to overlook the financial disparities between the parties and thus fail to provide redress against the blatant legal abuses that frequently accompany physical abuse, verbal harassment, and financial abuse. Miller and Smolter concluded that "paper abuse" should be recognized as a form of coercive control, that in their interviews with survivors this issue was frequently raised as a debilitating problem, and that attorneys for survivors also voiced this concern. The women interviewed reported having to sit in court waiting rooms where they overheard batterers' often derogatory and false allegations. Many women were forced to bring their children to court when unable to arrange child care and reported that their children also overheard the conversations. Finally, these researchers noted that women reported that because of multiple court appearances they were forced to take excessive time off from work, thus suffering further financial harm.

Unfortunately, these experiences are all too familiar. My clients frequently report that they have used up all their accrued vacation and personal days off from work for court appearances. Many frantically search for child care so they can appear repeatedly in court and are forced to incur costs for these expenses. While many states provide for legal fees, these awards rarely include child care expenses, adequately cover legal expenses, or answer the problem of multiple absences from work. Furthermore, while many states require employers to provide victims of domestic violence with time off for court appearances to obtain orders of protection, such leave does not include time off for court appearances in custody or child support proceedings. While legal abuse does not constitute the crime of stalking because of the legality of the court proceedings, many battered women experience fear, retraumatization, and economic abuse during litigation.

It is important for the mental health and legal systems to identify legal abuse as part of the tactics of economic abuse that are seen during divorce litigation. Many women report that batterers use this approach to cause them to incur needless legal fees, and more research is needed in this area. Strategies such as repeated frivolous motions, delays, and missed court appearances mean that the opposing party is forced to respond. Anecdotally, legal abuse has a devastating impact that is rarely discussed in the literature. However, most women struggling with divorce, with or without children, can attest to the devastation of their finances after divorce and the impact of post-divorce litigation to enforce frequently ignored financial orders.

It is easy to mischaracterize domestic violence as a problem that impacts only the poor; economic abuse devastates middle- and upper-income women as well. There are many legal decisions regarding custody, support, and the distribution of property which reference the abusive partners' endless motions and demands to relitigate custody, spousal support, and child support. In families with a history of coercive control, more affluent men can spend enormous sums of money during the divorce process. While court-ordered awards of counsel fees to the needier spouse are helpful, these do not always cover all the expenses of litigation. Some batterers may become skilled at legal representation and can be given considerable leeway by the judges. Self-help groups on the Internet offer advice to men who proceed without legal representation. In my practice, I have even seen instances in which the husbands are attorneys who either elect to represent themselves or have nominal representation from a colleague or friend. In these instances, the batterers may employ a range of tactics to intimidate their spouses. These tactics may include cross-examining their spouse directly on the witness stand and making unreasonable settlement demands to extort money to avoid their financial responsibilities. This is a subject that cries out for more research so that women are not blindsided when they enter the legal system. An informed judicial response includes recognition of such behaviors as toxic and debilitating.

Divorce, Separation, and Economic Abuse

Many abusive men must be forced to pay basic child support, child care, and medical expenses. Changes in child support collection practices on a national level mean that women can utilize government services to garnish wages and collect money judgments. However, payment of medical, child care, or education expenses continues to be problematic as the child support services rarely collect funds intended for these purposes. Abusive fathers may not pay college tuition and related expenses. In my practice, I have frequently heard fathers of significant means argue that, because they were not involved in the selection of a college, they will not pay for their children's higher education. Refusal to properly provide for their children's higher education has long-term implications. Adult children may be saddled with excessive student loans or have difficulty completing their education because they must work.

Wallerstein et al. also noted that, in most households, higher education is a major expense that requires both parents' economic contribution.[32] All too often, I have noticed that many of my graduate students are working two or even three jobs while struggling to complete their studies. Simply put, children without the support of both parents may have to make difficult economic decisions about the kind of professional or educational training they can afford. Economic abuse impacts more than battered mothers; it has the potential to impact her children for decades.

In discussions of divorce and separation, it is essential to understand the importance of a legal system that provides avenues by which women can achieve financial independence. As indicated previously, there is a significant body of research on economic abuse that highlights the importance of women's financial independence in leaving abusive relationships. Sanders has found that women without adequate housing, child care, and income are also less likely to be able to leave abusive relationships and to achieve such economic freedom.[33]

Also, Sanders noted the very vulnerable status of women seeking to enter the work force to obtain financial independence, a move that may spark a backlash from their abusive spouse.[34] This problem is particularly acute for battered women during divorce and separation, when their spouses may inflict more physical and economic abuse to prevent them from becoming fully independent.

Furthermore, Sanders noted that financial disagreements can trigger other forms of abuse. This is particularly important for mental health professionals and the courts to understand in the context of divorce and separation so that battered women are not prevented from achieving financial independence.

Thus, we find that intimate partner violence takes many forms, and the courts must clearly identify incidents of economic or legal abuse. Even when women are initially financially independent, it is impossible to remain so when confronted with having to repeatedly defend against expensive and even frivolous applications for custody, unsupervised visitation, and support. In my practice, many women with professional employment have been forced to sell their homes or rely on their extended families to continue to meet the costs of litigation. While women with financial independence and resources have more options about ending abusive relationships, they are still at risk of economic, verbal, physical, and sexual abuse following their separation.

We can conclude that when abusive men feel threatened by women and their growing economic independence they will employ a wide array of tactics to control them. These tactics may lead to abusers' underemployment, voluntary unemployment, excessive debts, and legal abuse—all frequently seen during divorce or custody litigation, regardless of economic status, class, ethnicity, and race.

In my practice, many clients find that abusive husbands underreport their income, fail to disclose their assets to their spouse, and sometimes refuse to work or take care of the children. Furthermore, I have recently begun to see a growing number of women in advanced middle age who have been separated from their abusive husbands for decades suddenly initiating legal proceedings to ensure their economic survival during their retirement.

In my practice, when there is an order of protection, I have found that judges are unwilling to order my clients to pay spousal support to an underemployed abusive spouse. However, in most states, the courts retain discretion, and orders of spousal support may reflect the length of the marriage, even if the wives have left their husbands because of abuse. The plight of these women again exemplifies the enduring impact of financial abuse throughout their lifetimes.

Another aspect of economic abuse may be seen in a review of the literature, that will be discussed in Chapter 8, on the division of household tasks. Parker and Wang concluded that women still spend more time on housework, child care, and the like, making it more difficult to take advantage of career opportunities that require longer hours or absences from home.[35] These researchers concluded in the Pew Study (2013) that the "roles converge, but gaps remain" between men and women in the time spent on child care.[36] A recent study by Davis and Greenstein, using data from the International Social Justice Project, found that gender continues to be the single predictor of the time spent doing housework.[37] Significantly, these researchers found that although men may divide their time between work and home more equitably, their assumption of child care and household tasks has not caught up with their spouses' efforts.[38] While in some families men may elect to stay home to raise their children or work reduced hours when the children are young, in economically abusive situations, mothers will frequently have the expense of full-time child care although the fathers are physically available for much of the day.

Child Support Enforcement

In my practice at a battered women's program, on Friday afternoons the social workers routinely distributed food from the pantry to women who had just filed for orders of protection but had not yet obtained orders of child support. In this way, they and their children could eat over the weekend. Some of these women, confronted by stark financial choices, returned to their abusers because they simply could not feed their families without orders of temporary child and spousal support. While many states allow for temporary orders of child support as part of the relief that can be granted in an order of protection, I have found that judges were frequently reluctant to order such support when women first petitioned the court for relief unless the fathers were present. Such orders of child support are essential to help women leave abusive relationships.

Federal efforts to require uniform child support enforcement began in 1974, when Congress enacted Title IV-D of the Social Security Act. This effort was intended largely to allow the federal government to recover Aid to Families with Dependent Children's (AFDC) funds and thus requires the states to establish child support enforcement programs to trace the whereabouts of fathers.[39] Bridges indicated that the federal government also established the Child Support Enforcement Program, requiring the states to operate such agencies with federal funds.[40]

During the 1980s and 1990s, a series of laws was passed that again increased child support enforcement. The Full Faith and Credit for Child Support Order Act (FFCCSOA) recognized that each state must give full faith and credit to another state's order of child support.[41] Prior to this Act, the home state could reduce another state's child support orders. However, passage of additional federal legislation emphasized the need for increased child support enforcement. Passage of the Family Support Act (FSA) amended Title IV-D of the Social Security Act to increase interstate child support efforts and allowed the states to garnish salaries and follow strict guidelines for the amounts of child support awards (Uniform Interstate Family Support Act 1992).[42] By way of example, New York State adopted child support guidelines, or a statutory formula, requiring the noncustodial parent to pay a designated amount of his income in child support, and such payments could be garnished by his employer.[43] Previously, child support orders varied greatly, judges generally used their discretion to determine the correct amounts, and orders could vary. Efforts to provide for interstate recognition and enforcement of child support orders also resulted in the Uniform Interstate Family Support Act of 1992.[44] This legislation provided for child and spousal support orders, enforcement, registration of an out-of-state order, paternity determinations, and long-arm jurisdiction over nonresident parents.[45]

Finally, following the passage of a series of federal amendments to the Social Security Act and related legislation, enforcement of child support became a reality for many women. If the father worked on the books, his income could be garnished so enforcement was made easier. Child support awards were more consistent as they followed an established statutory formula and were less subjective. However, when fathers are self-employed, skillful advocacy is needed on the part of an attorney to impute income based on expenses or gifts. In domestic violence cases, fathers may deliberately reduce or underreport their income on their income taxes to avoid their obligations to support their children. Some researchers argue that such child support enforcement is punitive for men without sufficient income. However, enforcement of child support has lifted many women out of poverty and has done a great deal to alleviate economic abuse.

The Distribution of Marital Property

Much has been written about the division of marital property in divorce. To summarize, the states have adopted several different legal principles to divide marital property in divorce.[46] Lee noted that initially it was common for the various states to employ a title theory: that the spouse who held property was the sole owner, regardless of the length of the marriage or the other spouse's contributions.[47] California first adopted the concept of community property, which is based on the concept of marriage as an economic partnership. Except for property obtained before the marriage, inheritances, or gifts, the courts divided the marital property equally during divorce. Several states—including Washington, Wisconsin, Texas, Arizona, Louisiana, New Mexico, Nevada, and Iowa—have also followed the precepts of community property. Garrison indicated that New York originally adhered to the title theory of property distribution in which, absent fraud, the person who held title to the property was deemed the rightful owner.[48] Some states, including New York, adopted the doctrine of equitable distribution—a standard that allowed judges to divide property without regard to title of the property. This doctrine encouraged judges to consider the unpaid or nonmonetary work of women who were not in the work force but had raised children and otherwise contributed to their spouses' careers.[49]

However, after adoption of the principle of equitable distribution, critics argued that this was a subjective standard by which women could be treated unfairly.[50] These critics argued that *equal* distribution and not *equitable* distribution would better provide for women following divorce.[51] In New York, many community property principles were incorporated into the concept of equitable distribution so that property acquired during the marriage was considered marital, while gifts and premarital property were deemed to be separate.[52] For example, California, New Jersey, Arizona, Louisiana, Nevada, New Mexico, Texas, Washington, and Wisconsin use the principles of community property to divide marital property equally. Other states, like New York, have included some principles of community property, so that judges now consider separate and marital property while using the standard of equitable distribution.[53] Thus, in many states, matrimonial judges can equitably divide the value of the marital residence, summer home, retirement savings, pensions, and sometimes professional degrees and licenses. The nonmonetary contributions of women who did not enter the work force but instead made contributions to their husband's careers and child-rearing can be recognized through equitable distribution.

However, the states have not adopted a uniform approach to the division of marital property in households in which one partner has been abusive. The concepts of marital partnerships and equitable division of the assets and debts do not routinely allow exceptions in circumstances in which women have been abused economically. Lee also noted that abused women continue to have difficulty leaving the marital relationship because they will be unable to support themselves and their children. This researcher noted that women without children may not have sufficient assets and income to support themselves in their retirement, yet such women are blamed for not leaving abusive relationships regardless of the economic price they may be forced to pay. Like Stark, this researcher further noted that battered women suffer even more during divorce because batterers frequently interfere with their employment and finances.[54]

The Impact of No-Fault Divorce

With the advent of "no-fault" divorce, concerns were raised that the courts were less likely to consider adultery or abuse in dividing marital property or awarding spousal support. In fact, some theorists argue that the concept of no-fault divorce—if applied without exceptions—does not allow judges to consider fault at all when dividing property or providing spousal support.[55] Swisher opposed the strict application of no-fault divorce, in which conduct is not a factor in the division of assets or allocation of support. This researcher also noted that such provisions of divorce could be adapted, similar to, no-fault workers' compensation statutes and no-fault automobile insurance, to provide victims with more compensation in egregious situations.[56]

Most states have adopted no-fault divorce. Rather than having litigants prove the grounds for divorce, the issue of fault becomes less important in judicial determinations regarding the division of marital property and awards of spousal support. More recently, however, many states have provided for exceptions to the no-fault provisions, allowing for economic redress when there is a history of domestic violence. Swisher noted that thirty-two states had retained fault-based grounds along with their no-fault provisions to allow the courts to hold one spouse liable for serious or egregious marital conduct. States could thus provide orders of compensatory spousal support and the appropriate division of marital property.

However, states have adopted varying standards in considering domestic violence and the distribution of property. In New York, only in cases when the domestic violence "shocks the conscience of the court" will judges provide more spousal support or a larger share of the marital assets to abused spouses. *Havell v. Islam.*[57] With the exception of providing redress when the spouse has wasted marital assets, the courts do not consider economic abuse. The burden to prove that one spouse has wasted marital assets falls on the spouse who is economically constrained by the other's actions.

Guidelines for child support and enforcement efforts have improved financial circumstances for women with children. However, the matrimonial and bankruptcy laws have not developed a similar approach to economic abuse to protect the injured spouse. Furthermore, legislation is needed so that the courts have the leeway they need to consider the existence of domestic violence in the distribution of marital property.

Alimony, Spousal Support, and Maintenance

The American Academy of Matrimonial Lawyers has called the resolution of spousal support the most complicated economic concern for the courts during divorce.[58] Wide disparities exist as to how the amounts and duration of support should be determined. Furthermore, judges may also consider the impact of the distribution of marital property, and now child support, in their determinations of spousal support.

Historically, the British courts ordered alimony payments when there were religious divorces that provided for legal separations, or divorces from bed and board: that is, during separation.[59] Significantly, the couple remained legally married, and alimony was intended to ensure that the husband continued to support his wife after separation.[60] Collins noted the importance of alimony because the law barred women from holding property, signing contracts, or keeping whatever wages they might earn.[61] Thus, while it was difficult to enforce the payment of alimony, it was particularly important in terms of the wife's economic survival. When reforms of Great Britain's matrimonial laws in the nineteenth century made civil divorce accessible to ordinary citizens, the practice of alimony awards continued. Collins noted that the courts did not grant alimony to women who were thought to be at fault; only wives who were perceived as the innocent party were granted such assistance. This researcher noted that, in the United States, many aspects of matrimonial law, including the award of alimony, have followed the English model.[62]

Kisthardt indicated that, during the 1970s, many states developed equitable distribution and community property distribution schemes that looked at fairness and equity—and not simply the title holder—when awarding property during a divorce.[63] However, this researcher noted that this approach often led to smaller awards of spousal support.

Conversely, during this same time, many states also adopted the concept of no-fault divorce, which eliminated fault as grounds for divorce and distribution of property.[64] Many states, including California and Arizona, developed guidelines for temporary spousal support that was determined using mathematical formulas. California's guidelines for temporary support were computed by calculating 40% of the net income of the more affluent spouse, minus 50% of the net income of the needy spouse, with adjustments for any tax considerations.[65] This approach did not address the policy issue of the impact of economic abuse or other forms of domestic violence on women. At the same time, the various states addressed the issue of domestic violence as a consideration in determining spousal support in conflicting and confusing ways.

During the 1990s, most states passed legislative reforms that allowed judges to consider more than need in determining the amount and duration of spousal support. While the term "alimony" is rarely used now, most states have developed legislation that delineates the factors courts should consider when ordering spousal support or maintenance. These statutory factors are in place to allow the trial court to determine the economic impact of one spouse, typically the wife, leaving the work force to care for children or to make non-monetary contributions to her husband's career. Many states began to consider the need to continue the standard of living enjoyed by the parties before the divorce, the amount of the award of equitable distribution, and other financial resources in determining spousal support.[66] Additionally, some states also enacted legislation that viewed spousal support as a form of remediation to allow one party time to obtain an education or training to enable her to become self-supporting.[67] More research is needed to quantify the economic impact of abuse to provide for increased orders of spousal support.

The advent of no-fault divorce in the states also raised concerns that women would not receive adequate spousal support. Furthermore, legal scholars have criticized the factors considered by courts as being vague and subjective, providing little guidance to judges.[68]

No-fault divorce also changed how the courts viewed alimony as women entered the work force. Although alimony was replaced with spousal support or maintenance, we cannot assume that women now earn as much as men. In fact, substantial inequities persist in women's earnings, as acknowledged in the research.[69] However, the American Law Institute (ALI) criticized the needs-based approach to spousal support and advocated that spousal support be a form of compensation for economic hardships that occur as the result of the divorce.[70] Kisthardt noted that the ALI's principles adopted an approach that assumed that, in the matrimonial partnership, one spouse incurred losses because of the divorce and that these losses should be shared by both partners.[71]

Collins noted that many states enacted legislation that reduced judicial discretion and provided for the application of a financial formula to determine the amount and duration of spousal support. Thus, where there is a significant income disparity, the more affluent spouse can be directed to pay a designated amount of support for a specific duration depending on the length of the marriage. Longer marriages typically meant that the spouses received support for more extended periods of time.

Finally, Collins called for a different approach that allowed for postmarital income adjustments that gradually dissolved the couple's economic partnership over a predetermined period until financial separation was complete.[72] This theory viewed spousal support as a kind of marital residual in which incomes would originally be shared at an equal level by transferring income. Such payments were to be reduced by 10% at designated intervals until they were phased out entirely. This approach viewed spousal support as a financial formula that assumes that women and men have equal capacities to become self-supporting.

During the 1990s, Bussayabuntoon noted that some states enacted legislation that allowed judges to consider other, more subjective factors in determining spousal support, including the age and health of the parties.[73] Failure to understand the connection between the impact of domestic violence and health of the abused spouse can be problematic. Judges do not necessarily view abused women as having additional financial, psychological, and medical needs that could cause them to be economically vulnerable for the rest of their lives. Here, a review of the literature on adverse childhood experiences (ACEs) and the resulting mental health and medical costs, as presented in Chapter 4, has indicated a demonstrated correlation between exposure to abuse and health care costs.[74] Individuals subjected to abuse are more likely to experience psychological symptoms, including depression, substance abuse, and posttraumatic stress disorder (PTSD), and they could need psychological treatment for many years. Persons abused as children also may have increased health care costs and require more treatment and hospitalizations for decades.[75] These circumstances should be routinely considered in divorces when families have a history of abuse. In my practice, I have met women with PTSD, autoimmune diseases, and traumatic brain injuries that resulted from the physical and psychological abuse they endured. Some have difficulty working. Many have significant health problems, with their attendant costs. Thus, the impact of domestic violence on all aspects of health should be a factor that the courts should consider when determining spousal support.

The research on domestic violence as a source of traumatic exposure and the resulting impact on women's wage earnings, medical, or psychiatric needs should also be considered in determining the amount and duration of spousal support. The adoption of mathematical formulas in establishing spousal support has some benefits. It is intended to level the playing field and does remove some of the impact of judicial bias. However, mathematical formulas do not provide for circumstances in which batterers have petitioned the court for spousal support. Burkett argues that convicted batterers should not be permitted to make such applications.[76] But this prohibition does not go far enough. In my practice, I have had cases in which battered women are the primary wage earners. In those instances, they may only have civil, not criminal, orders of protection. In some cases they may have never requested an order of protection. They may have requested relief for the first time during the divorce. In those cases, the courts should consider the underlying social policy of protecting women who have been abused when batterers request spousal support. If battered women are faced with the threat of having to pay spousal support to their abusive partners, this could deter them from leaving the abusive relationship. Furthermore, when there is a history of economic abuse, the abusive spouses may hide their assets, refuse to turn over financial information, and evade their financial obligations, making it difficult to fairly distribute the marital assets and obtain adequate child or spousal support. While mathematical formulas are helpful in eliminating judicial bias in determinations of spousal support, it is important to provide clear guidance to the courts if there is also domestic violence, so that judges consider the impact of physical and economic abuse on battered women.

Counsel Fees

The award of counsel fees in which the more affluent spouse pays the other's counsel fees during litigation is essential in ensuring a just outcome. Hecht Schafran noted that the majority of the states' Gender Bias Task Force reports included recommendations that women receive counsel fees to ensure that they obtain equal treatment and justice.[77] The premise behind an interim award is that women should not be disadvantaged by their inability to obtain legal representation because they do not have access to sufficient funds.[78] In cases of domestic violence, Martin advocated that the courts appoint counsel for battered women to guarantee the victim a meaningful opportunity to be heard.[79] Because of legislative changes, many states now require judges to direct the more well-off spouse to pay the less-affluent spouse's legal fees. In New York, statutory amendments provide for counsel fees, along with temporary maintenance during the divorce, adding to a body of caselaw that provides that "the matrimonial scales of justice are not unbalanced by the weight of the wealthier litigant's wallet." *O'Shea v. O'Shea;* N.Y. Dom. Rel. Law 237.[80]

Much more research is needed to determine the impact of awards of counsel fees during divorce litigation in cases that include domestic violence. Furthermore, to protect the family's assets, it is important for the courts to determine whether economic abuse has taken place. In many instances in my practice, the abusive party underreports his income or hides his assets, in which case the courts are frequently reluctant to order counsel fees. In those situations, only at the end of the action will the courts consider such an award, although women remain at risk economically. The problems of legal abuse, in which abusers may repeatedly file frivolous motions requiring the abused spouse to waste significant financial resources in answering papers or unnecessary court appearances, must be considered in awarding counsel fees. Some jurisdictions are reluctant to restrict the parties' access to the courts. Such access is extremely important; however, the courts should also consider the devastating impact of such abuses and can fashion remedies that prevent economic exploitation.

Federal Civil Remedies

Federal civil remedies for battered women and their children are limited. The original provisions of the Violence Against Women Act (VAWA 1994) provided for federal civil remedies for the victims of gender-motivated violence.[81] Prior to this, the US Supreme Court had barred a claim under the Fourteenth Amendment's Due Process Clause against child protective services for failing to protect a child from his father's violence, although the agency was aware of the abusive history. *DeShaney v. Winnebago County Department of Social Services.*[82] However, the Court struck down the provisions of VAWA that provided for money damages, in a five-to-four decision in 2000, using a narrow view of the provisions of the Commerce Clause, holding that these provisions were unconstitutional. *United States v. Morrison.*[83] Justice Souter, in his dissenting opinion, noted the multiple hearings on the economic impact of domestic violence in which survivors, doctors, and mental health professionals had testified about the costs of such abuse, and he believed this justified Congressional regulation.

Because of the Court's decision in *Morrison*, the responsibility to provide protection from abuse rests predominantly with the states. While it may be possible to file state personal injury claims against abusers in cases of domestic violence, many women are barred by the statute of limitations and must demonstrate significant incapacity to overcome this procedural hurdle.[84] Recognition of economic abuse during the process of divorce would minimize the exploitation of many women and prevent their long-term economic instability.

Conclusion

While there have been efforts made to pass legislation that makes spousal main-tenance and counsel fee awards mandatory when there is a significant income discrepancy, the divorce process is often a financial minefield for women. This is particularly true in cases of domestic violence, requiring that the courts also consider physical and economic abuses more readily when contemplating awards of counsel fees, spousal support, and the division of the marital property.

The continuing problem of economic abuse of battered women is particularly acute during divorce and custody litigation. An informed judicial response requires statutory provisions and advocacy that recognizes legal abuse, interference with employment opportunities, and the impact of damaged credit. Even women who have stable, professional employment can be devastated financially by having to defend against years of litigation. In these instances, we must consider the differential impact of such economic abuse on women that makes it difficult for battered women to leave abusive relationships and undermines their financial stability.

8

An Integrated Mental Health
Response in Custody Litigation

Effective and informed mental health treatment is essential for parents and children during separation and divorce. Mental health professionals frequently lack an understanding of the legal system, custody jurisprudence, and their own importance in custody disputes in deciphering the extent of trauma and abuse in high-risk families. This is further complicated by the lack of graduate training on domestic violence and child maltreatment and its relationship to trauma, posttraumatic stress disorder (PTSD), and the growing body of research on traumatic memories and the brain.

For many parents and children struggling with the trauma of divorce, their therapist is their first point of contact as they begin the process. The information they receive, rightly or wrongly, becomes their guidebook for approaching this crisis. When divorce is complicated by high-risk factors of domestic violence, mental illness, or substance abuse, the process is rife with difficulties in traumatic divorce. The legal system has difficulty identifying these high-risk factors or in fashioning appropriate remedies that protect the children from continued exposure to trauma.[1]

In prosecutions of domestic violence charges, the criminal justice system has made enormous progress. However, when women raise concerns regarding domestic violence in the context of a divorce or a custody dispute, the courts frequently allow unsupervised visitation, joint legal custody, or even full custody to fathers accused of being abusive. Through extensive litigation, batterers often demand custody or visitation, effectively engaging in "legal abuse."[2] It is problematic that allegations of domestic violence and child maltreatment by battered women are minimized and that until recently, very few graduate mental health programs provide clinical training in the identification of such abuse. Further complications arise out of the public's widespread belief that allegations of sexual abuse during separation or divorce have a low level of credibility, although Trocmé and Bala have indicated that the actual rate of deliberately false allegations is very low.[3]

Many mental health providers are struggling to understand the complexity of the legal system and its response to families in crisis. Family law is state-specific, complex, and requires an analysis of the individual facts and circumstances of each family, as well as an understanding of the relevant state laws. The therapist must help the client navigate conflicting advice while the client may be still exposed to the abusive spouse. To do this without collaboration between the therapist and attorney causes enormous confusion for the client. Divorcing parents must approach their situation strategically as they enter an adversarial process. Even if there is collaboration between attorneys and mental health professionals, there may not be a common language or understanding of the complexities of the problems these families experience.

Despite the gaps in communication between these professions, it is not always advisable to steer parents away from litigation. For women who have experienced abuse or the psychological effects of living with a spouse who is mentally ill or has a substance abuse problem, litigation is often the most effective means to ensure their stability and safety and that of their children. Despite the complexity and difficulty in navigating the legal system, an experienced and knowledgeable therapist can be an important advocate for the children.

The Development of Custody Jurisprudence

The US Supreme Court "recognized on numerous occasions that the relationship between parent and child is constitutionally protected." *Troxel v. Granville; Parham v. J.R.*[4] The Court has consistently developed jurisprudence that acknowledges the "fundamental liberty interest of natural parents in the care, custody, and management of their child." *Washington v. Glucksberg.*[5] The states have developed conflicting lines of reasoning that address the issue of custody. In this confusing context of custody jurisprudence, it is important to consider not only whether there are any extraordinary circumstances, such as domestic violence, substance abuse, or untreated mental illness, but also the families' normal child-rearing patterns.

Historically, custody determinations were based on English common law and the Roman law concept of "natural law," which indicated that children were the property of their fathers.[6] Gradually, in the late nineteenth century, the "natural law" approach yielded to an approach which determined marital fault and awarded custody to the more virtuous parent. This fault-based approach was succeeded by the "tender years" presumption, which assumed that mothers were the primary caretaker of the children and thus should be the custodial parent—provided that they were virtuous.[7]

In the mid-1970s, Ronner noted that the emphasis shifted again as most states adopted the "best interests of the child" standard, which was thought to be gender-neutral.[8] This has been criticized for being subjective and, thus, the courts in many states began to clarify their definition of this standard. *Bennett v. Jeffreys.*[9] By way of example, in the 1980s, the New York Court of Appeals articulated factors to be considered in determining the best interests that included the child's preferences, the need to place siblings together, the economic stability of the parents, the lifestyle the parent would offer, and the likelihood that the parent would foster a relationship with the noncustodial parent. *Friederwitzer v. Friederwitzer.*[10] The courts also carefully considered past custody agreements and arrangements before modifying existing arrangements, believing that this would provide children with needed stability. *Eschbach v. Eschbach.*[11]

Domestic Violence and Child Custody Determinations

Determining the best interests of the child is subjective. Thus, a body of law has developed to guide judicial determinations of custody. Lemon's analysis of the legislative response to the challenge of domestic violence is instructive.[12] This researcher noted that while historically divorces were rare, the shift in the 1970s from fault-based divorce to no-fault divorce also meant that women were no longer assured custody of the children when men were abusive. Lemon also noted that the trend of no-fault divorce also coincided with many fathers' rights groups that advocated for statutory presumptions of joint legal custody.[13]

Significantly, the U.S. Congress enacted a joint Congressional Resolution in 1994 that declared that evidence of physical abuse of a spouse "should create a statutory presumption that it is detrimental to the child to be placed in the custody of the abusive spouse."[14] Furthermore, the National Council of Juvenile and Family Court Judges (1994) also released a Model Code on Domestic and Family Law Violence that stated in pertinent part:

> In every proceeding where there is at issue a dispute as to the custody of children, a determination by the court that domestic or family violence has occurred raises a rebuttable presumption that it is detrimental to the child and not in the best interest of the child to be placed in sole custody, joint legal custody or joint physical custody with the perpetrator of family violence.[15]

The American Bar Association (ABA 1994) also issued a report in which it advocated that there should be a presumption of unfitness in custody cases when there is a history of domestic violence.[16] The ABA also warned that batterers are unfit because of their efforts to harm the other parent and that they will take advantage of their access to the children to control their spouse.

In response, sixteen states and the District of Columbia adopted rebuttable presumptions against granting custody to batterers.[17] Other states have enacted legislation that extends the rebuttable presumptions to joint legal custody in domestic violence cases. Finally, a small number of states, including New York, allow for the consideration of domestic violence as a factor in determining custody and visitation. The distinguishing aspects of the various state laws regarding custody and domestic violence are beyond the scope of this chapter. Suffice it to say that, in most states, family court judges have ample legislation to rely on to protect children in custody and domestic violence cases.

Thus, as part of the pattern of legislative reforms, in New York, the courts were required to give "weighty consideration" to domestic violence in determining custody.[18] In California, Lemon has indicated that a presumption of unfitness was mandated if a parent was found to be abusive. Some states follow a "primary caretaker" standard in which the primary caretaker is presumed to be the best choice for custodial parent, absent evidence of unfitness.[19] However, Mercer's review of the "primary caretaker" standard in West Virginia found that where there was ambiguity over child care responsibilities or in cases where the judge clearly disapproved of the mother's sexual conduct, they were more likely to use the best interests standard.[20] Many theorists continue to believe that judicial discretion and a less rule-bound approach fosters increased litigation. Custody determinations are complex and should be based on clear factors regarding the child's primary attachment and need for safety, not the parent's financial well-being, sexual orientation, sexual conduct, or other factors that are capable of subjective interpretation or manipulation.

It could be expected that, statistically, we would see an increase in mothers' being awarded custody, particularly when there was a history of domestic violence, but also in cases in which substance abuse or untreated mental illness were at issue. However, it is difficult to identify the subsequent outcomes of custody litigation because of the private nature of the family courts and lack of public documentation. However, more recent studies of gender bias research and the discriminatory practices against battered mothers discussed earlier, along with the many anecdotal reports of battered women reported to domestic violence advocates across the country, indicate that there is a backlash against women in the courts.[21]

Competing Legal Presumptions and Custody Decisions

The question remains whether competing legislative mandates have undermined the mandate to protect battered women and their children in custody litigation. Many states have adopted "friendly parent" provisions, in which the parent who encourages "frequent and continuing contact" with the noncustodial parent is the preferred choice in custody determinations.[22] Jaffe et al. also observed that fathers' rights groups were instrumental in advocating for laws that provided a presumption in favor of joint custody. Lemon also noted this conflicting trend regarding custody, in which many states have passed legislation requiring family courts to consider domestic violence in custody and visitation decisions while conversely passing laws that stressed the importance of joint legal custody.[23] The conflicting legislative trends, including the presumption of joint legal custody and the requirement that the family courts consider domestic violence, have created tension and confusion for family court judges.

As a family law attorney, I believe that it is important for parents to communicate with each other about their children. They remain parents for many years after the divorce. However, it is unreasonable to make blanket assumptions about the appropriateness of such communication. When there is a history of domestic violence, such communication is not appropriate and may be unsafe. Abusive fathers should be informed when children are sick, hospitalized, or in emergencies. But we must remember that such abusers are completely incapable of negotiations, and battered mothers should not have constraints placed on their ability to parent their children. Bancroft et al. have discussed at length the characteristics of batterers and the harm they inflict as parents.[24]

Determinations of access and decision-making authority when one parent is abusive raises significant questions. In my practice, I have noticed an alarming trend of abusive fathers' obtaining access to the children for virtually half of the time, with little regard for the age and developmental appropriateness of these decisions. In many of these families, the fathers have not had significant interest previously in parenting their children. Many family court judges are comfortable with taking a more activist role by increasing the time fathers have historically spent with their children regardless of whether the children are comfortable with this process. Such decisions should be informed by the developmental stage of the children involved and their wishes, but most importantly, their safety. As discussed in Chapter 4, the research on toddlers and overnight visitation in less-distressed families has indicated that more than one weekly overnight with the noncustodial parent has had a detrimental developmental impact.[25] Furthermore, children under the age of seven may also have difficulty with these arrangements. Much more research is needed with elementary school-aged children to determine the long-term impact of shared physical custody on children's educational and psychological adjustment. I have watched with concern as many young children struggle to organize their belongings as they move from house to house, something that would be stressful for an adult, let alone a child. Homework, shoes, raincoats, and school books are frequently left behind in the other parent's home, causing anxiety and stress for everyone involved.

Stark noted that many judges interpret intimate partner violence as simply high-conflict divorce and that episodes of physical abuse are simply considered an extension of the conflict.[26] This approach may result in custody decisions that minimize the father's abusive history and allow for joint custody with abusive fathers. Finally, Portwood and Heany agreed that how we understand domestic violence—whether this is viewed as situational or gendered violence against women—has impacted the ability of our legal system to address domestic violence in custody and visitation cases.[27]

Even in divorces that are not traumatic, given the criticisms of the best interests standard, it is important to review its effectiveness.[28] Ronner argues that this standard is subjective, and, as a result, the judges can be influenced by their own individual biases in viewing protective mothers, high-risk allegations, and deviant behavior. This researcher concluded that if judges have traditional ideas about gender, mothers—particularly those who work—may be discriminated against.[29] Such judges can be unduly protective of fathers and lose sight of the children's physical and emotional needs. Nor can we rely on children to assess the risks to their safety of an unsupervised relationship with an abusive father. The children's emotional connection with their fathers should be only one of many factors to be considered in determining a safe custody resolution.

For mental health professionals, understanding custody or visitation disputes requires a basic understanding of the legal system and competing psychological perspectives. Furthermore, custody jurisprudence, or the reasoning courts apply in determining custody of the children, continues to reflect our prevailing cultural attitudes about gender roles and family. While therapists cannot give legal advice, knowing when to refer a client to an ethical attorney and offering help to navigate the legal system can minimize the damage of traumatic divorce.

Stark also noted that family courts continue to be the only place where discredited psychological and family systems theories thrive, regardless of the extensive data to support the harm done to children and their mothers from continued exposure to domestic violence.[30] To comprehend the advantage of batterers in custody litigation, it is essential to understand the level of manipulation employed by abusive fathers, the subjective nature of the best interests standard, and the reluctance of mental health professionals and the courts to limit fathers' access to their children. These factors are compounded by misconceptions in the family courts regarding domestic violence and its impact on children.[31]

There is an enormous amount of research on the effects on children who have lived with domestic violence. Despite this, during a custody evaluation, the child's relationship with an abusive father is frequently misunderstood. Children yearn for their fathers and hope that the court's intervention will cause their fathers to "get better." The interview of the children and batterer in the forensic office is not typical of their relationship, as children are frequently manipulated.

In my law practice, I have seen how fathers can manipulate their children by not visiting with them for extended periods. Then, the batterer's first contact with them may be in the forensic expert's office, during the custody evaluation. The children typically will be excited to see their fathers and will be openly affectionate toward them. On their best behavior during forensic interviews, the batterers fuel their children's hopes that their father is "better" and that life will change. Invariably, the fathers blame the mothers for their own absence, saying that she kept the children away from him, although she may have been forced to flee with her children to a domestic violence shelter. The custody evaluator, expecting to see children who are fearful of their fathers, given the extent of the high-risk allegations, can be misled by the children's behavior.

In these instances, the fathers' inability to put their children's needs above their own should be considered in making custody and visitation recommendations. Such manipulative behavior does not bode well for the parenting of children. Also, children frequently fear that their fathers will abandon them if they disclose abuse to the custody evaluator, and their behavior may cause the courts to distrust the mothers' allegations. Thus, it should be assumed that children are ambivalent about their fathers and long for a normalization of their relationship with them. These children need the support of the courts in the form of clear orders of custody to the protective parent, orders of protection when necessary, counseling, and supervised visitation.

Attorneys for the Children

This process may be complicated by assignment of an attorney for the child who will articulate the children's wishes to the court. Some states allow the attorney for the child to substitute their own judgment on the record for the child's, if they believe the child is at risk of harm, and such attorneys can even take positions that are inconsistent with the children's stated wishes.[32] In other states, these attorneys are considered *guardians ad litem* who articulate the children's best interests. The mental health professional can clarify the child's statements and behavior to the assigned attorney and explain that the behavior seen may be a result of the child's ambivalence toward an abusive parent's manipulation or fear of their abandonment.

In my law practice, I have frequently known young children to articulate their longing for their fathers while being unable to describe the abuse they have witnessed to an attorney whom they have seen for a minimum period in the courthouse. In one instance, a five-year-old girl whose mother had fled from the father's abuse informed her attorney that she wanted to live with him after not having seen her father for some time. The counselor assigned to work with the child's attorney reported that the child missed her father and had eagerly asked to live with him. Moments after hearing from this counselor, the judge ordered that the child be turned over immediately to the father for a two-week visit. This little girl looked back at her mother—bewildered and frightened—while being led away from her to the father for a two-week visit. No arrangements were made for contact between the mother and child during this time. Upon the child's return, she reported that the father was openly contemptuous of the mother, angry, spent little time with her, and was abusive to his new girlfriend. The mother reported that the child began to experience nightmares, difficulty sleeping alone, and other related behavioral problems. The judge and attorney for the child were well-meaning but failed to understand the risk of reexposing this child to her father's traumatic behavior. Undermining the mother's ability to create protective boundaries can deprive the child of necessary safety and refuge, as articulated by Herman, by allowing the traumatic exposure to continue unsupervised.[33] Later, the mother reported that the child confided in her that she asked to live with her father because he threatened that she would never see him again if she did not say this to her attorney, the custody evaluator, or the judge.

In New York, legislation directs that a protective parent cannot be deprived of custody or contact with her children if she makes "good-faith allegations, supported by the facts" to the courts that the children are the victims of child abuse, neglect, or the effects of witnessing domestic violence.[34] Nevertheless, allegations of such abuse are still distrusted and used as a basis for depriving mothers of custody of their children and even for losing financial support. This fear of losing custody if the allegations are not believed has a chilling effect on women's willingness to fight for their children. Mothers may settle for joint custody arrangements that include parental coordination, mediation, and the like to avoid the risk of losing their children altogether.[35]

Custody Determinations and Trauma

The well-established concepts of attachment theory, trauma, and the documented harm to children exposed to domestic violence have not been translated into a legal approach that protects children and their mothers. Divorce even without domestic violence can be difficult for children, with long-term implications.[36]

Visitation and custody arrangements should reflect the developmental needs of the children on a case-by-case basis. If instead a one-size-fits-all schedule is implemented, very young children subjected to overnight visitation or split custody arrangements with the noncustodial parent may experience significant levels of anxiety.[37] Research that bolsters the understanding of the impact of domestic violence as a form of trauma for children and adults should be included in all graduate mental health education curricula. Many custody evaluators have limited clinical experience in working with children or child maltreatment, or they fail to interview the children about the abuse or assume a posture of disbelief when allegations of high-risk factors arise in a custody dispute.

For victims of trauma, a therapist or custody evaluator who approaches concerns about high-risk factors with skepticism can compound the traumatic effects of the abuse. For a patient suffering from the life-altering impact of PTSD, it is essential that the therapist accepts her experience with thoughtfulness and respect. Physical injuries can be seen and documented. By contrast, psychic wounds are largely invisible. Mental health professionals must look carefully for the symptoms associated with PTSD, which vary according to the age and developmental phase of the patient. Children often cannot tell us what has happened in one interview. Rather, this is information that can be gathered over time in a caring, child-friendly environment.

The effects of trauma can have a life-long effect on the physical and psychological health of the survivor, and this can even be life-threatening if unidentified and untreated. Even very small children have been shown to suffer neurological changes because of exposure to domestic violence and may have life-long difficulty regulating the intensity of their feelings and responses.[38] Researchers agree that such children may suffer a wide range of psychological and physical symptoms including sleep disorders, headaches, stomachaches, diarrhea, ulcers, asthma, and enuresis, and many researchers estimate that in 50% of families where the mother is the victim of domestic violence, the children are also abused.[39]

The Primary Caretaker and Custody

While there are many reasons to support a gender-neutral approach to custody determinations, the courts should not overlook the family's history of child care, the children's need for stability, and the high-risk factors discussed. This is not to say that there are not fathers who are more nurturing and more stable than mothers and should be awarded custody. However, custody determinations should not be made in disregard of the research about working parents, the division of child-caring tasks, or the history of high-risk factors in the family.

While mothers increasingly work outside of the home, they are still predominantly the caregivers for children. Although studies indicate that fathers do spend more time with child-rearing tasks than in the past, women still spend more time on this care and on other household tasks.[40] A closer look at the research in a study by Parker and Wang indicates that "roles converge, but gaps remain" between men and women in the time spent on child care.[41] Davis and Greenstein's research using data from the International Social Justice Project, found that "although the amount and proportion of household labor spouses perform have changed since the 1960s, gender continues to be the single predictor of the time spent doing housework."[42] While fathers spend more time engaged in housework and child care than they did in the 1950s, these authors concluded that they "have by no means caught up to mothers in terms of time spent caring for children and doing household chores, but there has been some gender convergence in the way they divide their time between work and home."[43]

It can be inferred from the Pew Study's findings that many women continue to feel responsible for their children, arranging child care, medical appointments, and schooling although employed outside the home.[44] Simply put, many mothers now have two jobs.

Current Trends in Child Custody

Traditionally, one parent received physical and legal custody of the children, which meant that not only would the children reside primarily with that parent, but that he or she would make all of the decisions regarding the children's education, health, religious upbringing, and day-to-day lives. Joint legal custody has many different permutations. Typically, joint legal custody may mean that both parents make decisions regarding the children's health, education, and welfare and that parents must agree before a decision is made. Each parent has equal access to medical, educational, and psychological records. Thus, both parents may attend parent–teacher conferences, attend doctors' appointments, or speak with the children's medical providers. However, the children may still reside primarily with one parent while the noncustodial parent has a visitation or parental access schedule.

Joint legal decision-making is frequently not the same as joint physical custody, in which the children reside with both parents equally. This should be distinguished from arrangements in which children have a primary residence and contact with their noncustodial parent is organized around overnights, weekends, and vacation access. Beginning in the 1970s, Bauserman has indicated that there has been an increasing trend for children to spend large amounts of time with both parents.[45] In some instances, the children have no primary residence but spend virtually equal amounts of time with both parents. Simultaneously, many states have developed "joint custody presumptions" indicating that joint custody is the preferred arrangement and in the best interests of the children unless there is a proven impediment, such as the existence of domestic violence.[46] While contact with both parents in families without high-risk factors has been found to be helpful for children, in cases in which there has been abuse, this is far more problematic. Furthermore, it can be argued that, even without a history of domestic violence and substance abuse, a one-size-fits-all approach to custody and visitation should not be applied unilaterally. There are many other considerations including the age of the children, the specific vulnerabilities of each child (particularly when children have special needs), and their attachment to each parent to be considered in fashioning an access schedule for parents and children. These issues are more properly addressed in the therapeutic process and not in the courts when parents disagree.

Joint Legal Custody Presumptions

Many states have enacted laws creating a statutory presumption that joint legal custody is best for children because it encourages fathers' participation in their children's lives. Douglas noted that nine states had state laws which presumed that joint legal custody—where no one parent has decision-making authority—is best for children. Louisiana has a statutory presumption in favor of joint physical custody, whereas Washington, DC's laws assume that shared physical and legal custody is best for children.[47] Following New Hampshire's enactment of the statutory presumption that joint legal custody was best for children, Douglas found that 93% of divorced families had joint legal custody of the children.[48] However, comparing families in New Hampshire to those in Maine, where there was no such legislation, Douglas concluded that there were no differences in paternal involvement following divorce. This study did not review the adjustment levels of children but simply reviewed the extent of the fathers' contact with the children.

As discussed in Chapter 2, children in homes where there is no domestic violence and substance abuse have an easier time adjusting to their parents' divorce. In such families, the children can benefit from a strong, stable relationship with their fathers. However, the research is inconclusive as to whether joint legal custody—that is, joint decision-making alone—has a significant impact on fathers' relationships with their children. Questions remain regarding how much contact fathers should have, at what age, and whether the courts should modify the existing relationships to impose schedules that are not consistent with the families' history of caretaking.

A review of the research on joint legal custody by Bauserman noted the two disparate arguments in opposition and support of joint custody. Specifically, those who opposed joint custody argued that it could expose children to more conflict, while those who supported joint custody indicated that this would provide children with frequent access to both parents.[49] His analysis of the research concluded that children in joint custody arrangements spent substantial time with both parents and were better adjusted than those in single-parent sole custody households, although he did not conclude that joint physical custody was necessary for children. However, Bauserman found many deficits in the studies he reviewed concerning the reporting of statistical results and called for more research.

Crosbie-Burnett noted that it is the quality of the co-parent–child relationship, and not the custody arrangement, that creates stress for children. This researcher did note that adolescents are particularly vulnerable to parental remarriage. Finally, Crosbie-Burnett concluded that there was a connection between the adolescents' adjustment, their parents' remarriage, and introduction of stepfamily relationships.[50]

A statutory presumption that joint custody is best for children fails to take into consideration the many different types of relationships that existed before and after the divorce. Even if there is an absence of domestic violence and abuse, some parents may have a difficult time working together. Relying on Hetherington and Stanley-Hagan's research, it takes time for parents and children to adjust to the divorce in less-distressed families.[51] Parents may initially experience significant anger at their former spouses, yet, over time, the intensity of their feelings may subside. For many divorcing couples in less-distressed families, divorce remains a life crisis. This is not to say that in less-distressed families those parents may not eventually develop a way to work together and that this is ultimately best for the children. However, it can be argued that the imposition of joint physical or legal custody on parents in crisis may only exacerbate their initial conflicts and that much more research is needed in this area.

Custody and Domestic Violence

Kernic et al. noted the dearth of studies on child custody and visitation decisions in households with a history of intimate partner violence.[52] Stark has warned that continued post-separation contact is the most common context for such abuse.[53] Kernic et al. indicated the extensive body of research on the kinds of abuses that accompany continued unsupervised contacts with an abusive father; for example, children not being returned on time and their continued psychological and physical abuse.[54] A study of domestic violence agencies in California found that between 10% and 25% of the women reported threats of child kidnapping and incidents of verbal and physical abuse, indicating that visitation can become a venue for further abuse.[55]

The study by Kernic et al. examined custody outcomes when male-perpetrated domestic violence was alleged. To that end, the researchers examined court files for three groups: those with unsubstantiated but alleged intimate partner violence, those with allegations of intimate partner violence that are substantiated by police or orders of protection that were identified during the custody dispute, and those with substantiated allegations of intimate partner violence that were not identified during the custody dispute.[56] The researchers focused exclusively on restrictions to the fathers' access and custody of the children, and their study focused primarily on male violence against women. It is interesting to note that this population included instances in which women were initially described as the perpetrators, but later it was revealed that their actions were largely in self-defense against male violence. These divorce cases were compared to a control group of randomly selected divorcing couples with children in which there were no allegations of intimate partner violence. Significantly, the researchers found that in divorcing couples where intimate partner violence had been substantiated, the women were no more likely to receive custody of their children than women in households where there was no history of such abuse.[57] The researchers also studied visitation outcomes for the fathers, finding that 46% of fathers in relationships where intimate partner violence was substantiated and known to the courts had some restrictions placed on their visitation in terms of the length and time of the visits, and 51% were referred to court-mandated treatment, counseling, or some other requirements.[58] However, when intimate partner violence was substantiated and known to the courts, only 25% of the fathers received supervised visitation.[59]

Kernic et al. correctly noted that domestic violence is poorly understood. Without sufficient training in domestic violence, judges, custody evaluators, and other mental health professionals are skeptical of women who have not sought help before and question why there was an absence of documentation of the abuse. They also question why the allegations are being raised for the first time in the context of a custody or divorce proceeding.[60]

Although Jaffe et al. acknowledged that the research on parent–child relationships and parenting styles in families with a history of domestic violence is sparse, they propose parenting arrangements that have the potential to provide batterers with extensive access to their children.[61] Utilizing a number of different typologies of domestic violence, they propose a spectrum of access plans, including co-parenting, parallel parenting, the supervised exchanges of children, and supervised visitation.[62] While not all domestic violence is the same, the literature on assessment of the possibilities of continued abuse is not conclusive, and there are many risks associated with these approaches that should not be dismissed.

Despite the lack of outcome studies, such parenting arrangements are currently being widely adopted in the family courts. In particular, the Report from the Wingspread Conference on Domestic Violence and Family Courts (2007) called for the development of such parenting plans even while calling for more research on whether domestic violence could be defined as a typology of behaviors.[63] This raises significant concerns.

In my practice, I have had clients who have joint custody or co-parenting arrangements with batterers. Co-parenting requires that parents communicate about the children. In families in which there is an absence of domestic violence, this is important. However, in my practice, when there has been a history of domestic violence, substance abuse, or untreated mental illness and joint legal custody, my clients have reported that they receive multiple emails or texts each day, frequently accusing them of failing to communicate sufficiently even if they have already responded. Some of the batterers demand a daily log of their children's activities. Many of my clients have found it impossible to obtain necessary mental health treatment for the children because batterers will refuse to select a therapist or will intimidate mental health providers to such an extent that the therapists frequently refuse to treat the children. Just the number and length of daily emails or texts is unusual. Most divorced parents communicate only when necessary in succinct communications about the logistics of the children's arrangements, choice of schools, or medical providers. Sometimes they speak on the phone about matters related to the children's care. This behavior evinces a growing respect for the boundaries that the other parent needs to reestablish his or her life.

Batterers seek control. Such a level of control precludes their being flexible or capable of negotiations. It is precisely these same characteristics that are an essential part of being a parent. I have observed how many of my clients' lives become a war zone. Many of these emails, texts, and other communications are reused by the batterers in their efforts to relitigate custody of the children and are attached to their petitions to obtain sole custody. It is this author's position that when the courts promote these types of parenting arrangements, not only do we place women and children in untenable situations, but we also encourage continued litigation. I have also found that, in many cases in which there is co-parenting—even with those who have sufficient means—the batterers are not required to pay child support as no one has primary physical custody of the children. In short, these parenting plans undermine federal public policies that seek to ensure that children receive adequate child support or that domestic violence be given serious consideration in custody and visitation determinations.

Parallel parenting may also minimize the contact between the parents but allow for maximum participation of both parents in their children's lives. However, Bancroft et al. noted the ways in which batterers undermine their children's relationship with their mothers not only because they are abusive to her but also because they ignore or denigrate her role.[64] In this environment, it is difficult for the mothers to set limits with their children, take away privileges when necessary, or establish clear routines. Some of my clients report that batterers take the children on expensive vacations while paying minimum child support. Finally, Jaffe et al. cautioned that the research on such parenting arrangements is subjective and that therefore these types of arrangements should be viewed as preliminary recommendations.[65]

However, it is disturbing that this latest trend fails to integrate our understanding of domestic violence as a source of traumatic exposure for women and children. It is also my opinion that only where the parents freely chose such arrangements and neither parent has been victimized by the other should there be any form of joint legal custody. In short, these arrangements should never be considered when there is a history of domestic violence.

Conclusion

An understanding of children's healthy separation and attachment needs should also inform recommendations for custody and visitation schedules.

While liberal overnights and extensive vacation schedules are generally appropriate for school-aged children, preschool children are often rushed into overnight schedules prematurely during litigation. Mental health professionals are frequently confronted by children who display anxiety at the abrupt imposition of overnight or vacation visitation before they are ready. Case-by-case assessments should be given significant consideration by the courts and litigants so that schedules reflect the children's needs. Nor should the mother's anxiety about the imposition of such schedules on her children be treated with distrust or contempt.

If mental health professionals are armed with a thorough history of parenting in the family, they can empower their patients to bring this to their attorneys' attention and, in traumatic divorce, advocate for those clients as well. There is a significant body of work in which therapists actively help young children cope with the separation from their primary caretaker as they transition between their families during scheduled visitation.[66] While this can be helpful, we need to consider whether such uniformly implemented schedules are not causing children to pay a very high price.

A thorough family history includes a review of who took parental leave when the child was born; who arranged for the child care; who communicates with the caretaker; who takes off from work when the child is sick, or, if the caretaker is unavailable, who takes the child to the doctor and attends parent–teacher conferences; who selects and visits the schools and summer programs; and, finally, who gets up in the middle of the night with the child.

I once represented a professional woman whose husband had significant mental health issues. The husband worked as a consultant and scheduled his work so that it appeared that he was home full-time. Although he did work, he refused to fully contribute to the family finances and frequently threatened the mother with loss of custody. Despite his constant verbal and economic abuse, she was intimidated into staying in the relationship for many years even though the children experienced emotional difficulties.

Upon inquiry, I learned that the parties had always hired full-time child care and that although the husband could have been fully involved with the children, he was not. I was able to obtain documentation from the parties' tax returns proving that they deducted the cost of full-time child care until the children were of school age. When the children entered school, the couple continued to deduct child care costs for after-school programs and the like. Although the husband continued to threaten to get custody and referred to himself as the primary caretaker, my client had always borne full responsibility for juggling the needs of their children while continuing to work full-time.

This kind of manipulation is not uncommon and demonstrates the importance of a thorough history of the family to counteract a parent's psychological and financial abuse. In this case, the courts offered an arena where the children were protected. With preparation, the mother was able to provide documentation to the court-appointed custody evaluator that challenged the father's view of himself as the primary caretaker. The husband's mental illness was carefully documented in the forensic report, and the client obtained full legal custody, with the father's access limited to unsupervised weekly visits.

In another instance in my practice, a father who had chosen to reside in another state some distance away rarely visited his three-year-old daughter. After suddenly filing for custody in the child's home state, the father demanded immediate overnight visits on the first court date—although he had never cared for the child alone. Without investigation, the judge awarded the father over-night weekend visitation, although the father had refused the mother's offer of several day-visits during this same time period. The child was brought abruptly to her father's home where, without preparation, she was introduced to the father's new family, including a stepbrother. Upon return to her mother, the child informed her of the father's new marriage and relationships.

This little girl had spent a difficult weekend in which she was forced to nav-igate her new family without the assistance of her mother, who was shocked and bewildered by the news of the father's new family. Upon return to her mother's care, the child immediately curled up into a fetal position, developed nightmares, and regressed in toilet training.

In this instance, the judge's bias—that fathers should almost always have overnight visits—caused her to make an impulsive decision that was not informed by the facts of the case and was not developmentally appropriate for such a young child who had not seen her father in close to a year. The father's sudden demand for overnight visitation and custody, accompanied by his refusal to see his daughter on someone else's terms or to pay child support, indicated that while there was a minimal history of physical abuse, he was psy-chologically abusive and unable to meet his daughter's emotional needs.

It is also important for mental health professionals to be aware of other markers of an abusive relationship. It is essential to know whether one adult has exhibited unusual control of the family finances and whether one parent has been verbally abusive, engaged in stalking and harassment, or exercised other forms of coercive control.[67] The protective mother may also be at an increased risk of physical abuse during the separation and divorce, requiring help with safety planning and protective orders.

Questions remain as to whether the laws that require judges to consider domestic violence in custody and visitation cases have been undermined by the passage of "friendly parent" and joint custody presumptions. Furthermore, the question of how, or whether, the mental health and legal systems can change the relationship between an abusive parent and their children is one that can-not be solved without input from victims' services providers and survivors of domestic violence. This issue must be informed by the research on trauma and children. Finally, it is important to consider whether making family court more transparent and open to observers will help make the courts more accountable.

Battered mothers are clearly the better custodial parent when the alternative is to ignore or minimize the harm caused by a parent who is abusive and exposes the children to harm. When partnerships exist with trained professionals, the protective parent has a better chance of successfully traversing the divorce process. However, therapists do not operate in a vacuum and cannot control many of the variables of litigation. Nevertheless, with an understanding of the legal system, a therapist can communicate effectively in "legal speak" and provide information on the existence and effect of these high-risk factors to the court or its forensic expert, thus helping to minimize the damage to children.

It is also essential for the healthy parent to have an attorney who is committed to advocating for the client. Their attorney will need to be armed with information that can be provided by the client's therapist. The attorney should be able to understand the ramifications of high-risk factors to provide the client with valuable information about appropriate legal remedies and an understanding of the ramifications of their legal choices.

The models of shared parenting arrangements, including joint physical custody or joint legal custody, are susceptible to manipulation and conflict-ridden parenting. The courts should recognize that, given major conflict between parents, it is best to designate one parent as the primary decision-maker or custodial parent. A protective mother, with the support of her therapist, can make a reasoned decision to request sole custody of the children and supervised visitation with the noncustodial parent. When the custodial parent has learned the hard way that decisions cannot be made with her former partner because of ongoing abuse, sole decision-making should be the norm.

A clear determination of custody ensures that child support obligations are established. If children divide their time equally between their parents, the courts are less likely to impose an obligation to pay child support. Nor can very young children be separated from their primary caretakers for extended periods of time without experiencing significant levels of stress and anxiety. The mental health professionals need to be keenly aware of the emotional and financial consequences for the children they treat.

Finally, clear boundaries regarding decision-making, visitation, and orders tailored to the children's needs for safety and security can foster realistic relationships and are essential for all family members. In traumatic divorces, it is particularly important to safeguard children. Psychological assessments must be based not only upon individual psychopathology, but also on the current research in the social sciences, rates of interfamilial violence, trauma, and its impact on children. While mental health professionals have been reluctant to enter divorce litigation, the information they provide, along with effective mental health care, has the potential to inform the legal system and prevent further trauma.

9

The Response to Families Engaged in Traumatic Divorce

JUDICIAL TRENDS AND REFORMS

The family courts struggle to balance the competing needs of families seeking assistance each day. The problems of these families are multifaceted, including issues of domestic violence, mental health, and substance abuse. The courts are typically underfunded and have limited resources in civil cases of custody and divorce. To be effective, researchers have noted that differential case management of domestic violence cases requires coordination with other courts, government agencies, and community-based service providers.[1] This chapter will discuss the current resources available to the family courts, including the model of the problem-solving courts and supervised visitation services. Finally, this chapter will address the appropriateness of the various forms of alternative dispute resolution (ADR) that have been developed to address the concerns of high-risk families, including mediation, parenting coordination, and collaborative law and related safety concerns.

The Problem-Solving Model Court Response

The philosophy of therapeutic jurisprudence—a judicial approach that seeks to use social science research and the delivery of services to change the legal process for offenders—has led to the development of problem-solving courts.[2] These specialized courts address specific community safety concerns and have access to specialized community resources to address the problems of offenders and victims.[3]

Criminal courts have utilized various judicial models, including problem-solving model courts, to address the problems of domestic violence, substance abuse, and mental health concerns. Increasingly, such problem-solving courts have provided significant resources to judges for both perpetrators and victims in the form of treatment programs and counseling services.[4] The defendants are directed to comply with court-mandated programs, and there are consequences should they fail to do this. Many of these agencies working with the courts monitor the status of the defendants in the various programs, providing information about their compliance with court orders and victim safety to the judges. In cases involving allegations of criminal domestic violence, some model courts provide an integrated response, in which the judges exercise subject matter jurisdiction to also hear the various related issues of custody and divorce.

The model courts have developed to address the problems of substance abuse, mental health issues, and domestic violence. The clear majority of such programs developed in the criminal courts. However, many of these families have problems that also are heard in the civil courts in the form of civil orders of protection, custody, visitation, divorce, and housing. In the federal courts, many women are forced to file for bankruptcy because of economic abuse.[5] Model family courts should have the authority to address child custody, visitation, divorce, support, and consumer debt to prevent the need for bankruptcies.

However, some families have not had contact with the criminal justice system. This may occur for a variety of reasons, either because the victims have never reported the criminal behavior, or the abusers may have focused primarily on sexual or economic abuse or threats that are less likely to come to the attention of law enforcement. In some instances, the police may have been called to the home, but there may not have been arrests or prosecutions, either because the perpetrator was not present when they arrived or the victim may have declined to prosecute.

The criminal courts can be distinguished from civil family courts not only because the legal burden of proof and penalties are greater, but also because the prosecutors' office presents their cases on behalf of the state, and, as a result, victims do not have control over decisions. While there is a growing trend to focus on the victims' needs, the emphasis in the criminal courts is largely on punishment and rehabilitation of perpetrators. Custody and visitation are typically heard in the family courts, which are civil proceedings. While problem-solving criminal courts, typically referred to as *model courts*, are designed to provide services as an alternative to incarceration, it is striking that in most family courts such resources are not uniformly available. There have been some drug treatment courts in child welfare cases in which treatment is made available to parents. However, in the family courts, the only remedy currently available to battered mothers, should the batterers not comply with court-ordered visitation or custody, is to return to court to file a violation petition. Many women find this process prohibitively expensive and risky because their allegations may not be believed. Services to families in the form of supervised visitation programs or substance abuse treatment after divorce or custody litigation are a scarce resource. Many court-related programs do not continue to provide supervised visitation after the case is completed. When services continue privately, it is unusual to find a supervisor or treatment provider who continues to report to the courts regarding closed cases. Best practices include long-term monitoring and notice to all parties of any communications to the courts. However, the failure to provide any follow-up leaves a vacuum in which women and children remain at risk. This problem is particularly acute when batterers have unsupervised visitation, overnights, or some form of shared decision-making. It is for these reasons that the model of problem-solving courts is essential in custody and divorce litigation, particularly if there are multiple allegations of mental illness, substance abuse, and domestic violence.

We should assume that, when there are allegations of domestic violence in civil cases of divorce and custody, these may represent very serious allegations regardless of whether there is prior criminal court involvement. Buzawa et al. found in a study of the Quincy, Massachusetts, district court that most of the defendants charged with domestic violence crimes were more likely to be brought to court by their victims seeking *civil* orders of protection and not to the *criminal* courts.[6] Given the vulnerability of children in such households, it is essential that we provide sufficient resources to address these problems.

As awareness of domestic violence has increased, so, too, has the caseload for the family courts. In 2003, the National Center for State Courts found that over the past ten years custody cases involving domestic violence had increased by 14%.[7] Similarly, these researchers indicated that the American Bar Association reported that cases involving domestic violence in the family courts had increased by 79%.[8] Ver Steegh and Dalton noted that the family courts have attempted to implement differential case management that included family assessments, screening on an expedited basis, development of service plans so that appropriate referrals and court services could be put in place, the development of parenting plans, and long-term monitoring.[9] While there is a need for continued monitoring after a judicial determination has been made, pretrial development of parenting plans, without a hearing, raises significant concerns as to whether the judges have adequate information and evidence to make such determinations. Expedited hearings in which both sides can present evidence and the judge can assess the witnesses' credibility require additional hearing officers, staffing, and courtrooms. Thus, protective orders and supervised visitation could be implemented to ensure safety.

The role of the judge in the family courts is to hold a hearing in which both sides can present evidence, testify, and raise legal arguments. Following a hearing, the judge must make findings of fact and apply the relevant laws to their determinations. This is how the legal process works, and the family courts should be no different from other courts. However, because family courts are so overloaded, the courts seek other ways of resolving their cases. Implementing unsupervised access plans may take place months, or even longer, before a hearing is held. Furthermore, many divorce researchers have formed a belief that parental conflict is exacerbated by the culture of litigation.[10] In contrast, however, Pruett et al. noted that mothers reported that their children had fewer symptoms of anxiety, depression, and somatic complaints when there were attorneys involved in their children's legal cases.[11]

Problem-Solving Substance Abuse and Mental Health Courts

There are several model courts utilized in the criminal courts to handle cases of domestic violence. Some states have adopted specialized domestic violence courts to handle criminal and civil issues regarding the same family, and these will be heard before the same judge.[12] Former New York State Chief Judge Lippman stressed the importance of providing battered women with legal representation in civil cases, indicating that this saved the state 85 million dollars in medical and mental health care costs.[13] Any court-based program to manage domestic violence and abuse cases in the family courts must provide civil legal representation from lawyers trained in domestic violence advocacy and related mental health services to victims.

As part of court reform, the legal system and community agencies have looked at innovative ways to respond to various social problems including substance abuse, mental health problems, and domestic violence.[14] Fay-Ramirez reported that, as of 2012, there were more than 3,000 problem-centered courts, sometimes called *problem-solving courts*, in the United States that have developed over the past twenty years and that many such courts handle criminal drug offenses.[15] In comparison to traditional courts, problem-centered courts are intended to offer alternatives to incarceration in the form of diversionary programs such as drug treatment or mental health treatment.[16] Fay-Ramirez also noted that the judges in such courts provide decisions that demonstrate flexibility to the defendants' needs.[17] In such courts, the judge is a central figure and can provide services for both the victims and offenders.[18] Duffy indicated the importance of judicial training in handling these problems to enable judges to be more effective.[19] Berman and Feinblatt noted that the various problem-solving courts have common elements but differ in many ways.[20] Utilizing nontraditional approaches, these courts attempt to impose accountability on offenders sentenced to alternative rehabilitative services while addressing community concerns and service delivery.[21] In problem-solving courts, there are a team of mental health and legal professionals, headed by the judge, who make assessments and an alternate diversion or sentencing plan. In the criminal context, these recommendations can result in different outcomes from traditional criminal courts, so that sentences may be reduced, cases diverted, or charges dismissed if there is successful compliance with court orders.[22] Such courts seek to view the problems of the offenders in a broader context, balancing the needs of the community and individuals. Similarly, Castellano and Anderson noted that mental health courts developed because of the poor conditions for the mentally ill in the prisons.[23]

In such a court, an offender with a substance abuse problem may be required to complete a residential drug program or see a psychiatrist on a regular basis. The mental health agencies monitor compliance with these services, and cases are brought back to court for more serious intervention if the offender fails to comply with the treatment plan. For those offenders with serious mental illnesses, the mental health courts are specialized criminal courts that help offenders enroll in community-based treatment programs.[24]

Recidivism and Effectiveness

Assessing recidivism in the mental health courts has been difficult. Castellano and Anderson noted the significant comorbidity of mental health and substance abuse problems.[25] Concerns about the effectiveness of the assigned treatment programs remain as not every program is suitable for every participant. Some researchers have questioned whether the mental health courts divert scarce funds from other forms of mental health treatment.[26] Finally, they raised the question of whether mandating that the offenders take prescribed psychotropic drugs is undermining their motivation and self-determination.[27] It is significant that Keator et al. found that offenders in three mental health courts accessed community-based treatment more quickly than mentally ill offenders upon release from jail.[28] Finally, the due process concerns of offenders with mental health problems must be balanced against the need for community safety.

Belenko's study at the national Center on Addiction and Substance Abuse (CASA) at Columbia University found that there were substantial reductions in drug use and crime-related activities during the offender's participation in drug court programs.[29] Similarly, Berman and Feinblatt's study of forty-eight drug courts and the rates of completion of drug treatment found that those offenders mandated to attend drug treatment had a higher rate of drug treatment completion than those offenders who participated voluntarily.[30]

Significantly, the CASA study also found that, during the time that the offenders were participating in these drug courts, drug use and recidivism rates were reduced.[31] Similarly, Oehme and O'Rourke's research involving participants in supervised visitation programs found that recidivism was reduced during such participation. Court monitoring is effective on many levels.[32]

The provision of services in the drug courts includes the increased use of supervision, drug testing, and monitoring of participation in treatment programs.[33] Inherent in the use of drug treatment programs as an alternative to incarceration is the implicit threat of more severe penalties if the offender does not cooperate fully.[34] Sung and Belenko noted that the original evaluations of drug treatment programs found that more offenders sentenced in drug courts to treatment completed these programs, in comparison to those offenders sentenced in traditional criminal courts.[35] However, later research revealed that many offenders who had completed residential drug treatment did not stay crime-free.[36] More research is needed to determine the reasons behind the increase in recidivism and whether some groups of drug users are impacted by other influences in their lives.

However, in Dade County, Florida, the National Institute of Justice research found that defendants in the drug courts had fewer drug-related arrests compared with those sentenced in more traditional courts.[37] Given this finding, more research is needed to determine the quality of the individual drug courts, the impact of the role of a nontraditional judge, and the availability and appropriateness of the prescribed drug treatment programs.[38]

Berman and Feinblatt also noted the need for extensive evaluations of all problem-solving courts to determine their effectiveness.[39] Significantly, these researchers found that there were common elements in problem-solving courts, whether these courts addressed the problems of domestic violence, drugs, or mental health. They noted that the judges were actively involved in the supervision of the offenders, whether they were mandated to attend drug, mental health, or domestic violence programs.[40] Furthermore, these courts have strong relationships with service providers and are frequently less adversarial because, in some courts, the offender must enter a guilty plea before a treatment plan is developed.

Berman and Feinblatt also observed that criticisms of the problem-solving courts focus on the question of whether offenders are afforded sufficient due process.[41] In many courts, offenders cannot participate in these courts without entering guilty pleas or enrolling in court-monitored treatment programs and foregoing the right to a trial. Offenders must also sign releases of medical and treatment records that allow the courts to review their progress in the programs and drug testing results. These are important due process concerns that must be addressed by providing competent legal representation in such problem-solving courts.

Domestic Violence Courts

Berman and Feinblatt further noted that more research is needed on the effectiveness of domestic violence courts, family treatment, and mental health courts to determine long-term outcomes.[42] While clerking for a state judge, I helped to organize one of the first problem-solving domestic violence courts that handled criminal charges in New York State in the early 1990s. Having visited and practiced in other such courts over the years, I note that these courts have changed and that there is more awareness of the need for monitoring of any treatment provided. Dade County, Florida; New York State's Center for Court

Innovation; and Quincy, Massachusetts' District Court have developed specific problem-solving courts. The courts and service providers have begun to identify various programmatic changes that were necessary to address the need for monitoring and accountability for offenders. Alternate sentencing is very much a part of problem-solving courts so that, rather than incarceration and probation, offenders in drug courts may be sentenced to substance abuse programs. In many instances, batterers are sentenced to complete an anger management or batterers' treatment program. When offenders do not comply with such court-ordered programs, there must be collaboration with service providers and consequences for noncompliance. More research is needed to determine the effectiveness of the treatment offered in such problem-solving courts. Finally, Berman and Feinblatt concluded that, in Dade County, Florida, defendants in drug courts had fewer drug-related arrests compared with those sentenced in more traditional courts.[43]

The research on domestic violence model courts in criminal cases is equivocal as to whether they reduce the rate of recidivism.[44] Cissner et al. found that when court policies attempted to increase victims' safety and to hold offenders accountable using rehabilitation, recidivism was reduced.[45]

Implementation of civil custody and divorce courts with domestic violence allegations requires extensive training of judges, court personnel, and service providers on trauma, domestic violence, mental health, and substance abuse.[46] Bancroft et al. argued that the full impact of the batterers' behavior is not simply the physical abuse, as domestic violence impacts family functioning in myriad ways.[47] Mental health professionals who understand the impact of abuse and the other high-risk factors of mental illness and substance abuse on parenting can more effectively evaluate the batterers' behaviors. Finally, the proceedings in drug courts and criminal domestic violence courts are different from those in civil custody litigation. The incentives for offenders in drug courts—that is, to avoid incarceration—are very different from those in custody litigation. It is conceivable that domestic violence civil courts will require judges, in collaboration with mental health professionals, to refer the parents for a variety of services. For example, while domestic violence is not caused by substance abuse, drug use does have an impact on violence in the home, and researchers agree that male batterers who are alcoholics cause more serious injuries than those who are sober.[48] Therefore, we should consider that it is sometimes appropriate for a domestic violence court to make referrals to substance abuse programs or mental health treatment. Victims and children need mental health counseling and a treatment plan that sensitively helps them with their trauma and related psychological concerns that could benefit from early interventions. In situations where the mothers and children will not be further endangered, supervised visitation programs over the long term may reduce post-separation violence.

In custody and divorce cases when there are allegations of domestic violence, mental illness, and substance abuse, the courts must be motivated first and foremost by the need to protect victims of domestic violence and the children of these families. Research on the length of time these families spend in the legal system and whether there was continued litigation after custody and visitation decisions were rendered would be helpful. Over the long term, what would this mean in terms of the health and mental health care for the family members? Could we potentially minimize trauma by implementing monitoring of visitation issues, and would batterers behave more appropriately if they were subjected to such long-term supervision? Finally, specialized model courts to address custody and divorce litigation could focus attention on the long-term needs of the families seeking help. With adequate training, resources, and attention, this could be a substantial improvement from the traditional judicial response.

There is much we can learn from the research on mental health and drug courts. The research on such problem-solving courts concluded that recidivism is reduced and completion of drug treatment enhanced during the offenders' participation in these courts. This suggests that, in family court, where families seek help with the problems of domestic violence, mental illness, and substance abuse, there are no short-term solutions. Real planning requires a significant investment of resources. Court rulings and programs that provide batterers with consistent and informed guidelines for their behavior, with consequences if they disregard the courts' directives, can only be possible with a judicial approach that allows for such resources, along with appropriate training of all personnel.[49]

Schwarz has noted that domestic violence victims are frequently involved in multiple court proceedings at the same time, making the process overwhelming and confusing.[50] In my practice, I have frequently represented battered women who have filed for child support before one magistrate, only to be served with custody petitions or a divorce action before another judge. The concept of one family-one judge, where a jurist trained in intimate partner abuse hears all the families' problems, is also the basis for many of the integrated domestic violence courts where the civil and criminal cases are heard together. This researcher also noted that not only battered women can benefit from unifying family court proceedings but that this is also helpful for all family members.[51]

Mediation

The overwhelmed court systems have looked beyond litigation to alternative ways to resolve the issues of custody and visitation. Thus, the courts refer families to mediation, diverting them from the traditional approach of litigation. Waldman and Ojelabi describe the increase in mediation globally in which parties engage in facilitated negotiations rather than litigation.[52] Mediation is premised on the concept that self-determination and autonomous decision-making will bring about a fair and reasonable result in the form of a negotiated agreement.[53] Campbell and Johnston believed that couples were more satisfied and more likely to comply with mediated agreements than if decisions had been heard by a judge.[54]

Historically, Campbell and Johnston noted that mediation in custody disputes grew out of the process first utilized in labor disputes but modified for family law purposes.[55] Different models of mediation have emerged. Among them is the pragmatic process, where the facilitators utilize a rational, issue-driven, goal-oriented approach to conflict resolution based on the economic model of mediation and resulting in the development of a final agreement. Discussion of emotional issues is discouraged. These researchers also found that some mediators address emotional issues, assisting the parties in coming to terms with the separation and divorce, by utilizing a family system's approach to reach an agreement with lawyers and mental health professionals. Here, the mediator may model conflict resolution strategies so that the parties can resolve later difficulties while arriving at legal solutions. Campbell and Johnston described the use of mediation in what they have termed high-conflict divorce, in which they posit that disagreements about children and finances are an expression of the underlying tensions between the parents.[56] Finally, some mediators have developed an interdisciplinary approach with lawyers and mental health professionals to teach conflict resolution skills in a family system's approach.[57]

Waldman and Ojelabi concluded that there is significant controversy about whether mediators are responsible for the fairness of these final agreements.[58] There are also significant disagreements in the field of mediation about whether and how much mediators should intervene if the agreements seem blatantly unjust. These researchers further noted that there are frequently vast disparities between the parties in mediation. Some parties are more affluent, with more effective legal representation. Thus, these researchers call for an ethical approach in which mediators intervene to prevent unjust agreements.

Mediation with high-risk families presents many problems. In my practice, some clients have been referred to mediation by judges during litigation. Many attorneys have noted how difficult it is to reject such referrals for fear of angering the judges. In many instances, well-meaning judges with an overloaded court calendar objectively believe that mediation may present a swifter and less traumatic approach to traditional litigation. However, in my practice, I have also seen instances in which judges threaten the litigants to agree to mediation without supervision of the actual results, informing the less affluent party of the costs and risks involved in litigation while overlooking the safety concerns raised.

When there has been intimate partner violence, substance abuse, or untreated mental illness, this means that women are negotiating to protect their children's safety and their own. But safety should be nonnegotiable. In these situations, restrictions on overnights or unsupervised visitation should not be lifted. Mediation regarding financial matters when one party has more experienced counsel and the funds to prolong litigation frequently results in the less affluent spouse's capitulation. Traumatized women in mediation frequently feel pressured to acquiesce to an agreement that may not be in their children's best interest and may present significant risks to their own safety to avoid incurring extensive legal fees and the risk of losing at trial.

I have occasionally attended mediation sessions with my clients, particularly when they have felt bullied by their spouses. In a case where there had been significant psychological and financial abuse and the children strongly resisted overnight visitation, a mediator shouted at my client when she would not agree to a schedule of overnights and weekends. Such a schedule is typical in less-distressed divorcing families. However, in this case, the father's mental health problems interfered with his ability to attend to the children's basic needs during visitation or engage in appropriate child-oriented activities with the children. Only after repeated displays of the father's disregard for his children's needs was the mediator able to understand. Until then, my client and I had spent hours in mediation in which she incurred unnecessary legal expenses. What is significant about this case is that there were no allegations of physical abuse. The father had a serious untreated mental health problem and engaged in the verbal and economic abuse of my client. In such circumstances, mediation is inappropriate.

Ellis and Stuckless addressed the question of whether mediation lends itself to increased risks. These researchers found that, with adequate safety protocols informed by careful assessments of the history of domestic violence, battered women were not at greater risk of post-separation abuse.[59] These researchers utilized the Domestic Violence Evaluation (DOVE), a research tool developed to screen for the risks of abuse, in response to criticisms that the process of mediation left women exposed to further harm.[60] Ellis and Stuckless sought to evaluate the level of risks of such contact, under the assumption that some abuse is conflict-driven while other forms are the result of coercive control.[61] The researchers developed safety measures that were commensurate with the level of risks they found. For example, these researchers recommended that the parties arrive and leave separately when there was a moderate risk of physical assaults.[62]

In cases where the researchers believed there to be a minimal risk of further abuse, the mediator established rules regarding respectful communications and prohibited coercive conduct.[63] In high-risk cases, the researchers recommended telephone mediation sessions or escorts to and from the mediation program for the parties.[64] These are sensible and reasonable recommendations that allow battered women to feel safe in the courthouse and have nothing to do with participation in mediation. In my practice, there have been several times when I had to ask court personnel to delay the batterer while my client and I fled the courthouse after he exhibited threatening or explosive behavior. I am grateful to the court officers who immediately understood and escorted us out of the courthouse so that we did not encounter the batterer on the courthouse stairs, in the waiting rooms, or on the street.

However, in mediation, the theoretical framework behind this risk assessment is that the physical abuse was a result of the couple's mutual inability to manage their conflicts, placing blame on both parties for the abuse. Campbell and Johnston noted that domestic violence had been found in 75% of intractable custody conflicts.[65] Finally, the DOVE assessment is based on the premise that some forms of physical abuse are simply poor conflict resolution skills. As discussed in greater depth in Chapter 3, domestic violence is not conflict, but is part of a constellation of coercively controlling behaviors.[66] I have noted again and again that even when the incidents of physical abuse are few, other forms of abuse continue to reinforce the victim's vulnerability. In this environment, it is difficult for the victimized spouse to advocate for her needs or her children's safety. Unfortunately, the Uniform Collaborative Law Act (2009) sets forth proposed guidelines to recommend that, in some instances of domestic violence, this form of ADR is appropriate.[67]

The larger question is not whether battered women are placed at risk during the process of mediation, but whether the conditions of their agreements lead to a higher rate of traumatization and abuse through inappropriate contact and inadequate financial stability. Research on male partner violence indicates that risks continue after the separation and that one of the primary reasons for separation is this abuse.[68] The research of Ellis and Stuckless focused on whether mediation exposed battered women to increased risks of post-separation physical abuse. These researchers found that in cases in which there was a history of domestic violence, women with mediated agreements were no more likely to experience post-separation abuse than women who had more traditional litigation.[69] Their concerns about physical safety are important. However, even if the mediators provide a physically safe place for such sessions to take place, is mediation appropriate if a parent has been abusive? Understanding batterers means that we should be aware of their manipulative behaviors and inflated sense of entitlement. Bancroft and Silverman have repeatedly noted that the dynamic of the batterer's abusive behavior interferes with the mother's ability to parent her children.[70]

Questions remain regarding batterers' ability to parent and negotiate and whether battered women are strong enough and have sufficient resources to withstand proposals that undermine their financial, physical, and psychological well-being. Finally, we must ask whether the agreements reached in mediation are fair, and what safeguards exist to ensure that basic levels of safety, financial security, and justice are attainable (in mediation) when one party has a significant physical, psychological, and financial advantage.

Parenting Coordination

Parenting coordination is referred to as a hybrid form of ADR that is used in the family court system. Coates et al. referred to the increased use of parenting coordination to provide case management for the small portion of families deemed to be high-conflict who spent enormous time relitigating their concerns over custody and visitation in the courts.[71] While mediation is typically used by the courts to reach settlement agreements, parenting coordinators are frequently employed privately by the parties after the divorce to help them resolve disagreements regarding their children. In some instances, these researchers acknowledged that parenting coordinators make decisions for the family when ordered by the court or if the parents agree.[72] This practice raises significant due process concerns as the process of parenting coordination becomes an extrajudicial proceeding.

The Report of the Task Force on Parenting Coordination (2005) issued by the Association of Family and Conciliation Courts (AFCC) indicated that the process could be led by either a mental health or legal professional with training in mediation to work with high-conflict families.[73] Furthermore, the report indicated that the goals of parenting coordination with such families was to assist in the implementation of their parenting plans, to mediate disagreements, or, by court order or consent of the parties, to make final decisions. The Task Force noted the quasi-legal nature of parenting coordination, where parenting coordinators have significant responsibilities, including mediation, education, case management, and decision-making. The Task Force acknowledged the risks involved in working with families in which one parent had been abusive and that, where the abuser was coercively controlling, it was important to have staff trained in domestic violence or to refrain from working with such parents. Finally, the Task Force recommended that parenting coordinators withdraw if they cannot maintain their neutrality but failed to put into place any mechanism for removal of coordinators should this not occur.[74]

These recommendations are troubling. Assessing for a history of domestic violence should be done by a trained mental health professional. Domestic violence advocates and the Task Force agree that parenting coordination will not work when one party is intimidated by the other in abusive situations, making it essential that this not take place in any cases of domestic violence. Furthermore, when abused parents have full decision-making authority over decisions regarding their children, there is no need for such parenting coordination or mediation. When abusers seek mental health or substance abuse treatment, this should be done individually and need not involve other family members.

It is also not clear whether attorneys working without the assistance of trained mental health professionals, and without such a background, should be considered trained parenting coordinators and skilled in case management, assessment, and education. In most instances, the insertion of a parenting coordinator is part of the agreement and final judgment and is thought to be necessary where the agreement or court order provides for joint legal custody and the parties cannot work together. In some cases, parenting coordinators act as decision-makers.[75] At other times, they are only available to provide case management to help negotiate the conflicts over decisions regarding the health, education, and welfare of the children.

Coates et al. describe parenting coordination in a favorable light as this takes place outside of the courtroom in a nonadversarial setting.[76] Henson stressed the importance of having parenting coordinators follow the guidelines already in place when they make their decisions for the families.[77]

All the researchers agree that there is little research on whether parenting coordination is effective or has any impact on more-distressed families. Much of the literature on parenting coordination has stressed the need for standardization of training and credentials and has pointed to the diverse range of mental health professionals, certified mediators, and attorneys who do this work without agreed upon graduate training.[78] Although there is little research on the effectiveness of parenting coordination, there is widespread acknowledgment that this hybrid form of ADR is, at least in part, used to minimize time for the families in the court system. Scott et al. found that there was no link between the use of brief parenting coordination programs and relitigation of custody cases.[79]

A report by the American Psychological Association discussed a pilot project in Washington DC that provided parenting coordination for low-income families. This project used an interdisciplinary approach working with practitioners with a significant degree of psychological training and supervision.[80] The report did not provide long-term findings about the effectiveness of parenting coordination. It did indicate that the coordinators provided intensive case management and assistance in navigating conflicts and decision-making regarding schools and medical providers.[81] However, case management and advocacy for distressed families are a valuable resource that need not be tied to parenting coordination.

In my practice, many of my clients have had great difficulty in participating in face-to-face meetings with their abuser and find this traumatic. In some instances, the parenting coordinator has agreed to meet separately with the parents because of the safety concerns raised. On the face of it, this sounds like a solution to the problem of the enforced communication between the parents when there is a history of domestic violence, untreated mental illness, or substance abuse. However, I have frequently heard complaints about the costs and time spent in revisiting issues in parenting coordination. The courts typically direct that the parties share the costs of the parenting coordinator in middle- and upper-income families. Many of my clients have complained that the batterer used the parenting coordinator to abuse them financially by scheduling unnecessary meetings or by making frequent telephone calls, and my clients were forced to share this cost. Of concern is the tendency of the batterers to insist on renegotiating issues that were determined by court order, revisiting decisions about selection of doctors, specialists, schools, and overnight visitation. Henson is correct that it is essential that parenting coordinators adhere to the guidelines for the areas in which they are to assist in decision-making. However, batterers can be highly manipulative, and parenting coordinators may be swayed by such tactics.

There are discrepancies among the individual states as to whether a parenting coordinator can decide issues regarding custody and visitation. In New York, the courts have rejected the idea of parenting coordinators as decision-makers, finding this to be an impermissible delegation of judicial authority. *Edwards v. Rothschild*; *Silbowitz v. Silbowitz*.[82] Thus, we can conclude that such delegation raises due process concerns.

Similarly, the Pennsylvania Superior Court recently enacted a rule specifically holding that any order appointing a parenting coordinator was to be vacated, finding that only judges could make decisions in child custody cases.[83] The constitutionality of parenting coordinators making decisions regarding the health, education, and welfare of the children represents a significant intrusion into the family's right to privacy that has not been fully resolved by the courts. Finally, it is important to note that the use of parenting coordination with traumatized families has not been linked to lower rates of relitigation.

Collaborative Law

Collaborative law is part of the growing worldwide trend toward ADR in family law cases.[84] The model for this form of ADR is one in which the parties engage in negotiations to resolve their differences. Before beginning this process, the parties must sign an agreement in which their attorneys will be disqualified from representing them if the parties are unable to resolve their differences out of court.[85] Thus, both parties retain attorneys who are committed to the collaborative law process. The goal of the parties' negotiations is to shift the focus from position-based to problem-solving approaches to their negotiations to reach a result without judicial intervention.[86] The National Conference of the Commissioners on Uniform State Laws' Drafting Committee noted that, unlike mediation, a neutral party is not present to mediate the parties' concerns.[87] Furthermore, the Drafting Committee observed that both parties must be represented by attorneys to avoid manipulation of the unrepresented party.[88] Roddy noted that a growing number of states and the District of Columbia have enacted legislation providing for collaborative law.[89]

While collaborative law requires the parties to fully disclose their income and assets, in all forms of ADR, this financial disclosure is voluntary. It is assumed that both parties will be motivated to provide such information without the need for court orders.

However, in my family law practice, while litigating property settlements or child support, I have frequently had to seek assistance from the courts when abusive fathers refuse to provide proof of their income and assets, thus requiring motion practice and court orders. No such recourse is available in collaborative law. Finally, the model of the Uniform Collaborative Law Act that is recommended for adoption by the states does not advocate collaborative law or other forms of ADR when there is a history of coercion and violence.[90] However, it is troubling that the writers of the Uniform Collaborative Law Act accepted as fact that there are instances in which one of the parties exaggerates claims of abuse and that, in those cases, ADR may be appropriate and even that many actual victims want to participate.[91] Sadly, this position demonstrates a serious lack of understanding of the dynamics of domestic violence and the profound impact that the resulting power imbalance will have on any attempted negotiations.

Supervised Visitation Programs

Meyer observed that while parents have a fundamental Constitutional right to raise their children, the states also have a compelling interest in ensuring the other family members' safety and best interests of the children when there is a need for supervised visitation.[92] As a result, supervised visitation in families in which there is a history of domestic violence remains an alternative forum in which children can maintain a safe relationship with their abusive fathers. However, for mental health professionals who supervise visits, the guidelines for their roles, whether they are advocates, neutral observers, or working therapeutically to repair the parent–child relationship, has not been fully resolved.

Supervised visitation programs were originally utilized in child protective proceedings to facilitate access and reunification between biological parents and their children when there were safety concerns about such contacts.[93] In the 1990s, Pearson et al. noted that child support agencies also referred families to supervised visitation programs to facilitate fathers' involvement.[94] In 2000, supervised visitation programs were provided through federal funds in the Violence Against Women Act of 2000.[95] However, Maxwell and Oehme noted that child protective proceedings and family law cases involving domestic violence are very different, and normalization of parent–child visitation is not always appropriate.[96] Strauss noted the growing importance of temporary orders of supervised visitation as the courts become more aware of allegations of domestic violence, mental illness, substance abuse, or parental unfitness.[97] Brandt noted that supervised visitation may be used by judges as a temporary measure to reestablish parent–child relationships (as in prolonged separations) until they have determined the veracity of the allegations or as a case management tool.[98]

Supervised Visitation in Domestic Violence Cases

Supervised visitation programs attempt to provide an opportunity for children to have a relationship with their parent within the confines of a safe setting. In the 1990s, the family courts began increasingly to use supervised visitation programs when there were allegations of domestic violence, substance abuse, and mental illness. However, programs vary in designs and the populations they serve. Thoennes and Pearson found that the safety needs of the family members are very different in families with a history of domestic violence, noting that 43–53% of the mothers in their study reported being abused by the children's fathers after separation.[99] Scaia and Connelly stressed the importance of ensuring the safety of battered women and urged visitation supervisors to forego neutrality where this issue was concerned.[100] Birnbaum and Alaggia have called for increased research in the use of supervised visitation and the need for substantial changes in public policy.[101]

In practice, the courts may order supervision to be conducted by a family member, friend, private mental health professional, or designated nonprofit agency. Some visits take place in an agency setting or therapist office, or parents may be accompanied to public places. Not all visitation supervision programs are the same. Only recently, the Supervised Visitation Network (SNV) developed standards for practice for supervised exchanges and therapeutic supervision that included case reviews, written policies, and avoidance of conflicts of interest.[102] However, without sufficient funding, implementation of such visitation is difficult as many agencies have limited staff and thus must supervise several families at once. In such agencies, one or two staff members may be unable to hear the communications between parent and child. Programs that provide one-on-one supervision are costlier and much in demand. As of this writing, I am not aware of any graduate programs that provide clinical training in supervised visitation.

Children benefit from established routines during these visits, and therefore the supervisors must have the clinical skills to determine why and how the rules are being circumvented and, without hostility, set limits. For example, most visitation programs prohibit gift-giving to avoid the manipulation of the children's emotions. However, in my practice, in virtually all the cases in which the batterers were ordered to participate in supervised visitation, the fathers gave the children expensive gifts and sometimes even cash. In some instances, the supervisors had to limit the amount of gifts to no more than two per visit despite rules to the contrary.

Safety is also a significant concern as batterers may use the visitation to stalk the mothers following the visit or to question the children about her activities. Maxwell and Oehme noted that fathers frequently exhibit controlling and aggressive behaviors during visits.[103] This requires basic safety measures to ensure that batterers do not bring weapons to the visits and that the parents arrive and leave at separate times to avoid contact and additional violence.[104] For children, someone must explain the process to them and the reasons for this supervision. Many children are pleased to see their fathers, particularly in the confines of a safe space.

To effectively address the long-term effects of domestic violence on children and their relationship with their fathers, there is a dramatic need for sufficient public funds to expand the research in this area and fund effective programs. Having worked closely with visitation supervisors in my practice, their hands-on interventions and assessments are invaluable for my clients and their children. However, there is considerable confusion among visitation supervisors as to whether they are neutral observers, advocates for safety, or working therapeutically to repair the parent–child relationship.

The review by Maxwell and Oehme of behaviors exhibited in supervised visitation programs in Florida noted that batterers frequently deny or minimize their abusive behavior.[105] These researchers noted that the programs' rules about gifts, food, arriving and departing at the designated times, and recording the visits were frequently violated. In my practice, I have even had clients report that batterers attempted to record the visits and later attempted to introduce these recordings into evidence at trial. Bancroft et al. have found that when batterers break rules there should be consequences, even if these are slight.[106] In my practice, the supervisors have from time to time reported their concerns and observations to the courts, but, even when they are concerned about the children's reaction, the courts have not suspended the visits. Without a united front, it is difficult for supervisors to be effective.

Moore and Ford's report on supervised visitation and best practices recommends frequent communication between the courts and visitation staff and that the courts determine the level of safety precautions and protocols in place before using such providers.[107] Given the risks that visitation presents to battered women, it is essential that there be timely and consistent reports before each court date to ensure that batterers comply with agency protocols and court orders. In my practice, there have been times when the supervisors needed guidance from the court but had no mechanism to communicate their concerns. With this troubled population, we can expect that problems will occur during visits, and there needs to be sufficient collaboration between the court personnel and the supervisors to ensure safety. Without such structure and safety, it is unclear why children are subjected to such contacts.

Supervised Visitation with Traumatized Children

Without limits, consequences, and clinically informed practice, batterers can manipulate the process, resulting in further trauma for women and children. In my practice, there have been several incidents in which the children's emotional safety and the mother's privacy were jeopardized. In one instance, a father accused of sexual abuse attempted to engage the child in sexualized play. In another incident, the father followed the mother and child to her home after the visit, in violation of the order of protection. Both instances were not reported to the courts for several weeks, and visits continued until the next court date.

Researchers have called for more study on whether exposure to supervised visitation may increase the harm to battered women and children.[108] Johnston and Straus noted that many children in supervised visitation programs have been subjected to trauma related to exposure to domestic violence, serious mental illness, or substance abuse.[109] These researchers stressed the importance of children feeling safe in supervised visitation, both physically and psychologically.[110] Johnston and Straus also noted that the children in supervised visitation may have a delayed response to the trauma and exhibit symptoms later, and that the supervisors should be particularly clinically astute to determine if the children are uncomfortable or anxious during the visits.[111]

Jaffe and Crooks observed that some courts will order only supervised exchanges of the children out of concern that mothers could be abused during the pick-ups and drop-offs of the children.[112] In some instances, courts direct the parents to exchange the children for visitation at the local police precinct. However, the precinct environment is uncomfortable and does not ensure safety. Notably, the police are not scrutinizing the exchanges, and, in my practice, I have found that there is less ability to control what happens during the visit and any surrounding incidents when only the exchanges are supervised.

In my practice, in a case involving the custody of a preschool-aged boy with developmental delays, the judge initially directed that the father would have supervised visitation during the pendency of the custody litigation. After several months in which the visitation supervisor continued to express her concerns about the father's visits, the judge modified this order to indicate that only the exchanges between parent and child would be supervised. Immediately after this modification, the child became terrified and had nightmares. In those instances, it is difficult to know what caused their son's distress. Notably, the court had not held a hearing to determine whether unsupervised visitation was safe or appropriate for this father. The visitation supervisor had not appeared in court to testify about the appropriateness of this plan and later indicated that she felt ineffectual once her role was limited. Small children typically cannot explain what happened during their visits, what frightened them, or if the visiting parent behaved inappropriately. Significantly, Bancroft and Silverman, who have worked with many batterers, found supervised exchanges

to be inappropriate and noted that if there were sufficient concerns to supervise the exchange that the remainder of the visits should also be observed.[113]
Furthermore, in line with the concerns of Johnston and Straus regarding the
importance of children feeling safe during supervised visitation, it should be
noted that feelings of safety are not simply based on an absence of physical
aggression but also reflect children's need for a sense of psychological well-
being. Thus, it is difficult for supervisors to ensure that children are safe and
feel secure when they are unaware of what transpires during most of the visits.

Johnston and Straus concluded that children in supervised visitation programs are some of the most vulnerable children and, most importantly, that
such programs should not retraumatize children.[114] Furthermore, the question of how, or whether, the mental health and legal systems can change the
relationship between an abusive parent and his children is one that cannot be
solved without input from victims' services providers and survivors of domestic
violence and must be informed by the research on trauma and children. Finally,
it is important to consider whether making family court more transparent and
open to observers will help make the courts more accountable.

Frequently, many judges have been willing to overlook domestic violence
because of their preconceptions about the mental health concerns of battered
women. It is disturbing that there are many cases in which supervised visitation
is viewed as a transition to "normalized access," which can range from a schedule of alternating weekends to two weeks out of every month. Research on battered women in the Australian family courts indicated that, in most instances,
batterers received unsupervised visitation in the final custody determination
regardless of whether their behavior improved.[115] In my practice, I have found
that abusive fathers, after a period of supervised visitation and at the close
of the litigation, generally receive unsupervised visitation or even overnights
regardless of whether their behavior substantially improved. The problem may
be that the courts view supervised visitation as a punishment for fathers while
underestimating the long-term safety concerns or are stymied by the lack of
low-cost visitation programs. The question of whether visits should be suspended is a difficult one that must be determined on a case-by-case basis after
hearings in which both parents have representation and the safety and emotional needs of the child are addressed.

Post-Separation Risks of Abuse

There is substantial agreement by social scientists that the risks of domestic
violence increase after separation; Jaffe and Crooks have starkly noted the elevated risks to battered women following separation.[116] These risks are not limited to physical violence but are also reflected in batterers' manipulation of
the children and, as noted in one parenting program, use of litigation of child

custody to terrorize their partners.[117] Furthermore, these families have a history of trauma and abuse. Rosen and O'Sullivan's small study of women in a domestic violence program, in which one-half were still living with their batterers, found that level of abuse was the same, that more than 50% of the fathers had threatened to take the children, and that more than 40% had threatened to kill the mothers.[118] In those families in which the parents were not separated, 100% of the children either witnessed or overheard the abuse, and, in separated families, 87% of the children were aware of the abuse.

The risks continue as contact with the children leaves the mothers further exposed to abuse. Rosen and O'Sullivan conducted a larger study of New York City Family Courts and found that when mothers were granted orders of protection they were more likely to obtain custody, but the fathers received visitation in 64% of such cases. In some instances, following separation, Jaffe and Crooks correctly noted that there have been shocking instances of domestic homicides during supervised visitation. This is particularly troubling because it is not always possible to determine the level of risks in separating families during custody and divorce litigation. Finally, it is encouraging that Oehme and O'Rourke found that, in their study of battered mothers and their children in supervised visitation programs, there was a significant reduction in violence during the litigation.[119] Only 14.5% of the batterers were arrested for violent crimes during this time. These research findings may have significant implications for the effectiveness of long-term supervised visitation. Hopefully, if model courts that address custody and domestic violence continue to provide monitoring after cases are completed, the rate of post-separation violence could be reduced. This possibility has significant promise for children in families during and after traumatic divorce and requires more research and public funding.

It is important for mental health professionals and the legal system to recognize the significance of even one incident of physical violence. However, for the legal system and the mental health professionals working with them, it is sufficient for us to say that continuing exposure to an abusive parent—even if the children are not the direct targets of the abuse—is unhealthy for children and can have long-term implications.

Due process also requires hearings in which parents are represented and testimony can be provided. Unfortunately, the level of parental access is frequently determined by the more informal method of oral argument at the first court appearance rather than utilizing an evidence-based approach. As will be discussed in Chapter 11, the provision of adequate judicial personnel to hold expedited hearings on the appropriate safety measures needed is essential to ensure adequate due process protections for adults and children.

The very first court date is critical because the courts will not have heard testimony or evaluated the evidence but will render decisions about temporary visitation. Given the lack of supervised visitation providers and the disagreement about the merits and training of the individual providers, children and mothers frequently remain at-risk during the pendency of the court case. There is general agreement among researchers in domestic violence that a considerable number of mothers are subject to further abuse during post-separation contacts that can include visitation.[120]

In my practice, I have found that it is essential to marshal convincing arguments on the first court appearance regarding the safety concerns, the history of domestic violence, and reasons for supervised visitation and to provide the court a list of proposed agency or individual providers. Opposing counsel will typically oppose such plans and argue against the need for restrictions. It is also important to understand the visitation supervisors' possible biases and level of experience.

Furthermore, even if supervised visitation is immediately ordered when the parties enter the court system, because of the backlog of cases and length of time between adjournments, judges frequently implement gradual modifications of their orders so that the abusive parent has increasing amounts of unsupervised contact with his children. Thus, well before the hearing has taken place, the father may have unrestricted visitation with the children even while the mothers have orders of protection. Much more research is needed to address the question of the length of time such families linger in court and whether restrictions on visitation—or what is now called "access"—are lifted prior to a hearing and whether these rulings raise long-term safety concerns.

In practice, the judges make their decisions in reliance on the supervisors' reports. Given the lack of standardization of the visitation supervisors' training on domestic violence, this is problematic. It is widespread practice that, on subsequent court dates, the fathers' attorneys will argue for unsupervised access, overnights, and extended weekend access based on the content of the supervisors' reports. Again, these decisions are typically made before a hearing takes place. On the date of the hearing, visitation may already be unsupervised, and there can be considerable pressure brought to bear on mothers to agree to the fathers' having extensive overnights and joint decision-making. Many attorneys are afraid to raise the issue of domestic violence and ask for supervised visitation, fearing that their clients will be accused of parental alienation. In other instances, battered women or their attorneys may agree to informal supervision by family members, friends, or babysitters. Unfortunately, if there are problems, they are unable to issue a report or provide expert testimony to the courts. It is generally better to have the benefit of a licensed mental health professional's report.

Conclusion

The concept of the model courts has significant potential to address the concerns of families in custody or divorce litigation when there are histories of domestic violence, mental illness, and substance abuse. Extensive training for judges is an important aspect of such courts and will be discussed in greater detail in Chapter 11. Significantly, a review of the research indicates that supervised visitation programs that provide continued monitoring after the case is completed have the potential to decrease separation violence for battered women and their children. This is an important finding that could have widespread implications for public health and safety, and it warrants increased funding and research. Problems such as domestic violence, mental illness, and substance abuse cannot be solved overnight or even during litigation. Families enduring abuse and traumatic divorce require long-term sustained help from the courts and public institutions. Thus, public policy research must focus on methods to ensure the long-term safety of women and children.

Furthermore, the controversy over the use of ADR methods begins with the question of how we define families in which there is a history of domestic violence, substance abuse, or mental health problems. Unfortunately, if we view these families as engaging in high-conflict then we ignore the possible traumatic impact of domestic violence, untreated mental illness, and substance abuse. These are programs that appear to be very well meaning and that have significant appeal because they espouse alternatives to traditional litigation. However, a clinical understanding and identification of families in which there is domestic violence, substance abuse, or untreated mental illness require more safety precautions and boundaries than these programs can provide. Again, it is important to understand that abuse and other high-risk factors are not conflicts in which both parents must learn how to engage in more constructive approaches to conflict resolution. Abuse is not simply a matter of physical safety. Victims of intimate partner violence, in which mental illness and substance abuse may play a significant part, must be protected from all forms of coercive control: economic and sexual abuse, threatening and harassing behavior, and physical abuse. Without recognition of the pervasive impact of such abuse, victims will be pressured into alternative forms of dispute resolution that continue their traumatization.

Many divorce researchers view custody and divorce litigation in a negative light in which the families' difficulties are exacerbated. However, we can again review the research by Pruett et al. that suggests that children did not suffer more when attorneys were involved in their cases.[121] Given the safety concerns inherent in the enforcement of continuous contact in traumatic divorce and the concerns raised by the AFCC, the appropriateness of ADR with traumatized families should be reevaluated. Furthermore, the research on high conflict divorce and parenting coordination does not provide rigorous outcome data if one parent has a significant mental health or substance abuse problem, as discussed in Chapter 3. Several researchers have noted the existence of domestic violence and substance abuse in families termed high-conflict.[122] Programs such as mediation, parenting coordination, and, finally, collaborative law emphasize the importance of furthering co-parenting skills with high-conflict families. Accurate identification of domestic violence, untreated mental illness, and substance abuse would avoid confusion and help the courts develop a streamlined approach to litigation of these cases that emphasizes public health and safety.

An informed interdisciplinary response in which facts and evidence are heard at an expedited hearing by judicial personnel who are trained in high-risk factors, with the assistance of similar mental health professionals who can provide necessary services, may help to bring finality to these cases. Considerable resources have been brought to bear in the courts to address criminal cases that involve domestic violence and substance abuse problems through the development of model courts. Families involved in civil litigation in which the courts are typically underfunded, with scarce resources and inadequate training in the accurate identification of these high-risk factors, will result in more medical and mental health costs for traumatized children and mothers.

10

Expert Testimony and Custody Evaluations

Family court judges rely heavily on the opinions of professionals who perform custody evaluations. Custody evaluators are usually mental health professionals, such as counselors, social workers, psychologists, or psychiatrists, but in some states attorneys may take on this role. At the heart of the current controversy regarding the family courts' reliance on these mental health professionals' opinions is the reliability of the evaluators' methods of collecting data, their supporting theories, training, and the relevance of these factors to the facts and issues presented.

Expert witnesses are permitted to offer testimony that goes beyond that of typical witnesses, who can testify only regarding things that they directly experienced and not their opinions. Expert witnesses provide the courts with their assessments and opinions. In the context of custody litigation, mental health professionals may give the court their expert opinions about parental fitness, the children's needs and wishes, and the presence of intimate partner abuse or child maltreatment that can assist the court in making decisions regarding custody and visitation.

Beginning in the 1970s, the family courts increasingly relied on court-appointed mental health professionals' expertise rather than the opinions of professionals hired by the parents. This practice was codified in proposed model legislation called the Uniform Marriage and Divorce Act (UMDA), which recommended that courts order investigations and reports to assist them in their determinations of child custody.[1] However, in New York, in the seminal case of *Bennett v. Jeffreys*, the Court of Appeals cautioned that:

> In custody matters parties and courts may be very dependent on the auxiliary services of psychiatrists, psychologists, and trained social workers. This is good. But it may be an evil when the dependence is too obsequious or routine or the experts too casual.[2]

This statement provides insight into the current concerns regarding interdisciplinary practice in the family courts, where judges rely heavily on custody evaluations by mental health professionals. Informed interdisciplinary practice between mental health and legal professionals requires that there be procedures in place limiting the admission of unproven theories, misinterpretation of data, and reports that are not tainted by bias. While most attorneys are not educated in psychology, opposition to the evaluator's conclusions requires that they question the evaluators' level of knowledge through cross-examination on complex issues. This process is the only mechanism by which judges in custody litigation can weigh the relevance and reliability of the evaluators' testimony.

The controversies regarding the competing theories espoused by custody evaluators—including parental alienation—are unresolved. The underlying question as to whether these evaluators can accurately assess parenting abilities or have sufficient training in the high-risk areas that impact parenting, including abuse and child maltreatment, is fraught with controversies.

The Court's Use of Expert Testimony

Historically, in a variety of civil and criminal cases, judges and juries relied on expert professional testimony to make their ultimate decisions. Schuman noted that the courts required professionals to have sufficient qualifications before being allowed to provide expert opinions on any topic to the court.[3] However, this researcher also noted that knowledge, professional background, and training alone are not sufficient to qualify the professional as an expert. In the case of scientific expert testimony, professionals must also have obtained their knowledge by scientifically accepted methods supported by adequate empirical evidence.[4] In the family courts, mental health professionals must have complied with scientifically sound methods of collecting data before their findings are admitted into evidence.

Some problems occur when custody evaluators with impressive curriculum vitae may not have training or experience in the specific area that is a concern for the judge. For example, not all mental health professionals have specific training and expertise in substance abuse, domestic violence, or sexual abuse. Shuman warned that evaluators may draw conclusions from carefully collected data that have an empirically weak basis.[5] In some instances, their methods of collecting data may be flawed or even invalid.

Gross's discussion of expert witnesses noted the inherent paradox of admitting expert testimony at trial.[6] Such witnesses are called to testify about matters that are well beyond the scope of the judge's or jury's understanding, while the courts are also required to evaluate the reliability of their opinions. Ivkovic and Hans commented that judges and jurors have difficulty separating sound scientific evidence from flawed junk science.[7] Huber observed that the practice of admitting such evidence can result in the acceptance of opinions that have no basis in empirical research.[8] Finally, Faigman et al. observed that while the admission of expert scientific evidence is technically intended to assist the trier of fact in making determinations, in actuality, judges and jurors are in a very poor position to determine the validity and relevance of the proffered testimony.[9]

The American Bar Association's study (ABA 1989) of jurors' acceptance of expert testimony is revealing. The ABA study found that most jurors rejected the opinions of what they called "hired guns" retained by the litigants to give expert opinions. However, this study also found that the jurors were more respectful of professionals' opinions when the professional had hands-on experience with the parties. Thus, jurors found the treating physician's opinion to be more reliable than those of professionals hired by the litigants.[10] This finding is particularly important in the context of custody litigation in which evaluators interview parents, children, extended family members, teachers, therapists, and doctors and synthesize this information into a report in which they formulate conclusions about who is the better parent and whether the allegations made are true. The question remains whether the judges would be better served by hearing unfiltered direct testimony from these individuals.

Guidelines for Psychologists in Custody Evaluations

Haselschwerdt et al. noted that while many guidelines for the practice of custody evaluations exist, there are no universal standards for conducting such evaluations. Qualifications vary across the states, and California is the only state at this juncture that requires training in domestic violence.[11] Keilin and Bloom were the first researchers to study the methods used by psychologists in preparing custody evaluations.[12] Their findings reflected the lack of structure and guidelines in this emerging area of practice; some professionals were privately retained by one or both parties, while most evaluators preferred the practice of court appointments to maintain their neutrality.[13] These early evaluations were shorter, and the evaluators took far less time to compile them as compared to more current practices. Keilin and Bloom found that evaluators' recommendations of sole legal custody were most influenced by older children's preferences, parental alienation, the parent and child bond, parental mental health, and parenting skills.[14] In joint legal custody determinations, the mental health professionals indicated that the older child's wishes were quite influential, followed by the quality of the relationship the children had with both parents, the parents' willingness to work together, the quality of their relationships, and their mental stability. Historically, custody evaluators have not given sufficient consideration to the problems of domestic violence, physical or sexual abuse, and neglect.

Ackerman and Ackerman sought to replicate Keilin and Bloom's study of custody evaluators, polling psychologists and other mental health professionals' methodologies and practice. They found that evaluators preferred joint custody arrangements, relying on the parents' ability to work together.[15] In their sole custody recommendations, the evaluators considered current substance abuse problems, parental alienation, parenting skills, psychological stability, and attachment. Only in instances where the evaluators recommended either joint or sole custody was physical and sexual abuse considered.[16]

The American Psychological Association (APA) drafted the first guidelines and recommendations for best practices in custody evaluations.[17] These guidelines included recommendations for practice and ethical standards. To that end, the APA recommended that all evaluators consider their data using the best interests of the child standard. They stressed the need to determine the child's wishes, but shifted their primary focus to the parents, indicating that evaluators should assess the "parents' ability to plan for the child's future needs, capacity to provide a stable and loving home, and any potential for inappropriate behavior or misconduct that may negatively influence the child."[18] Significantly, the APA recommendations addressed evaluator bias, recommending self-awareness concerning the impact of race, age, gender, language, sexual orientation, and class. Informed consent, transparency regarding the limits of confidentiality in the context of a forensic report to the court, and clarification of billing practices were recommended as well. Evaluators were also advised against having multiple relationships with family members. Finally, the APA agreed that custody evaluations should assess three critical areas: parenting capacities, the developmental and psychological needs of the children, and the subsequent "fit" between parenting abilities and the children's needs.[19]

The APA guidelines stressed the importance of obtaining information from more than one source to avoid bias that could result from obtaining unverified, one-sided information.[20] Some evaluators also conducted home visits where children can be observed in more natural circumstances. Pepiton et al. indicated that a significant part of the evaluation was to also include a review of the original judicial order of referral and supporting court documents.[21]

Bow and Quinnell conducted research on custody evaluators' practices and compliance with the APA guidelines.[22] Overall, these researchers found that, in comparison with earlier research, there was adherence to the APA guidelines. These researchers found that evaluators considered more factors, obtained data from a variety of sources, and spent much more time on their evaluations. However, these researchers noted that ethical issues remained and, finally, that evaluators had concerns about the legal risks involved.

The Association of Family and Conciliation Courts (AFCC 2006), published what was referred to as the Model Standards of Practice for Child Custody Evaluations.[23] These new standards recommended that evaluators have a minimum of a master's degree in a mental health field and that they remain current in areas related to child custody. The AFCC recommended that evaluators establish a record-keeping system and that they inform the litigants of their procedures for payment and release of their reports. Substantively, the AFCC guidelines recommended that the evaluators be competent in assessing the developmental needs of children, family dynamics, and the impact of divorce, separation, domestic violence, alienation of the child, child maltreatment, and substance abuse, to name a few. More specialized areas of practice included assessments of sexual abuse and substance abuse. It is notable that the AFCC cautioned that evaluators not educated in specialized areas refrain from evaluating such issues.

Guidelines for Psychiatry

The American Academy of Child and Adolescent Psychiatry (AACAP) also developed guidelines for child custody evaluation.[24] These included recommendations about best practices for interviewing children and clear prohibitions against dual relationships. This very practical guide called for relevant information about court appearances, testifying, and what types of materials the evaluator should review, specifically admonishing evaluators not to listen to recordings taken without permission.[25] The AACAP also recommended that evaluators include interviews with children, parent–child observations, and collateral contacts with stepparents, caregivers, and the like.[26]

Social Work Guidelines

Luftman et al. developed clinical guidelines for custody evaluations for social workers that are grounded in an understanding of the dynamics of divorce. These researchers focused on some of the essential issues before the court: the quality of the parent–child relationship, parenting styles, social functioning, and domestic violence.[27] Significantly, these authors highlighted the risk to children in homes in which there is domestic violence and post-separation risks for mothers and advocated that contact between the parents in such cases should be minimized. This is an important safety mechanism. Their emphasis on trauma, safety, and the potential for batterers to be manipulative provides a clinical framework for custody evaluations that is worth emulating. The National Association of Social Work's Ethical Principles and Standards also provides robust practice guidelines as it reiterates practitioners' ethical obligations and responsibility to practice in an unbiased, culturally competent manner.[28]

Recent Guidelines for Custody Evaluators

The APA (2010) recently revised its guidelines for custody evaluations, expanding on many of the basic requirements of informed consent and avoidance of multiple relationships, conflicts of interest to maintain neutrality, and the need for culturally competent investigations.[29] The revised guidelines articulated a more nuanced understanding of the context in which custody evaluations take place, distinguishing them from clinical practice and evaluations in child welfare proceedings.[30] The guidelines stressed the importance of understanding the context of the evaluations, in which mental health professionals are not simply required to provide personality assessments but to address the strengths and weaknesses of the parties' parenting abilities.[31] The APA concluded that best practices for the collection of data included testing, clinical interviews, observations, and interviews with health care and child care providers and extended family.[32] Finally, the APA concurred with its earlier standards advising that custody evaluator's recommendations should be based on the evaluators' assessment of the children's best interests.[33]

Ackerman and Pritzl conducted a poll of 213 psychologists in which they included questions about the demographics of the participants. Their study concluded that the clear majority of psychologists who performed custody evaluations—95%—were self-trained, having no formal graduate coursework in forensic psychology and relying instead on workshops and seminars.[34] Ninety-five percent of these custody evaluators were male.[35] These researchers concurred with Bow and Quinnell's earlier conclusions that time spent on interviewing, reviewing documentation, and writing reports had increased significantly. Conversely, the practice of testing children and adults had become more widespread. Furthermore, the use of tests such as the Ackerman-Schoendorf Scales for Parent Evaluation (ASPECT), the Parent–Child Relationship Inventory (PCRI), Parent Awareness Skills Survey (PASS), and the Bricklin Scales had increased, although there were issues raised about their admissibility in court.[36] Finally, Ackerman and Pritzl found that a surprising number of the evaluators interviewed—49.5%—had had at least one licensing board complaint lodged against them, 9% had had state ethics complaints, and 19% had had malpractice claims filed against them.[37]

The APA's revised guidelines called for self-awareness on the part of evaluators to avoid bias; an understanding of the context of the forensic evaluation, in which litigants are under heightened stress; and the need to have culturally informed, nondiscriminatory practices for gathering data.[38] Because of the subjectivity of custody determinations and the disparate training and professional backgrounds of evaluators, parents with significant financial means may even retain other evaluators to critique the original report when displeased with the results.[39] Finally, the APA (2010) recommendations continued to call for evaluators to be neutral and culturally aware. Despite this recommendation, Chiu has indicated that there is a lack of research on the impact of culture and ethnicity in custody evaluations and argued that this lack could result in biased custody reports.[40] This is a significant concern and warrants more research on the disparate impact such testing and evaluations may have on immigrants, people of color, or families from diverse socioeconomic backgrounds.

Domestic Violence and Custody Evaluators

Oberlander noted the difficulties in conducting forensic evaluations in custody litigation when there are competing allegations of abuse, mental illness, parental alienation, and substance abuse, particularly when both parents are trying to present themselves in the best possible light.[41] Not every custody evaluator has experience and the appropriate educational background to assess and identify domestic violence and child maltreatment, or even to determine whether the mental health problems seen are the result of such abuse. The significance of this cannot be overemphasized as this translates into situations in which families struggle alone with addiction, abuse, and related mental health concerns, without proper services, and custody evaluators may recommend custody to a parent who is harmful to the child.

Judicial Guidelines for Custody and Domestic Violence

The National Council of Juvenile and Family Court Judges (NCJFC 2006) developed judicial guidelines that displayed a profound understanding of domestic violence and articulated the need to determine the safety risks of domestic violence on parenting and children. The authors utilized a broader definition of domestic violence, describing it as a complex "pattern of assaultive and coercive behaviors that operate at a variety of levels—physical, psychological, emotional, financial and/or sexual—that perpetrators use against their intimate partners."[42] The guide further questioned the need for psychological testing, recommending that judges be aware of the qualifications of the evaluators and pointing out that there were no validated psychological tests that can directly assess parenting capabilities.[43]

Finally, the NCJFC acknowledged that evaluating the existence of and risks associated with domestic violence required specialized skills and training and that many practitioners did not have such background.[44] It is not uncommon to have custody evaluators provide curriculum vitae in which they have documented postgraduate seminars in domestic violence. However, the NCJFC indicated that basic training in domestic violence is not enough to qualify the evaluator as an expert or even to assure that they have basic competence in this area.[45] To that end, they advised judges to actively question the evaluators' qualifications. Finally, the NCJFC stressed the importance of cultural competence in custody evaluations, including linguistic capabilities when parents are not fluent in English.[46] Similarly, the guide noted that certain issues are "red flags" for custody evaluators. Such warning signs include the presence of domestic violence, substance abuse, mental illness, symptoms of posttraumatic stress disorder (PTSD), and the estrangement of children.[47] The implications of such factors are complex and interrelated: for example, substance abuse by the perpetrator may increase violence in the home, or, conversely, being abused may cause battered women to self-medicate. Thus, it is essential that custody evaluators identify these issues while also understanding their implications.

In the context of custody evaluations, it is helpful to the courts if the custody evaluator has training and experience in identifying risks, and it is problematic for judges when such evaluators begin with assumptions that there are minimal levels of abuse that are not safety risks. Zorza noted that assessment of domestic violence requires specialized knowledge so that evaluators can recognize all the nonphysical manifestations of abuse, including social isolation, intimidation, and financial and sexual abuse.[48] These are predictors of future dangerousness and risks that should not be ignored.

The AFCC (2016) also issued guidelines on intimate partner violence as a supplement to its Model Standards of Practice for Child Custody Evaluations.[49] The Intimate Partner Violence Supplement appears to emphasize the need for safety but also posits that there are many contexts for abuse during separation, including violence caused by poor impulse control, conflict management skills, or a reaction to the separation or divorce.[50]

Evaluating Domestic Violence

Life in a household where there is a history of domestic violence is dangerous, and these risks should never be minimized. Davis et al. argued that evaluators should consider children to be at greater risk of harm when their protective parent has separated from the abuser and the children continue to see him without her protection.[51] These researchers reviewed sixty-seven custody case files of custody or visitation litigation from 1997 to 2007.[52] In these cases, evaluators had concluded that the allegations of domestic violence were accurate in 53% of the cases when they could review documentary evidence, such as medical or court records. However, 21% of the evaluators failed to find that there was a history of domestic violence, even when there was documented evidence.[53] When evaluators observed instances of the child's estrangement from one parent, as in child abuse or domestic violence, in 73% of these cases the evaluators attributed this to parental alienation.[54] Davis et al. went further, finding that in one-fourth of the cases where the parents had not made claims of parental alienation, the evaluators concluded that this was a problem.[55]

In comparison, Haselschwerdt et al. polled a small group of twenty-three custody evaluators who had completed at least one forensic evaluation in the past ten years.[56] The participants ranged in age from forty-one to seventy-one years and were composed of fourteen psychologists, four social workers, one psychiatrist, two attorneys, and two counselors of unknown backgrounds. Most of the participants in the research had not been required to have completed training on domestic violence, although a majority reported having some education in this area. The researchers divided the evaluators into those who they termed "feminist evaluators" and family violence evaluators. The family violence evaluators were predominantly male, with a mean age of fifty-seven years, and had virtually no formal training in domestic violence. The authors found that all of those described as feminist evaluators believed that domestic violence could not be separated from the abusers' ability to parent, but because of their belief in categories of abusive behavior would recommend day-time visits.[57]

Araji conducted a small study in Alaska of thirty-four victims of domestic violence who had been involved in custody litigation.[58] Given the small size of her sample population, she also compared her findings to several others, including the Arizona Coalition Against Domestic Violence and the Battered Mothers' Testimony Project.[59] Her findings concurred with the other research, which indicated that joint and sole legal custody was awarded even when the perpetrators abused drugs or alcohol or were abusive in the presence of the children. Many battered women reported that evaluators used parental alienation theory against them. Significantly, custody evaluators appeared to lack training in domestic violence and displayed bias in favor of perpetrators, often holding battered women responsible for their abuse.[60]

Finally, Stahl and Martin noted the lack of formal training in forensic evaluations while concluding that most evaluators did not address the critical issue of parent–child attachment.[61] It is of concern that these researchers found that most evaluators obtained forensic training from the same organization and that many such trainings have not provided sufficient information on trauma, intimate partner violence, and attachment.

The national study of custody evaluators' training, education, and underlying beliefs about women and domestic violence by Saunders et al. is instructive.[62] The respondents in this research included judges, custody evaluators, private attorneys, and domestic violence program workers. These researchers sought to determine the respondents' level of knowledge of domestic violence, post-separation risks, and assessments of dangerousness. Saunders et al. also measured beliefs about domestic violence survivors, including whether the evaluators believed that women made false allegations or alienated their children. These researchers further analyzed whether their subjects believed that domestic violence survivors' resistance to co-parenting was harmful to children and, finally, whether domestic violence was relevant to custody and visitation decisions.[63]

The researchers concluded that 90% of each professional group had acquired some training on the impact of domestic violence on children, and, except for private attorneys, 90% of these same professionals had acquired information regarding the prevalence and causes of domestic violence. However, Saunders et al. found that the average age of most custody evaluators ranged from fifty to sixty years, indicating that they received their professional education well before domestic violence was consistently part of the graduate mental health curriculum. In comparison, a smaller group of judges, custody evaluators, and private attorneys had knowledge of the post-separation risks of violence, screening, and assessments of dangerousness.[64] There is a significant need for a graduate curriculum in domestic violence and child maltreatment, which will be discussed in Chapter 11.

The post-separation risk to battered women and children has been well documented in the literature, including the Canadian Violence Against Women Survey, which found that 19% of women were physically assaulted following separation.[65] A smaller study by Morrison of continued contact with children and abusive fathers in Scotland found that both children and the mothers remained at risk following separation.[66] Both Ellis and Saunders et al. have discussed the problems and risks of post-separation abuse.[67]

Saunders et al. also noted that judges and private attorneys were less likely to report that their custody cases included allegations of domestic violence allegations.[68] Custody evaluators had the highest rate of believing that mothers made false allegations of domestic violence (22%) followed by 13–16% of judges and private attorneys, as compared to 7–8% of legal aid attorneys and domestic violence workers. These authors reported that 29–36% of the judges, evaluators, and private attorneys believed that abuse victims alienated the other parent from their children, compared to 19–20% of legal aid attorneys and domestic violence workers. In fact, 70–76% of domestic violence workers and legal aid attorneys believed that it was batterers who alienated the children from the other parent, as compared to only 58% of private attorneys and 49–51% of judges and evaluators.[69]

In response to a vignette of a domestic violence incident, custody evaluators and private attorneys were most likely to believe that these mothers exaggerated domestic violence, a finding that has much to do with their relative lack of understanding of current and postjudgment risks. Finally, Saunders et al. found that custody evaluators, judges, and private attorneys were the least likely to believe that battered women should have sole custody and were the most likely to believe that fathers should have sole legal and physical custody.

The research by Bow and Boxer on custody evaluators also confirmed the lack of graduate-level education in domestic violence found in the research of Saunders et al. Bow and Boxer's sent a questionnaire to those psychologists, most of whom had doctorates, who conducted custody evaluations. The respondents indicated that 68.2% had not taken any graduate courses in domestic violence and that their sole method of training consisted of seminars and articles.[70] Some of these respondents indicated that they taught such seminars.

These findings are similar to the research of Saunders et al. in that graduate course work in domestic violence did not exist when most of the evaluators received their advanced degrees.[71] Furthermore, only 29% of the respondents in Bow and Boxer's study utilized any risk measurements for screening of domestic violence, and, of these respondents, the majority developed these instruments themselves.[72] Although the researchers concluded that these psychologists considered domestic violence in their evaluations, their difficulty in gauging the safety of the children brings this conclusion into question. Furthermore, even now, many graduate programs in psychology and psychiatry offer little in the way of training on domestic violence, and many do not address the differing definitions and controversies surrounding custody, divorce, gender, and domestic violence.

Are Custody Evaluations Accurate?

The primary question regarding custody evaluators is not simply whether these mental health evaluators have the requisite clinical skills to make custody determinations but also whether they may have biases that interfere with their clinical judgment. Tippins and Wittman question whether custody evaluators can control for their own biases, which may be subtle but pervasive.[73] These authors also questioned the accuracy of the reporting of the evaluations.

In my practice, while most judges allow litigants to read these reports in their attorneys' offices, they are not allowed to have a copy, which would allow them to study the report in more detail. Clients typically are overwhelmed when they first read the report and need time to absorb information that is highly personal, frequently traumatic, and sometimes contains widespread factual inaccuracies. When parents are prohibited from reading the actual report, it is difficult for them to assist their attorneys in rebutting reports when there may be factual errors or discernable biases.

Flawed as family court may be, there are certain due process protections, both procedural and substantive, that are part of all court proceedings. Litigants are permitted to have written notice of the charges against them. In the context of a family court proceeding, this means that they will receive a copy of the petitions. A transcript of the proceedings will ensure that there is a record of what has transpired. Statements from other persons can be verified by cross-examination; however, it is difficult to contest the data, analysis, and recommendations in custody evaluations when litigants have very restricted access to these reports and underlying notes. Such problems with transparency and due process can make it difficult to refute any biases and possible factual errors embedded in these reports.

Custody evaluators routinely raise issues of parental alienation theory, which creates an environment in which battered women's allegations are often discounted or minimized. Parental alienation, as discussed in more depth in Chapter 4, is a gender-biased theory, whether described as a syndrome or disorder, in which many mental health professionals primarily refer to women as the source of false allegations. It is also important that the mental health and legal professionals develop ways to avoid the incipient gender, class, cultural, and racial biases that have permeated the family courts.

The Role of Attachment

To promote the children's best interests, custody evaluations should provide to the court information about primary attachments. It should be expected that children have intense emotions about their parental relationships, and particularly concerning their primary caretaker. Bowlby, the seminal researcher on children's attachment with their primary caretaker, described this relationship as central to children's long-term development and well-being.[74] Bowlby's research speaks of one parental figure being the primary attachment figure. This does not preclude children from having close relationships with other important persons in their lives.[75] However, interference with the relationship with their primary attachment figure in terms of forced separations may activate children's desperate need to obtain physical closeness—seen as clingy behavior—with their attachment figure. Children under one year of age may experience distress when their primary attachment figure leaves or be fearful of strangers.[76] In my practice, I have observed that children as old as five or six may be reluctant to separate from their primary caretaker overnight and may have very intense anxiety about such schedules.

Bryne et al. argued that attachment as discussed in the courtroom means something entirely different from these theories of attachment.[77] Assessing children's development and attachment takes a significant level of clinical expertise and experience. However, the current measurements of attachment have not been validated for use with children of divorce, and there is a paucity of research on custody evaluations and attachment.[78]

Edleson and Williams observed that children have complex relationships with fathers who have been physically abusive.[79] Peled found that boys had more difficulty than girls in reconciling these two aspects of their father: the violent abusive father and the good loving father.[80] This is something that I have observed in my practice as well; boys are frequently confused and struggle to come to terms with their fathers' abuse. Mental health professionals must have considerable clinical training in the dynamics of domestic violence and parenting to understand the ambivalence of children in such custody disputes.

The first and foremost question must not be whether the children love their fathers—most children love their parents—but how their parent's abuse impacted their caregiver and their lives. For custody evaluators, the question that must be addressed is whether, by imposing extensive overnight schedules with young children, even without the high-risk factors of domestic violence, mental illness, and substance abuse, the courts may be interfering with the children's normal attachment and development. McIntosh noted the vulnerability of infants and toddlers to overnight visitation because of their fast-paced physical, cognitive, language, social, and emotional development coinciding with their critical formation of attachments.[81]

We are now in uncharted territory—in which children are spending extensive time, including overnights at young ages, going back and forth between two homes—without sufficient research to support this practice. Little is known about the outcome of these legal practices. The nebulousness of the best interests standard may have contributed to this problem. Custody evaluators have struggled to understand attachment and to find ways to measure it through testing and parent–child observations and may not always understand what they were observing.

These evaluations become more complex when the relationships between children and their primary caretaker may have been damaged by exposure to abusive behavior or other problems that existed prior to the separation. For example, as discussed previously, Bancroft et al. described how batterers are not just physically abusive but also frequently denigrate mothers to their children, thereby undermining their parental role and their children's attachment.[82] In some instances, mental health and substance abuse problems exacerbated by the abuse may impact the parent–child attachment.

Many of my clients with children aged 5–7 years have reported that they return from visits teary and clingy, insisting on immediate hugs and their mothers' undivided attention even when there is no history of abuse. It is essential that evaluators observe behavior and, particularly, the interaction between parents and children, but assessments of emotional bonds and attachments require much more. The ability to identify attachment depends on the education, training, and clinical expertise of the evaluator.

Interviewing Children

There is no clear consensus about the age at which children should be interviewed. The AACAP established parameters regarding interviews of children for psychiatrists who conduct child custody evaluations. These parameters indicated that children as young as three years of age can be interviewed and noted that some children can be interviewed alone if they are able to easily separate from their parent.[83] Herman et al. also noted the importance of interviewing children in a child-friendly atmosphere, engaging in developmentally appropriate activities, and that the use of a doll house could be helpful in eliciting information about the family. Despite this, it is important for the evaluators to remember that some children are more comfortable than others about leaving their attachment figure, and a child's reluctance or anxiety should not be exacerbated by the evaluation process. Many custody evaluators have concluded that children should be five years of age or older to be interviewed, and, in practice, many evaluators do not directly interview very young children. However, this rule should be applied with flexibility because some preschool children may be extremely verbal.

Powell and Lancaster, in their review of the literature, indicated that many mental health professionals do not have expertise in interviewing children. Furthermore, the literature on interviewing children in custody evaluations typically discusses what information must be obtained, rather than how to interview children.[84] Powell and Lancaster stressed the importance of establishing comfort and a rapport with children during the process that includes a nonjudgmental, welcoming, and child-friendly atmosphere.[85] They noted that the evaluator should use open-ended questions to address children's concrete concerns about their living arrangements and continued relationship with their parents.[86]

Evaluators have not resolved the issue of when and how to interview children who have witnessed abuse or were themselves the target of such behavior. Pepiton et al. noted the reluctance many custody evaluators have about interviewing children regarding allegations of intimate partner violence.[87] In my practice, I have noted that many custody evaluators never asked the children about violence in their homes. Children are highly familiar with their family life, and, while their perceptions are linked to their level of development, their observations can provide a window into the dynamics of power and control that frequently permeate their households. Nonetheless, interviewing a child should take into consideration the child's age and language development. Younger children will be more comfortable in a child-friendly atmosphere, with age-appropriate activities available. Very young children may demonstrate anxiety and anger in their play, which should be discussed in the reports, even while there may be different theories on the underlying reasons for such behavior. Asking children to explain drawings of their families can tell us a lot about the history of family conflicts and abuse. It is also necessary to interview caretakers and teachers to determine how the child is functioning outside of the forensic examination.

Furthermore, children are very aware of the problems in their homes. I have observed mothers carefully explain to their children why they will be entering a battered women's shelter. It is a difficult position for battered mothers who do not want to speak badly about their children's father, and one that many of my clients have faced with sensitivity and discretion. However, several of these children immediately responded by acknowledging their awareness of the domestic violence, making comments such as: "Oh, because Daddy hits." These same children were not asked later by the custody evaluators about their parents' separation or their fathers' abuse, although this could have elicited information that would be invaluable for judges in determining the best interests of the child. Custody evaluators can be visibly uncomfortable with the subject of family violence or may minimize the seriousness of such allegations, thus giving children the message that such problems should not be discussed.

Faller, one of the seminal writers on sexual abuse of children, has addressed the issues of the validity of the children's memories of such behavior, finding that children and adults have variations in their ability to recall.[88] Some researchers have indicated that children with higher verbal intelligence have better memory recall and are less suggestible than those with lower verbal intelligence scores.[89] Bruck and Melnyk did not support this concept, finding that, except for children with intellectual delays, they could find no evidence to indicate that some children were more suggestible.[90] Faller noted that memory and suggestibility vary within each person, making it difficult to come to blanket statements about children and their ability to recall their allegations.[91] However, she also noted that having children repeat their memories multiple times may cause them to develop a script of their memory in which the supporting details become less vivid while the overall picture remains.[92] Evaluators should be aware of the limitations and weaknesses in many earlier investigations and their impact on the children's memory. The issues about interviewing children who may have been sexually abused and their symptomatology have been addressed in Chapter 4.

Pepiton et al. indicated that in custody evaluations when there have been allegations of sexual abuse, it is particularly important that the professionals be qualified to investigate these reports, warning that it is an ethical violation to render an opinion about the veracity of abuse allegations without such training. While this recommendation should be obvious to most evaluators, the extent of the distortions and myths that surround the subject of sexual abuse in the family courts is a significant concern.

Separate and apart from the issue of children being directly abused, concerns remain about how custody evaluators respond to children who may have been exposed to domestic violence. Pepiton et al. noted that many evaluators simply assumed that when children did not volunteer information about abuse that these allegations were false.[93] These researchers noted the importance of including behavioral observations—particularly observations of parent–child interactions—in their final report and expressed concern that many evaluators did not spend sufficient time observing such interactions.[94] These authors recommended that evaluators should provide structured and unstructured activities for children so they have more opportunities to observe the parent–child relationship.[95] However, given that families are being observed during custody evaluations, there should be some understanding of the constraints and tensions that prevent these observations from being truly spontaneous. Parents are typically on their best behavior during these interviews and present their story in a manner that they hope will win the evaluator's approval. Some parents will lie or minimize the impact of their substance abuse or violence.

Oberlander noted the problems associated with involving children in custody litigation.[96] Children's involvement may be limited to meetings with their own attorneys. However, when forensic evaluations are ordered, children participate in forensic interviews and observations and may even be interviewed by judges in closed *in camera proceedings*. These procedures are intrusive for all family members but may be difficult for vulnerable children. Evaluators have reported that the wishes of the children significantly influence their recommendations regarding custody. However, children may be subject to pressure from one parent or another. It is important to have children express in language that is age-appropriate the reasons behind their choices when they express a wish to live with one parent or the other. Follow-up questions about what their lives would then be like as a result can help determine if they are being influenced. It is also important to assess the children's developmental stages and language abilities. In one instance in my practice, a young child spontaneously informed the custody evaluator that visits with his dad were "great," and he wanted overnights. When asked why he had said this, he replied that his father told him to do so.

Stark also warns that judges, evaluators, and attorneys are hampered by a limited understanding of the impact of domestic violence on children and victims, noting the problems associated with a more limited definition of intimate partner violence.[97] Stark noted that the spectrum of domestic violence goes beyond physical and emotional abuse. By way of example in my practice, even when a mother described the sexual and economic abuse that she endured, the evaluator recommended unsupervised visitation for a very young child with special needs, finding the abuse to be merely "situational."

In my practice, I have also observed a custody evaluator, who admitted not being qualified to assess sexual abuse allegations, proceed to discount a mother's allegations because he believed that the timing of the report was suspect. In this case, the mother filed for divorce after reporting the allegations to the child's pediatrician. The evaluator's conclusion disregarded the body of research which indicates that false allegations are rare and relied instead on Gardner's Sexual Abuse and Related Stressors (SAR-S) scale.[98] This instrument, made popular by Gardiner in his writings about sexual abuse, has been repeatedly debunked in the research.[99] The evaluator also used the child's attachment to her sexually abusive father as evidence that the child had not been abused. However, evaluators who understand the dynamics of sexual abuse will also realize that children in such families frequently have an emotional bond to their abusive parents.[100] This case highlights the need for evaluators to possess the highest level of understanding of that research.

Psychological Testing and Custody Evaluations

The use of psychological testing in custody evaluations is by far the most bewildering aspect of the process for attorneys and clients, and many researchers have commented on this practice. Ackerman and Ackerman noted that as the field of custody evaluations progressed, several psychological tests were developed, including ASPECT, the Bricklin Perceptual Scales (BPS), and the Custody Quotient, that were considered experimental.[101] These researchers also noted that these tests were designed to be used with clinical populations and not with families experiencing custody conflicts. Although these authors found that custody evaluators considered many factors in making their custody recommendations—not simply test results—this does not mean that the test results of custody evaluations should be accepted without question. Nor should we assume that they are accurate measurements of parenting or attachment. Much of what has been discussed in the literature seems to indicate that many competent mental health professionals can provide assessments without the use of psychological testing. Indeed, psychiatrists and social workers do not use tests at all.

Historically, the emphasis on obtaining data from many sources, including the use of psychological testing, was encouraged by the APA guidelines to prevent evaluator bias, although they cautioned against inappropriately interpreting assessment data in custody disputes.[102] Testing was expected to provide an additional source of data that would provide neutral, unbiased information for the court. Research has indicated that the overall use of psychological tests in forensic evaluations is rising.[103] Quinnell and Bow found that while testing of adults has increased in custody evaluations, testing of children is done more selectively and typically only when there are specific developmental concerns.[104] In their review of the research, they reported that the Minnesota Multiphase Personality Inventory (MMPI), the Rorschach, and Thematic Apperception Test (TAT) were the most commonly used tests in custody evaluations with adults. In a study of the testing practices of custody evaluators, 52% of whom were males between the ages of 32 to 71 years, with an average of 13.6 years of practice in child custody, the evaluators were found to test approximately 90% of the adults and 60% of the children. This represents a significant reduction in testing of children as noted in Ackerman and Ackerman's prior research.[105]

Emery et al. criticized many of the forensic assessment instruments, particularly those used for children. These researchers analyzed the BPS, in which children are presented with a stylus and rating cards and are asked to rate their parents on thirty-two activities. Those parents who receive the most positive ratings were considered the "parent of choice" under the premise that the speed of the test ensures that children give their "unconscious choice."[106] These researchers also noted that the Perception of Relationships Test (PORT), which scores children's drawings, has also been widely criticized as having unclear test administration and scoring guidelines.

In contrast, Ackerman and Ackerman's early research on custody evaluations noted that the MMPI and modification (MMPI-2) were the most frequently administered personality tests with adults.[107] Erickson questioned the validity of the MMPI on battered women because of the possibility that the responses measured in this test could more accurately be attributed to exposure to domestic violence and the heighten stress experienced.[108] This raises questions as to whether the test truly measures the respondent's reactions to abuse, the level of stress experienced, or identifies actual personality traits or psychopathology.[109] She noted the growing recognition of the impact of trauma, PTSD, and complex PTSD, in connection to domestic violence. In my practice, I have observed that those evaluations that utilize tests such as the MMPI-2 do not address trauma, its impact, or whether clients are struggling with PTSD, even if there were allegations of abuse. Given the general acceptance of the impact of trauma in the APA's *Diagnostic and Statistical Manual of Mental Disorders* (DSM-5), it is significant that most custody evaluations do not assess the extent of traumatic exposure in children and related symptomatology.

Some researchers have questioned the use of the Millon Clinical Multiaxial Inventory III (MCMI-3), the most recent form of this personality measure, noting that its use of double negatives, among other issues, could be confusing.[110] Concerns have also been raised that the MCMI-III exaggerates psychopathology.[111] Bow et al. were also concerned to find that many evaluators used computer-generated reports to interpret their data. The percentage of evaluators using such programs to interpret the MMPI-2 was significant—61%—and an additional 79% of the evaluators utilized these programs to interpret the MCMI-III.[112] They observed that the use of computer-generated interpretative reports for the MCMI-III could result in overdiagnosing psychopathology because of evaluators' poor understanding of the cutoffs used to determine areas of concern.[113] Recently, to address these concerns, a newer form of the computer-generated interpretative report for the MMPI-2 RF has been developed. However, there continue to be questions as to whether the psychologists who performed the testing accurately interpreted the data. Yeamans also criticized the use of computer-generated reporting of personality tests and noted that the scoring may be done by a computer scoring service through the Internet, citing the need for quality control.[114] Khan et al. found that custody evaluators may also interpret the test themselves by purchasing a computer program without truly understanding the underlying formulas that produce the computer-generated results.[115]

Ackerman and Ackerman observed that such tests were intended for use in the clinical population and had not been validated for use with parents during custody litigation. Notably, the Academy of Child and Adolescent Psychiatry's Practice Parameters advised against the use of MMPI, the TAT, and the

Rorschach because these were not designed for use in custody evaluations, thus raising questions about their validity.[116]

Some parents are more comfortable than others in testing situations, and some are more knowledgeable test-takers than others. I represented a client who had recently left an abusive situation but was sufficiently savvy to note that the test she took was assessing for paranoia. Thus, while she was legitimately concerned that her abuser was stalking her, she carefully framed her answers in such a way that she would not receive such a diagnosis. Tests results can be manipulated, but evaluators should understand the legitimacy of a battered woman's concerns for her safety.

Nor is such testing appropriate in cases of domestic violence. In 1993, in a review of the research, Khan et al. found that scoring for battered women in transition indicated a potential to abuse drugs or alcohol and to have low ego strengths.[117] These results may have led some researchers to believe that battered women have a propensity for greater psychopathology. Significantly, these researchers also observed that their sample population had higher levels on the paranoia scale, noting that the women's fearfulness and suspicions could be appropriate reactions to abuse.[118] Erickson also concurred with this understanding of battered women's heightened anxiety in response to being terrorized.

These factors should be seen in the context of a clinical assessment, in which testing is simply one part of the whole, to determine whether a traumatized parent may be self-medicating with alcohol and may require counseling, support, and sometimes medication. Misuse of alcohol, while not a good thing, is not the same as an addiction. It is also not clear whether the earlier tests or more recent modifications adequately take into consideration responses to trauma and stress. Furthermore, it is difficult to determine on the face of the test results whether the evaluators have training and experience in trauma and abuse and whether their understanding of these factors would impact their recommendations. It should be noted that there is disagreement among psychologists as to whether the responses of elevated defensiveness frequently seen in the MMPI-2 can alternatively be ascribed as a response to the stress of custody litigation or other potentially traumatic factors.[119]

Medoff cautions against misinterpretation of the MMPI-2 results, noting that statistically elevated scores in one area are not necessarily of clinical significance and may not be indicative of psychopathology.[120] However, misinterpretation of the test results can result in the overdiagnosis of parents under extreme stress.[121] It should be noted that, in the context of custody litigation, evaluations will be read by lawyers and judges who have no clinical training in psychology and can easily draw erroneous conclusions about the test results.

Roseby stressed a clinical and scientific approach to custody evaluations. She also noted that there are difficulties in personality testing because some psychologists do not have the requisite skills to correctly interpret the data.[122] She cautioned against the use of computer-generated interpretations of the data and indicated that testing must be viewed considering all other data available, including information collected from collateral contacts, parent–child observations, and interviews. This researcher noted that without sufficient understanding of the test results divorcing parents may be held to a higher standard of mental health than those from intact families and that parents' difficulties may not interfere with their parenting.

Roseby recommended a further step—having a meeting at the end of the evaluation in which clients can review the results with their attorney and the evaluator—rather than in a courtroom where the mutual tensions between the parties would only increase with such exposure. While this is not an opportunity to argue for a different evaluation result, clients are frequently anxious and overwhelmed, and the presence of their attorney might make this a more positive situation. It is significant that in my many years of representing battered women in custody cases, this option was never made available in any of my cases. Finally, this researcher observed that evidence of mental health problems, such as those identified in the psychological tests, is not a measure of parenting capacities.

Heinze and Grisso studied the use of several instruments that have been specifically used in custody evaluations to measure parenting capabilities.[123] They studied the ASPECT, which attempts to quantify the results of psychological testing, interviews and scoring of observations of parent and child, to determine custody. These results were found to be consistent with the judges' determinations of custody, although the results of these instruments were not shared with judges. However, this research was based on married, white, well-educated parents and may not measure the effectiveness of this instrument with other races and socioeconomic classes. Furthermore, the researchers noted that some parents are manipulative and present themselves in a falsely positive light. This finding is of concern because ASPECT includes the evaluators' observations, and batterers are extraordinarily manipulative and can be extremely charming. Consider a traumatized battered woman, disassociating while discussing the abuse, presenting with a flat affect, depressed, and suffering from the effects of trauma. What would be the evaluators' response?

Schleuderer and Campagna's research on substance abuse and custody evaluations indicated that while there are blood tests to determine the physical presence of uncontrolled substances, these are not reliable measurements because these substances are excreted at different rates depending on the individual's health, amount ingested, and the normal variability of physiology. These researchers also found that psychological tests did not reliably screen for substance abuse and noted that the MacAndrews Alcoholism Scale-Revised (MAC-R) Index on the MMPI-2 only detected the potential for addiction, not the level of current usage.[124]

Turning to parents with physical disabilities, the research by Breeden et al. is instructive, indicating that the clear majority of psychologists surveyed did not seek out consultation, supervision, or specialized knowledge when conducting custody evaluations with parents with physical disabilities.[125]

Legal Standards of Admissibility

The original test to determine the reliability of scientific evidence and its admissibility in federal courts was established in *Frye v. United States*.[126] In *Frye*, the court noted the need for expert witnesses under the following circumstances:

> The rule is that the opinions of experts or skilled witnesses are admissible in evidence in those cases in which the matter of inquiry is such that inexperienced persons are unlikely to prove capable of forming a correct judgment upon it, for the reason that the subject-matter so far partakes of a science, art, trade as to require a previous habit or experience or study in it, in order to acquire a knowledge of it.[127]

After setting out the need for expert opinions, the court turned to the question of when scientific opinions were sound enough to be admissible evidence. Noting the development of new theories and technology, the court in *Frye* wrestled with the question of "[j]ust when a scientific principle or discovery crosses the line between the experimental and demonstrable."[128] To avoid considering testimony that lacked scientific validity and that might be experimental in nature, the *Frye* decision established a *bright line standard* for determining the admissibility of expert testimony, requiring that the underlying theories upon which the opinions were based must have gained "general acceptance" in the particular field of inquiry.[129] Most state courts have come to accept this standard.

   Frye was overruled in the federal courts in the US Supreme Court case of *Daubert v. Merrell Dow Pharmaceuticals, Inc.*, in response to the passage of the Federal Rules of Evidence.[130] The Court held that the rule established in *Frye*, requiring that the proffered testimony be based upon general acceptance, was overruled by Section 702 of the Federal Rules of Evidence, which called for a more flexible view of scientific expert opinion.[131] In *Daubert*, the Court weighed the importance of expert testimony and articulated a new "reliability approach" to expert evidence that called for the underlying scientific theories to be both reliable and relevant. Reviewing the Federal Rules of Evidence in their entirety, the Court in *Daubert* found that the trial courts were gatekeepers, and, as such, the court must determine the reliability and relevance of the proffered evidence. The Court found that to be reliable, scientific knowledge must have appropriate validation that supports the scientist's conclusions. The trial courts were also required to determine the relevancy of the proffered testimony; that is, whether the proffered testimony was sufficiently tied to the facts of the case. The Court clarified this issue, finding that there needed to be a sufficient "fit" or relevance between the facts and the opinion.[132]

The Court set forth factors that may be considered to determine the admissibility of the proffered evidence. These include whether the theory or technique has been empirically tested and subjected to peer review and publication, the error rate of the particular theory, the existence and maintenance of standards controlling the technique's operation, and whether there has been widespread acceptance within the relevant scientific community.[133] This ruling was expanded further on remand, as the Ninth Circuit of the Federal Court of Appeals also found that, to qualify as an expert without having published, this testimony must be based on some other objective evidence that could demonstrate that their testimony was based on scientifically valid principles.[134] In 1999, the Supreme Court in *Kumho Tire Co. v. Carmichael* expanded the use of this test to engineers providing technical information to the court.[135]

The Supreme Court also clarified that trial judges have considerable discretion when considering the admission of expert testimony. Appellate courts are required to give credence to the trial judges' determinations on the admissibility of expert testimony and will only overrule if the trial courts failed to consider other relevant theories before admitting such testimony. *General Electric Co. v. Joiner.*[136] Owen noted that the use of this standard of review indicated that appellate courts will generally give deference to the trial court's findings regarding admissibility of proffered testimony, but, even when judges had reviewed and accepted the experts' methodology, they were still not precluded from rejecting the expert's conclusions.[137]

In 2011, the Federal Rules were amended to clarify the standard and procedures to be used in evaluating the relevance and reliability of the proposed expert testimony by embodying the ruling of *Daubert,* supra, and its progeny.[138] However, several states continue to adhere to the *Frye* standard in determining the admissibility of expert opinions, including California, Illinois, Maryland, New Jersey, New York, Pennsylvania, and Washington.

In New York, in *People v. Wernick,* the Court of Appeals upheld the continued use of the "general acceptance" of *Frye.*[139] However, the New York Second Department, in 2000, held that the defendant was entitled to summary judgment as a matter of law, finding that the plaintiff had failed to demonstrate its expert had "the requisite skill, training, education, knowledge, or experience to render the opinion." *Houck v. Simoes; Hofmann v. Toys "R" Us, NY Ltd.*[140] The appellate courts in New York have not necessarily abandoned the *Frye* standard; however, the concept of judicial discretion dictates that the trial judge should hold an inquiry to first establish the bona fides of the expert witness. Thus, even under *Frye,* to prevent unscientific or misleading expert testimony, the trial court should still determine how much weight to give the experts' testimony.

The role of the judge as gatekeeper over expert testimony has expanded, requiring much more of the trial judge.[141] While some states continue to adhere to *Frye*, increased flexibility to determine whether the opinion offered meets certain evidentiary criteria, to avoid testimony that has no basis in science, is important. Increasingly, the trial courts rely on motions, or preferably hearings, in which witnesses can be cross-examined and opposing views can be presented. In jury trials, the trial judge can give careful instructions regarding the burden of proof to assist the jurors in determining how much weight to give the expert testimony. These are essential components to ensure that testimony and reports are sufficiently reliable and relevant.[142]

Allegations of parental alienation are made every day in the family courts and are used primarily against women. Katz indicated correctly that such claims are typically made to draw attention away from the dangerous behavior—such as abuse or child maltreatment—of the parent making the claims of parental alienation.[143] In my practice, I have observed that parental alienation charges are now being used even when my clients have not made any claims of abuse. These charges are simply part of the repertoire of attorneys representing fathers when mothers object to extended overnights with very young children or complain of children returning from visits late, tired, and without their homework. Given that in many states the "friendly parent" doctrine requires the custodial parent to encourage the relationship with the other parent, claims of any interference with the father's relationship, for whatever reason, can form the basis for a change in custody. Katz has correctly noted that by means of the "friendly parent" doctrine, interference with the other parent's relationship with the child has been incorporated into the requirements of parental fitness embodied in the best interests of the child standard.[144] This is a powerful weapon to give to fathers who may not want to pay child support or have difficulty placing their children's needs above their own, even in families with an absence of domestic violence, substance abuse, or mental illness. Fink noted that separating parents typically may be angry with each other and may speak badly of the other parent in the presence of the children.[145] This can occur in less-distressed families without a history of abuse. In these cases, the family could be helped by mental health professionals to overcome the stresses of divorce and separation without the use of the more punitive parental alienation theory.

The admissibility of psychological theories with a fragile empirical basis should be questioned and judges should scrutinize their acceptance and application. Under the *Frye* standard, which requires general acceptance, parental alienation, whether as a syndrome or a disorder, has not achieved this status. There are some courts that have upheld parental alienation theory. However, Fink noted that, in most courts when they hold hearings on the admissibility of expert testimony under either *Frye* or *Daubert*, such evidence has been excluded.[146] Therefore, careful presentation of the weakness of the empirical data and opposing theories is essential. Hoult advocates that parental alienation syndrome as a novel scientific theory be subjected to the gatekeeping rules of expert testimony under *Daubert*.[147]

Conclusion

The practice of custody evaluations is very common, yet there is very little in the way of regulation, laws, and professional scrutiny of the evaluators' professional practices. The problems of bias on the part of some custody evaluators, lack of validity of some psychological testing, and educational deficits of evaluators who have not had graduate-level education in domestic violence and child maltreatment calls into question their ability to provide neutral, informed guidance to the family courts.

In practice, hearings or even motion practice regarding the admissibility of the expert's testimony rarely take place. Evaluators called as court witnesses testify virtually unchallenged. At times, there may be cross-examination regarding the custody evaluators' educational backgrounds and credentials, but most attorneys are not comfortable questioning them. Questions using the *Daubert* guidelines, including but not limited to questions regarding the empirical basis of the evaluator's theories, the error rate, or their methodology typically are not asked in custody hearings. There are many legal decisions in which mothers lose custody after making allegations of abuse and evaluators wrongly conclude that they have alienated the children simply because the mother cannot provide sufficient evidence of the abuse. Custody evaluators who have little or no training in identifying sexual abuse, who use testing to determine whether a parent abuses drugs or alcohol, and who have weak training in domestic violence and the known risks after separation should not provide expert testimony in these areas.

Finally, while mental health professionals can provide very important support to the courts in custody proceedings, the acceptance of custody evaluators as experts should be scrutinized. Some cases call for the testimony of experts; for example, a mental health professional trained and experienced in the identification of sexual abuse in children could be enormously helpful to judges faced with such serious allegations. In cases where there are allegations of substance abuse, the testimony of mental health clinicians who specialize in the treatment of addiction would again be very helpful for the judge and the family members. In cases where one family member has been severely traumatized and displays significant mental health symptoms, an expert in trauma and PTSD would also be helpful. These types of experts with such knowledge and education are frequently absent from custody litigation. In cases without such symptomatology and allegations, trial judges could be better served by hearing the direct testimony of witnesses.

11

Recommendations and Conclusions

BUILDING AN INTEGRATED RESPONSE

This chapter will briefly discuss the need for model courts that address domestic violence, substance abuse, and mental illness during divorce and custody litigation. An informed judicial response requires adequate judicial personnel to permit expedited hearings, attorneys who have training in domestic violence, court monitoring, and continued judicial oversight of these families following separation. The need for immediate risk assessments and safety planning requires unbiased and knowledgeable mental health professionals so that meaningful interdisciplinary collaboration can take place. Thus, supervised visitation programs must be viewed as a long-term need and not a temporary stop-gap measure. Finally, building an informed interdisciplinary practice in the family courts must be based on graduate education that has focused on domestic violence, child maltreatment, substance abuse, and trauma. Mental health educators are in a unique position to contribute to the resolution of this crisis. The hands-on approach of social workers to clinical practice and a broader view of the family can also help to advocate for systemic changes and services to enhance parenting and children's adjustment.

Systemic Change in the Family Courts

The criminal courts, law enforcement, and medical profession have made substantial progress in confronting domestic violence as a public health and safety concern. At the same time, the family courts have lagged in their response to battered women amid significant controversy. Many researchers have written about the problem of the treatment of women in the family courts because of gender bias.[1] Significantly, the family courts are structured less around due process, the admissibility of evidence, and legal processes. The family courts' focus on private family life and the subjective standards of custody and the division of property has created a climate in which decisions about children appear arbitrary, without an empirical basis.

To summarize, there is a significant body of research on the impact of gender bias toward women in the family courts.[2] Zeoli et al. compellingly argue that women without independent evidence of domestic violence are terrorized by their abusers during the family court litigation and afterward.[3] Similarly, Faller has criticized the theory of parental alienation empirically, even though it is widely used in the family courts to discredit allegations of abuse.[4] Stark concluded that women as a class are discriminated against in the institution of the family courts.[5]

Dalton discussed the different paradigms regarding abuse and conflict, noting that many mental health professionals in the court system are trained to see conflict and, only when provided with considerable evidence of abuse, does this alter their views of the same incidents.[6] Thus, the systemic impact of such beliefs has had a profound impact on battered women in custody cases.

In my practice, a woman separated from her husband and filed for divorce after an incident in which he was abusive. Several years later, when she consulted with my office, I learned that although the courts originally indicated that the father's visits should be supervised, she reported to me that after several months the judge modified the original order and granted him unsupervised visitation. My client began to observe that their son had difficulty urinating and made statements that indicated that his father had inappropriately touched his genitals. However, the custody evaluator, who acknowledged having no training in sexual abuse, concluded, as did child protective services, that the timing of my client's allegations, which coincided with her filing for divorce, was suspect.

Significantly, the judge had not held an initial hearing to determine whether the father was abusive or if supervised visitation was necessary and for how long. Once supervised visitation was ordered, absent a hearing on this issue, the decision to grant the father unsupervised access was arbitrary and had no evidentiary basis. Furthermore, custody evaluators who have no specialized training in sexual abuse allegations should not be used to determine the veracity of such concerns and must refrain from such conclusions.

A systemic review of this case indicates that neither parent was provided with sufficient due process protections. Allegations of abuse are typically made on an emergency basis and relief—by necessity—is granted that same day, typically excluding the abusive party from the home. This is an important safety measure. However, when the father first appeared in court, or shortly thereafter, a hearing should have been held in which both parties were represented to determine the appropriate visitation plan. Furthermore, the need for supervised visitation is one that is long-term, and any modification of this form of access should not occur without substantial evidence of change. Finally, specialized courts that hear cases of domestic violence, substance abuse, or child maltreatment should provide long-term monitoring of such cases, requiring significant public funding.

Conversely, the criminal courts focus on specific acts has moved forward with an evidence-based approach to the prosecution of incidents of violence, menacing, and harassment. Dalton noted the failure of the family courts to integrate the positive changes in the laws regarding domestic violence and custody and their use of psychological theories to refute claims of abuse. Dalton and Stark agree that trainings alone are not sufficient to change court-appointed evaluators' views of abuse.[7]

The need for change is urgent. It is of concern that the National Institute of Justice (NIJ) found in a large-scale study that a significant percentage of judges, private attorneys, and custody evaluators failed to believe battered women's allegations of abuse, even when they were provided with supporting documentation.[8] These researchers found that evaluators' beliefs that women made false allegations of domestic violence strongly coincided with other core attitudes. Such attitudes included their belief that abused women made false allegations of abuse regarding their children and alienated the children from their fathers. These evaluators also indicated that they did not believe that domestic violence was important in custody determinations and, finally, that children are hurt when battered women do not want to co-parent.[9] Such attitudes indicate that change must come from the graduate mental health programs, which include a diverse curriculum that covers domestic violence, child maltreatment, and divorce.

Studies regarding the lack of acceptance of domestic violence allegations might be easier to understand if these issues were found in criminal court, where the evidence must meet the highest legal burden of proof to determine guilt. In the criminal courts, prosecutors must establish that the defendant is guilty beyond a reasonable doubt. In the family court, the lesser legal burden of proof of a preponderance of the evidence means that victims must prove that it is more likely than not that the offense was committed. Intuitively, one would assume that it is easier for battered women to obtain civil orders of protection, custody of her children, and orders limiting visitation. The fact that in the family courts the allegations of battered women are frequently minimized or unsubstantiated alerts us to the presence of bias. This is a grave concern that requires profound adaptations in graduate education to address abuse and child maltreatment and systemic reform of public and private institutions. Stark noted that the kind of evidence-gathering required in the criminal courts is not a part of the family courts' investigations of abuse.[10] Mental health professionals who understand all the implications and symptoms of traumatic exposure are needed so that women and children in crisis have the services they need to minimize the impact of traumatic behavior and the risks to their safety.

Kourlis et al. advocated for an increase in parent education, mediation services, and parenting coordination in the family courts, arguing that litigation is harmful to separating or divorcing families.[11] However, families overwhelmed with untreated mental illness, domestic violence, and substance abuse are at risk and will need judges who can hold expedited hearings to hear emergency applications and provide court orders that provide immediate protection for women and children. Unfortunately, mediation and parenting coordination are not appropriate in such families as they require continued contact between the parents, thus ignoring the safety risks that accompany separation. The problems of domestic violence, mental illness, and substance abuse cannot be solved through parent education. Families with such concerns require protective orders and specialized trauma-informed services.

These families also desperately need a legal environment in which their attorneys have access to interdisciplinary consultation with mental health professionals who can provide assessments and referrals to substance abuse treatment and mental health counseling. Providing access to referrals and resources in the courts would ensure an informed public health response. Service delivery cannot take place in the courthouse because of privacy and safety concerns of battered women, and their confidentiality would need to be assured. However, confidentiality can be maintained if the courthouse provided access to information and referrals, and, in some instances, this takes place. Protocols and clinical review of mandated reporting, while beyond the scope of this book, would also need to be addressed. The problems of protecting client confidentiality in the context of working across professional disciplines must also be addressed so families can receive the services they need.

Stark correctly noted that scatter-shot short-term trainings for attorneys and judges are not sufficient to address these significant and complex problems.[12] The same is true for mental health professionals. However, researchers have found that social workers and marriage-family therapists were more likely than psychologists to believe battered women's allegations of abuse and to consider such abuse in custody determinations and less likely to find parental alienation.[13] These findings are consistent with social work graduate education in which social workers are taught to look at the whole picture and to understand the interrelationships among hardships, inequities, trauma, and their impact on parenting and public health. Significantly, Saunders et al. also found that social workers were more likely to find that supervised visitation was beneficial for families and believed domestic violence was a significant factor in determining custody and visitation.

Attitudes and training matter. Significantly, virtually three-quarters (74.9%) of the evaluators in the national study by Saunders et al. were over fifty years of age, indicating that they received their graduate education at a time when the study of domestic violence and trauma was virtually absent from the curricula of graduate mental health programs. The lack of empirically based education in these significant areas has contributed to the adoption of concepts about families that are steeped in biases. Similarly, in law enforcement, the tendency of police to arrest both perpetrators and victims was found to be closely linked to traditional attitudes about the roles of women.[14] However, the solution of primary aggressor laws that directed law enforcement to review the history of violence in the family before arresting the victim, along with significant funding for law enforcement training through the Violence Against Women Act, has led to a decrease in dual arrests of battered women. This chapter will also discuss the need for graduate education on domestic violence and child maltreatment to address the problem of conflicting theories of trauma and abuse.

There are many key players in the family courts, including custody evaluators, court personnel, and attorneys for the children, and it will be difficult to ensure that they all have the requisite understanding of trauma, domestic violence, and the interrelationship with substance abuse. Gentile noted that the Voices of Women Organizing Project concluded not only that a judicial process that protects women requires court observers, but also that the involvement of battered women's advocacy groups and survivors in the judicial selection process is an important safeguard.[15] To those who would argue that this is one-sided, in many jurisdictions, committee members are part of the legal elite, members of law firms that have had little experience litigating in the family courts. The process of judicial selection must be more diverse and transparent. Stark noted the tensions between the attitudes and ideology of the family courts and necessary results that require safety and moral judgments about right and wrong.[16] The family courts should not ignore the message that they send to children in traumatized families: that abusive behavior is acceptable. Finally, Stark noted that when the family courts are more just and require law-biding behavior of all parents, then it is more likely that we will have stronger joint parenting following separation.

The Model Court Movement

The philosophy of therapeutic jurisprudence—a judicial approach that seeks to use social science research and the delivery of services to change the legal process for offenders—has led to the development of problem-solving courts.[17] These specialized courts address specific community safety concerns and have access to specialized community resources to address the problems of offenders and victims.[18]

In the past three decades, model courts have developed to address the problems of substance abuse, mental health issues, and domestic violence. The clear majority of such programs have developed in the criminal courts, as discussed in Chapter 9. However, many of these same families have problems that appear primarily in the civil courts, in the form of civil orders of protection, custody, visitation, divorce, and housing. A considerable number of women are forced to file for bankruptcy because of abuse that includes not only physical assaults but also coerced debt.[19] Model family courts should have the authority to address child custody, visitation, divorce, support, and consumer debt to prevent the need for bankruptcies.

As of this writing of this chapter, there are a limited number of model courts that handle only civil cases that address divorce and custody complicated by issues of domestic violence, substance abuse, or mental illness. Several pilot projects exist that can generate empirical research.[20] These are important projects that warrant attention paid to issues that include expedited interim hearings on orders of protection, custody, and visitation; legal representation of parents; and expedited referrals for domestic violence counseling. Furthermore, courts providing access to referrals to legal representation and counseling services will need to resolve the issues of confidentiality to protect victims. For parents accused of being abusive, expedited hearings in which they are represented can provide them with the opportunity to confront their accusers and the charges against them and, if necessary, to access supervised visitation. The drug and domestic violence model courts require defendants to enter guilty pleas, after which they are directed to obtain services and their compliance is monitored. Adaptation of this model in specialized custody and matrimonial courts requires an expedited hearing in which parents are represented by counsel so the courts can determine the level of safety measures necessary for parental access and, in extreme situations, whether such visits should be suspended. This approach will require evaluation and research to ensure that there are due process protections for the parents. However, the enormity of the problems in the family courts requires a trauma-informed judicial response.

Finally, programmatically, judicial and mental health training should include an awareness that there is an enormous need for long-term supervised visitation programs. Given the dearth of long-term, low-cost supervised visitation programs, public and private funding is essential to ensure safety.

Mirchandani also observed that battered women need to access the civil and criminal courts for a variety of problems that arise out of the same facts and that civil remedies are frequently necessary to complement criminal remedies, including custody, child support, and visitation.[21] These are remedies not available in the criminal courts. This researcher acknowledged the problems of litigants appearing in multiple courts and receiving conflicting orders. For example, an order of protection received by the victim during a criminal case may indicate that the defendant must stay away from the children, while a similar order in the family courts might only protect the mother. However, this researcher argues that the solution is not an integrated court but that there should be systemic court reforms. Such reforms could provide for communications between civil and criminal judges and ensure that judges had stable judicial assignments so that they would be more familiar with their caseload.[22]

The judicial response to domestic violence has focused primarily on criminal cases and, in the past decades, integrated domestic violence courts, in which cases that involve criminal charges and divorce or custody are seen together. This programmatic change was implemented to address families who were in multiple courts at the same time.[23]

Consider that a battered woman needing an order of protection, child support, and custody of her children could now have one judge address these concerns. This concept of integration of the criminal and civil courts was developed to avoid multiple conflicting orders of protection and to provide "one-stop" shopping for battered women where services and legal assistance were provided before one judge. Mirchandani found that the domestic violence courts were among the earliest form of problem-solving courts.[24] Furthermore, while more communication between the courts is important, given the level of stress involved in litigation of multiple cases for battered women in multiple courts and their vulnerability to medical and mental health issues, "one-stop" shopping is the preferred response. Those pilot projects that address only custody and abuse are a small part of the family court systems and a short step in what Stark refers to as the "long march" to justice.[25]

Battered Women's Experiences in Court

Moe Wan conducted a qualitative study of an advocacy program for battered women seeking civil restraining orders in which she observed advocates, court personnel, and judges during this process.[26] Using Ptacek's typology of judicial demeanor, this researcher classified behaviors of court personnel.[27] In instances in which hearing officers displayed good-natured demeanor, Moe Wan found that they made women comfortable, spent time explaining the process, clarified allegations of domestic violence, and drafted orders that reflected the safety concerns raised in the preliminary hearing. Significantly, this sometimes involved the hearing office using very direct questioning during *ex parte* hearings to clarify the need for an order of protection. Taking the time to do this is no small thing, as I have frequently observed battered women being afraid to speak out in court and therefore not providing sufficient details about the abuse to warrant their obtaining a temporary order of protection. In some instances, Moe Wan observed that court personnel and advocates demonstrated bureaucratic demeanor in which hearing officers took on a more passive and neutral approach. However, this researcher also observed that it was these same personnel who frequently appeared impatient and disinterested, and they rarely asked questions or explained the process to the litigants. In one instance, this researcher observed hearing officers refusing to answer questions raised by victims concerning visitation. While this issue is not directly related to the issuance of a temporary order of protection, when left unresolved, it could lead to concerns about safety for the children and further litigation. Finally, this researcher used Ptacek's classification of firm or condescending demeanor to describe instances in which hearing officers were authoritarian and unsupportive and asserted their power over victims.[28] Moe Wan concluded that most interactions observed could be classified as either good-natured or, alternatively, firm and condescending, with very few court personnel displaying bureaucratic demeanor. However, there was a small number of court personnel who, through their comments and attitudes, consistently degraded and humiliated these women. In these situations, such behavior can mirror batterers' behavior and has the potential to retraumatize victims, causing them to be unwilling to follow through on their applications or to seek help in the future. These findings require more research on whether such harsh behaviors affect women's decision to complete the process of obtaining protective orders.

As an attorney for battered women and a former court employee, this research finding about the behavior of some, but not all, attorneys, court personnel, and judges is not news. These findings support my own anecdotal experiences in the courtroom, that there are professionals who display courtesy, helpfulness, and an awareness of domestic violence. This has mattered enormously to my clients, making them feel safe and receptive to the help they receive. However, not infrequently, I have observed court personnel and judges displaying poor judicial and court demeanor. This includes shouting, disparaging behavior, indifference, and refusal to answer requests for information. Less experienced lawyers may be intimidated, and such intimidation can have a negative impact on their ability to zealously represent their clients. Battered women can lose trust in the legal system. Furthermore, it is important to consider whether judges and court personnel are also impacted by vicarious trauma in ways that negatively affect their job performance and the treatment of litigants. High caseloads, insufficient administrative support, scarce resources, and the lack of training in the family courts have all contributed to the current situation. It would be important to determine whether the supportive behavior of advocates for battered women on the part of attorneys or other mental health professionals can mitigate the damage caused by intemperate behavior on the part of some court personnel. In my practice, I have seen clients display enormous resilience and competence in parenting after receiving supportive mental health services and good lawyering.

An informed model court response to custody and domestic violence should include training for court personnel, attorneys for the children, and judges to prevent the display of behaviors that are indifferent or actively hostile. Furthermore, court administrators who make staffing determinations should choose staff and judges who understand the importance of responding to litigants—who may be unrepresented—with information, courtesy, and resources. While hearing officers and judges cannot provide legal advice, they can refer litigants to court facilities and community services where they can receive such assistance. Supporting court personnel can provide lists of referrals and agencies, and placement of such agencies in the courthouse is a crucial step in this process that has been adopted in many model courts.

The study by Bell et al. of 406 women seeking help in cases of domestic violence in the civil and criminal courts concluded that 55% found the courts to be fair, 36% indicated that the court's response was very helpful, and 10% found the courts to be unhelpful.[29] Their concerns about their court experience included the impact of lengthy delays in the process and having to make multiple unnecessary appearances. Battered women reported that these delays meant that they had to take off excessive time from work and arrange for child care to cover their court appearances. While these issues may seem trivial, many of my clients over the years have found litigation extremely stressful financially and professionally as multiple court appearances meant taking off considerable time from work, sometimes without compensation and with extra legal fees and child care expenses. Although many courts provide on-site child care, the regulations for such "drop in" facilities are often stringent. Frequently, parents must show their children's immunization records and their own personal identification, something that many litigants who are in crisis do not have readily available. Finally, many women felt that the delays were due to incompetence and thus they felt unsafe. Significantly, many women in this study found it was helpful when court staff connected them to community resources and battered women's shelters. The court day is long and unpleasant for children forced to be in waiting room facilities without access to cafeterias, vending machines, or a child-friendly environment. Imagine a family courthouse in which every waiting room had child-friendly programing as well as public information for all adults on the availability of services.

Davis noted that the courts are hindered by conflicting theories of abuse, as has been discussed in Chapter 3.[30] This researcher noted that many professionals in the family court system had differing ideas about their functions and roles, creating significant confusion. As a result, the Battered Women's Justice Project (BWJP) has developed a framework for the identification and direction of custody cases involving domestic violence allegations.[31] This project stressed the importance of early identification of abuse using a screening instrument that could detect the various forms of abuse, including all forms of coercive control, that warrants further study. Davis observed that there are different forms of domestic violence and ample research demonstrating significant post-separation risks. This author's research did not address long-term safety planning for families in custody litigation with a history of domestic violence and abuse.

Walker et al. noted that partner abuse before and during separation could cause significant physical and mental health consequences for these women and that the experience of navigating the different systems, including the criminal justice system, was particularly stressful.[32] Hardesty and Chung found that battered women also experience fear during the separation and post-separation period.[33] Researchers not only indicated that women are fearful but that this fear is often warranted as violence may continue after they leave and even escalate.[34] Hardesty and Chung concluded that the court's response to domestic violence is limited by its misconceptions of abuse as conflict.[35] Thus, many courts require parents to attend mediation or parenting classes while there is no mechanism to identify battered women or to uniformly exempt them from such programs. Furthermore, these researchers found that, even when exempted from mediation or parenting classes, the courts do not make appropriate services available to battered women.

Procedurally, the use of problem-solving model courts in the family courts for child custody with families impacted by domestic violence, substance abuse, and mental illness has the potential to include routine screening, safety planning, and ongoing services for battered women and their children. Furthermore, in the context of divorce and custody litigation, Hardesty and Chung also stressed the need for culturally competent services and that such services should be an integral part of safety planning. These are important safety measures that can impact public health and safety and should be a routine part of the court's response, even when allegations of abuse are not disclosed. Finally, to avoid the problems of custody and visitation arrangements that fail to consider the risks of exposure to domestic violence, substance abuse, and untreated mental illness, the safety plans developed for battered women can be incorporated into the parenting plans. Protective orders, visitation plans that include supervised visitation, as well as referrals to battered women's services should all be available in the same place to facilitate "one-stop" shopping for programs.

Winick and Wexler have argued that therapeutic jurisprudence, characterized by the centrality and involvement of the presiding judge, has been used to reduce social problems by providing services in the context of a legal case.[36] Typically, the use of therapeutic jurisprudence is closely linked to the interdisciplinary delivery of services and, in fact, generally provides services for offenders at the onset of the court case, often as an alternative to incarceration. However, Stark warned against therapeutic jurisprudence and argued instead that the family court model of custody litigation should become more like criminal court investigations.[37] Keeping this in mind, having one judge who is familiar with the problems of these litigants can be helpful if this person is educated in this area. Only recently has domestic violence become part of law school clinical education, and it is important to have supporting personnel to provide the presiding judge with specialized training and resources.

Battered women can benefit from an informed judicial response that includes referrals to domestic violence advocates. Fathers can benefit from an expedited hearing in which they are afforded due process protections. Children will benefit from supervised visitation programs when appropriate. Such model courts should be focused on child safety. Thus, the supervised visitation programs can provide intakes, assessments, ongoing case management, and supervision of visitation, as well as long-term monitoring. This requires a different approach, one that emphasizes safety and the prevention of long-term traumatic exposure. To ensure safe families, there needs to be long-term solutions in which supervised visitation is more than a temporary measure. While initial assessments are important, not all the information about the family's history is immediately available as battered women may have difficulty identifying themselves as abused or feel uncomfortable discussing very personal problems. Thus, follow-up contact with social services should be an essential part of the court intervention. However, the problems of confidentiality and due process will also need to be addressed.

Judicial Reforms

The research of Cuthbert et al. on the treatment of battered women and their children in Massachusetts family courts concluded that these conditions rose to the level of human rights violations.[38] These researchers advocated for continued auditing of the Massachusetts family courts every three to five years. They also called for several systemic reforms to these family courts. These reforms included establishment of an independent office of the state ombudsperson, where litigants can bring complaints; a study of Massachusetts' current supervised visitation systems and the existing programs in other states for the development of a model program; and replacement of their guardian ad litem system in which attorneys represented children. These researchers not only called for additional training on domestic violence, child maltreatment, child development, and mental health, but also for a multidisciplinary team that could provide assessments and investigations for custody evaluations. Finally, Cuthbert et al. called for legislative and court reforms, including a requirement that an abusive parent attend supervised visitation for a minimum of one year and that such attendance take place in a state-approved batterers' treatment program. Finally, these researchers called for increased legal services for battered women and children and the funding of battered women's programs to support women during litigation.[39]

These recommendations indicate the scope of the systemic reforms that must take place to protect battered women and their children. However, the use of an interdisciplinary team to provide evaluations is problematic, and a better response would be to selectively use evaluations for substance abuse and sexual abuse interventions from mental health professionals with academic expertise in these areas.

Green refers to the presumption of openness in court proceedings.[40] In particular, the Sixth Amendment provides that defendants in the criminal courts shall have a public trial.[41] While a public and fair trial in criminal cases is an essential part of due process protections, in the family courts, the right to a public hearing is often subject to the court's discretion. Green observed that a restrictive view of the need for privacy, and thus a closed proceeding, in civil cases involving allegations of domestic violence is problematic. Given the problems of gender and other forms of bias that have been documented in the family courts, closing the courthouse doors prevents public scrutiny of this problem. Green noted the success of court watch programs (Women at the Court House, WATCH) acting as observers in twenty-nine states as of the writing of her article.[42] This program developed as part of an effort to respond to problems encountered by battered women in the court system. While these observers did not interfere with the court proceedings, they did compile reports about the outcomes of the domestic violence cases and sometimes wrote to attorneys who had advocated zealously for their clients, providing them with positive feedback. In other instances, they contacted judges, attorneys, and the media to bring the problems of the family courts to the public's attention. In one instance, the Florida Watch project compiled a report about a judge who was particularly biased in his behavior toward battered women. Thus, this judge was reassigned to work on other types of cases.[43] Having court observers can enhance the atmosphere and professionalism of the family courts. As a former law clerk to a judge in the criminal courts, where the proceedings are public, I have observed how court monitors and jurors were welcomed in the courthouse and their presence was viewed as a public service by concerned members of the public.

Considering the many studies of gender bias in the courts, discussed more fully in Chapter 5, current efforts to create change have not fully remedied the inadequate treatment of battered women in the courts. Robust reform of the family court system requires an ombudsman office that is run by a council of interdisciplinary professionals and community and domestic violence advocates with investigators who have the authority to obtain court records and to recommend changes. While many in the mental health and legal profession argue that families require privacy, these concerns can be addressed with orders that prohibit outside disclosure, in which names are redacted, and the press could be excluded.

Interdisciplinary Collaboration and the Provision of Services in the Family Courts

The family courts provide little in the way of social services, support, or treatment for the families they serve. This paucity of services may be linked to a variety of factors, including the lack of funding, confidentiality concerns, and systemic problems. Given that many attorneys for battered women work alongside social workers, as well as the development of law school clinics in which social workers may be assigned, this portion of the discussion will focus primarily on the collaboration between these two professions.

While both lawyers and social workers work under ethical requirements that ensure client confidentiality, social workers are mandated reporters of child maltreatment. Albrandt noted that while some states provide that attorneys may also report child abuse and neglect, this author concluded that the statutory requirements of attorney–client privilege exempted attorneys from reporting.[44] Thus, best practices indicate that the sharing of confidential information between attorneys and social workers must be carefully screened to avoid sabotaging their legal representation. Having to report a client who was medicating herself by abusing alcohol, for example, would make it impossible for an attorney to continue to zealously represent her interests. However, helping clients to obtain counseling before their drinking became a genuine problem can be couched in a way that prevents risks to the children while allowing the attorneys to continue their representation.

St. Joan described a clinical model in the University of Denver Law School that established boundaries between law and social work students while promoting continued collaboration.[45] This law school clinic adopted an approach that allowed law students to inform clients of the opportunity to work with a social worker and explained the associated risks of working with a mandated reporter. Students and faculty received notice of the written policies regarding client confidentiality and the procedures in place to provide ethical representation and advocacy. Significantly, this meant that information must be protected, and, to that end, separate files and offices were maintained. This author noted the inherent dilemma in collaboration as attorneys wanted to protect clients from mandated reporting while also protecting the children. It is this balancing act that attorneys struggle with when we represent battered women in custody cases. A client traumatized by abuse may drink at night but may not be impaired by alcohol. However, when attorneys obtain such information, it is important to make the necessary referrals in a nonjudgmental manner. Clients will then have a place to talk about the stresses of litigation, parenting, and their own traumatization. Attorneys can advise the client of the risks involved in drinking during a custody case, and, unless there is a significant problem with alcohol, the clients typically respond to this level of support and legal advice.

St. Joan observed that there were three models of interdisciplinary collaboration. These included the consultant approach, the law firm model, and the consent model.[46] The consultant model required independent delivery of mental health services without the sharing of offices, files, or case information. The employee model was premised on the belief that social workers in a legal agency are exempt from the requirements of mandated reporting and obligated to follow attorney–client privilege guidelines. The consent model also allows social workers to collaborate closely with attorneys, with the clients' written consent and confirmation that they are aware of the social workers' obligations as a mandated reporter.[47] Use of the employee model is not a viable option everywhere because, in many states, social workers have an independent obligation to report child maltreatment. A better practice is to have protocols in place that include supervision and interdisciplinary consultation if circumstances should develop in which a social worker feels obligated to report possible child maltreatment. Informing clients of their role as a mandated reporter should be, and generally is, routine practice among most social workers, visitation supervisors, and custody evaluators.

The model of family justice centers that provide one-stop linkages to prosecutors, civil legal assistance, shelters, and social services has been a significant source of assistance for battered women. At the same time, the need to maintain client confidentiality and to provide a safe space for victims of domestic violence has meant that these programs are not court-based.[48] The question becomes whether a model court that addresses domestic violence, substance abuse, and mental health concerns can be connected to the services offered by the family justice centers, and, if so, what privacy protections need to be in place. Criticisms of the family justice centers cite the lack of confidentiality and the reliance on the criminal justice approach to domestic violence.[49] In the context of custody and divorce litigation, while clients can receive referrals from the family justice projects, the lack of immediate availability of social services represents a gap in service delivery. A review of existing programs is needed to determine whether client confidentiality can be maintained while still allowing for brief assessments, referrals to domestic violence shelters, and domestic violence programs that provide counseling with collaborative agencies present in the courthouse.

One-stop models of services for victims of domestic violence have increased because of the Family Justice Projects that are funded by the Violence Against Women Act.[50] Some programs have begun to bring community-based domestic violence service providers into the court system to provide access to legal representation for battered women and referrals or entry into battered women's shelters, counseling, and mentoring programs. Such programs are helpful in providing emergency services but can also provide increased social support. There is disagreement among researchers about how to measure the presence or perception of social supports, yet there is agreement that such support is helpful. Bauman et al. noted that the presence or perception of social support led to a higher quality of life, lower levels of depression, and enhanced mental health outcomes.[51] Given the isolation of many battered women, enhancing social supports may help them to marshal the resources necessary to withstand the stress of litigation and separation. Bauman et al.'s study compared battered women seeking help through the courts or shelters with those identified in hospital emergency rooms or clinics, finding that those seeking help had more social supports. We can assume that battered women can benefit from the provision of mental health services in multiple ways. Mancoske et al.'s early research is instructive on battered women from diverse backgrounds who sought short-term counseling services at a battered women's program with social workers.[52] This study found that, following the provision of short-term eight-week group treatment, those women who received counseling from a grief resolution per-spective experienced an improvement in self-esteem and self-efficacy.

Assessment of Batterers' Intervention Programs

The question of whether the judicial response to custody and intimate part-ner violence should include services for men in the form of batterers' interven-tion programs (BIPs) requires a thoughtful analysis of the effectiveness of such programs, standardization, attrition, recidivism, and how we assess change. To date, measuring the effectiveness of such programs tends to focus on the rate at which batterers complete these programs and whether they have reoffended or been arrested again during a designated time. It is difficult to determine the extent of any change as some batterers are rarely physically abusive.[53] Babcock et al. reviewed the evolution of batterers' programs, finding that many pro-grams ranged in duration from twelve to fifty-two weeks, used a group interven-tion model, and required that facilitators have some experience in working in domestic violence.[54] It is also important to remember that batterers' treatment programs are typically used in the context of criminal court, where convicted batterers may be mandated to attend such programs or face incarceration.

Silvergleid and Mankowski's research sought to identify and analyze those aspects of the BIPs that were effective in reducing batterers' violence.[55] Significantly, the program participants and facilitators agreed that a primary motivation for changing abusive behavior was the external influence of the courts and not the content of the program. While at times batterers referred to the influence of the courts as a positive—helping them to recognize their problems and facilitating change—it is significant that the program's content was not their primary motivating factor for stopping their abusive behavior.

While clerking for a judge, I helped to organize one of the first New York state criminal courts to address domestic violence and learned that BIPs did not work without monitoring and enforcement.[56] Batterers who agreed to attend such programs in lieu of incarceration frequently failed to attend or complete these programs. This problem has been well documented in the liter-ature, and researchers estimate that between 50% and 75% of all such batter-ers who are enrolled failed to complete their programs.[57] Notably, a graduate degree in mental health was not needed to lead these programs. Babcock et al. described the range of treatment approaches in such programs that included psychoeducational men's groups, the Duluth Model, cognitive behavior groups, and anger management.[58] These researchers conducted a meta-analysis of the diverse types of batterers' programs and found that there was a small positive impact on recidivism in batterers' programs. However, conceptually, it is difficult to understand how such brief interventions, sometimes limited to a maximum of six months, could facilitate lasting change. Furthermore, a review of the research by Babcock et al. noted the consensus that attrition rates in such programs remained a significant problem.

In my experience, without such collaboration and monitoring between the courts and the BIPs, batterers rarely attended these programs. While such programs are typically groups in which the participants are to support and help each other address their concerns, the female therapists frequently spoke about how difficult it was to work with this population. Silvergleid and Mankowski discussed the importance of the facilitators in BIPs, whose role shifted from providing support to confrontation. Participants in the study spoke positively about the balance of support and confrontational styles of their facilitators. However, Silvergleid and Mankowski could not conclude based on their research whether BIPs significantly reduced violence or recidivism.[59] There is also a lack of research on the efficacy of group treatment for batterers as parents. Finally, the question of what types of curriculum are most effective has not been resolved.

Since the 1990s, the states have become increasingly concerned with regulating BIPs and thus most states are developing standards for such treatment. Boa and Mankowski compared these programs prior to the Oregon's adoption of such guidelines and two years afterward.[60]

Typically, BIPs strove to prevent future incidents of intimate partner violence by developing self-awareness in batterers, so that they understand the patterns of power and control involved, and finally to hold them accountable for their behavior. To that end, while content varied from program to program, the key element of external control was obtained through judicial monitoring and repercussions when batterers fail to attend, dropped-out, or were rearrested. Furthermore, while most states have guidelines for BIPs, there is variation from state to state in terms of the length of such programs, with a consensus being that these programs should be no less than sixteen weeks in duration, while, on average, programs were twenty-four to twenty-six weeks in duration.[61] Maiuro et al. concluded that, while there was compliance with the required length of the programs, there was an absence of external monitoring or enforcement. These researchers concluded that there was a need for empirically based treatment, standardization, and critical monitoring of program compliance with state regulations.

Buttell and Carney also analyzed the problem of the rate of attrition among batterers in completing such programs.[62] This research studied the attrition rate in a twelve-week psychoeducational program broken up into three modules. These modules focused first on educating group participants to identify their defense mechanisms to foster change, followed by a module that challenged batterers' beliefs and values and, finally, a module that attempted to provide the participants with alternative behavioral responses. These researchers found only slight differences between those batterers who completed treatment and those who dropped out of the programs.

DeHart et al.'s research found that attendance in batterers' programs could be enhanced using internal and external motivations and hypothesized that the presence of judicial sanctions for failure to attend and complete these programs could be effective in lowering attrition.[63] These researchers also noted that many batterers never appear for even the initial intake appointment following the telephone screening and called for more research to determine the reasons behind their failure to engage at all in treatment.

Buzawa et al. observed that while there is considerable research on batterers, we should not assume that all batterers are alike.[64] These researchers indicated that some batterers use violence in response to substance abuse, stress, or the need to be in control. Sherman found that one subgroup of batterers tended to be employed, had other community ties, and were less likely to have ever been involved with law enforcement.[65] Researchers have argued that more research is needed on the types of men who batter to better understand whether they will respond to treatment.

The Family Violence Council's Domestic Violence Abuser Research Collaborative (2002) noted that measurements used in the criminal court context to indicate improvement may not accurately account for changes in batterers' behaviors as not all acts of abuse come to the attention of law enforcement and the criminal courts. Similarly, the Family Violence Council called for research that included interviews of victims and other family members to better determine the effectiveness of such programs, although they concluded that such programs do not harm. Notably, Gondolf raised concerns that the use of batterers' treatment programs may lull battered women into a false sense of complacency as incidents of violence may be as much as a year or more apart.[66]

Therefore, it is inevitable that questions surround the use and effectiveness of batterers' programs. Edleson's discussion of batterers' programs highlighted some of the concerns about the goals of these programs and how we measure success.[67] This researcher noted the lack of clarity concerning the programs' goals and whether it was sufficient to reduce the number of times each week that a batterer physically attacks his spouse or whether the goal should be to eliminate all incidents of abuse. Edleson raised questions as to whether batterers simply employed other forms of abuse after completion of these programs. These questions indicate how difficult it is to change not simply behavior, but attitudes and values. In the context of parenting and custody litigation, the harm caused by exposure to batterers' abuse is not simply a matter of physical risks but also the other related risks for children of exposure to this kind of parenting.[68] As discussed previously, Bancroft and Silverman describe the rippling effect of destruction because abuse impacts all areas of family life and functioning.[69]

Edelson and Williams have noted the lack of research on parenting by fathers who are abusive, although there is a significant body of research on the parenting of battered mothers.[70] We do know that batterers not only abuse women but that children are also at a greater risk of physical harm. Edleson and Williams concluded in an empirical review of the research in this area of more than thirty studies that the median rate of the co-occurrence of child abuse and domestic violence was 41%.[71] As has been discussed in Chapter 4, children in families with a history of domestic violence are more at risk of multiple long-term problems, and Jaffe et al. noted the high level of posttraumatic stress disorder (PTSD) seen in even very young children because of exposure to domestic violence.[72]

Finally, given that men who complete BIPs have only marginally less recidivism rates, and the lack of empirical evidence to support this form of treatment to modify their parenting, the inclusion of such programs is not warranted in model courts that address domestic violence and custody.

The Study of Victimology

Dussich discussed the growing field of victimology, in which the focus is shifted away from perpetrators to a study of victims and their injuries, recovery, and treatment.[73] Because of this movement, educational programs have developed to provide training to practitioners and researchers at all levels. Victimology has encompassed many areas of study, including sexually abused children, crime victims, maltreated children, battered women, victims of hate crimes, and torture in war-torn countries, to name a few. Notably, the First American Symposium on Victimology (2003) provided forums for discussion of the development of academic programs, victim services, and curricula for first responders and mental health professionals, among others.[74] Such programs continue to develop and are an important part of understanding the experience of victimization and recovery along with systemic responses that enable growth, recovery, and resilience.

The Medical Profession and Domestic Violence

Much of graduate-level and postgraduate education on domestic violence addresses the issues of screening, identification of abuse, and risk assessment. In medical and social work schools, screening for domestic violence has become an important part of education. Many patients are now routinely asked if "they feel safe in their home" during doctor's visits. Phelps observed that simply taking a patient's painful history of abuse in a nonjudgmental manner could have therapeutic value.[75] For patients seeking medical care in emergency rooms, doctors' offices, clinics, or hospitals, this may be their first experience of requesting help. The importance of an informed unbiased response at this juncture cannot be overemphasized for victims of abuse. In teaching medical students to interview victims of domestic violence, I have found that it is important to stress using open-ended questions that are respectful, concerned, and nonjudgmental. Training in this area should stress the importance of unbiased and full documentation of the injuries and supporting allegations in affirmative statements and quotes, frequently in the patients' own words, describing their abuse. Too often, physician's document abuse by indicating that the patient "alleges" that they have been injured because of an assault, not aware that, when couched in such terms, the statements may later be viewed skeptically when medical records are reviewed at trial. Teaching medical students to routinely photograph injuries, which then become part of the medical record, is also important. Phelps also noted that medical students may experience painful emotional responses after taking their patients' history of abuse. As a result, all training of medical students whenever possible should include practice-based programs that provide supervision.

Graduate Education

Identifying domestic violence requires a clinical leap involving critical listening to hear the symptoms of abuse. Furthermore, the field of domestic violence is complex and one in which there are competing ideas of divorce, separation, parenting, violence, and post-separation risks. Graduate curriculum in psychiatry, psychology, social work, and counseling should include an overview of the different theories of domestic violence, divorce, and separation that is enhanced by empirically supported data. Only by having empirically grounded, practice-based graduate work in domestic violence, child maltreatment, substance abuse, and trauma can we overcome the obstacles that battered women face in the courts.

Furthermore, screening without appropriate action can expose clients to greater harm, while effective screening with referrals to appropriate community resources can prevent future incidents of violence.[76] In a study of social work professionals, Tower found that while 35.7% of social work graduates reported having no training in domestic violence, a sizable portion indicated that they had such training during their foundation year. Additionally, the remaining students reported that this material was covered in their field placement, and the remainder responded that the material was also covered in their coursework.[77] This researcher concluded that education alone is not sufficient to ensure that appropriate screening takes place and that other reminders of the importance of completing documentation could help.

McNiel et al. found that when psychiatric and clinical psychology interns were provided with formal training on violence risk assessment, they increased their documentation of patient risks and experienced more self-confidence in this area.[78] It should be noted that this research project compared participants who attended a five-hour workshop as compared to those who did not attend. There was no attendant study to determine whether those who attended the workshop identified more at-risk patients or whether this increased patient safety. Education in domestic violence and substance abuse must be an inherent part of graduate training for all mental health and medical professionals, and it should consist of more than a limited workshop. However, it is encouraging that the participants became more aware of the problem as a result of even this brief training. For social workers, an understanding of intimate partner violence must become part of their clinical expertise, independent of forms and reporting requirements.

Dragiewicz et al. noted the significant growth of university-level courses that address domestic violence as well as graduate-level programs in public administration and criminal justice that also focus on such abuse.[79] While faculty found that these courses were challenging to teach because of the intense nature of the subject matter and student experiences, these programs were well received. Furthermore, the link to community programs helped to ground the theory with practice.

Legal Education

Forgey and Colarossi addressed the importance of interdisciplinary education for lawyers and social workers in their development of a course for both disciplines to address the issue of domestic violence.[80] This course focused on a historical analysis of domestic violence, theories of causation, and, finally, the legal response. While noting the differences in ethics and mandated reporting requirements for social workers, these authors thought that interdisciplinary collaboration and education was important. Significantly, these researchers noted that some social work students dropped out of this course, and grades for social workers were not as high as in their other areas of concentration.

St. Joan observed that there may be discomfort on the part of social work students as a result of a perceived power imbalance when working in a law clinic as attorneys have the ultimate authority over case decisions.[81] Social workers can provide attorneys with valuable assistance in understanding their client's emotional needs and providing support while allowing the attorneys to concentrate on legal representation. In my teaching, it is important to provide social workers with positive feedback about the skills they bring to their collaboration, and, with experience and supervision, these students begin to experience more professional confidence. I have also rarely successfully represented a battered woman without the help of a social worker, as I have explained to my students on many occasions. Finally, the challenge of maintaining client confidentiality should not be a barrier to the provision of services within the court system. Careful releases, informed collaboration, and an understanding of the different professions' ethical obligations should help to overcome the obstacles in working together to assist clients.

Winick and Wexler discussed the use of therapeutic jurisprudence to enhance legal education that would provide not only practical experiences, but also training in client interviewing and some understanding of the behavioral sciences.[82] By working alongside social workers, law students can learn more about the context of their clients' difficulties and hone their interviewing skills. Social workers can benefit from learning about the legal system and the stresses that clients experience as a result. It is in these areas that interdisciplinary education can be effective. Social work students also need an understanding of trauma that is integrated into their field placement and course work, along with intensive supervision to assist them in their work with battered women and their children. The pitfalls of interdisciplinary practice are significant, but when students feel confident in their clinical judgment they can hold their own.

Bell and Goodman reviewed whether battered women experienced any positive effects because of the involvement of law school advocacy programs in which law students receive clinical training in domestic violence.[83] Such education included coursework and seminars in domestic violence and work with trained attorneys in representing battered women in court. These researchers conducted a small study of the short-term effectiveness of law school advocacy programs in which students were paired with battered women seeking civil orders of protection. Contact between victims and law students enrolled in the clinics occurred frequently during the legal process through in-person meetings or telephone communications. Many of the law students provided additional help to battered women that was not part of their assigned tasks, including helping to prepare their testimony and exhibits and assistance with safety planning. Notably, the survivors of domestic violence reported significantly lower levels of psychological and physical reabuse and experienced slightly marginal increases in levels of emotional support.[84] This study is significant not only for the training of law students in domestic violence but also because increases in client perceptions of social supports has helped to reduce isolation and lessen the risks of continued exposure to abuse for battered women.

McQueeney's discussion of domestic violence coursework and curricula focused on the need to provide an intersectional approach to the problems of domestic violence among women of color and in the LGBT community, noting the connection between gender, race, class, and sexuality.[85] This author also discussed the challenges of teaching about domestic violence because of the sensitive subject matter and the preconceived notions that some students bring to the classroom. In my teaching, I have found that students challenge preexisting ideas about divorce and domestic violence and raise questions as to whether men and women are violent at the same rate. They do not want to be told what to think, but respond to assigned readings of original research and benefit from their own research and opportunities for engagement. Repeatedly, my work as their teacher is to give them an opportunity for critical thinking that is informed by empirical data and to also provide them an opportunity for problem-solving in small- and large-group discussions on such difficult issues.

Vicarious Trauma

Finklestein et al. observed that there is a body of research on the impact of vicarious trauma, or the risk of mental health professionals developing symptoms like PTSD through indirect exposure to client narratives and clinical histories.[86] Vicarious trauma, sometimes referred to as *secondary trauma*, has also been found in other helping professions, including nursing and emergency room staff.[87] Finklestein et al. noted that specialized training, supervision, and peer support can ameliorate some of the impact of such secondary trauma. Some research has indicated that high caseloads can increase the risks of such traumatization among mental health professionals.[88] High caseloads and a lack of supervision are not limited to the mental health fields, and the legal and medical professions also needs help in identifying risks for vicarious trauma. The legal profession has not kept pace with the medical and mental health professions in assisting students, new attorneys, and colleagues with the risks involved in working with traumatized clients. There is a need for interdisciplinary collaboration with mental health professionals to address such concerns that should be part of any custody and domestic violence model courts.

Conclusion

To envision a solution to violence and coercion in the private domain is a daunting goal, and I recognize the vast amount of research and advocacy in this area. There are many researchers and practitioners who have spent their lives researching, writing, and working with survivors. Their work has laid the groundwork for a more trauma-informed systemic response to the problems of domestic violence, substance abuse, and untreated mental illness in family life. Abuse is toxic and results in the increased use of medical and mental health services over the course of decades.[89] Substance abuse is also a significant problem, and the misuse of alcohol has been found to escalate incidents of domestic violence in which women are often severely injured. Abused women may have mental health concerns requiring referrals for treatment, and batterers may have significant psychiatric symptoms that should be assessed to determine the risks and, when possible, to receive treatment. These issues are interrelated and require resources and informed interdisciplinary collaboration. Today's children can become tomorrow's victims and perpetrators if we do not make the necessary changes.

This book is an effort to change the conversation from empirically weak and gender-biased theories to data-supported public health policies and education that protect mothers and children. There may even be a time when students look back incredulously on the family courts' failure to protect women and children. The new normal must be centered primarily on child safety in which public health and safety risks are treated with utmost gravity. For this reason, this chapter addressed the interdisciplinary resources, graduate education, systemic changes, and due process concerns that are an essential component for any long-term strategy to combat these problems.

Domestic violence is inextricably linked to gender. When women are abused, their children are taught that their mothers have no value in their lives, that violence is an acceptable method of control, and that fathers are permitted a wide range of coercive behaviors. Many of these patterns of coercive control represent criminal activities that would not be tolerated in the public domain but are still minimized in the private sphere. This book has discussed the impact of gender bias against women in the courts, the public health impact of trauma on women and children, and the systemic changes that are necessary in graduate education to address the reforms needed.

The legal and mental health professions have approached the problems that accompany divorce and separation in ways that mirror many of the gender, class, and racial inequities that are part of many battered women's experiences in their family life. Poverty and economic disparities are often part of the problem, but not always. While I initially represented clients from victim services agencies, over the past decade, I have also represented women who are doctors, lawyers, accountants, journalists, teachers, and nurses, all of whom have been abused. Addressing the complex problems of gender bias in the courts and among some mental health professionals requires a leap of understanding about this all too frequent problem.

Providing services to families that have been impacted by domestic violence, substance abuse, and mental illness means that the mental health and legal systems must begin to understand the essential role the courts can play in enhancing recovery and resilience for battered women and their children. A review of the research on gender bias in the courts indicates that this remains an enormous challenge. The gender bias task force movement of the past gathered information and held hearings in which professionals and community advocates were heard. As a result of this movement, there were changes made in laws regarding support and the division of property. For the first time, the courts were directed to specifically consider domestic violence as a factor in determining custody and visitation. Combatting the current inequities requires public funding, education, attention, and systemic changes because battered women need more than physical safety: they also need emotional and financial dignity to raise their children. The problems cannot be solved by the courts alone and require implementation of model courts, judicial monitoring, social supports, and long-term supervised visitation programs.

Finally, court-based referrals for battered women's services must begin with assessments of their abuse, safety risks, and safety planning. Battered women need legal advocacy that quickly addresses their needs for health care and child support and appropriate referrals for children and adults. In short, the goal of such courts must be to provide and rebuild a safety net for battered women and their children.

NOTES

Chapter 1

1. E. Stark, *Coercive Control: How Men Entrap Women in Personal Life* (New York: Oxford University Press, 2007).

2. P. R. Amato, L. S. Loomis, and A. Booth, "Parental Divorce, Marital Conflict and Offspring Well-being During Early Adulthood," *Adulthood, Social Forces* 73, no. 3 (1995): 895–915.

3. E. M. Hetherington, and M. Stanley-Hagen, "The Adjustment of Children with Divorced Parents: A Risk and Resiliency Perspective," *Journal of Child Psychology and Psychiatry* 40, no. 1 (1999): 129–140.

4. E. M. Hetherington, M. Cox, and R. Cox, "Divorced Fathers," *The Family Coordinator* (October 1976): 417–428.

5. J. R. Johnston, V. Roseby, and K. Kuehnle, *In the Name of the Child: A Developmental Approach to Understanding and Helping Children of Conflicted and Violent Families,* 2nd ed. (New York: Springer Publishing, 2009).

6. Amato et al., "Parental Divorce, Marital Conflict and Offspring Well-Being During Early Adulthood" (1995).

7. Ibid.

8. J. Herman, *Trauma and Recovery: The Aftermath of Violence—From Domestic Abuse to Political Terror* (New York: Basic Books, 1997).

9. K. Kendall-Tackett, *Treating the Lifetime Health Effects of Childhood Victimization*, 2nd ed. (Kingston, NJ: Civic Research Institute, 2013).

10. L. Jones, M. Hughes, and U. Unterstaller, "Post-Traumatic Stress Disorder (PTSD) in Victims of Domestic Violence," *Trauma, Violence, & Abuse* 2, no. 2 (2001): 99–119.

11. S. Griffing et al., "Exposure to Interpersonal Violence as a Predictor of PTSD Symptomatology in Domestic Violence Survivors," *Journal of Interpersonal Violence* 21, no. 7 (2006): 936–954.

12. Jones et al. "Post-Traumatic Stress Disorder (PTSD) in Victims of Domestic Violence" (2011).

13. Herman, *Trauma and Recovery* (1997).

14. L. Hourani et al., "Gender Differences in the Expression of PTSD Symptoms Among Active Duty Military Personnel," *Journal of Anxiety Disorders* 29 (January 2015): 101–108.

15. Ibid.

16. Herman, *Trauma and Recovery* (1997).

17. J. S. Volpe, "Effects of Domestic Violence on Children and Adolescents: An Overview," 1996, The American Academy of Experts in Traumatic Stress, accessed on March 22, 2017, http://www.aaets.org/article8.htm

18. American Psychiatric Association, *Diagnostic and Statistical Manual of Mental Disorders*, 5th ed. (Arlington, VA: American Psychiatric Publishing, 2013).

19. E. Alisic and R. J. Kleber, "Measuring Posttraumatic Stress Reactions in Children: A Preliminary Validation of the Children's Responses to Trauma Inventory," *Journal of Child and Adolescent Trauma* 3, no. 3 (2010): 192–204; D. Kaminer, S. Seedat, and D. J. Stein, "Post-Traumatic Stress Disorder in Children," *World Psychiatry* 4, no. 2 (2005):121–125.

20. Griffing et al., "Exposure to Interpersonal Violence as a Predictor of PTSD Symptomatology in Domestic Violence Survivors" (2006).

21. Stark, *Coercive Control* (2007).

22. Joan S. Meier, "Domestic Violence, Child Custody, and Child Protection: Understanding Judicial Resistance and Imagining the Solutions," *Am. U. J. Gender Soc. Pol'y & L.* 11, no. 2 (2003): 657–731.

23. A. E. Adams, C. Sullivan, D. Bybee, and M. R. Greeson, "Development of the Scale of Economic Abuse," *Violence Against Women* 14, no. 5 (2008): 563–588.

24. K. Parker and W. Wang, *Modern Parenthood: Roles of Moms and Dads Converge as They Balance Work and Family* (Washington, DC: Pew Research Center, 2013).

25. Kendall-Tackett, *Treating the Lifetime Health Effects of Childhood Victimization* (2013).

26. M. Juodis, A. Starzomski, S. Porter, and M. Woodworth, "A Comparison of Domestic and Non-Domestic Homicides: Further Evidence for Distinct Dynamics and Heterogeneity of Domestic Violence Perpetrators," *Journal of Family Violence* 29, no. 3 (2014): 299–313.

27. Stark, *Coercive Control* (2007).

28. E. Stark, "Reframing Child Custody Decisions in the Context of Coercive Control," in *Domestic Violence, Abuse, and Child Custody: Legal Strategies and Policy Issues*, edited by M. Hannah and B. Goldstein (Kingston, NJ: Civic Research Institute, 2010), 11:1–11:31.

29. K. Gentile, "'You Don't Recognize Me Because I'm Still Standing': The Impact of Action Research with Women Survivors of Domestic Violence," in *Domestic Violence: Methodologies in Dialogue*, edited by C. Raghavan and S. J. Cohen (Boston: Northeastern University Press, 2013), 171–199; Leigh Goodmark, "Telling Stories, Saving Lives: The Battered Mothers' Testimony Project, Women's Narratives and Court Reform," *Ariz. St. L.J.* 37, no. 3 (2005): 709–757; K. Y. Slote et al., "Battered Mothers Speak Out: Participatory Human Rights Documentation as a Model for Research and Activism in the United States," *Violence Against Women* 11, no. 11 (2005): 1367–1395.

30. N. Trocmé and N. Bala, "False Allegations of Abuse and Neglect when Parents Separate," *Child Abuse and Neglect* 29, no. 12 (2005): 1333–1345.

31. Meier, "Domestic Violence, Child Custody, and Child Protection" (2003).

32. M. Dragiewicz, "Gender Bias in the Courts: Implications for Battered Mothers and Their Children," in *Domestic Violence, Abuse, and Child Custody: Legal Strategies and Policy Issues*, edited by M. Hannah and B. Goldstein (Kingston, NJ: Civic Research Institute, 2010), 5:2–5:19.

33. L. Bancroft, J. G. Silverman, and D. Ritchie, *The Batterer as Parent: Addressing the Impact of Domestic Violence on Family Dynamics*, 2nd ed. (Los Angeles: Sage Publications, 2012).

34. M. K. Alvord and J. J. Grados, "Enhancing Resilience in Children: A Proactive Approach," *Professional Psychology: Research and Practice* 36, no. 3 (2005): 239.

35. D. Saunders, K. C. Faller, and R. Tolman, *Child Custody Evaluators' Beliefs About Domestic Abuse Allegations: Their Relationship to Evaluator Demographics, Background, Domestic Violence Knowledge and Custody-Visitation Recommendations* (Washington, DC: National Institute of Justice, 2011).

36. Jane C. Murphy and Robert Rubinson, "Domestic Violence and Mediation: Responding to the Challenges of Crafting Effective Screens," 39 *Fam. L. Q.* 53 (2005–2006); Andrew Schepard, "The Model Standards of Practice for Family and Divorce Mediation," in *Divorce and Family Mediation: Models, Techniques and Applications*, ed. Jay Folberg, Ann L. Milne, and Peter Salem (New York: Guilford Publications, 2004), 516–541; American Bar Association, American Arbitration Association, and Association for Conflict Resolution, *Model Standards of Conduct for Mediators* (August 2005), accessed on July 31, 2017 https://www.mediate.com/articles/model_standards_of_conflict.cfm#comments.

37. Nancy Ver Steegh, "Yes, No, and Maybe: Informed Decision Making About Divorce Mediation in the Presence of Domestic Violence," 9 *Wm. & Mary J. Women & L.* 145 (June 2006).

38. Bancroft et al., *The Batterer as Parent* (2012).

Chapter 2

1. P. H. Shiono and L. Sandham Quinn, "Epidemiology of Divorce, The Future of Children," *Children and Divorce* 4, no. 1 (1994): 15–28.

2. American Psychiatric Association, *Diagnostic and Statistical Manual of Mental Disorders*, 5th ed. (Arlington, VA: American Psychiatric Publishing, 2013).

3. C. R. Ahrons, "Family Ties After Divorce: Long-Term Implications for Children," *Family Process* 46, no. 1 (2006): 53–65.

4. J. R. Johnston et al., "Allegations and Substantiations of Abuse in Custody-Disputing Families," *Family Court Review* 43, no. 2 (2005): 283–294.

5. P. R. Amato, L. S. Loomis, and A. Booth, "Parental Divorce, Marital Conflict and Offspring Well-Being During Early Adulthood," *Adulthood, Social Forces* 73, no. 3 (1995): 895–915.

6. M. L. Haselschwerdt, J. L. Hardesty, and J. D. Hans, "Custody Evaluators' Beliefs About Domestic Violence Allegations During Divorce: Feminist and Family Violence Perspectives," *Journal of Interpersonal Violence* 26, no. 8 (2011): 1694–1719.

7. S. H. Patel and L. Hensley Choate, "Conducting Child Custody Evaluations: Best Practices for Mental Health Counselors who are Court-Appointed as Child Custody Evaluators," *Journal of Mental Health Counseling* 36, no. 1 (2014): 18–30

8. S. P. Herman et al., "Practice Parameters for Child Custody Evaluation," *Journal of the Academy of Child & Adolescent Psychiatry* 36, no. 10 (1997): 57S–68S; American Psychological Association, "Guidelines for Child Custody Evaluations in Family Law Proceedings," *American Psychologist* 65, no. 9 (2010): 863–867; V. Luftman et al., "Practice Guidelines in Child Custody Evaluations for Licensed Clinical Social Workers," *Clinical Social Work Journal* 33, no. 3 (2005): 327–357.

9. Patel and Choate, "Conducting Child Custody Evaluations" (2014).

10. J. Herman, *Trauma and Recovery: The Aftermath of Violence — from Domestic Abuse to Political Terror* (New York: Basic Books, 1997).

11. E. M. Hetherington, M. Cox, and R. Cox, "Divorced Fathers," *The Family Coordinator* (October 1976): 417–428.

12. E. M. Hetherington, "An Overview of the Virginia Longitudinal Study of Divorce and Remarriage with a Focus on Early Adolescence," *Journal of Family Psychology* 7, no. 1 (1993): 39–56.

13. Ibid.

14. Hetherington et al., "Divorced Fathers" (1976)

15. E. M. Hetherington, "Intimate Pathways: Changing Patterns in Close Personal Relationships Across Time," *Family Relations* 52, no. 4 (2003): 318–331.

16. E. M. Hetherington and M. Stanley-Hagen, "The Adjustment of Children with Divorced Parents: A Risk and Resiliency Perspective," *Journal of Child Psychology and Psychiatry* 40, no. 1 (1999): 129–140.

17. E. M. Hetherington, M. Cox, and R. Cox, "Long-Term Effects of Divorce and Remarriage on the Adjustment of Children," *Journal of the American Academy of Child Psychiatry* 24, no. 5 (1985): 518–530.

18. M. H. Bornstein, *Handbook of Parenting Volume 4: Social Conditions and Applied Parenting* (Mahwah, NJ: Lawrence Erlbaum Associates, 2002); Hetherington and Stanley-Hagen, "The Adjustment of Children with Divorced Parents" (1999).

19. P. R. Amato and J. G. Gilbreth, "Nonresident Fathers and Children's Well-Being: A Meta-Analysis," *Journal of Marriage and Family* 61, no. 3 (1999): 557–573.

20. Hetherington and Stanley-Hagen, "The Adjustment of Children with Divorced Parents" (1999).

21. Hetherington et al., "Long-Term Effects of Divorce and Remarriage on the Adjustment of Children" (1985).

22. J. S. Wallerstein and J. B. Kelly. *Surviving the Breakup: How Children and Parents Cope with Divorce* (New York: Basic Books, 1980).

23. J. S. Wallerstein, J. M. Lewis, and S. Blakeslee, *The Unexpected Legacy of Divorce: A 25 Year Landmark Study* (New York: Hyperion, 2000).

24. Ibid.

25. J. E. Lansford, "Parental Divorce and Children's Adjustment," *Perspectives on Psychological Science* 4, no. 2 (2009): 140–152.

26. P. R. Amato, "Reconciling Divergent Perspectives: Judith Wallerstein, Quantitative Family Research, and Children of Divorce," *Family Relations* 52, no. 4 (2003): 332–339.

27. Ibid.

28. Ibid.

29. J. R. Johnston, V. Roseby, and K. Kuehnle, *In the Name of the Child: A Developmental Approach to Understanding and Helping Children of Conflicted and Violent Families,* 2nd ed. (New York: Springer Publishing, 2009).

30. E. M. Hetherington, "Coping with Family Transitions: Winners, Losers, and Survivors," *Child Development* 60, no. 1 (1989): 1–14; J. Kiecolt-Glaser et al., "Marital Quality, Marital Disruption, and Immune Function," *Psychosomatic Medicine* 49, no. 1 (1987): 13–34.

31. M. S. Forgatch and D. S. DeGarmo, "Adult Problem Solving: Contributor to Parenting and Child Outcomes in Divorced Families," *Journal of Social Development* 6, no. 2 (1997): 237–253; Hetherington, "An Overview of the Virginia Longitudinal Study of

Divorce and Remarriage with a Focus on Early Adolescence" (1993); R. L. Simons et al., "The Impact of Mothers' Parenting, Involvement by Nonresidential Fathers, and Parental Conflict on the Adjustment of Adolescent Children," *Journal of Marriage and Family* 56 (May 1994): 356–374.

32. Hetherington, "An Overview of the Virginia Longitudinal Study of Divorce and Remarriage with a Focus on Early Adolescence" (1993).

33. Hetherington and Stanley-Hagen, "The Adjustment of Children with Divorced Parents," (1999): 130.

34. Ibid.

35. Ibid.

36. Hetherington and Stanley-Hagen, "The Adjustment of Children with Divorced Parents" (1999): 133; Amato et al., "Parental Divorce, Marital Conflict and Offspring Well-Being During Early Adulthood" (1995).

37. Hetherington and Stanley-Hagen, "The Adjustment of Children with Divorced Parents" (1999): 133; Amato et al., "Parental Divorce, Marital Conflict and Offspring Well-Being During Early Adulthood" (1995).

38. Amato, "Reconciling Divergent Perspectives" (2003).

39. Simons et al., "The Impact of Mothers' Parenting" (May 1994).

40. Forgatch and DeGarmo, "Adult Problem Solving" (1997).

41. E. E. Maccoby, C. E. Depner, and R. H. Mnookin, "Coparenting in the Second Year After Divorce," *Journal of Marriage and Family* 52 (February 1990): 141–155.

42. E. E. Maccoby et al., "Postdivorce Roles of Mothers and Fathers in the Lives of Their Children," *Journal of Family Psychology* 7, no. 1 (1993): 24–38.

43. Linda Nielsen, "Shared Residential Custody: Review of the Research," 27 *Amer. J. Fam. L.* 123 (Spring 2013).

44. Maccoby et al. "Coparenting in the Second Year After Divorce" (1990).

45. Ibid.

46. Maccoby et al. "Postdivorce Roles of Mothers and Fathers in the Lives of Their Children" (1993).

47. Wallerstein et al. *The Unexpected Legacy of Divorce* (2000); Hetherington and Stanley-Hagen, "The Adjustment of Children with Divorced Parents (1999).

48. J. McIntosh, "Special Considerations for Infants and Toddlers in Separation/Divorce: Developmental Issues in the Family Law Context," in *Encyclopedia on Early Childhood Development* [online], edited by R. E. Tremblay, M. Boivinm and R. Peters (Montreal: Center of Excellence for Early Childhood Development, 2011), 1–6. http://.enfant- encyclopedie.com/pages/PDF/Henninghausen-LyonsRuthANGxp_rev.pdf

49. Ibid.

50. Ibid.

51. McIntosh, "Special Considerations for Infants and Toddlers in Separation/Divorce" (2011); J. McIntosh, B. M. Smyth and M. Kelaher, "Overnight Care Patterns and Psycho-emotional Development in Infants and Young Children," in *Post Separation Parenting Arrangements and Developmental Outcomes for Children*, edited by J. McIntosh, J. Smyth, B. Kelaher, Y. Wells, and C. Long (Canberra: Report to the Australian Government Attorney General's Department, May 2010): 85–169.

52. McIntosh, "Special Considerations for Infants and Toddlers in Separation/Divorce" (2011).

53. M. van Ijzendoum and P. Kroonenberg, "Cross-cultural Patterns of Attachment: A Meta-Analysis of the Strange Situation," *Child Development* 59, no. 1 (1988): 147–156.

54. Hetherington, "An Overview of the Virginia Longitudinal Study of Divorce and Remarriage with a Focus on Early Adolescence" (1993).

55. Hetherington and Stanley-Hagen, "The Adjustment of Children with Divorced Parents" (1999).

56. C. M. Buchanan, E. E. Macobby, and S. M. Dorrnbusch, *Adolescents After Divorce* (Cambridge, MA: Harvard University Press, 1996), 55–56.

57. Ibid.

58. Wallerstein et al., *The Unexpected Legacy of Divorce* (2000).

59. Simons et al., "The Impact of Mothers' Parenting, Involvement by Nonresidential Fathers, and Parental Conflict on the Adjustment of Adolescent Children" (1994).

60. Simons et al., "The Impact of Mothers' Parenting, Involvement by Nonresidential Fathers, and Parental Conflict on the Adjustment of Adolescent Children" (1994): 372.

61. Buchanan et al., *Adolescents After Divorce* (1996).

62. O. Karaaslan, "Comparison of Social Engagement of Children Having Disabilities with Their Mothers and Fathers," *Educational Sciences: Theory & Practice* 16, no. 5 (2016): 1649–1670.

63. McIntosh, "Special Considerations for Infants and Toddlers in Separation/Divorce" (2011).

64. J. R. Johnston and L. E. G. Campbell, *Impasses of Divorce* (New York: Free Press, 1988).

65. M. F. Ehrenberg et al., "Adolescents in Divorcing Families: Perceptions of What Helps and Hinders," *Journal of Divorce & Remarriage* 45, no. 3/4 (2006): 69–91.

66. Buchanan et al., *Adolescents After Divorce* (1996).

67. Wallerstein et al., *The Unexpected Legacy of Divorce* (2000).

68. Amato and Keith, "Parental Divorce and the Well-Being of Children" (1991).

69. A. J. Cherlin et al., "Longitudinal Studies of Effects of Divorce on Children in Great Britain and the United States," *Science* 252, no. 5011 (1991): 1386–1389.

70. Amato and Keith, "Parental Divorce and the Well-Being of Children" (1991).

71. Amato et al. "Parental Divorce, Marital Conflict and Offspring Well-Being During Early Adulthood" (1995).

72. Amato et al., "Parental Divorce, Marital Conflict and Offspring Well-Being During Early Adulthood" (1995); P. R. Amato and A. Booth, "Consequences of Parental Divorce and Marital Unhappiness for Adult Well-Being," *Social Forces* 69, no. 3 (1991): 895–914.

73. P. R. Amato and B. Hohmann-Marriott, "A Comparison of High- and Low-Distress Marriages that End in Divorce," *Journal of Marriage and Family* 69 (August 2007): 621–638.

74. Johnston and Campbell, *Impasses of Divorce* (1988).

75. J. R. Johnston, "High-Conflict Divorce," *Children and Divorce* 4, no. 1 (1994): 165–182.

76. Ibid.

77. Ibid.

78. P. G. Jaffe and C. V. Crooks, "Understanding Women's Experiences Parenting in the Context of Domestic Violence: Implications for Community and Court-Related Service

Providers," *Violence Against Women Online Resources* (February 2005) http://citeseerx.ist. psu.edu/viewdoc/download?doi=10.1.1.192.3729&rep=rep1&type=pdf

79. J. R. Johnston and J. R. Goldman, "Outcomes of Family Counseling Interventions with Children Who Resist Visitation: An Addendum to Friedlander and Walters," *Family Court Review* 48, no. 1 (2010): 112–115.

80. Johnston et al., "Allegations and Substantiations of Abuse in Custody-Disputing Families" (2005).

81. M. Juodis, A. Starzomski, and M. Woodworth, "What Can Be Done About High-Risk Perpetrators of Domestic Violence?" *Journal of Family Violence* 29, no. 4 (2014): 381–390.

82. R. Walker et al., "An Integrative Review of Separation in the Context of Victimization: Consequences and Implications for Women," *Trauma, Violence, & Abuse* 5, no. 2 (2004): 143–193.

83. L. Bancroft and J.G. Silverman, *The Batterer as Parent: Addressing the Impact of Domestic Violence on Family Dynamics* (Los Angeles: Sage Publications, 2002): 132–133.

84. Bancroft and Silverman, *The Batterer as Parent* (2002); J. L. Hardesty and G. H. Chung, "Intimate Partner Violence, Parental Divorce, and Child Custody: Directions for Intervention and Future Research," *Family Relations* 55, no. 2 (2006): 200–210.

85. Johnston et al., "Allegations and Substantiations of Abuse in Custody-Disputing Families" (2005).

86. N. Trocmé and N. Bala, "False Allegations of Abuse and Neglect when Parents Separate," *Child Abuse and Neglect* 29 (2005): 1333–1345.

87. Amato et al., "Parental Divorce, Marital Conflict and Offspring Well-Being During Early Adulthood" (1995).

88. J. R. Johnston and R. B. Straus, "Traumatized Children in Supervised Visitation: What Do They Need?" *Family Court Review* 37, no. 2 (1999): 135–158.

89. American Psychiatric Association, DSM-5 (2013).

90. Herman, *Trauma and Recovery* (1997).

91. L. Jones, M. Hughes, and U. Unterstaller, "Post-Traumatic Stress Disorder (PTSD) in Victims of Domestic Violence," *Trauma, Violence, & Abuse* 2, no. 2 (2001): 99–119.

92. Herman, *Trauma and Recovery* (1997).

93. Johnston and Straus, "Traumatized Children in Supervised Visitation" (1999).

94. L. Fischel-Wolovick, "Police Response: Mandatory Arrest Primary Physical Aggressor," in *Lawyer's Manual on Domestic Violence: Representing the Victim*, 6th ed., edited by M. R. Rothwell Davis, D. A. Leidholdt, and C. A. Watson (New York: Supreme Court of the State of New York, Appellate Division, First Department, 2015), 52–61; Steven D. Epstein, *The Problem of Dual Arrest in Family Violence Cases* (Wethersfield, CT: Connecticut Coalition Against Domestic Violence, 1987); D. Hirschel et al., "Domestic Violence and Mandatory Arrest Laws: To What Extent Do They Influence Police Arrest Decisions?," *Journal of Criminal Law and Criminology* 98, no. 1 (2007): 255–298.

Chapter 3

1. C. Raghavan and S. J. Cohen, "Introduction," in *Domestic Violence: Methodologies in Dialogue*, edited by C. Raghavan and S. J. Cohen (Boston: Northeastern University Press, 2013), vi–xi.

2. R. J. Gelles and M. A. Straus, "Violence in the American Family," *Journal of Social Issues* 35, no. 2 (1979): 15–39.

3. R. J. Gelles, "Methodological Issues in the Study of Family Violence," in *Physical Violence in American Families: Risk Factors and Adaptions to Violence in 8,145 Families*, edited by M. A. Straus, R. J. Gelles and C. Smith (New Brunswick, NJ: Transaction Publishers, 1990), 17–28.

4. S. K. Burge et al., "Using Complexity Science to Examine Three Dynamic Patterns of Intimate Partner Violence," *Family Systems and Health* 34, no. 1 (2016): 4–14.

5. Gelles, "Methodological Issues in the Study of Family Violence" (1990); L. E. Walker, *The Battered Woman* (New York: Harper and Row, 1979); J. Giles-Sims, *Wife Battering: A Systems Theory Approach* (New York: Guilford Press, 1983); E. Pence and M. Paymar, *Education Groups for Men Who Batter: The Duluth Model* (New York: Springer Publishing, 1993).

6. E. Stark, *Coercive Control: How Men Entrap Women in Personal Life* (New York: Oxford University Press, 2007).

7. Ibid., 5.

8. J. Woodhouse and N. Dempsey, "Domestic Violence in England and Wales," *House of Commons Library, Briefing Paper 6337* (May 6, 2016); "Extended Definition of Domestic Violence Takes Effect," news release from the UK Government Home Office, March 31, 2013. https://www.gov.uk/government/news/extended-definition-of-domestic-violence-takes-effect.

9. K. Candela, "Protecting the Invisible Victim: Incorporating Coercive Control in Domestic Violence Statutes," *Family Court Review* 54, no. 1 (2016): 112–125; Domestic Violence, Crime and Victims (Amendment) Act of 2012, 5c and 6c s.76 (Eng. Wales).

10. Martin Evans, "New Domestic Violence Law Will Outlaw Coercive Control," *Telegraph (London)*, November 28, 2014 http://www.telegraph.co.uk/news/uknews/law-and-order/11244275/New-domestic-violence-law-will-outlaw-coercive-control.html

11. Domestic Violence, Crime and Victims (Amendment) Act of 2012, 5c and 6c, s. 76 (Eng. Wales).

12. Ibid.

13. Council of Europe Convention on Preventing and Combating Violence Against Women and Domestic Violence, art. 210, November 5, 2011 (Istanbul Convention).

14. Istanbul Convention (2011).

15. K. Libal and D. Parekh, "Reframing Violence Against Women as a Human Rights Violation: Evan Stark's Coercive Control," *Violence Against Women* 15, no. 2 (2009): 1477–1489.

16. Ibid.

17. J. R. Johnston and L. E. G. Campbell, "A Clinical Typology of Interparental Violence in Disputed-Custody Divorces," *American Journal of Orthopsychiatry* 63, no. 2 (1993): 190–199.

18. E. Stark, "Rethinking Custody Evaluation in Cases Involving Domestic Violence," *Journal of Child Custody* 6, no. 3 (2009): 287–321.

19. M. P. Johnson, *A Typology of Domestic Violence: Intimate Terrorism, Violent Resistance, and Situational Couple Violence* (Boston: Northeastern University Press, 2008).

20. Johnson, *A Typology of Domestic Violence* (2008); J. B. Kelly and M. P. Johnson, "Differentiation Among Types of Intimate Partner Violence: Research update and implications for interventions," *Family Court Review* 46, no. 3 (2008): 476–499.

21. M. P. Johnson, "Conflict and Control: Gender Symmetry and Asymmetry," *Violence Against Women,* 12, no.11 (November 2006): 1003–1018.

22. Pence and Paymar, *Educational Groups for Men Who Batter* (1993); Kelly and Johnson, "Differentiation Among Types of Intimate Partner Violence" (2008).

23. Kelly and Johnson, "Differentiation Among Types of Intimate Partner Violence" (2008).

24. J. S. Meier, "Johnson's Differential Theory: Is It Really Empirically Supported?" *Journal of Child Custody* 12, no. 1 (2015): 4–24.

25. Kelly and Johnson, "Differentiation Among Types of Intimate Partner Violence" (2008).

26. Johnson, *A Typology of Domestic Violence* (2008).

27. E. Stark, "Commentary on Johnson's 'Conflict and Control: Gender Symmetry and Asymmetry in Domestic Violence,'" *Violence Against Women* 12, no. 11 (2006): 1019–1025.

28. K. Graham, M. Plant, and M. Plant, "Alcohol, Gender and Partner Aggression: A General Population Study of British Adults," *Addiction Research and Theory* 12, no. 4 (2004): 385–401.

29. M. S. Kimmel, "'Gender Symmetry' in Domestic Violence: A Substantive and Methodological Research Review," *Violence Against Women* 8, no. 11 (2002): 1332–1363.

30. L. Fischel-Wolovick, "Police Response: Mandatory Arrest Primary Physical Aggressor," in *Lawyer's Manual on Domestic Violence: Representing the Victim,* 6th ed., edited by M. R. Rothwell Davis, D. A. Leidholdt, and C. A. Watson (New York: Supreme Court of the State of New York, Appellate Division, First Department, 2015), 52–61.

31. Kimmel, "'Gender Symmetry' in Domestic Violence" (2002).

32. Johnston and Campbell, "A Clinical Typology of Interparental Violence in Disputed-Custody Divorces" (1993).

33. M. A. Dutton and L. A. Goodman, "Coercion in Intimate Partner Violence: Toward a New Conceptualization," *Sex Roles* 52, no. 11 (2005): 743–756.

34. J. I. H. Frieze and M. C. McHugh, "Power and Influence Strategies in Violent and Nonviolent Marriages," *Psychology of Women Quarterly* 16, no. 4 (1992): 449–465; Meier, "Johnson's Differential Theory" (2015).

35. Frieze and McHugh, "Power and Influence Strategies in Violent and Nonviolent Marriages" (1992).

36. Meier, "Johnson's Differential Theory" (2015).

37. M. A. Straus and R. J. Gelles, *Physical Violence in American Families - Codebook 7733* (Ann Arbor, MI: Institute for Social Research, 1980); Gelles, "Methodological Issues in the Study of Family Violence" (1990).

38. M. A. Straus, S. Hamby, S. Boney-McCoy, and D. Sugarman, "The Revised Conflict Tactics Scales (CTS2): Development and Preliminary Psychometric Data," *Journal of Family Issues* 17, no. 3 (1996): 283–316; M. A. Straus, "Blaming the Messenger for the Bad News About Partner Violence by Women: The Methodological, Theoretical, and Value Basis of the Purported Invalidity of the Conflict Tactics Scales," *Behavioral Sciences and the Law* 30, no. 5 (2012): 538–556.

39. Straus, "Blaming the Messenger for the Bad News About Partner Violence by Women" (2012).

40. J. Zorza, "New Typologies: A Reinvention or a Trivialization?" unpublished manuscript, undated, Microsoft Word file.

41. Kelly and Johnson, "Differentiation Among Types of Intimate Partner Violence" (2008).

42. Straus, "Blaming the Messenger for the Bad News About Partner Violence by Women" (2012).

43. Convention on the Elimination of All Forms of Discrimination Against Women, arts. 1, 2, Dec. 18, 1979, 1249 U.N.T.S. 13 (CEDAW Convention); D. Simonovic, "Global and Regional Standards on Violence Against Women: The Evolution and Synergy of the CEDAW and Istanbul Conventions," *Human Rights Quarterly* 36, no. 3 (2014): 590–606.

44. Kimmel, "'Gender Symmetry' in Domestic Violence" (2002).

45. Kimmel, "'Gender Symmetry' in Domestic Violence" (2002); M. S. Kimmel, *The Gendered Society* (New York: Oxford University Press, 2000).

46. Kimmel, "'Gender Symmetry' in Domestic Violence" (2002).

47. Stark, "Commentary on Johnson's 'Conflict and Control'" (2006).

48. P. Tjaden and N. Thoennes, *Full Report on the Prevalence, Incidence, and Consequences of Violence Against Women* (Washington, DC: National Institute of Justice, 2000).

49. Ibid.

50. Gelles, "Methodological Issues in the Study of Family Violence" (1990).

51. Tjaden and Thoennes, *Full Report on the Prevalence, Incidence, and Consequences of Violence Against Women* (2000).

52. Fischel-Wolovick, "Police Response: Mandatory Arrest Primary Physical Aggressor" (2015).

53. R. P. Dobash and R. E. Dobash, "Reflections of Findings from the Violence Against Women Survey," *Canadian Journal of Criminology* 37 (July 1995): 457–484.

54. Kimmel, "'Gender Symmetry' in Domestic Violence" (2002).

55. Dobash and Dobash, "Reflections of Findings from the Violence Against Women Survey" (1995).

56. Ibid.

57. Ibid.

58. R. P. Dobash and R.E. Dobash, "Women's Violence to Men in Intimate Relationships: Working on a Puzzle," *British Journal of Criminology* 44, no. 3 (2004): 324–349; D. A. Gaquin, "Spouse Abuse: Data from the National Crime Survey," *Victimology* 2, no. 3 (1978): 632–643; M. D. Schwartz, "Gender and Injury in Marital Assault," *Sociological Focus* 20, no. 1 (1987): 61–75; V. F. Sacco and H. Johnson, *Patterns of Criminal Victimization in Canada* (Ottawa: Statistics Canada, 1990).

59. J. Zorza, "On Navigating Custody & Visitation Evaluations in Cases with Domestic Violence: A Judge's Guide." *Journal of Child Custody* 6, no. 3/4 (2011): 258–286.

60. Stark, "Rethinking Custody Evaluation in Cases Involving Domestic Violence" (2009).

61. P. Lehmann, C. K. Simmons, and V. K. Pillai, "The Validation of the Checklist of Controlling Behaviors (CCB): Assessing Coercive Control in Abusive Relationships," *Violence Against Women* 18, no. 8 (2012): 913–933.

62. Dutton and Goodman, "Coercion in Intimate Partner Violence" (2005).

63. Ibid.

64. L. Fischel-Wolovick, "The Primary Aggressor Law: Dual Arrests and Self Defense," in *Lawyer's Manual on Domestic Violence: Representing the Victim,* 2nd ed., edited by R. E. Cohen and J. C. Neely (New York: Supreme Court of the State of New York, Appellate Division, First Department, 1998), 235–246.

Chapter 4

1. J. Herman, *Trauma and Recovery: The Aftermath of Violence—From Domestic Abuse to Political Terror* (New York: Basic Books, 1997).

2. American Psychiatric Association, *Diagnostic and Statistical Manual of Mental Disorders*, 5th ed. (Arlington, VA: American Psychiatric Publishing, 2013).

3. Ibid., 309.81.

4. Ibid.

5. R. Pat-Horenczyk et al., "Emotion Regulation in Mothers and Young Children Faced with Trauma," *Infant Mental Health Journal* 36, no. 3 (2015): 337–348.

6. C. M. Chemtob et al., "Impact of Maternal Posttraumatic Stress Disorder and Depression Following Exposure to the September 11 Attacks on Preschool Children's Behavior," *Child Development* 81, no. 4 (2010): 1129–1141.

7. J. D. Bremner, *Does Stress Damage the Brain? Understanding Trauma-Based Disorders from a Neurological Perspective* (New York: Norton Publishing, 2003).

8. D. Finkelhor, "The Victimization of Children: A Developmental Perspective," *American Journal of Orthopsychiatry* 65, no. 2 (1995): 177–193.

9. V. J. Felitti et al., "Relationship of Childhood Abuse and Household Dysfunction to Many of the Leading Causes of Death in Adults," *American Journal of Preventive Medicine* 14, no. 4 (1998): 245–258.

10. R. F. Anda et al., "The Enduring Effects of Abuse and Related Adverse Experiences in Childhood: A Convergence of Evidence from Neurobiology and Epidemiology," *European Archives of Psychiatry and Clinical Neuroscience* 256, no. 3 (2006): 174–186.

11. J. D. Bremner, "The Relationship Between Cognitive and Brain Changes in Posttraumatic Stress Disorder," *Annals of the New York Academy of Science* 1071 (July 2006): 80–86.

12. S. A. McPherson-Sexton, "Normal Memory Versus Traumatic Memory Formation: Does Traumatic Stress Damage the Brain?" *Journal of Police Crisis Negotiations* 6, no. 2 (2006): 65–78; R. S. Edelstein, K. W. Alexander, G. S. Goodman, and J. W. Newton, "Emotion and Eyewitness Memory," in *Memory and Emotion*, edited by D. Resiburg and P. Hertel (New York: Oxford University Press, 2004), 308–346; K. K. Shobe and J. F. Kihlstrom, "Is Traumatic Memory Special?" *Current Directions in Psychological Science* 6, no. 3 (1997): 70–74.

13. Shobe and Kihlstrom, "Is Traumatic Memory Special?" (1997): 72; McPherson-Sexton, "Normal Memory Versus Traumatic Memory Formation" (2006).

14. C. Spatz Widom, K. G. Raphael, and K. A. DuMont, "The Case for Prospective Longitudinal Studies in Child Maltreatment Research: Commentary on Dube, Williamson, Thompson, Felitti, and Anda," *Child Abuse and Neglect* 28, no. 7 (2004): 715–722.

15. K. Kendall-Tackett, *Treating the Lifetime Health Effects of Childhood Victimization*, 2nd ed. (Kingston, NJ: Civic Research Institute, 2013).

16. J. Gayle Beck et al., "Exploring Negative Emotion in Women Experiencing Intimate Partner Violence: Shame, Guilt and PTSD," *Behavior Therapy* 42, no. 4 (2011): 740–750.

17. C. R. Brewin, B. Andrews, and J. D. Valentine, "Meta-Analysis of Risk Factors for Posttraumatic Stress Disorder in Trauma-Exposed Adults," *Journal of Consulting and Clinical Psychology* 68, no. 5 (2000): 748–766; D. A. Lee, P. Scragg, and S. Turner,

"The Role of Shame and Guilt in Traumatic Events: A Clinical Model of Shame-Based and Guilt-Based PTSD," *The British Journal of Medical Psychology* 74, no. Pt4 (2001): 451–466.

18. C. Feiring, L. Taska, and M. Lewis, "The Role of Shame and Attributional Style in Children's and Adolescent's Adaptation to Sexual Abuse," *Child Maltreatment* 3, no. 2 (1998): 129–142.

19. Feiring et al., "The Role of Shame and Attributional Style in Children's and Adolescent's Adaptation to Sexual Abuse" (1998); M. Lewis, *Shame and Guilt in Neurosis* (New York: International Universities Press, 1992).

20. M. A. Pico-Alfonso, "Psychological Intimate Partner Violence: The Major Predictor of Posttraumatic Stress Disorder in Abused Women," *Neuroscience and Biobehavioral Reviews* 29, no. 1 (2005): 181–193.

21. Kendall-Tackett, *Treating the Lifetime Health Effects of Childhood Victimization* (2013): 1–5.

22. S. R. Dube et al., "Cumulative Childhood Stress and Autoimmune Diseases in Adults," *Psychosomatic Medicine* 71, no. 2 (2009): 243–250; Kendall-Tackett, *Treating the Lifetime Health Effects of Childhood Victimization* (2013).

23. Kendall-Tackett, *Treating the Lifetime Health Effects of Childhood Victimization* (2013): 1–7; E. A. Walker et al., "Adult Health Status of Women with Histories of Childhood Abuse and Neglect," *The American Journal of Medicine* 107, no. 4 (1999): 332–339.

24. A. F. Lieberman, "Infants Remember: War Exposure, Trauma, and Attachment in Young Children and Their Mothers," *Journal of the American Academy of Child & Adolescent Psychiatry* 50, no. 7 (2011): 640–641.

25. R. Feldman and A. Vengrober, "Posttraumatic Stress Disorder in Infants and Young Children Exposed to War-Related Trauma," *Journal of the American Academy of Child & Adolescent Psychiatry* 50, no. 7 (2011): 645–658.

26. J. Bowlby, *A Secure Base: Parent-Child Attachment and Healthy Human Development* (New York: Basic Books, 1988); Feldman and Vengrober, "Posttraumatic Stress Disorder in Infants and Young Children Exposed to War-Related Trauma" (2011).

27. E. Alisic, and R. J. Kleber, "Measuring Posttraumatic Stress Reactions in Children: A Preliminary Validation of the Children's Responses to Trauma Inventory," *Journal of Child and Adolescent Trauma* 3, no. 3 (2010).

28. R. S. Pynoos, A. K. Goenjian, and A. M. Steinberg, "Children and Disasters: A Developmental Approach to Posttraumatic Stress Disorder in Children and Adolescents," *Psychiatry and Clinical Neurosciences* 52, no. S1 (1998).

29. M. Bair-Merritt, B. Zuckerman, M. Augustyn, and P. Cronholm, "Silent Victims: An Epidemic of Childhood Exposure to Domestic Violence," *New England Journal of Medicine* 369, no. 18 (2013): 1673–1675; Lisa James and Sally Schaeffer to Interested Health Professionals, May 12, 2012, re: Interpersonal and Domestic Violence Screening and Counseling: Understanding New Federal Rules and Providing Resources for Health Providers.

30. Herman, *Trauma and Recovery* (1997).

31. M. Pagelow, "The Effects of Domestic Violence on Children and Their Consequences for Custody and Visitation Agreements," *Conflict Resolution Quarterly* 7, no. 4 (1990): 347–363.

32. L. E. Walker, *The Battered Woman Syndrome* (New York: Springer, 1984); J. Giles-Sims, "A Longitudinal Study of Battered Children of Battered Wives," *Family Relations*

34, no. 2 (1985): 205–210; E. Walker and L. Fischel-Wolovick, "Children Who Witness Domestic Violence," *N. Y. L. J.*, October 19, 1994.

33. J. H. Kashani and W. D. Allan, *The Impact of Family Violence on Children and Adolescents* (New York: Sage Publications, 1998); S. Holt, H. Buckley H, and S. Whelan, "The Impact of Exposure to Domestic Violence on Children and Young People: A Review of the Literature," *Child Abuse and Neglect* 32, no. 8 (2008): 797–810.

34. J. L. Edleson, "Children's Witnessing of Adult Domestic Violence," *Journal of Interpersonal Violence* 14, no. 8 (1999): 839–870; Kashani and Allan, *The Impact of Family Violence on Children and Adolescents* (1998); Holt et al., "The Impact of Exposure to Domestic Violence on Children and Young People" (2008).

35. Holt et al., "The Impact of Exposure to Domestic Violence on Children and Young People" (2008).

36. S. Schechter and J. L. Edleson, *Effective Intervention in Domestic Violence and Child Maltreatment Cases: Guidelines for Policy and Practice* (also known as the *Greenbook*) (Washington, DC: National Council of Juvenile and Family Court Judges, 1999).

37. J. McCord, "A Forty Year Perspective on Effects of Child Abuse and Neglect," *Child Abuse and Neglect* 7, no. 3 (1983): 265–270.

38. Ibid.

39. V. A. Foshee et al., "Shared Risk Factors for the Perpetration of Physical Dating Violence, Bullying, and Sexual Harassment Among Adolescents Exposed to Domestic Violence," *Journal of Youth and Adolescence* 45, no. 4 (2015): 672–686.

40. Ibid.

41. C. S. Stover et al., "The Effects of Father Visitation on Preschool-Aged Witnesses of Domestic Violence," *Journal of Interpersonal Violence* 18, no. 10 (2003): 1149–1166.

42. R. Bolen, *Child Sexual Abuse: Its Scope and Our Failure* (New York: Kluwer Academic/Plenum Publishers, 2001); D. Finkelhor, G. T. Hotaling, I. A. Lewis, and C. Smith, "Sexual Abuse in a National Survey of Adult Men and Women: Prevalence, Characteristics, and Risk Factors," *Child Abuse and Neglect* 14, no. 9 (1990): 19–28; D. E. Russell, "The Incidence and Prevalence of Intrafamilial and Extrafamilial Sexual Abuse," *Child Abuse and Neglect* 7, no. 2 (1983): 133–146; G. E. Wyatt, "The Sexual Abuse of Afro-American and White-American Women in Childhood," *Child Abuse and Neglect* 9, no. 4 (1985): 507–519.

43. Bolen, *Child Sexual Abuse* (2001); D. Finkelhor, *Childhood Victimization: Violence, Crime, and Abuse in the Lives of Young People* (New York: Oxford University Press, 2008).

44. A. J. Sedlak et al., *Fourth National Incidence Study of Child Abuse and Neglect (NIS-4): Report to Congress* (Washington, DC: US Department of Health and Human Services, Administration for Children and Families, 2010).

45. Sedlak et al., *Fourth National Incidence Study of Child Abuse and Neglect (NIS-4)* (2010): 5.

46. F. W. Putnam, "Ten-Year Research Update Review: Child Sexual Abuse," *Journal of the American Academy of Child & Adolescent Psychiatry* 42, no. 3 (2003): 269–278.

47. Ibid.

48. Bolen, *Child Sexual Abuse* (2001).

49. J. A. Arroyo, T. L. Simpson, and A. S. Aragon, "Childhood Sexual Abuse Among Hispanic and Non-Hispanic White College Women," *Hispanic Journal of Behavioral Sciences* 19, no. 1 (1997): 57–68; Bolen, *Child Sexual Abuse* (2001).

50. Putnam, "Ten-Year Research Update Review" (2003): 271.

51. Ibid., 272.

52. Mayo Clinic Staff, "Diseases and Conditions: Child Abuse," Mayo Clinic, accessed March 22, 2017, http://www.mayoclinic.org/diseases-conditions/child-abuse/basics/definition/con-20033789

53. Putnam, "Ten-Year Research Update Review" (2003): 272.

54. C. Stevens-Simon and S. Reichert, "Sexual Abuse, Adolescent Pregnancy, and Child Abuse: A Developmental Approach to an Intergenerational Cycle," *Archives of Pediatrics and Adolescent Medicine* 148, no. 1 (1994): 23–27; Putnam, "Ten-Year Research Update Review" (2003): 272.

55. Putnam, "Ten-Year Research Update Review" (2003).

56. Mayo Clinic Staff, "Diseases and Conditions: Child Abuse."

57. Putnam, "Ten-Year Research Update Review" (2003); F. W. Putnam and P. K. Trickett, "Psychobiological Effects of Sexual Abuse: A Longitudinal Study," *Annals of the New York Academy of Science* 821 (June 21, 1997): 150–159.

58. Pico-Alfonso, "Psychological Intimate Partner Violence" (2005)

59. K. McBride, *Child Sexual Abuse Investigations: A Joint Investigative Approach Combining the Expertise of Mental Health and Law Enforcement Professionals* (Ljubljana, Slovenia: College of Police and Security Studies, 1996). https://www.ncjrs.gov/policing/chi341.htm

60. Ibid.

61. Centers for Disease Control and Prevention (CDC), "Sexual Assault and Abuse and STDs," accessed March 22, 2017 https://www.cdc.gov/std/tg2015/sexual-assault.htm

62. C. A. Plummer and J. A. Eastin, "System Intervention Problems in Child Sexual Abuse Investigations," *Journal of Interpersonal Violence* 22, no. 6 (2007): 775–787.

63. J. Corcoran, "Treatment Outcome Research with the Non-Offending Parents of Sexually Abused Children: A Critical Review," *Journal of Child Sexual Abuse* 13, no. 2 (2004): 59–67.

64. K. C. Faller, *Interviewing Children About Sexual Abuse: Controversies and Best Practice* (New York: Oxford University Press, 2007).

65. Ibid.

66. B. Kroll and A. Taylor, "Invisible Children? Parental Substance Abuse and Child Protection: Dilemmas for Practice," *Probation Journal* 47, no. 2 (2000): 91–100; S. Margura and A. B. Laudet, "Parental Substance Abuse and Child Maltreatment: Review and Implications for Intervention," *Children and Youth Services Review* 18, no. 3 (1996): 193–220.

67. S. Golder, M. R. Gillmore, M. R. Spieker, and D. Morrison, "Substance Use, Related Problem Behaviors and Adult Attachment in a Sample of High-Risk Older Adolescent Women," *Journal of Child and Family Studies* 14, no. 2 (2005): 181–193; A. Cihan, D. A. Winstead, J. Laulis, and M. D. Feit, "Attachment Theory and Substance Abuse: Etiological Links," *Journal of Human Behavior in the Social Environment* 24, no. 5 (2014): 531–537.

68. A. Schindler and S. Broning, "A Review on Attachment and Adolescent Substance Abuse: Empirical Evidence and Implications for Prevention and Treatment," *Substance Abuse* 36, no. 3 (2015): 304–313.

69. Cihan et al., "Attachment Theory and Substance Abuse" (2014): 534.

70. L. Bancroft, J. G. Silverman, and D. Ritchie, *The Batterer as Parent: Addressing the Impact of Domestic Violence on Family Dynamics*, 2nd ed. (Los Angeles: Sage Publications, 2012).

71. W. Marsiglio et al., "Scholarship on Fatherhood in the 1990s and Beyond," *Journal of Marriage and Family* 62, no. 4 (2000): 1173–1191.

72. Stover et al., "The Effects of Father Visitation on Preschool-Aged Witnesses of Domestic Violence" (2003).

73. A. F. Lieberman and P. Van Horn, "Attachment, Trauma, and Domestic Violence: Implications for Child Custody," *Child and Adolescent Psychiatric Clinics of North America* 7, no. 2 (1998): 423–443.

74. Stover et al., "The Effects of Father Visitation on Preschool-Aged Witnesses of Domestic Violence" (2003).

75. J. S. Meier, "Getting Real About Abuse and Alienation: A Critique of Drozd and Olesen's Decision Tree," *Journal of Child Custody* 7, no. 4 (2010): 219–252.

76. E. Peled, "Children of Battering Men: Living in Conflicts of Loyalties and Emotions," (paper presented at the 4th International Family Violence Research Conference, Durham, NH, July 1995).

77. Bancroft et al., *The Batterer as Parent* (2012).

78. Ibid.

79. Stover et al., "The Effects of Father Visitation on Preschool-Aged Witnesses of Domestic Violence" (2003).

80. Ibid.

81. Ibid.

82. M. Shepard, "Child-visiting and Domestic Abuse," *Child Welfare* 71, no. 4 (1992): 357–367.

83. Ibid.

84. Ibid.

85. J. R. Johnston and R. B. Straus, "Traumatized Children in Supervised Visitation: What Do They Need?" *Family Court Review* 37, no. 2 (1999): 135–158.

86. Ibid.

87. R. A. Gardner, *Sex Abuse Hysteria: Salem Witch Trials Revisited* (Cresskill, NJ: Creative Therapeutics, 1991); R. A. Gardner, *The Parental Alienation Syndrome: A Guide for Mental Health and Legal Professionals* (Cresskill, NJ: Creative Therapeutics, 1992).

88. R. A. Gardner, "Does DSM-IV Have Equivalents for the Parental Alienation Syndrome (PAS) Diagnosis?" *American Journal of Family Therapy* 31, no. 1 (2003): 1–21.

89. P. Tjaden and N. Thoennes, *Full Report on the Prevalence, Incidence, and Consequences of Violence Against Women* (Washington, DC: National Institute of Justice, 2000); Bolen, *Child Sexual Abuse* (2001); Sedlak et al., *Fourth National Incidence Study of Child Abuse and Neglect (NIS–4): Report to Congress* (2010).

90. K. C. Faller, "Possible Explanations for Child Sexual Abuse Allegations in Divorce," *American Journal of Orthopsychiatry* 61, no. 1 (1991): 86–91.

91. Gardner, *Sex Abuse Hysteria* (1991).

92. Ibid.

93. Ibid.

94. Ibid.

95. R. A. Gardner, *True and False Allegations of Child Sex Abuse* (Cresskill, NJ: Creative Therapeutics, 1992).

96. K. C. Faller, "The Parental Alienation Syndrome: What Is It and What Data Support It?" *Child Maltreatment* 3, no. 2 (1998): 100–115.

97. Ibid.

98. Cheri L. Wood, "The Parental Alienation Syndrome: A Dangerous Aura of Reliability," 27 *Loy. L.A. L. Rev.*1367 (1994).

99. Wood, "The Parental Alienation Syndrome" (1994): 1375; J. R. Conte et al., "Evaluating Children's Reports of Sexual Abuse: Results from a Survey of Professionals," *American Journal of Orthopsychiatry* 61, no. 3 (1991): 428–437.

100. N. Trocmé and N. Bala, "False Allegations of Abuse and Neglect when Parents Separate," *Child Abuse and Neglect* 29, no. 12 (2005): 1333–1345.

101. Gardner, *Sex Abuse Hysteria* (1991); K. C. Faller, *Child Sexual Abuse: Intervention and Treatment Issues* (Washington, DC: US Department of Health and Human Services, National Center on Child Abuse and Neglect, 1993); Faller, "The Parental Alienation Syndrome" (1998); K. C. Faller, "False Accusations of Child Maltreatment: A Contested Issue," *Child Abuse and Neglect* 29, no. 12 (2005): 1327–1331.

102. Faller, "The Parental Alienation Syndrome" (1998).

103. J. D. Hans et al., "The Effects of Domestic Violence Allegations on Custody Evaluators' Recommendations," *Journal of Family Psychology* 28, no. 6 (2014): 957–966.

104. American Psychological Association, "Statement on Parental Alienation Syndrome," press release dated January 1, 2008, accessed March 22, 2017. http://www.apa.org/news/press/releases/2008/01/pas-syndrome.aspx

105. M. Clemente and D. Padilla-Racero, "Are Children Susceptible to Manipulation? The Best Interest of Children and Their Testimony," *Children and Youth Services Review* 51 (February 2015): 101–107.

106. W. Bernet, M. C. Verrochio, and S. Korosi, "Yes, Children Are Susceptible to Manipulation: Commentary on Article by Clemente and Padilla-Racero," *Children and Youth Services Review* 56 (September 2015): 135–138; M. Clemente and D. Padilla-Racero, "Facts Speak Louder than Words: Science Versus the Pseudoscience of PAS," *Children and Youth Services Review* 56 (September 2015): 177–184.

107. E. Stark, "Reframing Child Custody Decisions in the Context of Coercive Control," in *Domestic Violence, Abuse, and Child Custody: Legal Strategies and Policy Issues*, edited by M. Hannah and B. Goldstein (Kingston, NJ: Civic Research Institute, 2010), 11:1–11:31.

108. R. E. Cheit, *The Witch-Hunt Narrative: Politics, Psychology, and the Sexual Abuse of Children* (New York: Oxford University Press, 2014).

109. *Matter of Nicole V.,* 71 N.Y. 2d 112 (1987).

110. Ibid.

111. Trocmé and Bala, "False Allegations of Abuse and Neglect when Parents Separate" (2005); N. Trocmé et al., *Canadian Incidence Study of Reported Child Abuse and Neglect: Final Report* (Ottawa: Minister of Public Works and Government Services Canada, 2001).

112. Trocmé and Bala, "False Allegations of Abuse and Neglect when Parents Separate" (2005).

113. Ibid., 1341.

114. Trocmé and Bala, "False Allegations of Abuse and Neglect when Parents Separate" (2005).

115. E. Stark, "Rethinking Custody Evaluation in Cases Involving Domestic Violence," *Journal of Child Custody* 6, no. 3 (2009): 287–321.

116. McBride, *Child Sexual Abuse Investigations* (1996).

117. J. Hetherton and L. Beardsall, "Decisions and Attitudes Concerning Child Sexual Abuse: Does the Gender of the Perpetrator Make a Difference to Child Protection Professionals?" *Child Abuse and Neglect* 22, no. 12 (1998): 1265–1283; Bolen, *Child Sexual Abuse* (2001).

118. M. L. Haselschwerdt, J. L. Hardesty, and J. D. Hans, "Custody Evaluators' Beliefs About Domestic Violence Allegations During Divorce: Feminist and Family Violence Perspectives," *Journal of Interpersonal Violence* 26, no. 8 (2011): 1694–1719.

119. W. G. Austin et al., "Parental Gatekeeping and Child Custody/Child Access Evaluation: Part I: Conceptual Framework, Research, and Applications," *Family Court Review* 51, no. 3 (2013): 485–501.

120. Ibid.

121. Ibid.

122. Ibid.

123. Herman, *Trauma and Recovery* (1997).

124. Bancroft and Silverman, *The Batterer as Parent* (2002): 61.

125. Bancroft and Silverman, *The Batterer as Parent* (2002); Margolin, G. "Effects of Domestic Violence on Children." in *Violence Against Children in the Family and Community*, edited by P. Trickett and C. Schellenbach (Washington, DC: American Psychological Association, 1998), 57–101.

Chapter 5

1. E. Stark, *Coercive Control: How Men Entrap Women in Personal Life* (New York: Oxford University Press, 2007).

2. N. Bernstein, *The Lost Children of Wilder: The Epic Struggle to Change Foster Care* (New York: Vintage Books, 2001).

3. *Lassiter v. Dept. Social Services of Durham Co. North Carolina*, 452 U.S. 18 (1981).

4. *In re. Gault*, 387 U.S. 1 (1967).

5. Ibid.

6. *Wilder v. Sugarman*, 385 F. Supp. 1013 (U.S.D.N.Y. 1974); see also *Wilder v. Bernstein*, 499 F. Supp. 980 (U.S.D.N.Y. 1980).

7. U.S. Const. amend. I.

8. U.S. Const. amend. XIV, § 1.

9. *Wilder v. Bernstein* (1980); Bernstein, *The Lost Children of Wilder* (2001).

10. *Bruno v. Codd*, 47 N.Y. 2d 582 (1979).

11. Ibid.

12. *Nicholson v. Scoppetta*, 4 N.Y. 3d 357 (2004), 344 F.3d 154 (2d Cir. 2003).

13. Ibid.

14. Joan S. Meier, "Domestic Violence, Child Custody, and Child Protection: Understanding Judicial Resistance and Imagining the Solutions," 11 *Am. U. J. Gender Soc. Pol'y & L.* 657 (2003).

15. Ibid.

16. Meier, "Domestic Violence, Child Custody, and Child Protection" (2003): 3.

17. L. Bancroft, J. G. Silverman, and D. Ritchie, *The Batterer as Parent: Addressing the Impact of Domestic Violence on Family Dynamics*, 2nd ed. (Los Angeles: Sage Publications, 2012).

18. M. Dragiewicz, "Gender Bias in the Courts: Implications for Battered Mothers and Their Children," in *Domestic Violence, Abuse, and Child Custody: Legal Strategies and Policy Issues,* edited by M. Hannah and B. Goldstein (Kingston, NJ: Civic Research Institute, 2010), 5:2–5:19; National Judicial Education Program to Promote Equality for Women and Men in the Courts, "Understanding Sexual Violence: The Judge's Role in Stranger and Nonstranger Rape and Sexual Assault Cases," A Self-Directed Video Curriculum.

19. L. Hecht Schafran and N. J. Wikler, *Gender Fairness in the Courts: Action in the New Millennium* (New York: Legal Momentum [Formerly NOW Legal Defense and Education Fund], 2001).

20. J. Resnick, "Asking About Gender in Courts," *Signs* 21 (Summer 1996): 952–960.

21. Ibid.

22. Jeannette F. Swent, "Gender Bias at the Heart of Justice: An Empirical Study of State Task Forces," 6 *S. Cal. Rev. L. & Women's Stud.* 1 (1996).

23. L. Hecht Schafran and N. J. Wikler, *Operating a Task Force on Gender Bias in the Courts: A Manual for Action* (New York: Legal Momentum [Formerly NOW Legal Defense and Education Fund], 1986): 1.

24. Resnick, "Asking About Gender in Courts (1996).

25. Gender Bias Study Committee of the Massachusetts Supreme Judicial Court, *Gender Bias Study of the Supreme Judicial Court, Commonwealth of Massachusetts* (Washington, DC: National Institute of Justice, 1989).

26. Ibid.

27. United States Census Bureau, *Statistical Abstract of the United States: 1989* (Washington, DC: United States Census Bureau, 1989).

28. G. Danforth and B. Welling, *Achieving Equal Justice for Women and Men in the California Courts: Final Report* (New York: Legal Momentum [Formerly NOW Legal Defense and Education Fund], 1996).

29. K. Czapanskiy and T. O'Neill, *Report of the Maryland Special Joint Committee on Gender Bias in the Courts* (New York: Legal Momentum [Formerly NOW Legal Defense and Education Fund], 1989).

30. Resnick, "Asking About Gender in Courts" (1996); New York Task Force on Women, "Report of the New York Task Force on Women in the Courts," 15 *Fordham Urb. L.J.* 15 (1986), 17–18.

31. Gender Bias Study Committee of the Massachusetts Supreme Judicial Court, *Gender Bias Study of the Supreme Judicial Court, Commonwealth of Massachusetts* (1989).

32. Resnick, "Asking About Gender in Courts" (1996).

33. Lilia M. Cortina, "The Study of Gender in the Courts; Keeping Bias at Bay," 27 *Law & Social Inquiry* 199 (2002).

34. Kimberly A. Lonsway et al., "Understanding the Judicial Role in Addressing Gender Bias: A View from the Eighth Circuit Federal Court System," 27 *Law & Soc. Inquiry* 205 (2002).

35. Ibid.

36. Model Code for Judicial Conduct (Am. Bar Ass'n 1990), C- 3B, R-5, amended August 6, 1990, August 10, 1999, August 12, 2003, February 12, 2007, and August 10, 2010, C-2, R-2.3; Lonsway et al., "Understanding the Judicial Role in Addressing Gender Bias" (2002).

37. Gender Bias Study Committee of the Massachusetts Supreme Judicial Court, *Gender Bias Study of the Supreme Judicial Court, Commonwealth of Massachusetts* (1989); Lonsway et al., "Understanding the Judicial Role in Addressing Gender Bias" (2002).

38. Lonsway et al., "Understanding the Judicial Role in Addressing Gender Bias" (2002); Minnesota Supreme Court Task Force for Gender Fairness in the Courts, "Minnesota Supreme Court Task Force for Gender Fairness in the Courts, Final Report," 15 *Wm. Mitchell L. Rev.* 827 (1989).

39. Lonsway et al., "Understanding the Judicial Role in Addressing Gender Bias" (2002).

40. M. Dragiewicz, "Gender Bias in the Courts (2010).

41. Advisory Committee of the Conrad N. Hilton Foundation, *Model Code on Domestic and Family Violence* (Reno, NV: National Council of Juvenile and Family Court Judges, 1994): 33.

42. H. Davidson, *The Impact of Domestic Violence on Children: A Report to the President of the American Bar Association* (Washington, DC: ABA Center on Children and the Law, 1994).

43. A. C. Morrill et al., "Child Custody and Visitation Decisions when the Father Has Perpetrated Violence Against the Mother," *Violence Against Women* 11, no. 8 (2005): 1076–1107.

44. Morrill et al., "Child Custody and Visitation Decisions when the Father Has Perpetrated Violence Against the Mother" (2005): 1101.

45. C. O'Sullivan, *Domestic Violence, Visitations and Custody Decisions in New York Family Courts, Final Report* (New York: Safe Horizon, 2002).

46. D. Saunders, K. C. Faller, and R. Tolman, *Child Custody Evaluators' Beliefs About Domestic Abuse Allegations: Their Relationship to Evaluator Demographics, Background, Domestic Violence Knowledge and Custody-Visitation Recommendations* (Washington, DC: National Institute of Justice, 2011), 18.

47. Saunders et al., *Child Custody Evaluators' Beliefs About Domestic Abuse Allegations* (2011).

48. Ibid., 8.

49. Meier, "Domestic Violence, Child Custody, and Child Protection" (2003).

50. Dragiewicz, "Gender Bias in the Courts" (2010); Morrill et al., "Child Custody and Visitation Decisions when the Father Has Perpetrated Violence Against the Mother" (2005).

51. Dragiewicz, "Gender Bias in the Courts" (2010).

52. Stark, *Coercive Control* (2007).

53. "History of the National Judicial Education Program," Legal Momentum [Formerly NOW Legal Defense and Education Fund], accessed November 19, 2016, http://www.legalmomentum.org/history-national-judicial-education-program-0

54. Dragiewicz, "Gender Bias in the Courts" (2010).

55. C. K. Cuthbert et al., *Battered Mothers Speak Out: A Human Rights Report on Domestic Violence and Child Custody in the Massachusetts Family Courts* (Wellesley, MA: Battered Mothers' Testimony Project at the Wellesley Centers for Women, 2002); K. Y. Slote et al., "Battered Mothers Speak Out: Participatory Human Rights Documentation as a Model for Research and Activism in the United States," *Violence Against Women* 11, no. 11 (2005): 1367–1395; Leigh Goodmark, "Telling Stories, Saving Lives: The Battered Mothers' Testimony Project, Women's Narratives and Court Reform," 37 *Ariz. St. L.J.* 709 (2005).

56. Cuthbert et al., *Battered Mothers Speak Out* (2002); Slote et al., "Battered Mothers Speak Out" (2005).

57. Voices of Women Organizing Project, *Justice Denied: How Family Courts in New York City Endanger Battered Women and Children* (Brooklyn, NY: Battered Women's Resource Center, 2008); K. Gentile, "'You Don't Recognize Me Because I'm Still Standing': The Impact of Action Research with Women Survivors of Domestic Violence," in *Domestic Violence: Methodologies in Dialogue*, edited by C. Raghavan and S. J. Cohen (Boston: Northeastern University Press, 2013), 171–199; Alison Bowen, "Report: Abused Women See Danger in Family Court," WomensENews, May 8, 2008. http://womensenews. org/2008/05/report-abused-women-see-danger-in-family-court/

58. Voices of Women Organizing Project, *Justice Denied* (2008); Alison Bowen, "Report: Abused Women See Danger in Family Court" (2008).

59. Voices of Women Organizing Project, *Justice Denied* (2008).

60. Arizona Coalition Against Domestic Violence, *Battered Mothers' Testimony Project: A Human Rights Approach to Child Custody and Domestic Violence* (Phoenix, AZ: Arizona Coalition Against Domestic Violence, 2003).

61. M. F. Brinig, L. M. Frederick, and L. M. Drozd, "Perspectives on Joint Custody Presumptions as Applied to Domestic Violence," *Family Court Review* 52, no. 2 (2014): 271–281.

62. Gentile, "'You Don't Recognize Me Because I'm Still Standing'" (2013); Goodmark, "Telling Stories, Saving Lives" (2005); Cuthbert et al., *Battered Mothers Speak Out* (2002).

63. K. Y. Slote et al., "Battered Mothers Speak Out: Participatory Human Rights Documentation as a Model for Research and Activism in the United States," *Violence Against Women* 11, no. 11 (2005): 1367–1395; Arizona Coalition Against Domestic Violence, *Battered Mothers' Testimony Project: A Human Rights Approach to Child Custody and Domestic Violence* (Phoenix: Arizona Coalition Against Domestic Violence, 2003).

64. K. Y. Slote et al., "Battered Mothers Speak Out: Participatory Human Rights Documentation as a Model for Research and Activism in the United States," *Violence Against Women* 11, no. 11 (2005): 1367–1395; U. N. Convention on the Rights of the Child, art. 2, Nov. 20, 1989, 1577 U.N.T.S. 3; Convention on the Elimination of All Forms of Discrimination Against Women, arts. 1, 2, Dec. 18, 1979, 1249 U.N.T.S. 13 (CEDAW Convention).

65. Slote et al., "Battered Mothers Speak Out" (2005).

66. Ibid.

67. Dorchen Leidholdt (legal director, Center for Battered Women's Legal Services, Sanctuary for Families), in discussion with the author, July 2015.

68. R. M. Celorio, "The Case of Karen Atala and Daughters: Toward a Better Understanding of Discrimination, Equality and the Rights of Women." 15 *CUNY L. Rev.* 335 (2012); Organization of American States (OAS), American Convention of Human Rights, arts. 1(1),24, Nov. 22, 1969, O.A.S.T.S. No. 36, 1144 U.N.T.S. 123 (American Convention); Inter-American Convention on the Prevention, Punishment, and Eradication of Violence Against Women, arts. 6, 8(b), June 9, 1994, 27 UST. 3301, 1438 U.N.T.S. 63 (Convention of Belem do Para).

69. Celorio, "The Case of Karen Atala and Daughters" (2012).

70. Deborah Dinner, "The Divorce Bargain: The Fathers' Rights Movement and Family Inequalities," 102 *Va. L. Rev.* 79 (2016).

71. M. Flood, "Separated Fathers and the 'Fathers' Rights' Movement," *Journal of Family Studies* 18, no. 2–3 (2012): 235–245.

72. J. E. Crowley, "Adopting 'Equality Tools' from the Toolboxes of Their Predecessors: The Fathers' Rights Movement in the United States," in *Fathers' Rights Activism and Law Reform in Comparative Perspective*, edited by R. Collier and S. Sheldon (Oxford, UK: Hart Publishing, 2006), 79–100; Flood, "Separated Fathers and the 'Fathers' Rights' Movement" (2012).

73. Meier, "Domestic Violence, Child Custody, and Child Protection" (2003).

74. Ibid., 8.

75. K. C. Faller, "False Accusations of Child Maltreatment: A Contested Issue," *Child Abuse and Neglect* 29, no. 12 (2005): 1327–1331.

76. N. Trocmé and N. Bala, "False Allegations of Abuse and Neglect when Parents Separate," *Child Abuse and Neglect* 29, no. 12 (2005): 1333–1345.

77. Meier, "Domestic Violence, Child Custody, and Child Protection" (2003).

78. Ibid., 44.

79. Slote et al., "Battered Mothers Speak Out" (2005).

80. K. Kendall-Tackett, *Treating the Lifetime Health Effects of Childhood Victimization*, 2nd ed. (Kingston, NJ: Civic Research Institute, 2013).

81. L. Bancroft and J. G. Silverman, *The Batterer as Parent: Addressing the Impact of Domestic Violence on Family Dynamics* (Los Angeles: Sage Publications, 2002).

82. Meier, "Domestic Violence, Child Custody, and Child Protection" (2003): 15.

83. See Brinig et al., "Perspectives on Joint Custody Presumptions as Applied to Domestic Violence" (2014).

84. E. Stark, "Reframing Child Custody Decisions in the Context of Coercive Control," in *Domestic Violence, Abuse, and Child Custody: Legal Strategies and Policy Issues*, edited by M. Hannah and B. Goldstein (Kingston, NJ: Civic Research Institute, 2010), 11:1–11:29.

85. Stark, *Coercive Control* (2007).

86. Stark, "Reframing Child Custody Decisions in the Context of Coercive Control" (2010): 11:4.

87. Ibid.

88. Meier, "Domestic Violence, Child Custody, and Child Protection" (2003): 244.

Chapter 6

1. T. H. Styron et al., "Fathers with Serious Mental Illness: A Neglected Group," *Psychiatric Rehabilitation Journal* 25, no. 3 (2002): 215–222.

2. J. Risser et al., "Do Maternal and Paternal Mental Illness and Substance Abuse Predict Treatment Outcomes for Children Exposed to Violence," *Child Care in Practice* 19, no. 3 (2013): 221–236.

3. J. C. Campbell, D. W. Webster, and N. Glass, "The Danger Assessment: Validation of a Lethality Risk Assessment Instrument for Intimate Partner Femicide," *Journal of Interpersonal Violence* 24, no. 6 (2009): 653–674.

4. Ibid.

5. L. Laing, "Secondary Victimization: Domestic Violence Survivors Navigating the Family Law System," *Violence Against Women* (August 23, 2016): 1–22.

6. Ibid.

7. L. Bancroft, J. G. Silverman, and D. Ritchie, *The Batterer as Parent: Addressing the Impact of Domestic Violence on Family Dynamics*, 2nd ed. (Los Angeles: Sage Publications, 2012).

8. M. Juodis, A. Starzomski, and M. Woodworth, "What Can Be Done About High-Risk Perpetrators of Domestic Violence?" *Journal of Family Violence* 29, no. 4 (2014): 381–390.

9. R. Beasley and C. D. Stoltenberg, "Personality Characteristics of Male Spouse Abusers," *Professional Psychology: Research and Practice* 23, no. 4 (1992): 310–317.

10. Bancroft et al., *The Batterer as Parent* (2012): 8.

11. D. Dutton and S. Golant, *The Batterer: A Psychological Profile* (New York: Basic Books, 1995).

12. Bancroft et al., *The Batterer as Parent* (2012).

13. Ibid.

14. E. Echeburua and J. Fernandez-Montalvo, "Male Batterers With and Without Psychopathy: An Exploratory Study in Spanish Prisons," *International Journal of Offender Therapy and Comparative Criminology* 51, no. 3 (2007): 254–263.

15. Ibid.

16. Bancroft et al., *The Batterer as Parent* (2012).

17. Ibid.

18. Ibid.

19. E. W. Gondolf, "MCMI-III Results for Batterer Program Participants in Four Cities: Less 'Pathological' Than Expected," *Journal of Family Violence* 14, no. 1 (1999): 1–17.

20. Beasley and Stoltenberg, "Personality Characteristics of Male Spouse Abusers" (1992).

21. R. Brasfield, "The Absence of Evidence Is Not the Evidence of Absence: The Abusive Personality as a Disordered Mental State," *Journal of Aggression and Violent Behavior* 19, no. 5 (2014): 515–522.

22. D. Dutton, "Trauma Symptoms and PTSD-like Profiles in Perpetrators of Intimate Abuse," *Journal of Traumatic Stress* 8, no. 2 (1995): 299–316.

23. D. Dutton, "Witnessing Parental Violence as a Traumatic Experience Shaping the Abusive Personality," *Journal of Aggression, Maltreatment and Trauma* 3, no. 1 (2000): 59–67.

24. Gondolf, "MCMI-III Results for Batterer Program Participants in Four Cities" (1999).

25. Gondolf, "MCMI-III Results for Batterer Program Participants in Four Cities" (1999); D. Dutton, "MCMI Results for Batterers: A Response to Gondolf," *Journal of Family Violence* 18, no. 4 (2003): 253–255.

26. Dutton, "MCMI Results for Batterers" (2003).

27. D. Dutton, *The Abusive Personality: Violence and Control in Intimate Relationships* (New York: Guilford Press, 2007).

28. Dutton, "MCMI Results for Batterers" (2003).

29. Brasfield, "The Absence of Evidence Is Not the Evidence of Absence" (2014).

30. American Psychiatric Association, *Diagnostic and Statistical Manual of Mental Disorders*, 5th ed. (Arlington, VA: American Psychiatric Publishing, 2013).

31. Juodis et al., "What Can Be Done About High-Risk Perpetrators of Domestic Violence?" *Journal of Family Violence* 29, no. 4 (2014): 381–390.

32. Ibid.

33. Ibid.

34. S. D. Hart, "Preventing Violence: The Role of Risk Assessment and Management," in *Intimate Partner Violence Prevention and Intervention*, edited by A.C. Baldry and F.W. Winkel (Hauppauge, NY: Nova Science Publishers, 2008), 7–18; Juodis et al., "What Can Be Done About High-Risk Perpetrators of Domestic Violence?" (2014).

35. Juodis et al., "What Can Be Done About High-Risk Perpetrators of Domestic Violence?" (2014).

36. J. C. Campbell et al., "Risk Factors for Femicide in Abusive Relationships: Results from a Multisite Case Control Study," *American Journal of Public Health* 93, no. 7 (2003): 1089–1097.

37. M. Juodis et al., "A Comparison of Domestic and Non-Domestic Homicides: Further Evidence for Distinct Dynamics and Heterogeneity of Domestic Violence Perpetrators," *Journal of Family Violence* 29, no. 3 (2014): 299–313.

38. Campbell et al., "Risk Factors for Femicide in Abusive Relationships" (2003); Juodis et al., "What Can Be Done About High-Risk Perpetrators of Domestic Violence?" (2014).

39. Juodis et al., "A Comparison of Domestic and Non-Domestic Homicides" (2014).

40. Juodis et al., "What Can Be Done About High-Risk Perpetrators of Domestic Violence?" (2014); O. Marra, *Domestic Violence Death Review Committee Annual Report to the Chief Coroner* (Ontario: Office of the Chief Coroner, 2005).

41. Campbell et al., "The Danger Assessment" (2009).

42. E. Stark, *Coercive Control: How Men Entrap Women in Personal Life* (New York: Oxford University Press, 2007).

43. Ibid.

44. R. Goel and L. Goodmark, *Comparative Perspectives on Gender Violence* (New York: Oxford University Press, 2015).

45. R. Pierre-Louis, *New York City Domestic Violence Fatality Review Committee, 2014 Annual Report* (New York: Mayor's Office to Combat Domestic Violence, 2014).

46. K. Lapp and C. Watson, *Family Protection and Domestic Violence Intervention Act of 1994: Evaluation of the Mandatory Arrest Provisions* (Albany, NY: New York State Division of Criminal Justice Services, 2001).

47. Pierre-Louis, *New York City Domestic Violence Fatality Review Committee, 2014 Annual Report* (2014).

48. World Health Organization, *The World Health Report 2002: Reducing Risks, Promoting Healthy Life* (Geneva: World Health Organization, 2002).

49. P. G. Jaffe et al., "Custody Disputes Involving Allegations of Domestic Violence: Toward a Differentiated Approach to Parenting Plans," *Family Court Review* 46, no. 3 (2008): 500–522.

50. Styron et al., "Fathers with Serious Mental Illness" (2002).

51. J. Risser et al., "Do Maternal and Paternal Mental Illness and Substance Abuse Predict Treatment Outcomes for Children Exposed to Violence?" (2013).

52. S. J. Lee, "Paternal and Household Characteristics Associated with Child Neglect and Child Protective Services Involvement," *Journal of Social Service Research* 39, no. 2 (2013): 171–197.

53. J. Herman, *Trauma and Recovery: The Aftermath of Violence—From Domestic Abuse to Political Terror* (New York: Basic Books, 1997).

54. Ibid.

55. M. Cloitre et al., "A Developmental Approach to Complex PTSD: Childhood and Adult Cumulative Trauma as Predictors of Symptom Complexity," *Journal of Traumatic Stress* 22, no. 5 (2009): 399–408.

56. S. Griffing et al., "Exposure to Interpersonal Violence as a Predictor of PTSD Symptomatology in Domestic Violence Survivors," *Journal of Interpersonal Violence* 21, no. 7 (2006): 936–954.

57. K. Kendall-Tackett, *Treating the Lifetime Health Effects of Childhood Victimization*, 2nd ed. (Kingston, NJ: Civic Research Institute, 2013).

58. J. Herman, *Trauma and Recovery* (1997).

59. M. A. Pico-Alfonso et al., "The Impact of Physical, Psychological, and Sexual Intimate Male Partner Violence on Women's Mental Health: Depressive Symptoms, Posttraumatic Stress Disorder, State Anxiety, and Suicide," *Journal of Women's Health* 15, no. 5 (2006): 599–611.

60. Cloitre et al., "A Developmental Approach to Complex PTSD" (2009).

61. K. E. Leonard and H. T. Blane, "Alcohol and Marital Aggression in a National Sample of Young Men.," *Journal of Interpersonal Violence* 7, no. 1 (1992): 19–30; K. E. Leonard, "Alcohol and Intimate Partner Violence: When Can We Say that Heavy Drinking Is a Contributing Cause of Violence?" *Addiction* 100, no. 4 (2005): 422–425.

62. Juodis et al., "What Can Be Done About High-Risk Perpetrators of Domestic Violence?" (2014).

63. Risser et al., "Do Maternal and Paternal Mental Illness and Substance Abuse Predict Treatment Outcomes for Children Exposed to Violence?" (2013).

64. K. Corvo and E. H. Carpenter, "Effects of Parental Substance Abuse on Current Levels of Domestic Violence: A Possible Elaboration of Intergenerational Transmission Processes," *Journal of Family Violence* 15, no. 2 (2000): 123–135.

65. Ibid.

66. Ibid.

67. K. E. Leonard and H. T. Blane, "Alcohol and Marital Aggression in a National Sample of Young Men (1992); Leonard, "Alcohol and Intimate Partner Violence" (2005).

68. S. E. Martin and R. Bachman, "The Relationship of Alcohol to Injury in Assault Cases," *Recent Developments in Alcoholism* 13 (1997): 42–56.

69. K. Graham et al., "Alcohol May Not Cause Partner Violence but It Seems to Make It Worse: A Cross National Comparison of the Relationship Between Alcohol and Severity of Partner Violence," *Journal of Interpersonal Violence* 26, no. 8 (2011): 1503–1523.

70. K. Graham, M. Plant, and M. Plant, "Alcohol, Gender and Partner Aggression: A General Population Study of British Adults," *Addiction Research and Theory* 12, no. 4 (2004): 385–401.

71. Graham et al., "Alcohol May Not Cause Partner Violence But It Seems to Make It Worse" (2011).

72. Graham et al., "Alcohol, Gender and Partner Aggression" (2004).

73. Ibid.

74. Ibid.

75. Graham et al., "Alcohol, Gender and Partner Aggression" (2004); J. E. Stets, "Gender Differences in Reporting Marital Violence and Its Medical and Psychological Consequences," in *Physical Violence in American Families*, edited by M. A. Straus and R. J. Gelles (New Brunswick, NJ: Transaction Publishers, 1990): 151–165.

76. M. Testa, B. M. Quigley, and K. E. Leonard, "Does Alcohol Make a Difference? Within-participants Comparison of Incidents of Partner Violence," *Journal of Interpersonal Violence* 18, no. 7 (2003): 735–743.

77. Risser et al., "Do Maternal and Paternal Mental Illness and Substance Abuse Predict Treatment Outcomes for Children Exposed to Violence" (2013): 231.

78. Ibid.

79. S. A. Graham-Bermann, K. H. Howell, M. Lilly, and E. DeVoe, "Mediators and Moderators of Change in Adjustment Following Intervention for Children Exposed to Intimate Partner Violence," *Journal of Interpersonal Violence* 26, no. 9 (2011): 1815–1833; Risser et al., "Do Maternal and Paternal Mental Illness and Substance Abuse Predict Treatment Outcomes for Children Exposed to Violence" (2013).

80. Risser et al., "Do Maternal and Paternal Mental Illness and Substance Abuse Predict Treatment Outcomes for Children Exposed to Violence" (2013).

81. M. Keiley, P. S. Keller, and M. El-Sheikh, "Effects of Physical and Verbal Aggression, Depression and Anxiety on Drinking Behavior of Married Partners: A Prospective and Retrospective Longitudinal Examination," *Journal of Aggressive Behavior* 35, no. 4 (2009): 296–312.

82. Ibid.

83. Ibid.

84. Stark, *Coercive Control* (2007).

85. Herman, *Trauma and Recovery* (1997).

86. H. B. Macintosh, N. Godbout and N. Dobash, "Borderline Personality Disorder: Disorder of Trauma or Personality, a Review of the Empirical Literature," *Canadian Psychological Association* 56, no. 2 (2015): 227–241.

87. D. Oyserman et al., "Parenting Among Mothers with a Serious Mental Illness," *American Journal of Orthopsychiatry* 70, no. 3 (2000): 296–315.

88. Ibid.

89. Ibid.

90. Ibid.

91. Ibid.

92. M. Gelkopf and S. E. Jabotaro, "Parenting Style, Competence, Social Network, and Attachment in Mothers with Mental Illness," *Child and Family Social Work* 18, no. 4 (2013): 496–503; M. F. Brunette and W. Dean, "Community Mental Health Care for Women with Severe Mental Illness Who Are Parents," *Community Mental Health Journal* 38, no. 2 (2002): 153–165.

93. Gelkopf and Jabotaro, "Parenting Style, Competence, Social Network, and Attachment in Mothers with Mental Illness" (2013).

94. Ibid.

95. Ibid.

96. M. Lacey et al., "Parents with Serious Mental Illness: Differences in Internalized and Externalized Mental Illness Stigma and Gender Stigma Between Mothers and Fathers," *Psychiatry Research* 225, no. 3 (2015): 723–733.

97. Oyserman et al., "Parenting Among Mothers with a Serious Mental Illness" (2000).

98. E. Peled, K. Gueta, and N. Sander-Almoznino, "The Experience of Mothers Exposed to the Abuse of Their Daughters by an Intimate Partner: 'There Is No Definition for It'," *Violence Against Women* 22, no. 13 (2016): 1577–1596.

99. Oyserman et al., "Parenting Among Mothers with a Serious Mental Illness" (2000).

100. D. Oyserman et al., "Parenting Among Mothers with a Serious Mental Illness" (2000); D. Gelfand and D. Teti, "The Effects of Maternal Depression on Children," *Clinical Psychology Review* 10, no. 3 (1990): 329–353.

101. J. Bowlby, *A Secure Base: Parent-Child Attachment and Healthy Human Development* (New York: Basic Books, 1988); R. Marvin et al., "The Circle of Security Project: Attachment-based Intervention with Caregiver-Pre-School Child Dads," *Journal of Attachment and Human Development* 4, no. 1 (2002): 107–124.

102. Oyserman et al., "Parenting Among Mothers with a Serious Mental Illness" (2000).

103. Ibid.

104. B. L. Green, C. Furrer, and C. McAllister, "How Do Relationships Support Parenting? Effects of Attachment Style, and Social Support on Parenting Behavior in an At-Risk Population," *American Journal of Community Psychology* 40, no. 1–2 (2007): 96–108.

105. Green et al., "How Do Relationships Support Parenting? (2007); J. Bowlby, *A Secure Base* (1998).

106. Laing, "Secondary Victimization" (2016).

107. Ibid.

108. Ibid.

109. Ibid.

110. S. A. Graham-Bermann et al., "An Efficacy Trial of an Intervention Program for Children Exposed to Intimate Partner Violence," *Child Psychiatry and Human Development* 406, no. 6 (2015): 928–239.

Chapter 7

1. C. Warrener, J. M. Koivunen, and J. L. Postmus, "Economic Self-Sufficiency Among Divorced Women: Impact of Depression, Abuse, and Efficacy," *Journal of Divorce & Remarriage* 54, no. 2 (2013): 163–175; P. R. Amato, "The Consequences of Divorce for Adults and Children," *Journal of Marriage and Family* 62, no. 4 (2000): 1269–1287.

2. E. Stark, *Coercive Control: How Men Entrap Women in Personal Life* (New York: Oxford University Press, 2007).

3. S. L. Pollet, "Economic Abuse: The Unseen Side of Domestic Violence," *NYSBA Journal* 83, no. 2 (2011): 40–44.

4. M. Outlaw, "No One Type of Intimate Partner Abuse: Exploring Physical and Non-Physical Abuse Among Intimate Partners," *Journal of Family Violence* 24, no. 4 (2009): 263–272.

5. Ibid.

6. A. E. Adams et al., "Development of the Scale of Economic Abuse," *Violence Against Women* 14, no. 5 (2008): 563–588.

7. Ibid., 571.

8. Ibid., 569.

9. Ibid., 574.

10. N. Erickson, "Economic Abuse: A Form of Abuse That Needs More Scrutiny," *New York Family Law Monthly* 10, no. 2 (2008): 3–4; *Wissink v. Wissink*, 301 A.D. 2d 36 (N.Y. App. Ct. 2002).

11. Erickson, "Economic Abuse" (2008).

12. C. K. Sanders, "Economic Abuse in the Lives of Women Abused by an Intimate Partner: A Qualitative Study," *Violence Against Women* 21, no. 1 (2015): 3–29; L. C. Lambert and J. M. Firestone, "Economic Context and Multiple Abuse Techniques," *Violence Against Women* 6, no. 1 (2000): 49–67.

13. Sanders, "Economic Abuse in the Lives of Women Abused by an Intimate Partner" (2015).

14. Warrener et al., "Economic Self-Sufficiency Among Divorced Women (2013); Adams et al., "Development of the Scale of Economic Abuse" (2008).

15. S. Park, "Working Towards Freedom from Abuse: Recognizing a 'Public Policy' Exception to Employment-at-Will for Domestic Violence Victims," *New York University Annual Survey of American Law* 59 (March 14, 2003): 121–162.

16. S. Lloyd and N. Taluc, "The Effects of Male Violence on Female Employment," *Violence Against Women* 5, no. 4 (1999): 370–392.

17. Warrener et al., "Economic Self-Sufficiency Among Divorced Women" (2013).

18. GAO Report to Congressional Committees, *Domestic Violence: Prevalence and Implications for Employment Among Welfare Recipients* (Washington, DC: United States General Accounting Office, 1998); Park, "Working Towards Freedom from Abuse" (2003).

19. J. Goldscheid and R. Runge, *Employment Law and Domestic Violence: A Practitioner's Guide* (Chicago: American Bar Association Commission on Domestic Violence, 2009).

20. M. J. Hayes, "Leaving Maryland Workers Behind: A Comparison of State Employee Leave Statutes.," *University of Maryland Law Journal of Race, Religion, Gender, and Class* 9, no. 1 (2009): 19–31.

21. Adams et al., "Development of the Scale of Economic Abuse" (2008).

22. Adams et al., "Development of the Scale of Economic Abuse" (2008); R. A. Brandwein and D.M. Filiano, "Toward Real Welfare Reform: The Voices of Battered Women," *Affilia.* 15, no. 2 (2000): 224–243; Lloyd and Taluc, "The Effects of Male Violence on Female Employment" (1999).

23. M. A. Anderson et al., " 'Why Doesn't She Just Leave?': A Descriptive Study of Victim Reported Impediments to Her Safety," *Journal of Family Violence* 18, no. 3 (2003): 151–155.

24. Adams et al., "Development of the Scale of Economic Abuse" (2008); Anderson et al., " 'Why Doesn't She Just Leave?' " (2003); A. Coker et al., "Frequency and Correlates of Intimate Partner Violence Type: Physical, Sexual, and Psychological Battering," *American Journal of Public Health* 90, no. 4 (2000): 553–560; J. Davies and E. Lyon, *Safety Planning with Battered Women* (Thousand Oaks, CA: Sage Publications, 1998).

25. S. L. Staggs et al., "Intimate Partner Violence, Social Support, and Employment in the Post-Welfare Reform Era," *Journal of Interpersonal Violence* 22, no. 3 (2007): 345–367; R. L. Repitti, K. A. Mathews, and I. Waldron, "Employment and Women's Health: Effects of Paid Employment on Women's Mental and Physical Health," *American Psychologist* 44, no. 11 (1989): 1394–1401.

26. Staggs et al., "Intimate Partner Violence, Social Support, and Employment in the Post-Welfare Reform Era" (2007).

27. Angela Littwin, "Coerced Debt: The Role of Consumer Credit in Domestic Violence," 100 *Cal. L. Rev.* 951 (2012).

28. Ibid.

29. N.Y. Dom. Rel. Law § 236(B)(2) (2016).

30. S. L. Miller and N. L. Smolter, " 'Paper Abuse': When All Else Fails, Batterers Use Procedural Stalking," *Violence Against Women* 17, no. 5 (2011): 637–650.

31. Miller and Smolter, "'Paper Abuse'" (2011); T. K. Logan et al., "The Impact of Differential Patterns of Physical Violence and Stalking on Mental Health and Help-Seeking Among Women with Protective Orders," *Violence Against Women* 12, no. 9 (2006): 866–886; K. A. Roberts, "Women's Experience of Violence During Stalking by Former Romantic Partners," *Violence Against Women* 11, no. 1 (2005): 89–114.

32. J. S. Wallerstein, J. M. Lewis, and S. Blakeslee, *The Unexpected Legacy of Divorce: A 25 Year Landmark Study* (New York: Hyperion, 2000).

33. Sanders, "Economic Abuse in the Lives of Women Abused by an Intimate Partner" (2015).

34. Ibid.

35. K. Parker and W. Wang, *Modern Parenthood: Roles of Moms and Dads Converge as They Balance Work and Family* (Washington, DC: Pew Research Center, 2013).

36. Ibid.

37. S. Davis and T. Greenstein, "Cross-National Variations in the Division of Household Labor," *Journal of Marriage and Family* 66, no. 5 (2004): 1260–1271.

38. Ibid.

39. Nicole K. Bridges, "The 'Strengthen and Vitalize Enforcement of Child Support (SAVE Child Support) Act': Can the SAVE Child Support Act Save Child Support from the Recent Economic Downturn?" 36 *Okla. City U.L. Rev.* 679 (2011).

40. Bridges, "The 'Strengthen and Vitalize Enforcement of Child Support (SAVE Child Support) Act'" (2011); Social Services Amendments of 1974, Pub. L. No. 93–647, § 101, 88 Stat. 2337, 2351 (1975) codified as amended at 42 U.S.C. § 651 (2006).

41. Full Faith and Credit for Child Support Orders Act (FFCCSOA), 28 U.S.C. § 1738B (1994 & Supp. 1998); Bridges, "The Strengthen and Vitalize Enforcement of Child Support (SAVE Child Support) Act" (2011): 689.

42. Bridges, "The 'Strengthen and Vitalize Enforcement of Child Support (SAVE Child Support) Act'" (2011): 689; Uniform Interstate Family Support Act of 1992 (National Conference of Commissioners on Uniform State Laws, UIFSA).

43. N.Y. Dom. Rel. Law § 240 (2016); N.Y. Fam. Ct. 413 (2016).

44. Bridges, "The 'Strengthen and Vitalize Enforcement of Child Support (SAVE Child Support) Act'" (2011).

45. M. DeMaria, "Comment, Jurisdictional Issues Under the Uniform Interstate Family Support Act," *Journal of the American Academy of Matrimonial Lawyers* 16 (1999): 243–258, http://www.aaml.org/sites/default/files/jurisdictional%20issues%20 under-uifsa.pdf; Uniform Interstate Family Support Act of 1992 (National Conference of Commissioners on Uniform State Laws, UIFSA); see also Personal Responsibility and Work Opportunity Act, 42 U.S.C. § 666 (1996).

46. Cheryl J. Lee, "Escaping the Lion's Den and Going Back for Your Hat: Why Domestic Violence Should be Considered in the Distribution of Marital Property upon Dissolution of Marriage," 23 *Pace L. Rev.* 273 (2002).

47. Ibid.

48. Marsha Garrison, "Good Intentions Gone Awry: The Impact of New York's Equitable Distribution Law on Divorce Outcomes," 57 *Brook. L. Rev.* 621 (1991).

49. Ibid.

50. L. J. Weitzman, *The Divorce Revolution: The Unexpected Social and Economic Consequences for Women and Children in America* (New York: Free Press, 1985); Martha

Albertson Fineman, "Implementing Equality: Ideology, Contradiction, and Social Change." 1983 *Wis. L. Rev.* 789 (1983); Garrison, "Good Intentions Gone Awry" (1991).

51. Weitzman, *The Divorce Revolution* (1985).

52. Garrison, "Good Intentions Gone Awry" (1991).

53. Ibid.

54. Stark, *Coercive Control* (2007); Lee, "Escaping the Lion's Den and Going Back for Your Hat" (2002).

55. Peter N. Swisher, "The ALI Principles: A Farewell to Fault—But What Remedy for the Egregious Marital Misconduct of an Abusive Spouse?" 8 *Duke J. Gender L. & Pol'y* 213 (2001).

56. Ibid.

57. *Havell v. Islam*, 751 N.Y.S. 2d 339 (N.Y. App. Ct. 2002), lv. denied 100 N.Y. 2d 505. (2003).

58. M. K. Kisthardt, "Re-thinking Alimony: The AAML's Consideration for Calculating Alimony, Spousal Support or Maintenance," *Journal of the American Academy of Matrimonial Lawyers* 21 (June 16, 2008): 61–85.

59. Robert Kirkman Collins, "The Theory of Marital Residuals: Applying an Income Adjustment Calculus to the Enigma of Alimony," 24 *Harv. Women's L. J.* 23 (2001).

60. Ibid., 28.

61. Ibid., 30.

62. Ibid.

63. Kisthardt, "Re-thinking Alimony" (2008).

64. Stacia Rudiman, "Part Three: Contingencies Constraining Judicial Discretion in Awarding Alimony: Domestic Violence as an Alimony Contingency: Recent Developments in California Law," 22 *J. Contemp. Legal Issues* 498 (2015).

65. Kisthardt, "Re-thinking Alimony" (2008).

66. Collins, "The Theory of Marital Residuals" (2001): 35–36.

67. Ibid.

68. Ibid., 33.

69. Kisthardt, "Re-thinking Alimony" (2008); Jane Rutherford, "Duty in Divorce: Shared Income as a Path to Equality," 58 *Fordham L. Rev.* 549 (1990); United States Census Bureau, *Statistical Abstract of the United States: 1989* (Washington, DC: United States Census Bureau, 1989).

70. Collins, "The Theory of Marital Residuals" (2001).

71. Kisthardt, "Re-thinking Alimony" (2008).

72. Collins "The Theory of Marital Residuals" (2001): 50.

73. Joann Bussayabuntoon, "Age and Health as Factors for Court-Ordered Alimony Decisions," 22 *J. Contemp. Legal Issues* 309 (2015).

74. K. Kendall-Tackett, *Treating the Lifetime Health Effects of Childhood Victimization*, 2nd ed. (Kingston, NJ: Civic Research Institute, 2013).

75. Ibid.

76. Sarah Burkett, "Finding Fault and Making Reparations: Domestic Violence Conviction as a Limitation on Spousal Support Award," 22 *J. Contemp. Legal Issues* 492 (2015).

77. Lynn Hecht Schafran, "Overwhelming Evidence: Reports on Gender Bias in the Courts," *Trial* 26, no. 2 (1990): 28–35.

78. Lynn Hecht Schafran, "Gender and Justice: Florida and the Nation," 42 *Fla. L. Rev.* 181 (1990).

79. Lisa E. Martin, "Providing Equal Justice for the Domestic Violence Victim: Due Process and the Victim's Right to Counsel," 34 *Gonz. L. Rev.* 329 (1999).

80. *O'Shea v. O'Shea*, 93 N.Y. 2d. 187 (1999); N.Y. Dom. Rel. Law § 237(a) (2015).

81. Violence Against Women Act (VAWA), 42 U.S.C. § 14011 (1994).

82. *DeShaney v. Winnebago County Dept. of Social Services*, 489 U.S. 189 (1989).

83. *United States v. Morrison,* 529 U.S. 598 (2000).

84. B. Levinson, "Compensation for Domestic Violence Victims: Tort Remedies and Beyond," in *Lawyer's Manual of Domestic Violence*, 6th ed., edited by M. R. Rothwell Davis, D. A. Leidholdt, and C. A. Watson (Supreme Court of the State of New York, Appellate Division, First Department, 2015), 130–139.

Chapter 8

1. L. Bancroft, J. G. Silverman, and D. Ritchie, *The Batterer as Parent: Addressing the Impact of Domestic Violence on Family Dynamics*, 2nd ed. (Los Angeles: Sage Publications, 2012).

2. L. Bancroft and J. G. Silverman, *The Batterer as Parent: Addressing the Impact of Domestic Violence on Family Dynamics* (Los Angeles: Sage Publications, 2002): xiii; S. L. Miller and N. L. Smolter, " 'Paper Abuse': When All Else Fails, Batterers Use Procedural Stalking," *Violence Against Women* 17, no. 5 (2011): 637–650.

3. N. Trocmé and N. Bala, "False Allegations of Abuse and Neglect when Parents Separate," *Child Abuse and Neglect* 29, no. 12 (2005): 1333–1345.

4. *Troxel v. Granville*, 530 U.S. 57 (2000); *Parham v. J.R.*, 442 U.S. 584 (1979).

5. *Washington v. Glucksberg*, 521 U.S. 702, 719 (1997).

6. Kathryn. L. Mercer, "A Content Analysis of Judicial Decision-Making: How Judges Use the Primary Caretaker Standard to Make a Custody Determination," 5 *Wm. & Mary J. Women & L.* 1 (Winter 1998).

7. Amy D. Ronner, "Women Who Dance on the Professional Track: Custody and the Red Shoes," 23 *Harv. Women's L. J.* 179 at 183 (2000).

8. Ibid.

9. *Bennett v. Jeffreys*, 40 N.Y. 2d 543 (1976).

10. *Friederwitzer v. Friederwitzer*, 55 N.Y. 2d 89 (1982).

11. *Eschbach v. Eschbach*, 56 N.Y. 2d 167 (1982).

12. Nancy K. Lemon, "Statutes Creating Rebuttable Presumptions Against Custody to Batterers: How Effective Are They?" 28 *Wm. Mitchell L. Rev.* 2 (2001).

13. Ibid.

14. Morella Resolution, H.R. J. 172, 101st Cong. (1994).

15. Advisory Committee of the Conrad N. Hilton Foundation, *Model Code on Domestic and Family Violence* (Reno, NV: National Council of Juvenile and Family Court Judges, 1994): 33; see also Lemon, "Statutes Creating Rebuttable Presumptions Against Custody to Batterers" (2001).

16. American Bar Association, *The Impact of Domestic Violence on Children: A Report to the President of the American Bar Association* (Chicago: American Bar Association, 1994).

17. Lemon, "Statutes Creating Rebuttable Presumptions Against Custody to Batterers" (2001).

18. N.Y. Dom. Rel. Law § 240 (2016).

19. Lemon, "Statutes Creating Rebuttable Presumptions Against Custody to Batterers" (2001).

20. Mercer, "A Content Analysis of Judicial Decision-Making" (1998).

21. K. Y. Slote et al., "Battered Mothers Speak Out: Participatory Human Rights Documentation as a Model for Research and Activism in the United States," *Violence Against Women* 11, no. 11 (2005): 1367–1395; K. Gentile, "'You Don't Recognize Me Because I'm Still Standing': The Impact of Action Research with Women Survivors of Domestic Violence," in *Domestic Violence: Methodologies in Dialogue*, edited by C. Raghavan and S. J. Cohen (Boston: Northeastern University Press, 2013): 171–199; Leigh Goodmark, "Telling Stories, Saving Lives: The Battered Mothers' Testimony Project, Women's Narratives and Court Reform," 37 *Ariz. St. L.J.* 709 (2005).

22. P. G. Jaffe, N. K. D. Lemon, and S. E. Poisson, *Child Custody and Domestic Violence: A Call for Safety and Accountability* (New York: Sage Publications, 2003).

23. Lemon, "Statutes Creating Rebuttable Presumptions Against Custody to Batterers" (2001).

24. Bancroft et al., *The Batterer as Parent* (2012).

25. J. E. McIntosh, "Special Considerations for Infants and Toddlers in Separation/Divorce: Developmental Issues in the Family Law Context," in *Encyclopedia on Early Childhood Development*, edited by R. E. Tremblay, M. Boivin, and R. DeV. Peters (Montreal: Centre of Excellence for Early Childhood Development, 2011), 1–5.

26. E. Stark, "Rethinking Custody Evaluation in Cases Involving Domestic Violence," *Journal of Child Custody* 6, no. 3 (2009): 287–321.

27. S. Portwood and J. F. Heany, "Responding to Violence Against Women: Social Science Contributions to Legal Solutions," *International Journal of Law and Psychiatry* 30, no. 3 (2002): 237–247.

28. Ronner, "Women Who Dance on the Professional Track" (2000).

29. Ibid., 185.

30. Stark, "Rethinking Custody Evaluation in Cases Involving Domestic Violence" (2009).

31. Bancroft and Silverman, *The Batterer as Parent* (2002): 115.

32. R.C.J.N.Y. § 7.2(d) (2007); J. Waksberg, "Representing Children on Appeal: Changed Circumstances, Changed Mind," *The Journal of Appellate Practice and Process* 12, no. 2 (2011): 313–329.

33. J. Herman, *Trauma and Recovery: The Aftermath of Violence—From Domestic Abuse to Political Terror* (New York: Basic Books, 1997).

34. N.Y. Dom. Rel. Law § 240 (2016).

35. Bancroft and Silverman, *The Batterer as Parent* (2002): 115.

36. E. M. Hetherington and M. Stanley-Hagen, "The Adjustment of Children with Divorced Parents: A Risk and Resiliency Perspective," *Journal of Child Psychology and Psychiatry* 40, no. 1 (1999): 129–140.

37. J. R. Johnston, V. Roseby, and K. Kuehnle, *In the Name of the Child: A Developmental Approach to Understanding and Helping Children of Conflicted and Violent Families*, 2nd ed. (New York: Springer Publishing, 2009).

38. J. Briere, *Therapy for Adults Molested as Children*, 2nd ed. (New York: Springer Publishing, 1996); V. G. Carrion, C. F. Weems, and A. L. Reiss, "Stress Predicts Changes in Children: A Pilot Longitudinal Study on Youth Stress, Posttraumatic Stress Disorder, and the Hippocampus," *Pediatrics* 119, no. 3 (2007): 509–516.

39. E. Walker and L. Fischel-Wolovick, "Children Who Witness Domestic Violence," *N. Y. L. J.*, October 19, 1994; M. Pagelow, "The Effects of Domestic Violence on Children and Their Consequences for Custody and Visitation Agreements," *Conflict Resolution Quarterly* 7, no. 4 (1990): 347–363; J. Giles-Sims, "A Longitudinal Study of Battered Children of Battered Wives," *Family Relations* 34, no. 2 (1985): 205–210; L. E. Walker, *The Battered Woman Syndrome* (New York: Springer Publishing, 1984); R. P. Dobash and R. E. Dobash, *Violence Against Wives* (New York: Free Press, 1979).

40. K. Parker and W. Wang, *Modern Parenthood: Roles of Moms and Dads Converge as They Balance Work and Family* (Washington, DC: Pew Research Center, 2013).

41. Ibid.

42. S. Davis and T. Greenstein, "Cross-National Variations in the Division of Household Labor," *Journal of Marriage and Family* 66, no. 5 (2004): 1260–1271.

43. Ibid.

44. Ibid.

45. R. Bauserman, "Child Adjustment in Joint-Custody Versus Sole-Custody Arrangements: A Meta-Analysis Review," *Journal of Family Psychology* 16, no. 1 (2002): 91–102.

46. E. M. Douglas, "The Impact of a Presumption for Joint Legal Custody on Father Involvement," *Journal of Divorce & Remarriage* 39, no. 1/2 (2003): 1–10.

47. Ibid.

48. Ibid.

49. Bauserman, "Child Adjustment in Joint-Custody Versus Sole-Custody Arrangements" (2002).

50. M. Crosbie-Burnett, "Impact of Joint Versus Sole Custody and Quality of Co-Parental Relationship on Adjustment of Adolescents in Remarried Families," *Behavioral Sciences and the Law* 9, no. 4 (1991): 439–449.

51. Hetherington and Stanley-Hagen, "The Adjustment of Children with Divorced Parents" (1999).

52. M. A. Kernic et al., "Children in the Crossfire: Child Custody Determinations Among Couples with a History of Intimate Partner Violence," *Violence Against Women* 11, no. 8 (2005): 991–1021.

53. Stark, "Rethinking Custody Evaluation in Cases Involving Domestic Violence" (2009).

54. Kernic et al., "Children in the Crossfire" (2005).

55. Ibid.

56. Ibid.

57. Ibid.

58. Ibid.

59. Ibid.

60. Ibid.

61. P. G. Jaffe et al., "Custody Disputes Involving Allegations of Domestic Violence: Toward a Differentiated Approach to Parenting Plans," *Family Court Review* 46, no. 3 (2008): 500–522.

62. Ibid.

63. Nancy Ver Steegh and Clair Dalton, "Report from the Wingspread Conference on Domestic Violence and Family Courts," *Family Court Review* 46, no. 3 (2008): 454–475.

64. Bancroft et al., *The Batterer as Parent* (2012).

65. Jaffe et al., "Custody Disputes Involving Allegations of Domestic Violence" (2008).

66. Johnston et al., *In the Name of the Child* (2009).

67. E. Stark, *Coercive Control: How Men Entrap Women in Personal Life* (New York: Oxford University Press, 2007).

Chapter 9

1. Nancy Ver Steegh and Clair Dalton, "Report from the Wingspan Conference on Domestic Violence and Family Courts," *Family Court Review* 46, no. 3 (2008): 454–475.

2. U. Castellano and L. Anderson, "Mental Health Courts in America: Promise and Challenges," *American Behavioral Scientist* 57, no. 2 (2013): 163–173.

3. Greg Berman and John Feinblatt, "Problem-Solving Courts: A Brief Primer," 23 *Law & Pol'y* 125 (2001).

4. Jonathan Lippman, "Ensuring Victim Safety and Abuser Accountability: Reforms and Revisions in New York Courts' Response to Domestic Violence," 76 *Alb. L. Rev.* 1417 (2013).

5. Angela Littwin, "Coerced Debt: The Role of Consumer Credit in Domestic Violence," 100 *Cal. L. Rev.* 951 (2012).

6. E. Buzawa, G. Hotaling, and A. Klein, "The Response to Domestic Violence in a Model Court: Some Initial Findings and Implications," *Behavioral Sciences & the Law* 16, no. 2 (1998): 185–206.

7. Ver Steegh and Dalton, "Report from the Wingspread Conference on Domestic Violence and Family Courts" (2008): 465.

8. Ibid.

9. Ibid.

10. M. K. Pruett et al., "Family and Legal Indicators of Child Adjustment to Divorce Among Families with Young Children," *Journal of Family Psychology* 17, no. 2 (2003): 169–180; E. M. Hetherington, "An Overview of the Virginia Longitudinal Study of Divorce and Remarriage with a Focus on Early Adolescence," *Journal of Family Psychology* 7, no. 1 (1993): 39–56

11. Pruett et al., "Family and Legal Indicators of Child Adjustment to Divorce Among Families with Young Children" (2003).

12. Lippman, "Ensuring Victim Safety and Abuser Accountability" (2013).

13. Ibid.

14. Greg Berman and John Feinblatt, "Problem-Solving Courts: A Brief Primer," 23 *Law & Pol'y* 125 (2001).

15. Susanna Fay-Ramirez, "Therapeutic Jurisprudence in Practice: Changes in Family Treatment Court Norms Over Time," 40 *Law & Soc. Inquiry* 205 (2015).

16. Fay-Ramirez, "Therapeutic Jurisprudence in Practice" (2015); S. Burns and M. Peyrot, "Tough Love: Nurturing and Coercing Responsibility and Recovery in California Drug Courts," *Social Problems* 50, No. 3 (2003): 416–438.

17. Fay-Ramirez, "Therapeutic Jurisprudence in Practice" (2015).

18. M. King and B. Batagol, "Enforcer, Manager, or Leader? The Judicial Role in Family Violence Courts," *International Journal of Law and Psychiatry* 33, no. 5/6 (2010): 406–416.

19. James Duffy, "Problem-Solving Courts, Therapeutic Jurisprudence and the Constitution: If Two Is Company, Is Three a Crowd?" 35 *Melb. U. L. Rev.* 394 (2011).

20. Berman and Feinblatt, "Problem-Solving Courts" (2001).

21. Ibid.

22. Castellano and Anderson, "Mental Health Courts in America" (2013).

23. Ibid.

24. Berman and Feinblatt, "Problem-Solving Courts" (2001).

25. Castellano and Anderson, "Mental Health Courts in America" (2013).

26. Castellano and Anderson, "Mental Health Courts in America" (2013); N. Wolff, "Courting the Courts: Courts as Agents for Treatment and Justice," in *Community-Based Interventions for Criminal Offenders with Severe Mental Illness*, edited by W. H. Fisher (Boston: JAI Press, 2003): 165.

27. Castellano and Anderson, "Mental Health Courts in America" (2013).

28. K. Keator et al., "The Impact of Treatment on the Public Safety Outcomes of Mental Health Court Participants," *American Behavioral Scientist* 57, no. 2 (2013): 231–243; Castellano and Anderson, "Mental Health Courts in America" (2013).

29. S. Belenko, "Study Finds Drug Courts Reduce Recidivism During Treatment," *Alcoholism & Drug Abuse Weekly* 10 (June 8, 1998): 3.

30. Berman and Feinblatt, "Problem-Solving Courts" (2001).

31. Ibid.

32. Karen Oehme and Kelly O'Rourke, "Protecting Victims and Their Children Through Supervised Visitation: A Study of Domestic Violence Injunctions," 3 *Faulkner L. Rev.* 261 (2011).

33. Belenko, "Study Finds Drug Courts Reduce Recidivism During Treatment" (1998).

34. Richard Boldt and Jana Singer, "Juristocracy in the Trenches: Problem-solving Judges and Therapeutic Jurisprudence in Drug Treatment Courts and Unified Courts," 65 *Md. L. Rev.* 82 (2006).

35. H. Sung and S. Belenko, "Failure After Success: Correlates of Recidivism Among Individuals Who Successfully Completed Coerced Drug Treatment," *Journal of Offender Rehabilitation* 42, no. 1 (2005): 75–97.

36. Ibid.

37. Berman and Feinblatt, "Problem-Solving Courts" (2001).

38. Ibid.

39. Ibid.

40. Ibid.

41. Ibid.

42. Ibid.

43. Ibid.

44. Fay-Ramirez, "Therapeutic Jurisprudence in Practice" (2015); Burns and Peyrot, "Tough Love" (2003).

45. A. B. Cissner, M. Labriola, and M. Rempel, "Domestic Violence Courts," *Violence Against Women* 20, no. 9 (2015): 1102–1122.

46. Berman and Feinblatt, "Problem-Solving Courts" (2001).

47. L. Bancroft, J. G. Silverman, and D. Ritchie, *The Batterer as Parent: Addressing the Impact of Domestic Violence on Family Dynamics*, 2nd ed. (Los Angeles: Sage Publications, 2012).

48. K. Graham, M. Plant and M. Plant, "Alcohol, Gender and Partner Aggression: A General Population Study of British Adults," *Addiction Research and Theory* 12, no. 4

(2004): 385–401; K. Corvo and E. H. Carpenter, "Effects of Parental Substance Abuse on Current Levels of Domestic Violence: A Possible Elaboration of Intergenerational Transmission Processes," *Journal of Family Violence* 15, no. 2 (2000): 123–135.

49. Bancroft et al., *The Batterer as Parent,* 2nd ed. (2012).

50. C. D. Schwartz, "Unified Family Courts: A Saving Grace for Victims of Domestic Violence Living in Nations with Fragmented Court Systems," *Family Court Review* 42, no. 2 (2004): 304–320.

51. Ibid.

52. E. Waldman and L. A. Ojelabi, "Mediators and Substantive Justice: A View from Rawls' Original Position," *Ohio State Journal on Dispute Resolution* 30, no. 3 (2016): 391–430.

53. Ibid.

54. L. E. G. Campbell and J. R. Johnston, "Impasse-Directed Mediation With High Conflict Families in Custody Disputes," *Behavioral Sciences & the Law* 4, no. 2 (1986): 217–241.

55. Ibid.

56. Ibid.

57. Ibid.

58. Waldman and Ojelabi, "Mediators and Substantive Justice" (2016).

59. D. Ellis and N. Stuckless, "Domestic Violence, DOVE, and Divorce Mediation," *Family Court Review* 44, no. 4 (2006): 658–671.

60. Ibid.

61. Ibid.

62. Ibid.

63. Ibid.

64. Ibid.

65. Campbell and Johnston, "Impasse-Directed Mediation with High Conflict Families in Custody Disputes" (1986).

66. E. Stark, *Coercive Control: How Men Entrap Women in Personal Life* (New York: Oxford University Press, 2007).

67. Drafting Committee on Uniform Collaborative Law Act, "Uniform Collaborative Law Act," 38 *Hofstra L. Rev.* 421 (2009).

68. Buzawa et al., "The Response to Domestic Violence in a Model Court" (1998).

69. Ellis and Stuckless, "Domestic Violence, DOVE, and Divorce Mediation" (2006).

70. L. Bancroft and J. G. Silverman, *The Batterer as Parent: Addressing the Impact of Domestic Violence on Family Dynamics* (Los Angeles: Sage Publications, 2002).

71. C. A. Coates et al., "Parenting Coordination for High-Conflict Families," *Family Court Review* 42, no. 2 (2004): 246–262.

72. Ibid.

73. AFCC Task Force on Parenting Coordination, *Guidelines for Parenting Coordination* (Madison, WI: Association of Family Conciliation Courts, 2005).

74. Ibid.

75. Coates et al., "Parenting Coordination for High-Conflict Families" (2004).

76. Ibid.

77. B. L. Henson, "Parenting Coordinator: Understanding This New Role," *The Colorado Lawyer* 35, no. 2 (2006): 31–36.

78. M. de Jong, "Suggested Safeguards and Limitations for Effective and Permissible Parenting Coordination (Facilitation or Case Management) in South Africa," *Per/PeLJ* 18, no. 2 (2015): 150–178.

79. M. E. Scott et al., *The Parenting Coordination Project Implementation and Outcomes Study Report* (Washington, DC: Child Trends for the American Psychological Association Practice Directorate, 2010).

80. Ibid.

81. Ibid.

82. *Edwards v. Rothschild*, 60 A.D. 3d 675 (N.Y. App. Ct. 2009); *Silbowitz v. Silbowitz*, 88 A.D. 3d 687 (N.Y. App. Ct. 2011).

83. K. L. Menzano, "Parenting Coordination Eliminated in Pennsylvania," *The Legal Intelligencer* (July 9, 2013) http://www.hangley.com/news/parenting-coordination-eliminated-pennsylvania; S. B. Mashburn, "Throwing the Baby Out with the Bathwater: Parenting Coordination and Pennsylvania's Decision to Eliminate its Use," *Journal of Dispute Resolution* 2015, no. 1 (2015): 191–206.

84. Drafting Committee on Uniform Collaborative Law Act, "Uniform Collaborative Law Act" (2009).

85. Ibid.

86. Ibid.

87. Ibid.

88. Ibid.

89. S. Roddy, "Collaborative Practice: Survey of Emerging Case Law," *American Journal of Family Law* 30, no. 2 (2016): 110–111; Drafting Committee on Uniform Collaborative Law Act, "Uniform Collaborative Law Act" (2009)

90. Drafting Committee on Uniform Collaborative Law Act, "Uniform Collaborative Law Act" (2009).

91. Ibid.

92. David D. Meyer, "The Constitutional Rights of Non-Custodial Parents," 34 *Hofstra L. Rev.* 1461 (2006).

93. R. B. Straus, "Supervised Visitation and Family Violence," *Family Law Quarterly* 29, no. 2 (1995): 229–252.

94. J. Pearson, L. Davis, and N. Thoennes, "A New Look at an Old Issue: An Evaluation of the State Access and Visitation Grant Program," *Family Court Review* 43, no. 3 (2005): 372–386.

95. Oehme and O'Rourke, "Protecting Victims and Their Children Through Supervised Visitation (2011); 42 U.S.C. § 10420.

96. M. S. Maxwell and K. Oehme, "Strategies to Improve Supervised Visitation Services in Domestic Violence Cases," *Violence Against Women Online Resources* (2001) http://citeseerx.ist.psu.edu/viewdoc/download?doi=10.1.1.208.7126&rep=rep1&type=pdf

97. Straus, "Supervised Visitation and Family Violence" (1995).

98. Elizabeth B. Brandt, "Concerns at the Margins of Supervised Access to Children," 9 *J. L. & Fam. Stud.* 201 (2007).

99. N. Thoennes and J. Pearson. "Supervised Visitation: A Profile of Providers," *Family Court Review* 37, no. 4 (1999): 460–477.

100. M. Scaia and L. Connelly, "With Equal Regard: An Overview of How Ellen Pence Focused the Supervised Visitation Field on Battered Women and Children," *Violence Against Women* 16, no. 9 (2010): 1022–1030.

101. R. Birnbaum and R. Alaggia, "Supervised Visitation: A Call for a Second Generation of Research," *Family Court Review* 44, no. 1 (2006): 119–134.

102. S. LaBotte and N. Blaschak-Brown, "Standards for Supervised Visitation Practice," *Supervised Visitation Network* (July, 2006) http://www.afccnet.org/portals/0/publicdocuments/guidelines/supervised_visitation_nework-standardsfinal7-14-06.pdf

103. Maxwell and Oehme, "Strategies to Improve Supervised Visitation Services in Domestic Violence Cases" (2001).

104. Ibid.

105. Ibid.

106. Bancroft et al., *The Batterer as Parent* (2012).

107. Samantha Moore and Kathryn Ford, *Supervised Visitation: What Courts Should Know when Working with Supervised Visitation Programs* (New York: New York State Unified Court System, Center for Court Innovation, 2006).

108. Maxwell and Oehme, "Strategies to Improve Supervised Visitation Services in Domestic Violence Cases" (2001).

109. J. R. Johnston and R. B. Straus, "Traumatized Children in Supervised Visitation: What Do They Need?" *Family Court Review* 37, no. 2 (1999): 135–158.

110. Ibid.

111. Ibid.

112. P. G. Jaffe and C. V. Crooks, "Understanding Women's Experiences Parenting in the Context of Domestic Violence: Implications for Community and Court-Related Service Providers," *Violence Against Women Online Resources* (February 2005) http://citeseerx.ist.psu.edu/viewdoc/download?doi=10.1.1.192.3729&rep=rep1&type=pdf

113. Bancroft and Silverman, *The Batterer as Parent* (2002).

114. Johnston and Straus, "Traumatized Children in Supervised Visitation" (1999).

115. L. Laing, "Secondary Victimization: Domestic Violence Survivors Navigating the Family Law System." *Violence Against Women* (August 23, 2016); R. Alexander, "Moving Forwards or Back to the Future? An Analysis of Case Law on Family Violence Under the 'Family Law Act 1975' (Cth)," *The University of New South Wales Law Journal* 33, no. 2 (2010): 907–928.

116. Jaffe and Crooks, "Understanding Women's Experiences Parenting in the Context of Domestic Violence" (2005).

117. Ibid.

118. L. N. Rosen and C. S. O'Sullivan, "Outcomes of Custody and Visitation Petitions when Fathers are Restrained by Protection Orders," *Violence Against Women* 11, no. 8 (2005): 1054–1075.

119. Oehme and O'Rourke, "Protecting Victims and Their Children Through Supervised Visitation" (2011).

120. Moore and Ford, *Supervised Visitation* (2006); C. O'Sullivan et al., *Supervised and Unsupervised Parental Access in Domestic Violence Cases: Court Orders and Consequences* (Washington, DC: National Institute of Justice, 2006).

121. Pruett et al., "Family and Legal Indicators of Child Adjustment to Divorce Among Families with Young Children" (2003).

122. P. R. Amato, L. S. Loomis, and A. Booth, "Parental Divorce, Marital Conflict and Offspring Well-Being During Early Adulthood," *Adulthood, Social Forces* 73, no. 3 (1995): 895–915; Johnston and Straus, "Traumatized Children in Supervised Visitation" (1999).

Chapter 10

1. M. E. O'Connell, "Child Custody Evaluations: Social Science and Public Policy, Mandated Custody Evaluations and the Limits of Judicial Power," *Family Court Review* 47, no. 2 (2009): 304–320.

2. *Bennett v. Jeffreys*, 40 N.Y. 2d 543 (1976).

3. D. W. Shuman, "What Should We Permit Mental Health Professionals to Say About the 'Best Interests of the Child?': An Essay on Common Sense, Daubert, and the Rules of Evidence," *Family Law Quarterly* 31, no. 3 (1997): 551–569.

4. Ibid.

5. Ibid.

6. Samuel R. Gross, "Expert Evidence," 1991 *Wis. L. Rev.* 1113 (1991).

7. Sanja Kutnjak Ivkovic and Valerie P. Hans, "Jurors' Evaluations of Expert Testimony: Judging the Messenger and the Message," *Law & Soc. Inquiry* 28, no. 2 (2003): 441–482.

8. P. Huber, *Galileo's Revenge: Junk Science in the Courtroom* (New York: Basic Books, 1991); Ivkovic and Hans, "Jurors' Evaluations of Expert Testimony" (2003).

9. David L. Faigman, Elise Porter, and Michael J. Saks, "Check Your Crystal Ball at the Courthouse Door, Please: Exploring the Past, Understanding the Present, and Worrying About the Future of Scientific Evidence," 15 *Cardozo L. Rev.* 1799 (1994).

10. American Bar Association Special Committee of Jury Comprehension, Litigation Section, *Jury Comprehension in Complex Cases* (Chicago: American Bar Association, 1989).

11. M. L. Haselschwerdt, J. L. Hardesty, and J. D. Hans, "Custody Evaluators' Beliefs About Domestic Violence Allegations During Divorce: Feminist and Family Violence Perspectives," *Journal of Interpersonal Violence* 26, no. 8 (2011): 1694–1719.

12. W. G. Keilin and L. J. Bloom, "Child Custody Evaluation Practices: A Survey of Experienced Professionals," *Professional Psychology: Research and Practice* 17, no. 4 (1986): 338–346.

13. Ibid.

14. Ibid.

15. M. J. Ackerman and M. C. Ackerman, "Custody Evaluation Practices," *Professional Psychology: Research and Practice* 28, no. 2 (1997): 137–145.

16. Keilin and Bloom, "Child Custody Evaluation Practices" (1986).

17. American Psychological Association, "Guidelines for Child Custody Evaluations in Divorce Proceedings," *American Psychologist* 49, no. 7 (1994): 677–680.

18. Ibid.

19. M. C. Heinze and T. Grisso, "Review of Instruments Assessing Parenting Competencies Used in Child Custody Evaluations," *Behavioral Sciences and the Law* 14, no. 3 (1996): 293–313.

20. American Psychological Association, "Guidelines for Child Custody Evaluations in Divorce Proceedings" (1994); Heinze and Grisso, "Review of Instruments Assessing Parenting Competencies Used in Child Custody Evaluations" (1996).

21. M. B. Pepiton et al., "Ethical Violations: What Can and Does Go Wrong in Child Custody Evaluations?" *Journal of Child Custody* 11, no. 2 (2014): 81–100; S. P. Herman et al., "Practice Parameters for Child Custody Evaluation," *Journal of the American Academy of Child & Adolescent Psychiatry* 36, no. 10 (1997): 57S–68S.

22. J. N. Bow and F. A. Quinnell, "Psychologists' Current Practices and Procedures in Child Custody Evaluations: Five Years After American Psychological Association Guidelines," *Professional Psychology: Research and Practice* 32, no. 3 (2001): 261–268.

23. L. Martin et al., *Model Standards of Practice for Child Custody Evaluations* (Madison, WI: Association of Family and Conciliation Courts (AFCC), 2006).

24. Herman et al., "Practice Parameters for Child Custody Evaluation" (1997).

25. Ibid.

26. Ibid.

27. V. Luftman et al., "Practice Guidelines in Child Custody Evaluations for Licensed Clinical Social Workers," *Clinical Social Work Journal* 33, no. 3 (2005): 327–357.

28. National Association of Social Workers, *Ethical Principles and Standards: 55th Anniversary Edition* (Washington, DC: NASW Press, 2017).

29. American Psychological Association, "Guidelines for Child Custody Evaluations in Family Law Proceedings," *American Psychologist* 65, no. 9 (2010): 863–867.

30. Ibid.

31. Ibid.

32. Ibid.

33. Ibid.

34. Ackerman and Ackerman, "Custody Evaluation Practices" (1997); M. J. Ackerman and T. B. Pritzl, "Child Custody Evaluation Practices: A 20-Year Follow-up," *Family Court Review* 49, no. 3 (2011): 618–628.

35. Ackerman and Pritzl, "Child Custody Evaluation Practices" (2011).

36. Ibid.

37. Ibid.

38. American Psychological Association, "Guidelines for Child Custody Evaluations in Family Law Proceedings" (2010).

39. Pepiton et al., "Ethical Violations" (2014).

40. E. Y. Chiu, "Psychological Testing in Child Custody Evaluations with Ethnically Diverse Families: Ethical Concerns and Practice Considerations," *Journal of Child Custody* 11, no. 2 (2014): 107–127.

41. L. B. Oberlander, "Ethical Responsibilities in Child Custody Evaluations: Implications for Evaluation Methodology," *Ethics and Behavior* 5, no. 4 (1995): 311–332.

42. C. Dalton, L. M. Drozd, and F. Q. F. Wong, *Navigating Custody & Visitation Evaluations in Cases with Domestic Violence: A Judge's Guide* (Reno, NV: National Council of Juvenile and Family Court Judges, 2006).

43. Ibid.

44. Ibid.

45. Ibid.

46. Ibid.

47. Ibid.

48. J. Zorza, "On Navigating Custody & Visitation Evaluations in Cases with Domestic Violence: A Judge's Guide," *Journal of Child Custody* 6, no. 3/4 (2011): 258–286.

49. Association of Family and Conciliation Courts (AFCC), "Guidelines for Intimate Partner Violence: A Supplement to the AFCC Model Standards of Practice for Child Custody Evaluation," *Family Court Review* 54, no. 4 (2016): 674–686.

50. Ibid.

51. M. S. Davis et al., *Custody Evaluations when There Are Allegations of Domestic Violence: Practices, Beliefs, and Recommendations of Professional Evaluators* (Washington, DC: National Institute of Justice, 2010).

52. Ibid.

53. Ibid.

54. Ibid.

55. Ibid.

56. Haselschwerdt et al., "Custody Evaluators' Beliefs About Domestic Violence Allegations During Divorce" (2011).

57. Ibid.

58. S. K. Araji, "Contested Custody, and the Courts: A Review of Findings from Five Studies with Accompanying Documentary," *Sociological Perspectives* 55, no. 1 (2012): 3–15.

59. Araji, "Contested Custody, and the Courts" (2012); Arizona Coalition Against Domestic Violence. *Battered Mothers' Testimony Project: A Human Rights Approach to Child Custody and Domestic Violence* (Phoenix, AZ: Arizona Coalition Against Domestic Violence, 2003); C. Cuthbert et al., *Battered Mothers Speak Out: A Human Rights Report on Domestic Violence and Child Custody in the Massachusetts Family Courts* (Wellesley, MA: Battered Mothers' Testimony Project at the Wellesley Centers for Women, 2002).

60. Araji, "Contested Custody, and the Courts" (2012).

61. P. M. Stahl and L. Martin, "An Historical Look at Child Custody Evaluations and the Influence of AFCC," *Family Court Review* 51, no. 1 (2013): 42–47.

62. D. Saunders, K. C. Faller, and R. Tolman, "Beliefs and Recommendations Regarding Child Custody and Visitation in Cases Involving Domestic Violence: A Comparison of Professionals in Different Roles," *Violence Against Women* 22, no. 6 (2015): 722–744; D. Saunders, K. C. Faller, and R. Tolman, *Child Custody Evaluators' Beliefs About Domestic Abuse Allegations: Their Relationship to Evaluator Demographics, Domestic Violence Knowledge and Custody-Visitation Recommendations* (Washington, DC: National Institute of Justice, 2011).

63. Saunders et al., *Child Custody Evaluators' Beliefs About Domestic Abuse Allegations* (2011).

64. Saunders et al., "Beliefs and Recommendations Regarding Child Custody and Visitation in Cases Involving Domestic Violence" (2015); Saunders et al., *Child Custody Evaluators' Beliefs About Domestic Abuse Allegations* (2011).

65. C. Humphreys and R. K. Thiara, "Neither Justice Nor Protection: Women's Experiences of Post-Separation Violence," *Journal of Social Welfare and Family Law* 25, no. 3 (2003): 195–214.

66. F. Morrison, "All Over Now? The Ongoing Relational Consequences of Domestic Abuse through Children's Contact Arrangement," *Child Abuse Review* 24, no. 4 (2015): 274–284.

67. D. Ellis, "Post-Separation Woman Abuse: The Contribution of Lawyers as 'Barracudas,' 'Advocates,' and 'Counsellors'," *International Journal of Law and Psychiatry*

10, no. 4 (1987): 403–411; Saunders et al., *Child Custody Evaluators' Beliefs About Domestic Abuse Allegations* (2011).

68. Saunders et al., "Beliefs and Recommendations Regarding Child Custody and Visitation in Cases Involving Domestic Violence" (2015).

69. Ibid.

70. N. Bow and P. Boxer, "Assessing Allegations of Domestic Violence in Child Custody Evaluations," *Journal of Interpersonal Violence* 18, no. 12 (2003): 1394–1410.

71. Saunders et al., *Child Custody Evaluators' Beliefs About Domestic Abuse Allegations* (2011).

72. Bow and Boxer, "Assessing Allegations of Domestic Violence in Child Custody Evaluations" (2003).

73. T. M. Tippins and J. P. Wittman, "Empirical and Ethical Problems with Custody Recommendations: A Call for Clinical Humility and Judicial Vigilance," *Family Court Review* 43, no. 2 (2005): 193–222.

74. J. Bowlby, *The Making and Breaking of Affectional Bonds* (London: Tavistock Publications, 1979).

75. J. Bowlby, *A Secure Base: Parent-Child Attachment and Healthy Human Development* (New York: Basic Books, 1988).

76. Kathryn L. Mercer, "A Content Analysis of Judicial Decision-Making: How Judges Use the Primary Caretaker Standard to Make a Custody Determination," 5 *Wm. & Mary J. Women & L.* 1 (Winter 1998).

77. J. G. Byrne et al., "Practitioner Review: The Contribution of Attachment Theory to Child Custody Assessments," *Journal of Child Psychology and Psychiatry* 46, no. 2 (2005): 115–127; M. Ainsworth, "Attachments Across the Life Span," *Bulletin of the New York Academy of Medicine* 61, no. 9 (1985): 792–812; M. Ainsworth et al., *Patterns of Attachment: A Psychological Study of the Strange Situation* (Mahwah, NJ: Lawrence Erlbaum Associates, 1978).

78. Byrne et al., "Practitioner Review" (2005).

79. J. L. Edleson and O. J. Williams, *Parenting by Men Who Batter: New Directions for Assessment and Intervention* (New York: Oxford University Press, 2007).

80. E. Peled, "Parenting by Men Who Abuse Women: Issues and Dilemmas," *British Journal of Social Work* 30, no. 1 (2000): 25–36.

81. J. E. McIntosh, "Special Considerations for Infants and Toddlers in Separation/Divorce: Developmental Issues in the Family Law Context," in *Encyclopedia on Early Childhood Development*, edited by R. E. Tremblay, M. Boivin, and R. DeV. Peters (Montreal: Centre of Excellence for Early Childhood Development, 2011), 1–6.

82. L. Bancroft, J. G. Silverman, and D. Ritchie, *The Batterer as Parent: Addressing the Impact of Domestic Violence on Family Dynamics*, 2nd ed. (Los Angeles: Sage Publications, 2012).

83. Herman et al., "Practice Parameters for Child Custody Evaluation" (1997).

84. M. B. Powell and S. Lancaster, "Guidelines for Interviewing Children During Child Custody Evaluations," *Australian Psychologist* 38, no. 1 (2003): 46–54.

85. Ibid.

86. Ibid.

87. Pepiton et al., "Ethical Violations" (2014).

88. K. C. Faller, *Interviewing Children About Sexual Abuse: Controversies and Best Practice* (New York: Oxford University Press, 2007).

89. Y. Chae and S. J. Ceci, "Individual Differences in Children's Recall and Suggestibility: The Effects of Intelligence, Temperament, and Self-Perceptions," *Applied Cognitive Psychology* 19, no. 4 (2005): 383–407.

90. M. Bruck and L. Melnyk, "Individual Differences in Children's Suggestibility: A Review and Synthesis," *Applied Cognitive Psychology* 18, no. 8 (2004): 947–996.

91. Faller, *Interviewing Children About Sexual Abuse* (2007).

92. Ibid.

93. Pepiton et al., "Ethical Violations" (2014).

94. Ibid.

95. Ibid.

96. Oberlander, "Ethical Responsibilities in Child Custody Evaluations" (1995).

97. E. Stark, "Rethinking Custody Evaluation in Cases Involving Domestic Violence," *Journal of Child Custody* 6, no. 3 (2009): 287–321.

98. R. A. Gardner, *The Parental Alienation Syndrome: A Guide for Mental Health and Legal Professionals* (Cresskill, NJ: Creative Therapeutics, 1992).

99. K. C. Faller, "False Accusations of Child Maltreatment: A Contested Issue," *Child Abuse and Neglect* 29, no. 12 (2005): 1327–1331.

100. Oberlander, "Ethical Responsibilities in Child Custody Evaluations" (1995).

101. M. J. Ackerman and M. C. Ackerman, "Child Custody Evaluation Practices: A 1996 Survey of Psychologists," *Family Law Quarterly* 30, no. 3 (1996): 565–586.

102. American Psychological Association, "Guidelines for Child Custody Evaluations in Divorce Proceedings" (1994); American Psychological Association, "Guidelines for Child Custody Evaluations in Family Law Proceedings" (2010).

103. J. N. Bow, J. R. Flens, and J. W. Gould, "MMP1-2 and MCMI-III in Forensic Evaluations: A Survey of Psychologists," *Journal of Forensic Psychology Practice* 10, no. 1 (2010): 37–52.

104. F. A. Quinnell and J. N. Bow, "Psychological Tests Used in Child Custody Evaluations," *Behavioral Sciences and the Law* 19, no. 4 (2001): 491–501.

105. Ackerman and Ackerman, "Child Custody Evaluation Practices" (1996).

106. R. Emery, R. K. Otto, and W. T. O' Donohue, "A Critical Assessment of Child Custody Evaluations: Limited Science and a Flawed System," *Psychological Science in the Public Interest* 6, no. 1 (2005): 1–29.

107. Ackerman and Ackerman, "Child Custody Evaluation Practices" (1996).

108. N. S. Erickson, "Use of the MMPI-2 in Child Custody Evaluations Involving Battered Women: What Does Psychological Research Tell Us?" *Family Law Quarterly* 39, no. 1 (2005): 87–108.

109. Ibid.

110. Bow et al., "MMP1-2 and MCMI-III in Forensic Evaluations" (2010).

111. F. I. Khan, T. L. Welch, and E. A. Zillmer, "MMPI-2 Profiles of Battered Women in Transition," *Journal of Personality Assessment* 60, no. 1 (1993): 100–111.

112. Bow et al., "MMP1-2 and MCMI-III in Forensic Evaluations" (2010).

113. Ibid.

114. R. Yeamans, "Urgent Need for Quality Control in Child Custody Psychological Evaluations," in *Domestic Violence, Abuse, and Child Custody: Legal Strategies and Policy Issues*, edited by M. Hannah and B. Goldstein (Kingston, NJ: Civic Research Institute, 2010), 21:1–21:21.

115. Khan et al., "MMPI-2 Profiles of Battered Women in Transition" (1993).

116. Herman et al., "Practice Parameters for Child Custody Evaluation" (1997).

117. Khan et al., "MMPI-2 Profiles of Battered Women in Transition" (1993).

118. Ibid.

119. D. Medoff, "MMPI-2 Validity Scales in Child Custody Evaluations: Clinical Versus Statistical Significance," *Behavioral Sciences and the Law* 17, no. 4 (1999): 409–411; M. J. Ackerman, *Clinician's Guide to Child Custody Evaluations* (Hoboken, NJ: John Wiley & Sons, 1995).

120. Medoff, "MMPI-2 Validity Scales in Child Custody Evaluations"(1999).

121. Erickson, "Use of the MMPI-2 in Child Custody Evaluations Involving Battered Women" (2005).

122. V. Roseby, "Use of Psychological Testing in a Child-Focused Approach to Child Custody Evaluations," *Family Law Quarterly* 29, no. 1 (1995): 97–110.

123. Heinze and Grisso, "Review of Instruments Assessing Parenting Competencies Used in Child Custody Evaluations" (1996).

124. C. Schleuder and V. Campagna, "Assessing Substance Abuse Questions in Child Custody Evaluations," *Family Court Review* 42, no. 2 (2004): 375–383.

125. C. Breeden, R. Olkin, and D. J. Taub, "Child Custody Evaluations when One Divorcing Parent Has a Physical Disability," *Rehabilitation Psychology* 53, no. 4 (2008): 445–455.

126. *Frye v. United States*, 293 F. 1013, 34 A.L.R. 145 (D.C. Cir. 1923).

127. *Frye v. United States* (1923), 1014.

128. Ibid.

129. *Frye v. United States* (1923).

130. *Daubert v. Merrell Dow Pharmaceuticals, Inc.*, 509 US 579 (1993).

131. Ibid.

132. *Daubert v. Merrell Dow Pharmaceuticals, Inc.* (1993); see *United States v. Downing*, 753 F.2d 1224, 1243 (3rd Cir. 1985).

133. J. Eric Smithburn, "The Trial Court's Gatekeeper Role Under Frye, Daubert, and Kumho: A Special Look at Children's Cases," 4 *Whittier J. Child & Fam. Advoc.* 3 (Fall 2004); see *Daubert v. Merrell Dow Pharmaceuticals, Inc.* (1993).

134. Smithburn, "The Trial Court's Gatekeeper Role Under Frye, Daubert, and Kumho" (2004); see *Daubert v. Merrell Dow Pharmaceuticals, Inc.*, 509 U.S. 579 (1993), on remand to 43 F.3d 1311 (9th Cir. 1995).

135. *Kumho Tire Co. v. Carmichael*, 526 US 137 (1999); see also David P. Horowitz, "Will the Gatekeeper Let Daubert In?" 78 June *N.Y. St. B. J.* 18 (June 2006).

136. *General Electric v. Joiner*, 52 US 136 (1997); see W. Wendell Hall, "Standards of Appellate Review in Civil Appeals," 21 *St. Mary's L. J.* 865 (1990).

137. David G. Owen, "A Decade of Daubert," 80 *Denv. L Rev.* 345 (2002).

138. Fed. R. Evid. 702.

139. *People v. Wernick*, 89 N.Y. 2d 111,120 (N.Y. App. Ct. 1996); see also *People v. Johnston*, 273 A.D. 2d 514 (N.Y. App. Ct. 2000).

140. *Hofmann v. Toys "R" Us—NY Limited Partnership*, 272 A.D. 2d 641 (N.Y. App. Ct. 2000); *Houck v. Simoes,* 85 A.D. 3d 967 (N.Y. App. Ct. 2011).

141. Horowitz, "Will the Gatekeeper Let Daubert In?" (June 2006).

142. *Daubert v. Merrell Dow Pharmaceuticals, Inc.* (1993).

143. Alayne Katz, "Junk Science v. Novel Scientific Evidence: Parental Alienation Syndrome, Getting It Wrong in Custody Cases," 24 *Pace L. Rev.* 239 (Fall 2003).

144. Ibid.

145. P. J. Fink, "Parental Alienation Syndrome," in *Domestic Violence, Abuse, and Child Custody: Legal Strategies and Policy Issues*, edited by M. Hannah and B. Goldstein (Kingston, NJ: Civic Research Institute, 2010), 12:1–12:8.

146. Ibid.

147. Jennifer Hoult, "Evidentiary Admissibility of Parental Alienation Syndrome: Science, Law, and Policy," 26 *Children's Leg. Rights J.* 1 (Spring 2006).

Chapter 11

1. K. Y. Slote et al., "Battered Mothers Speak Out: Participatory Human Rights Documentation as a Model for Research and Activism in the United States," *Violence Against Women* 11, no. 11 (2005): 1367–1395.

2. Gender Bias Study Committee of the Massachusetts Supreme Judicial Court, *Gender Bias Study of the Supreme Judicial Court, Commonwealth of Massachusetts* (Washington, DC: National Institute of Justice, 1989); L. Hecht Schafran and N. J. Wikler, *Gender Fairness in the Courts: Action in the New Millennium* (New York: Legal Momentum [Formerly NOW Legal Defense and Education Fund], 2001).

3. A. M. Zeoli et al., "Post-Separation Abuse of Women and Their Children: Boundary-Setting and Family Court Utilization Among Victimized Mothers," *Journal of Family Violence* 28, no. 6 (2013): 547–560.

4. K. C. Faller, "False Accusations of Child Maltreatment: A Contested Issue," *Child Abuse and Neglect* 29, no. 12 (2005): 1327–1331.

5. E. Stark, "Reframing Child Custody Decisions in the Context of Coercive Control," in *Domestic Violence, Abuse, and Child Custody: Legal Strategies and Policy Issues*, edited by M. Hannah and B. Goldstein (Kingston, NJ: Civic Research Institute, 2010), 11:1–11:29.

6. C. Dalton, "When Paradigms Collide: Protecting Battered Parents and Their Children in the Family Court System," *Family and Conciliation Courts Review* 37, no. 3 (1999): 273–296.

7. Dalton, "When Paradigms Collide" (1999); Stark, "Reframing Child Custody Decisions in the Context of Coercive Control" (2010).

8. D. Saunders, K. C. Faller, and R. Tolman, *Child Custody Evaluators' Beliefs About Domestic Abuse Allegations: Their Relationship to Evaluator Demographics, Background, Domestic Violence Knowledge and Custody-Visitation Recommendations* (Washington, DC: National Institute of Justice, 2011).

9. Ibid.

10. Stark, "Reframing Child Custody Decisions in the Context of Coercive Control" (2010).

11. R. L. Kourlis et al., "Courts and Communities Helping Families in Transition Arising from Separation and Divorce: Honoring Families Initiative White Paper," *Family Court Review* 51, no. 3 (2013): 351–376.

12. Stark, "Reframing Child Custody Decisions in the Context of Coercive Control" (2010).

13. Saunders et al., *Child Custody Evaluators' Beliefs About Domestic Abuse Allegations* (2011); K. Lewis, *Child Custody Evaluations by Social Workers* (Washington, DC: NASW Press, 2009).

14. L. Fischel-Wolovick, "Police Response: Mandatory Arrest Primary Physical Aggressor," in *Lawyer's Manual on Domestic Violence: Representing the Victim*, 6th ed., edited

by M. R. Rothwell Davis, D. A. Leidholdt, and C. A. Watson (New York: Supreme Court of the State of New York, Appellate Division, First Department, 2015), 52–61; D. Saunders, "The Tendency to Arrest Victims of Domestic Violence: A Preliminary Analysis of Officer Characteristics," *Journal of Interpersonal Violence* 10 (June 1, 1995): 147–148; D. A. Ford, "The Impact of Police Officers' Attitudes Towards Victims on the Disinclination to Arrest Wife Beaters." (Paper presented at the Third National Conference for Family Violence Researchers, University of New Hampshire, Durham, NH, July 1987).

15. K. Gentile, "You Don't Recognize Me Because I'm Still Standing," in *Domestic Violence: Methodologies in Dialogue*, edited by C. Raghavan and S. J. Cohen (Boston: Northeastern University Press, 2013), 171–199.

16. Stark, "Reframing Child Custody Decisions in the Context of Coercive Control" (2010).

17. U. Castellano and L. Anderson, "Mental Health Courts in America: Promise and Challenges," *American Behavioral Scientist* 57, no. 2 (2013): 163–173.

18. Greg Berman and John Feinblatt, "Problem-Solving Courts: A Brief Primer," 23 *Law & Pol'y* 125 (2001).

19. Angela Littwin, "Coerced Debt: The Role of Consumer Credit in Domestic Violence," 100 *Cal. L. Rev.* 951 (2012).

20. Battered Women's Justice Project, *Guiding Principles for Effectively Addressing Child Custody and Parenting Time in Case Involving Domestic Violence* (National Council of Juvenile and Family Court Judges (NCJFCF), US Dept. of Justice: Center for Court Innovation, 2016).

21. R. Mirchandani, "Battered Women's Movement Ideals and Judge-Led Social Change in Domestic Violence Courts," *The Great Society* 13, no. 1 (2004): 32–37.

22. Elizabeth L. MacDowell, "When Courts Collide: Integrated Domestic Violence Courts and Court Pluralism," 20 *Tex. J. Women & L.* 95 (August 2011).

23. Jonathan Lippman, "Ensuring Victim Safety and Abuser Accountability: Reforms and Revisions in New York Courts' Response to Domestic Violence," 76 *Alb. L. Rev.* 1417 (2013).

24. Mirchandani, "Battered Women's Movement Ideals and Judge-Led Social Change in Domestic Violence Courts" (2004).

25. Stark, "Reframing Child Custody Decisions in the Context of Coercive Control" (2010).

26. A. Moe Wan, "Battered Women in the Restraining Order Process: Observations on a Court Advocacy Program," *Violence Against Women* 6, no. 6 (2000): 606–632.

27. J. Ptacek, "Disorder in the Courts: Judicial Demeanor and Women's Experience Seeking Restraining Orders," (PhD diss., Brandeis University, 1995); Moe Wan, "Battered Women in the Restraining Order Process" (2000).

28. Moe Wan, "Battered Women in the Restraining Order Process" (2000); Ptacek, "Disorder in the Courts" (1995).

29. M. E. Bell et al., "Battered Women's Perceptions of Civil and Criminal Court Helpfulness: The Role of Court Outcome and Process," *Violence Against Women* 17, no. 1 (2011): 71–88.

30. G. Davis, "A Systematic Approach to Domestic Abuse-Informed Child Custody Decision Making in Family Law Cases," *Family Court Review* 53, no. 4 (2015): 565–577.

31. Battered Women's Justice Project, *Guiding Principles for Effectively Addressing Child Custody and Parenting Time in Case Involving Domestic Violence* (2016).

32. R. Walker et al., "An Integrative Review of Separation in the Context of Victimization: Consequences and Implications for Women," *Trauma, Violence, & Abuse* 5, no. 2 (2004): 143–193.

33. J. L. Hardesty and G. H. Chung, "Intimate Partner Violence, Parental Divorce, and Child Custody: Directions for Intervention and Future Research," *Family Relations* 55, no. 2 (2006): 200–210; J. C. Campbell, *Assessing Dangerousness* (Newbury Park, CA: Sage, 1995).

34. R. Fleury, C. M. Sullivan, and D. Bybee, "When Ending the Relationship Doesn't End the Violence: Women's Experiences of Violence by Former Partners," *Violence Against Women* 6, no. 12 (2000): 1363–1383.

35. Hardesty and Chung, "Intimate Partner Violence, Parental Divorce, and Child Custody" (2006).

36. Bruce J. Winick and David B. Wexler, "The Use of Therapeutic Jurisprudence in Law School Clinical Education: Transforming the Criminal Law Clinic," 13 *Clinical L. Rev.* 605 (2006).

37. Stark, "Reframing Child Custody Decisions in the Context of Coercive Control, Domestic Violence, Abuse, and Child Custody" (2010).

38. C. Cuthbert et al., *Battered Mothers Speak Out: A Human Rights Report on Domestic Violence and Child Custody in the Massachusetts Family Courts* (Wellesley, MA: Battered Mothers' Testimony Project at the Wellesley Centers for Women, 2002).

39. Ibid.

40. Rebecca Green, "Privacy and Domestic Violence in Court," 16 *Wm. & Mary J. Women & L.* 237 (2010).

41. U.S. Const. amend. VI.

42. Green, "Privacy and Domestic Violence in Court" (2010).

43. Green, "Privacy and Domestic Violence in Court" (2010); Montana Coalition Against Domestic and Sexual Violence, *MCADSV Court Watch Training Manual* (Washington, DC: US Department of Justice, Office of Justice Programs, 2007).

44. Brooke Albrandt, "Turning in the Client: Mandatory Child Abuse Reporting Requirements and the Criminal Defense of Battered Women," 81 *Tex. L. Rev.* 655 (2002).

45. Jacqueline St. Joan, "Building Bridges, Building Walls: Collaboration Between Lawyers and Social Workers in a Domestic Violence Clinic and Issues of Client Confidentiality," 7 *Clinical L. Rev.* 403 (2001).

46. Ibid.

47. Ibid.

48. "An Open Letter to Our Community Regarding the Family Justice Center," SafePlace, accessed February 14, 2017, http://www.safeplaceolympia.org/2012/11/an-open-letter-to-our-community-regarding-the-family-justice-center/.

49. Ibid.

50. Violence Against Women Act (VAWA), 42 U.S.C. § 14011 (1994).

51. E. M. Bauman et al., "Measuring Social Support in Battered Women: Factor Structure of the Interpersonal Support Evaluation List (ISEL)," *Violence Against Women* 18, no. 1 (2012): 30–42.

52. R. J. Mancoske, D. Standifer, and C. Cauley, "The Effectiveness of Brief Counseling Services for Battered Women," *Research on Social Work Practice* 4, no. 1 (1994): 53–63.

53. L. Bancroft and J. G. Silverman, *The Batterer as Parent: Addressing the Impact of Domestic Violence on Family Dynamics* (Los Angeles: Sage Publications, 2002); R. Gelles and M. Straus, *Intimate Violence* (New York: Simon and Schuster, 1988).

54. J. C. Babcock, C. E. Green, and C. Robie, "Does Batterers' Treatment Work? A Meta-Analytic Review of Domestic Violence Treatment," *Journal of Clinical Psychology Review* 23, no. 8 (2003): 1023–1053.

55. C. S. Silvergleid and E. S. Mankowski, "How Batterer Intervention Programs Work: Participant and Facilitator Accounts of Processes of Change," *Journal of Interpersonal Violence* 21, no. 1 (2006): 139–159.

56. AP10, Bronx Criminal Court, New York State.

57. D. R. Tollefson, E. Gross, and B. Lundahl, "Factors that Predict Attrition from a State-Sponsored Rural Batterer Treatment Program," *Journal of Aggression, Maltreatment and Trauma* 17, no. 4 (2008): 453–477; Babcock et al., "Does Batterers' Treatment Work?" (2003); J. E. Daly and S. Pelowski, "Predictors of Dropout Among Men Who Batter: A Review of Studies with Implications for Research and Practice," *Violence and Victims* 15, no. 2 (2000): 137–160.

58. Babcock et al., "Does Batterers' Treatment Work?" (2003).

59. Silvergleid and Mankowski, "How Batterer Intervention Programs Work" (2006).

60. A. L. Boa and E. S. Mankowski, "The Impact of Legislative Standards on Batterer Intervention Program Practices and Characteristics," *American Journal of Community Psychology* 53 (March 2014): 218–230.

61. R. D. Maiuro et al., "Are Current State Standards for Domestic Violence Perpetrator Treatment Adequately Informed by Research? A Question of Questions," *Journal of Aggression, Maltreatment and Trauma* 5, no. 2 (2001): 21–44; Boa and Mankowski, "The Impact of Legislative Standards on Batterer Intervention Program Practices and Characteristics" (2014).

62. F. P. Buttell and M. M. Carney, "Psychological and Demographic Predictors of Attrition Among Batterers Court Ordered into Treatment," *Journal of Social Work Research* 26, no. 1 (2002): 31–41.

63. D. D. DeHart et al., "Predictors of Attrition in a Treatment Program for Battering Men," *Journal of Family Violence* 14, no. 1 (1999): 19–34.

64. E. Buzawa, G. Hotaling, and A. Klein, "The Response to Domestic Violence in a Model Court: Some Initial Findings and Implications," *Behavioral Sciences and the Law* 16, no. 2 (1998): 185–206.

65. L. Sherman, "The Influence of Criminology on Criminal Law: Evaluating for Misdemeanor Domestic Violence," *Journal of Criminal Law and Criminology* 83, no. 1 (1992): 1–45.

66. W. E. Gondolf, "Patterns of Re-Assault in Batterer Programs," *Violence and Victims* 12, no. 4 (1997): 373–387; J. C. Babcock and R. Steiner, "The Relationship Between Treatment, Incarceration, and Recidivism of Battering: A Program Evaluation of Seattle's Coordinated Community Response to Domestic Violence," *Journal of American Psychology* 13, no. 1 (1990): 46–59

67. J. L. Edleson, "Controversy and Change in Batterers' Programs," accessed February 9, 2017, http://www.academia.edu/26410751/Controversy_and_Change_in_Batterers_Programs

68. Bancroft and Silverman, *The Batterer as Parent* (2002); L. Bancroft, J. G. Silverman, and D. Ritchie, *The Batterer as Parent: Addressing the Impact of Domestic Violence on Family Dynamics*, 2nd ed. (Los Angeles: Sage Publications, 2012).

69. L. Bancroft and J. G. Silverman, *The Batterer as Parent* (2002).

70. J. L. Edleson and O. J. Williams, *Parenting by Men Who Batter: New Directions for Assessment and Intervention* (New York: Oxford University Press, 2007).

71. Edleson and Williams, *Parenting by Men Who Batter* (2007); A. Appel and G. Holden, "The Co-occurrence of Spouse and Physical Child Abuse: A Review and Appraisal," *Journal of Family Psychology* 12, no. 4 (1998): 578–599.

72. P. G. Jaffe, L. L. Baker, and A. J. Cunningham, *Protecting Children from Domestic Violence: Strategies for Community Intervention* (New York: Guilford Press, 2004).

73. J. P. J. Dussich, "Teaching Victimology in America: From on the Job Training (OJT) to PhD," *Journal of Criminal Justice Education* 25, no. 4 (2014): 486–500.

74. J. P. J. Dussich, "History, Overview and Analysis of American Victimology and Victim Services Education," in *Proceedings of the First American Symposium on Victimology: Exploration of Higher Education and Professional Practice* at Kansas City Kansas Community College, January 9–10, 2003, pp. 4–17.

75. B. P. Phelps, "Helping Medical Students Help Survivors of Domestic Violence," *Journal of the American Medical Association* 283, no. 9 (2000): 1199.

76. L. E. Tower, "Domestic Violence Screening: Education and Institutional Support Correlates," *Journal of Social Work Education* 39, no. 3 (2003): 479–494; J, Koziol-McLain, C. J. Coates, and S. R. Lowenstein, "Predictive Validity of a Screen for Partner Violence Against Women," *American Journal of Preventive Medicine* 21, no. 2 (2001): 93–100.

77. Tower, "Domestic Violence Screening" (2003).

78. D. E. McNiel et al., "Impact of Clinical Training on Violence Risk Assessment," *American Journal of Psychiatry* 16, no. 2 (2008): 195–200.

79. M. Dragiewicz et al., "Innovative University Programs for Teaching About Domestic Violence," *Journal of Criminal Justice Education* 24, no. 4 (2013): 594–611.

80. M. A. Forgey and L. Colarossi, "Interdisciplinary Social Work and Law: A Model for Domestic Violence Curriculum," *Journal of Social Work Education* 39, no. 3 (2003): 459–476.

81. St. Joan, "Building Bridges, Building Walls" (2001).

82. Winick and Wexler, "The Use of Therapeutic Jurisprudence in Law School Clinical Education" (2006).

83. M. E. Bell and L. A. Goodman, "Supporting Battered Women Involved with the Court System," *Violence Against Women* 7, no. 12 (2001): 1377–1404.

84. Ibid.

85. K. McQueeney, "Teaching Domestic Violence in the New Millennium: Intersectionality as a Framework for Social Change," *Violence Against Women* 22, no. 12 (2016): 1463–1475.

86. M. Finklestein et al., "Post-Traumatic Stress Disorder and Vicarious Trauma in Mental Health Professionals," *Journal of Health and Social Work* 40, no. 2 (2015): 25–31.

87. L. E. Morrison and J. P. Joy, "Secondary Traumatic Stress in the Emergency Department," *Journal of Advanced Nursing* 72, no. 11 (2016): 2894–2906.

88. Finklestein et al., "Post-Traumatic Stress Disorder and Vicarious Trauma in Mental Health Professionals" (2015); L. Pearlman and P. Mac Ian, "Vicarious Traumatization: An Empirical Study of the Effects of Trauma Work on Trauma Therapists," *Journal of Professional Psychology: Research and Practice* 26, no. 6 (1995): 558–565.

89. K. Kendall-Tackett, *Treating the Lifetime Health Effects of Childhood Victimization*, 2nd ed. (Kingston, NJ: Civic Research Institute, 2013).

BIBLIOGRAPHY

Ackerman, M. J. *Clinician's Guide to Child Custody Evaluations*. Hoboken, NJ: John Wiley & Sons, 1995.

Ackerman, M. J., and M. C. Ackerman. "Child Custody Evaluation Practices: A 1996 Survey of Psychologists." *Family Law Quarterly* 30, no. 3 (1996): 565–586.

Ackerman, M. J., and M. C. Ackerman. "Custody Evaluation Practices." *Professional Psychology: Research and Practice* 28, no. 2 (1997): 137–145.

Ackerman, M. J., and T. B. Pritzl. "Child Custody Evaluation Practices: A 20-Year Follow-up." *Family Court Review* 49, no. 3 (2011): 618–628.

Adams, A. E., C. Sullivan, D. Bybee, and M. R. Greeson. "Development of the Scale of Economic Abuse." *Violence Against Women* 14, no. 5 (2008): 563–588.

Advisory Committee of the Conrad N. Hilton Foundation. *Model Code on Domestic and Family Violence*. Reno, NV: National Council of Juvenile and Family Court Judges, 1994.

AFCC Task Force on Parenting Coordination. *Guidelines for Parenting Coordination*. Madison, WI: Association of Family Conciliation Courts, 2005.

Ahrons, C. R. "Family Ties After Divorce: Long-Term Implications for Children." *Family Process* 46, no. 1 (2006): 53–65.

Ainsworth, M. "Attachments Across the Life Span." *Bulletin of the New York Academy of Medicine* 61, no. 9 (1985): 792–812.

Ainsworth, M., M. Blehar, E. Waters, and S. Wall. *Patterns of Attachment: A Psychological Study of the Strange Situation*. Mahwah, NJ: Lawrence Erlbaum Associates, 1978.

Albrandt, Brooke. "Turning in the Client: Mandatory Child Abuse Reporting Requirements and the Criminal Defense of Battered Women." 81 *Tex. L. Rev.* 655 (2002).

Alexander, R. "Moving Forwards or Back to the Future? An Analysis of Case Law on Family Violence Under the 'Family Law Act 1975' (Cth)." *The University of New South Wales Law Journal* 33, no. 2 (2010): 907–928.

Alisic E., and R. J. Kleber. "Measuring Posttraumatic Stress Reactions in Children: A Preliminary Validation of the Children's Responses to Trauma Inventory." *Journal of Child and Adolescent Trauma* 3, no. 3 (2010): 192–204.

Alvord, M. K., and J. J. Grados. "Enhancing Resilience in Children: A Proactive Approach." *Professional Psychology: Research and Practice* 36, no. 3 (2005): 238–245.

Amato, P. R. "The Consequences of Divorce for Adults and Children." *Journal of Marriage and Family* 62, no. 4 (2000): 1269–1287.

Amato, P. R. "Reconciling Divergent Perspectives: Judith Wallerstein, Quantitative Family Research, and Children of Divorce." *Family Relations* 52, no. 4 (2003): 332–339.

Amato, P. R., and A. Booth. "Consequences of Parental Divorce and Marital Unhappiness for Adult Well-Being." *Social Forces* 69, no. 3 (1991): 895–914.

Amato, P. R., and J. G. Gilbreth. "Nonresident Fathers and Children's Well-Being: A Meta-Analysis." *Journal of Marriage and Family* 61, no. 3 (1999): 557–573.

Amato, P. R., and B. Hohmann-Marriott. "A Comparison of High- and Low-Distress Marriages that End in Divorce." *Journal of Marriage and Family* 69 (August 2007): 621–638.

Amato, P. R., and B. Keith. "Parental Divorce and the Well-Being of Children: A Meta-Analysis." *Psychological Bulletin* 110, no. 1 (1991): 26–46.

Amato, P. R., L. S. Loomis, and A. Booth. "Parental Divorce, Marital Conflict and Offspring Well-Being During Early Adulthood." *Adulthood, Social Forces* 73, no. 3 (1995): 895–915.

American Bar Association. *The Impact of Domestic Violence on Children: A Report to the President of the American Bar Association.* Chicago: American Bar Association, 1994.

American Bar Association, American Arbitration Association, and Association for Conflict Resolution. *Model Standards of Conduct for Mediators (August 2005).* Accessed on July 31, 2017 https://www.mediate.com/articles/model_standards_of_conflict.cfmcomments.

American Bar Association Special Committee of Jury Comprehension, Litigation Section. *Jury Comprehension in Complex Cases.* Chicago: American Bar Association, 1989.

American Psychiatric Association. *Diagnostic and Statistical Manual of Mental Disorders,* 5th ed. Arlington, VA: American Psychiatric Publishing, 2013.

American Psychological Association. "Guidelines for Child Custody Evaluations in Divorce Proceedings." *American Psychologist* 49, no. 7 (1994): 677–680.

American Psychological Association. "Guidelines for Child Custody Evaluations in Family Law Proceedings." *American Psychologist* 65, no. 9 (2010): 863–867.

Anda, R. F., V. J. Felitti, J. D. Bremner, J. D. Walker, C. Whitfield, B. D. Perry, S. R. Dubt, and W. H. Giles. "The Enduring Effects of Abuse and Related Adverse Experiences in Childhood: A Convergence of Evidence from Neurobiology and Epidemiology." *European Archives of Psychiatry and Clinical Neuroscience* 256, no. 3 (2006): 174–186.

Anderson, M. A., P. M. Gillig, M. Sitaker, K. McCloskey, K. Malloy, and N. Grigsby. "'Why Doesn't She Just Leave?': A Descriptive Study of Victim Reported Impediments to Her Safety." *Journal of Family Violence* 18, no. 3 (2003): 151–155.

Appel, A., and G. Holden. "The Co-occurrence of Spouse and Physical Child Abuse: A Review and Appraisal." *Journal of Family Psychology* 12, no. 4 (1998): 578–599.

Araji, S. K. "Contested Custody, and the Courts: A Review of Findings from Five Studies with Accompanying Documentary." *Sociological Perspectives* 55, no. 1 (2012): 3–15.

Arizona Coalition Against Domestic Violence. *Battered Mothers' Testimony Project: A Human Rights Approach to Child Custody and Domestic Violence.* Phoenix: Arizona Coalition Against Domestic Violence, 2003.

Arroyo, J. A., T. L. Simpson, and A. S. Aragon. "Childhood Sexual Abuse Among Hispanic and Non-Hispanic White College Women." *Hispanic Journal of Behavioral Sciences* 19, no. 1 (1997): 57–68.

Association of Family and Conciliation Courts (AFCC). "Guidelines for Intimate Partner Violence: A Supplement to the AFCC Model Standards of Practice for Child Custody Evaluation." *Family Court Review* 54, no. 4 (2016): 674–686.

Austin, W. G., M. K. Pruett, H. D. Kirkpatrick, J. R. Flens, and J. W. Gould. "Parental Gatekeeping and Child Custody/Child Access Evaluation: Part I: Conceptual

Framework, Research, and Applications." *Family Court Review* 51, no. 3 (2013): 485–501.

Babcock, J. C., C. E. Green, and C. Robie. "Does Batterers' Treatment Work? A Meta-Analytic Review of Domestic Violence Treatment." *Journal of Clinical Psychology Review* 23, no. 8 (2003): 1023–1053.

Babcock, J. C., and R. Steiner. "The Relationship Between Treatment, Incarceration, and Recidivism of Battering: A Program Evaluation of Seattle's Coordinated Community Response to Domestic Violence." *Journal of American Psychology* 13, no. 1 (1990): 46–59.

Bair-Merritt, M., B. Zuckerman, M. Augustyn, and P. Cronholm. "Silent Victims: An Epidemic of Childhood Exposure to Domestic Violence." *New England Journal of Medicine* 369, no. 18 (2013): 1673–1675.

Bancroft, L., and J. G. Silverman. *The Batterer as Parent: Addressing the Impact of Domestic Violence on Family Dynamics.* Los Angeles: Sage Publications, 2002.

Bancroft, L., J. G. Silverman, and D. Ritchie. *The Batterer as Parent: Addressing the Impact of Domestic Violence on Family Dynamics*, 2nd ed. Los Angeles: Sage Publications, 2012.

Battered Women's Justice Project. *Guiding Principles for Effectively Addressing Child Custody and Parenting Time in Cases Involving Domestic Violence.* Washington, DC: National Council of Juvenile and Family Court Judges (NCJFCF), US Dept. of Justice, Center for Court Innovation, 2016.

Bauman, E. M., D. A. F. Haaga, S. Kaltman, and M. A. Dalton. "Measuring Social Support in Battered Women: Factor Structure of the Interpersonal Support Evaluation List (ISEL)." *Violence Against Women* 18, no. 1 (2012): 30–42.

Bauserman, R. "Child Adjustment in Joint-Custody Versus Sole-Custody Arrangements: A Meta-Analysis Review." *Journal of Family Psychology* 16, no. 1 (2002): 91–102.

Beasley, R., and C. D. Stoltenberg. "Personality Characteristics of Male Spouse Abusers." *Professional Psychology: Research and Practice* 23, no. 4 (1992): 310–317.

Beck, J. Gayle, J. McNiff, J. D. Clapp, S. A. Olsen, M. L. Avery, and J. Houston Hagewood. "Exploring Negative Emotion in Women Experiencing Intimate Partner Violence: Shame, Guilt and PTSD." *Behavior Therapy* 42, no. 4 (2011): 740–750.

Belenko, S. "Study Finds Drug Courts Reduce Recidivism During Treatment." *Alcoholism & Drug Abuse Weekly* 10 (June 8, 1998): 3.

Bell, M. E., and L. A. Goodman. "Supporting Battered Women Involved with the Court System." *Violence Against Women* 7, no. 12 (2001): 1377–1404.

Bell, M. E., S. Perez, L. A. Goodman, and M. A. Dutton. "Battered Women's Perceptions of Civil and Criminal Court Helpfulness: The Role of Court Outcome and Process." *Violence Against Women* 17, no. 1 (2011): 71–88.

Berman, Greg and John Feinblatt. "Problem-Solving Courts: A Brief Primer." 23 *Law & Policy* 125 (2001).

Bernet, W., M. C. Verrochio, and S. Korosi. "Yes, Children Are Susceptible to Manipulation: Commentary on Article by Clemente and Padilla-Racero." *Children and Youth Services Review* 56 (September 2015): 135–138.

Bernstein, N. *The Lost Children of Wilder: The Epic Struggle to Change Foster Care.* New York: Vintage Books, 2001.

Birnbaum, R., and R. Alaggia. "Supervised Visitation: A Call for a Second Generation of Research." *Family Court Review* 44, no. 1 (2006): 119–134.

Boa, A. L., and E. S. Mankowski. "The Impact of Legislative Standards on Batterer Intervention Program Practices and Characteristics." *American Journal of Community Psychology* 53 (March 2014): 218–230.

Boldt, Richard and Jana Singer. "Juristocracy in the Trenches: Problem-solving Judges and Therapeutic Jurisprudence in Drug Treatment Courts and Unified Courts." 65 *Md. L. Rev.* 82 (2006).

Bolen, R. *Child Sexual Abuse: Its Scope and Our Failure.* New York: Kluwer Academic/ Plenum Publishers, 2001.

Bornstein, M. H. *Handbook of Parenting Volume 4: Social Conditions and Applied Parenting.* Mahwah, NJ: Lawrence Erlbaum Associates, 2002.

Bow, J. N., and P. Boxer. "Assessing Allegations of Domestic Violence in Child Custody Evaluations." *Journal of Interpersonal Violence* 18, no. 12 (2003): 1394–1410.

Bow, J. N., J. R. Flens, and J. W. Gould. "MMP1–2 and MCMI-III in Forensic Evaluations: A Survey of Psychologists." *Journal of Forensic Psychology Practice* 10, no. 1 (2010): 37–52.

Bow, J. N., and F. A. Quinnell. "Psychologists' Current Practices and Procedures in Child Custody Evaluations: Five Years After American Psychological Association Guidelines." *Professional Psychology: Research and Practice* 32, no. 3 (2001): 261–268.

Bowlby, J. *The Making and Breaking of Affectional Bonds.* London: Tavistock Publications, 1979.

Bowlby, J. *A Secure Base: Parent-Child Attachment and Healthy Human Development.* New York: Basic Books, 1988.

Brandt, Elizabeth B. "Concerns at the Margins of Supervised Access to Children." 9 *J. L. & Fam. Stud.* 201 (2007).

Brandwein, R. A., and D. M. Filiano. "Toward Real Welfare Reform: The Voices of Battered Women." *Affilia* 15, no. 2 (2000): 224–243.

Brasfield, R. "The Absence of Evidence Is Not the Evidence of Absence: The Abusive Personality as a Disordered Mental State." *Journal of Aggression and Violent Behavior* 19, no. 5 (2014): 515–522.

Breeden, C., R. Olkin, and D. J. Taub. "Child Custody Evaluations when One Divorcing Parent Has a Physical Disability." *Rehabilitation Psychology* 53, no. 4 (2008): 445–455.

Bremner, J. D. *Does Stress Damage the Brain? Understanding Trauma-Based Disorders from a Neurological Perspective.* New York: Norton Publishing, 2003.

Bremner, J. D. "The Relationship Between Cognitive and Brain Changes in Posttraumatic Stress Disorder." *Annals of the New York Academy of Science* 1071 (July 2006): 80–86.

Brewin, C. R., B. Andrews, and J. D. Valentine. "Meta-Analysis of Risk Factors for Posttraumatic Stress Disorder in Trauma-Exposed Adults." *Journal of Consulting and Clinical Psychology* 68, no. 5 (2000): 748–766.

Bridges, Nicole K. "The 'Strengthen and Vitalize Enforcement of Child Support (SAVE Child Support) Act': Can the SAVE Child Support Act Save Child Support from the Recent Economic Downturn?" 36 *Okla. City U.L. Rev.* 679 (2011).

Briere, J. *Therapy for Adults Molested as Children,* 2nd ed. New York: Springer Publishing, 1996.

Brinig, M. F., L. M. Frederick, and L. M. Drozd. "Perspectives on Joint Custody Presumptions as Applied to Domestic Violence." *Family Court Review* 52, no. 2 (2014): 271–281.

Bruck, M., and L. Melnyk. "Individual Differences in Children's Suggestibility: A Review and Synthesis." *Applied Cognitive Psychology* 18, no. 8 (2004): 947–996.

Brunette, M. F., and W. Dean. "Community Mental Health Care for Women with Severe Mental Illness Who Are Parents." *Community Mental Health Journal* 38, no. 2 (2002): 153–165.

Buchanan, C. M., E. E. Macobby, and S. M. Dorrnbusch. *Adolescents After Divorce.* Cambridge, MA: Harvard University Press, 1996.

Burge, S. K., D. A. Katerndahl, R. C. Wood, J. Beccho, R. L. Ferrer, and M. A. Talamantes. "Using Complexity Science to Examine Three Dynamic Patterns of Intimate Partner Violence." *Family Systems and Health* 34, no. 1 (2016): 4–14.

Burkett, Sarah. "Finding Fault and Making Reparations: Domestic Violence Conviction as a Limitation on Spousal Support Award." 22 *J. Contemp. Legal Issues* 492 (2015).

Burns, S., and M. Peyrot. "Tough Love: Nurturing and Coercing Responsibility and Recovery in California Drug Courts." *Social Problems* 50, no. 3 (2003): 416–438.

Bussayabuntoon, Joann. "Age and Health as Factors for Court-Ordered Alimony Decisions." 22 *J. Contemp. Legal Issues* 309 (2015).

Buttell, F. P., and M. M. Carney. "Psychological and Demographic Predictors of Attrition Among Batterers Court Ordered into Treatment." *Journal of Social Work Research* 26, no. 1 (2002): 31–41.

Buzawa, E., G. Hotaling, and A. Klein. "The Response to Domestic Violence in a Model Court: Some Initial Findings and Implications." *Behavioral Sciences and the Law* 16, no. 2 (1998): 185–206.

Byrne, J. G., T. G. O'Connor, R. S. Marvin, and W. F. Whelan. "Practitioner Review: The Contribution of Attachment Theory to Child Custody Assessments." *Journal of Child Psychology and Psychiatry* 46, no. 2 (2005): 115–127.

Campbell, J. C. *Assessing Dangerousness.* Newbury Park, CA: Sage, 1995.

Campbell, J. C., D. W. Webster, and N. Glass. "The Danger Assessment: Validation of a Lethality Risk Assessment Instrument for Intimate Partner Femicide." *Journal of Interpersonal Violence* 24, no. 6 (2009): 653–674.

Campbell, J. C., D. W. Webster, J. Koziol-McLain, C. R. Block, D. W. Campbell, and M. A. Curry. "Risk Factors for Femicide in Abusive Relationships: Results from a Multisite Case Control Study." *American Journal of Public Health* 93, no. 7 (2003): 1089–1097.

Campbell, L. E. G., and J. R. Johnston. "Impasse-Directed Mediation with High Conflict Families in Custody Disputes." *Behavioral Sciences and the Law* 4, no. 2 (1986): 217–241.

Candela, K. "Protecting the Invisible Victim: Incorporating Coercive Control in Domestic Violence Statutes." *Family Court Review* 54, no. 1 (2016): 112–125.

Carrion, V. G., C. F. Weems, and A. L. Reiss. "Stress Predicts Changes in Children: A Pilot Longitudinal Study on Youth Stress, Posttraumatic Stress Disorder, and the Hippocampus." *Pediatrics* 119, no. 3 (2007): 509–516.

Castellano, U., and L. Anderson. "Mental Health Courts in America: Promise and Challenges." *American Behavioral Scientist* 57, no. 2 (2013): 163–173.

Celorio, Rosa M. "The Case of Karen Atala and Daughters: Toward a Better Understanding of Discrimination, Equality and the Rights of Women." 15 *CUNY L. Rev.* 335 (2012).

Chae, Y., and S. J. Ceci. "Individual Differences in Children's Recall and Suggestibility: The Effects of Intelligence, Temperament, and Self-Perceptions." *Applied Cognitive Psychology* 19, no. 4 (2005): 383–407.

Cheit, R. E. *The Witch-Hunt Narrative: Politics, Psychology, and the Sexual Abuse of Children*. New York: Oxford University Press, 2014.

Chemtob, C. M., Y. Nomura, K. Rajendran, D. Schwartz, R. Yehuda, and R. Abramovitz. "Impact of Maternal Posttraumatic Stress Disorder and Depression Following Exposure to the September 11 Attacks on Preschool Children's Behavior." *Child Development* 81, no. 4 (2010): 1129–1141.

Cherlin, A. J., F. F. Furstenberg, Jr., P. L. Chase-Lansdale, K. E. Kiernan, P. K. Robins, and D. Ruane Morrison. "Longitudinal Studies of Effects of Divorce on Children in Great Britain and the United States." *Science* 252, no. 5011 (1991): 1386–1389.

Chiu, E. Y. "Psychological Testing in Child Custody Evaluations with Ethnically Diverse Families: Ethical Concerns and Practice Considerations." *Journal of Child Custody* 11, no. 2 (2014): 107–127.

Cihan, A., D. A. Winstead, J. Laulis, and M. D. Feit. "Attachment Theory and Substance Abuse: Etiological Links." *Journal of Human Behavior in the Social Environment* 24, no. 5 (2014): 531–537.

Cissner, A. B., M. Labriola, and M. Rempel. "Domestic Violence Courts." *Violence Against Women* 20, no. 9 (2015): 1102–1122.

Clemente, M., and D. Padilla-Racero. "Are Children Susceptible to Manipulation? The Best Interest of Children and Their Testimony." *Children and Youth Services Review* 51 (February 2015): 101–107.

Clemente, M., and D. Padilla-Racero. "Facts Speak Louder than Words: Science Versus the Pseudoscience of PAS." *Children and Youth Services Review* 56 (September 2015): 177–184.

Cloitre, M., B. C. Stolbach, J. L. Herman, B. van der Kolk, R. Pynoos, J. Wang, and E. Petkova. "A Developmental Approach to Complex PTSD: Childhood and Adult Cumulative Trauma as Predictors of Symptom Complexity." *Journal of Traumatic Stress* 22, no. 5 (2009): 399–408.

Coates, C. A., R. Deutsch, Hon. H. Starnes, M. J. Sullivan, and B. L. Sydik. "Parenting Coordination for High-Conflict Families." *Family Court Review* 42, no. 2 (2004): 246–262.

Coker, A., P. H. Smith, R. E. McKeown, and M. King. "Frequency and Correlates of Intimate Partner Violence Type: Physical, Sexual, and Psychological Battering." *American Journal of Public Health* 90, no. 4 (2000): 553–560.

Collins, Robert Kirkman. "The Theory of Marital Residuals: Applying an Income Adjustment Calculus to the Enigma of Alimony." 24 *Harv. Women's L. J.* 23 (2001).

Conte, J. R., E. Sorenson, L. Fogarty, and J. Dalla Rosa. "Evaluating Children's Reports of Sexual Abuse: Results from a Survey of Professionals." *American Journal of Orthopsychiatry* 61, no. 3 (1991): 428–437.

Corcoran, J. "Treatment Outcome Research with the Non-Offending Parents of Sexually Abused Children: A Critical Review." *Journal of Child Sexual Abuse* 13, no. 2 (2004): 59–67.

Cortina, Lilia M. "The Study of Gender in the Courts; Keeping Bias at Bay." 27 *Law & Soc. Inquiry* 199 (2002).

Corvo, K., and E. H. Carpenter. "Effects of Parental Substance Abuse on Current Levels of Domestic Violence: A Possible Elaboration of Intergenerational Transmission Processes." *Journal of Family Violence* 15, no. 2 (2000): 123–135.

Crosbie-Burnett, M. "Impact of Joint Versus Sole Custody and Quality of Co-Parental Relationship on Adjustment of Adolescents in Remarried Families." *Behavioral Sciences and the Law* 9, no. 4 (1991): 439–449.

Crowley, J. E. "Adopting 'Equality Tools' from the Toolboxes of Their Predecessors: The Fathers' Rights Movement in the United States." In *Fathers' Rights Activism and Law Reform in Comparative Perspective*, edited by R. Collier and S. Sheldon, 79–100. Oxford, UK: Hart Publishing, 2006.

Cuthbert, C., K. Slote, M. G. Driggers, C. Mesh, L. Bancroft, and J. Silverman. *Battered Mothers Speak Out: A Human Rights Report on Domestic Violence and Child Custody in the Massachusetts Family Courts*. Wellesley, MA: Battered Mothers' Testimony Project at the Wellesley Centers for Women, 2002.

Czapanskiy, K., and T. O'Neill. *Report of the Maryland Special Joint Committee on Gender Bias in the Courts*. New York: Legal Momentum (Formerly NOW Legal Defense and Education Fund), 1989.

Dalton, C. "When Paradigms Collide: Protecting Battered Parents and Their Children in the Family Court System." *Family and Conciliation Courts Review* 37, no. 3 (1999): 273–296.

Dalton, C., L. M. Drozd, and F. Q. F. Wong. *Navigating Custody & Visitation Evaluations in Cases with Domestic Violence: A Judge's Guide*. Reno, NV: National Council of Juvenile and Family Court Judges, 2006.

Daly, J. E., and S. Pelowski. "Predictors of Dropout Among Men Who Batter: A Review of Studies with Implications for Research and Practice." *Violence and Victims* 15, no. 2 (2000): 137–160.

Danforth, G., and B. Welling. *Achieving Equal Justice for Women and Men in the California Courts: Final Report*. New York: Legal Momentum (Formerly NOW Legal Defense and Education Fund), 1996.

Davidson, H. *The Impact of Domestic Violence on Children: A Report to the President of the American Bar Association*. Washington, DC: ABA Center on Children and the Law, 1994.

Davies, J., and E. Lyon. *Safety Planning with Battered Women*. Thousand Oaks, CA: Sage Publications, 1998.

Davis, G. "A Systematic Approach to Domestic Abuse-Informed Child Custody Decision Making in Family Law Cases." *Family Court Review* 53, no. 4 (2015): 565–577.

Davis, M. S., C. S. O'Sullivan, K. Susser, and Hon. M. D. Fields. *Custody Evaluations when There Are Allegations of Domestic Violence: Practices, Beliefs, and Recommendations of Professional Evaluators*. Washington, DC: National Institute of Justice, 2010.

Davis, S., and T. Greenstein. "Cross-National Variations in the Division of Household Labor." *Journal of Marriage and Family* 66, no. 5 (2004): 1260–1271.

DeHart, D. D., R. J. Kennerly, L. K. Burke, and D. R. Follingstad. "Predictors of Attrition in a Treatment Program for Battering Men." *Journal of Family Violence* 14, no. 1 (1999): 19–34.

de Jong, M. "Suggested Safeguards and Limitations for Effective and Permissible Parenting Coordination (Facilitation or Case Management) in South Africa." *Per/PeLJ* 18, no. 2 (2015): 150–178.

DeMaria, M. "Comment, Jurisdictional Issues Under the Uniform Interstate Family Support Act." *Journal of the American Academy of Matrimonial Lawyers* 16 (1999): 243–258. http://www.aaml.org/sites/default/files/jurisdictional20issues20under-uifsa.pdf

Dinner, Deborah. "The Divorce Bargain: The Fathers' Rights Movement and Family Inequalities." 102 *Va. L. Rev.* 79 (2016).

Dobash, R. P., and R. E. Dobash. "Reflections of Findings from the Violence Against Women Survey." *Canadian Journal of Criminology* 37 (July, 1995): 457–484.

Dobash, R. P., and R. E. Dobash. *Violence Against Wives*. New York: Free Press, 1979.

Dobash, R. P., and R. E. Dobash. "Women's Violence to Men in Intimate Relationships: Working on a Puzzle." *British Journal of Criminology* 44, no. 3 (2004): 324–349.

Douglas, E. M. "The Impact of a Presumption for Joint Legal Custody on Father Involvement." *Journal of Divorce & Remarriage* 39, no. 1/2 (2003): 1–10.

Drafting Committee on Uniform Collaborative Law Act. "Uniform Collaborative Law Act." 38 *Hofstra L. Rev.* 421 (2009).

Dragiewicz, M. "Gender Bias in the Courts: Implications for Battered Mothers and Their Children." In *Domestic Violence, Abuse, and Child Custody: Legal Strategies and Policy Issues*, edited by M. Hannah and B. Goldstein, 5:2–5:19. Kingston, NJ: Civic Research Institute, 2010.

Dragiewicz, M., A. R. Gover, S. L. Miller, J. Naccarelli, and B. Paradiso. "Innovative University Programs for Teaching About Domestic Violence." *Journal of Criminal Justice Education* 24, no. 4 (2013): 594–611.

Dube, S. R., D. Fairweather, W. S. Pearson, V. J. Felitti, R. F. Anda, and J. B. Croft. "Cumulative Childhood Stress and Autoimmune Diseases in Adults." *Psychosomatic Medicine* 71, no. 2 (2009): 243–250.

Duffy, James. "Problem-Solving Courts, Therapeutic Jurisprudence and the Constitution: If Two Is Company, Is Three a Crowd?" 35 *Melb. U. L. Rev.* 394 (2011).

Dussich, J. P. J. "History, Overview and Analysis of American Victimology and Victim Services Education." In *Proceedings of the First American Symposium on Victimology: Exploration of Higher Education and Professional Practice at Kansas City Kansas Community College*, January 9–10, 2003: 4–17.

Dussich, J. P. J. "Teaching Victimology in America: From on the Job Training (OJT) to PhD." *Journal of Criminal Justice Education* 25, no. 4 (2014): 486–500.

Dutton, D. *The Abusive Personality: Violence and Control in Intimate Relationships*. New York: Guilford Press, 2007.

Dutton, D. "MCMI Results for Batterers: A Response to Gondolf." *Journal of Family Violence* 18, no. 4 (2003): 253–255.

Dutton, D. "Trauma Symptoms and PTSD-like Profiles in Perpetrators of Intimate Abuse." *Journal of Traumatic Stress* 8, no. 2 (1995): 299–316.

Dutton, D. "Witnessing Parental Violence as a Traumatic Experience Shaping the Abusive Personality." *Journal of Aggression, Maltreatment and Trauma* 3, no. 1 (2000): 59–67.

Dutton, D., and S. Golant. *The Batterer: A Psychological Profile*. New York: Basic Books, 1995.

Dutton, M. A., and L. A. Goodman. "Coercion in Intimate Partner Violence: Toward a New Conceptualization." *Sex Roles* 52, no. 11 (2005): 743–756.

Echeburua, E., and J. Fernandez-Montalvo. "Male Batterers With and Without Psychopathy: An Exploratory Study in Spanish Prisons." *International Journal of Offender Therapy and Comparative Criminology* 51, no. 3 (2007): 254–263.

Edelstein, R. S., K. W. Alexander, G. S. Goodman, and J. W. Newton. "Emotion and Eyewitness Memory." In *Memory and Emotion*, edited by D. Resiburg and P. Hertel, 308–346. New York: Oxford University Press, 2004.

Edleson, J. L. "Children's Witnessing of Adult Domestic Violence." *Journal of Interpersonal Violence* 14, no. 8 (1999): 839–870.

Edleson, J. L. "Controversy and Change in Batterers' Programs." Accessed February 9, 2017. http://www.academia.edu/26410751/Controversy_and_Change_in_Batterers_Programs

Edleson, J. L., and O. J. Williams. *Parenting by Men Who Batter: New Directions for Assessment and Intervention.* New York: Oxford University Press, 2007.

Ehrenberg, M. F., L. L. Stewart, D. N. Roche, J. Pringle, and J. Bush. "Adolescents in Divorcing Families: Perceptions of What Helps and Hinders." *Journal of Divorce & Remarriage* 45, no. 3/4 (2006): 69–91.

Ellis, D. "Post-Separation Woman Abuse: The Contribution of Lawyers as 'Barracudas', 'Advocates', and 'Counsellors'." *International Journal of Law and Psychiatry* 10, no. 4 (1987): 403–411.

Ellis, D., and N. Stuckless. "Domestic Violence, DOVE, and Divorce Mediation." *Family Court Review* 44, no. 4 (2006): 658–671.

Emery, R., R. K. Otto, and W. T. O'Donohue. "A Critical Assessment of Child Custody Evaluations: Limited Science and a Flawed System." *Psychological Science in the Public Interest* 6, no. 1 (2005): 1–29.

Epstein, Steven D. *The Problem of Dual Arrest in Family Violence Cases.* Wethersfield, CT: Connecticut Coalition Against Domestic Violence, 1987.

Erickson, N. S. "Economic Abuse: A Form of Abuse That Needs More Scrutiny." *New York Family Law Monthly* 10, no. 2 (2008): 3–4.

Erickson, N. S. "Use of the MMPI–2 in Child Custody Evaluations Involving Battered Women: What Does Psychological Research Tell Us?" *Family Law Quarterly* 39, no. 1 (2005): 87–108.

Faigman, David L., Elise Porter, and Michael J. Saks. "Check Your Crystal Ball at the Courthouse Door, Please: Exploring the Past, Understanding the Present, and Worrying About the Future of Scientific Evidence." 15 *Cardozo L. Rev.* 1799 (1994).

Faller, K. C. *Child Sexual Abuse: Intervention and Treatment Issues.* Washington, DC: US Department of Health and Human Services, National Center on Child Abuse and Neglect, 1993.

Faller, K. C. "False Accusations of Child Maltreatment: A Contested Issue." *Child Abuse and Neglect* 29, no. 12 (2005): 1327–1331.

Faller, K. C. *Interviewing Children About Sexual Abuse: Controversies and Best Practice.* New York: Oxford University Press, 2007.

Faller, K. C. "The Parental Alienation Syndrome: What Is It and What Data Support It?" *Child Maltreatment* 3, no. 2 (1998): 100–115.

Faller, K. C. "Possible Explanations for Child Sexual Abuse Allegations in Divorce." *American Journal of Orthopsychiatry* 61, no. 1 (1991): 86–91.

Fay-Ramirez, Susanna. "Therapeutic Jurisprudence in Practice: Changes in Family Treatment Court Norms Over Time." 40 *Law & Soc. Inquiry* 205 (2015).

Feiring, C., L. Taska, and M. Lewis. "The Role of Shame and Attributional Style in Children's and Adolescent's Adaptation to Sexual Abuse." *Child Maltreatment* 3, no. 2 (1998): 129–142.

Feldman, R., and A. Vengrober. "Posttraumatic Stress Disorder in Infants and Young Children Exposed to War-Related Trauma." *Journal of the American Academy of Child & Adolescent Psychiatry* 50, no. 7 (2011): 645–658.

Felitti, V. J., R. F. Anda, D. Nordenberg, D. F. Williamson, A. M. Spitz, V. Edwards, M. P. Koss, and J. P. Marks J. P. Marks. "Relationship of Childhood Abuse and Household Dysfunction to Many of the Leading Causes of Death in Adults." *American Journal of Preventive Medicine* 14, no. 4 (1998): 245–258.

Fineman, Martha Albertson. "Implementing Equality: Ideology, Contradiction, and Social Change." 1983 *Wis. L. Rev.* 789 (1983).

Fink, P. J. "Parental Alienation Syndrome." In *Domestic Violence, Abuse, and Child Custody: Legal Strategies and Policy Issues*, edited by M. Hannah and B. Goldstein, 12:1–12:8. Kingston, NJ: Civic Research Institute, 2010.

Finkelhor, D. *Childhood Victimization: Violence, Crime, and Abuse in the Lives of Young People*. New York: Oxford University Press, 2008.

Finkelhor, D. "The Victimization of Children: A Developmental Perspective." *American Journal of Orthopsychiatry* 65, no. 2 (1995): 177–193.

Finkelhor, D., G. T. Hotaling, I. A. Lewis, and C. Smith. "Sexual Abuse in a National Survey of Adult Men and Women: Prevalence, Characteristics, and Risk Factors." *Child Abuse and Neglect* 14, no. 9 (1990): 19–28.

Finklestein, M., E. Stein, T. Greene, I. Bronstein, and Z. Solomon. "Post-Traumatic Stress Disorder and Vicarious Trauma in Mental Health Professionals." *Journal of Health and Social Work* 40, no. 2 (2015): 25–31.

Fischel-Wolovick, L. "Police Response: Mandatory Arrest Primary Physical Aggressor." In *Lawyer's Manual on Domestic Violence: Representing the Victim*, 6th ed., edited by M. R. Rothwell Davis, D. A. Leidholdt, and C. A. Watson, 52–61. New York: Supreme Court of the State of New York, Appellate Division, First Department, 2015.

Fischel-Wolovick, L. " The Primary Aggressor Law: Dual Arrests and Self Defense." In *Lawyer's Manual on Domestic Violence: Representing the Victim*, 2nd ed., edited by R. E. Cohen and J. C. Neely, 235–246. New York: Supreme Court of the State of New York, Appellate Division, First Department, 1998.

Fleury, R., C. M. Sullivan, and D. Bybee. "When Ending the Relationship Doesn't End the Violence: Women's Experiences of Violence by Former Partners." *Violence Against Women* 6, no. 12 (2000): 1363–1383.

Flood, M. "Separated Fathers and the 'Fathers' Rights' Movement." *Journal of Family Studies* 18, no. 2–3 (2012): 235–245.

Ford, D. A. "The Impact of Police Officers' Attitudes Towards Victims on the Disinclination to Arrest Wife Beaters." Paper presented at the Third National Conference for Family Violence Researchers, University of New Hampshire, Durham, NH, July 1987.

Forgatch, M. S., and D. S. DeGarmo. "Adult Problem Solving: Contributor to Parenting and Child Outcomes in Divorced Families." *Journal of Social Development* 6, no. 2 (1997): 237–253.

Forgey, M. A., and L. Colarossi. "Interdisciplinary Social Work and Law: A Model for Domestic Violence Curriculum." *Journal of Social Work Education* 39, no. 3 (2003): 459–476.

Foshee, V. A., H. L. McNaughton Reyes, M. S. Chen, S. T. Ennett, K. C. Basiole, S. DeGue, A. M. Vivolo-Kanter, K. E. Moracco, and J. M. Bowling. "Shared Risk Factors for the Perpetration of Physical Dating Violence, Bullying, and Sexual Harassment Among Adolescents Exposed to Domestic Violence." *Journal of Youth and Adolescence* 45, no. 4 (2015): 672–686.

Frieze, J. I. H., and M. C. McHugh. "Power and Influence Strategies in Violent and Nonviolent Marriages." *Psychology of Women Quarterly* 16, no. 4 (1992): 449–465.

GAO Report to Congressional Committees. *Domestic Violence: Prevalence and Implications for Employment Among Welfare Recipients*. Washington, DC: United States General Accounting Office, 1998.

Gaquin, D. A. "Spouse Abuse: Data from the National Crime Survey." *Victimology* 2, no. 3 (1978): 632–643.

Gardner, R. A. "Does DSM-IV Have Equivalents for the Parental Alienation Syndrome (PAS) Diagnosis?" *American Journal of Family Therapy* 31, no. 1 (2003): 1–21.

Gardner, R. A. *The Parental Alienation Syndrome: A Guide for Mental Health and Legal Professionals*. Creskill, NJ: Creative Therapeutics, 1992.

Gardner, R. A. *Sex Abuse Hysteria: Salem Witch Trials Revisited*. Creskill, NJ: Creative Therapeutics, 1991.

Gardner, R. A. *True and False Allegations of Child Sex Abuse*. Creskill, NJ: Creative Therapeutics, 1992.

Garrison, Marsha. "Good Intentions Gone Awry: The Impact of New York's Equitable Distribution Law on Divorce Outcomes." 57 *Brook. L. Rev.* 621 (1991).

Gelfand, D., and D. Teti. "The Effects of Maternal Depression on Children." *Clinical Psychology Review* 10, no. 3 (1990): 329–353.

Gelkopf, M., and S. E. Jabotaro. "Parenting Style, Competence, Social Network, and Attachment in Mothers with Mental Illness." *Child and Family Social Work* 18, no. 4 (2013): 496–503.

Gelles, R. J. "Methodological Issues in the Study of Family Violence." In *Physical Violence in American Families: Risk Factors and Adaptions to Violence in 8,145 Families*, edited by M. Straus, R. Gelles and C. Smith, 17–28. New Brunswick, NJ: Transaction Publishers, 1990.

Gelles, R. J., and M. Straus. *Intimate Violence*. New York: Simon and Schuster, 1988.

Gelles, R. J., and M. A. Straus. "Violence in the American Family." *Journal of Social Issues* 35, no. 2 (1979): 15–39.

Gender Bias Study Committee of the Massachusetts Supreme Judicial Court. *Gender Bias Study of the Supreme Judicial Court, Commonwealth of Massachusetts*. Washington, DC: National Institute of Justice, 1989.

Gentile, K. "'You Don't Recognize Me Because I'm Still Standing': The Impact of Action Research with Women Survivors of Domestic Violence." In *Domestic Violence: Methodologies in Dialogue*, edited by C. Raghavan and S. J. Cohen, 171–199. Boston: Northeastern University Press, 2013.

Giles-Sims, J. "A Longitudinal Study of Battered Children of Battered Wives." *Family Relations* 34, no. 2 (1985): 205–210.

Giles-Sims, J. *Wife Battering: A Systems Theory Approach*. New York: Guilford Press, 1983.

Goel, R., and L. Goodmark. *Comparative Perspectives on Gender Violence*. New York: Oxford University Press, 2015.

Golder, S., M. R. Gillmore, M. R. Spieker, and D. Morrison. "Substance Use, Related Problem Behaviors and Adult Attachment in a Sample of High-Risk Older Adolescent Women." *Journal of Child and Family Studies* 14, no. 2 (2005): 181–193.

Goldscheid, J., and R. Runge. *Employment Law and Domestic Violence: A Practitioner's Guide*. Chicago: American Bar Association Commission on Domestic Violence, 2009.

Gondolf, E. W. "Patterns of Re-Assault in Batterer Programs." *Violence and Victims* 12, no. 4 (1997): 373–387.

Gondolf, E. W. "MCMI-III Results for Batterer Program Participants in Four Cities: Less 'Pathological' Than Expected." *Journal of Family Violence* 14, no. 1 (1999): 1–17.

Goodmark, Leigh. "Telling Stories, Saving Lives: The Battered Mothers' Testimony Project, Women's Narratives and Court Reform." *Ariz. St. L.J.* 37, no. 3 (2005): 709–757.

Graham, K., S. Bernards, S. C. Wilsnack, and G. Gmel. "Alcohol May Not Cause Partner Violence But It Seems to Make It Worse: A Cross National Comparison of the Relationship Between Alcohol and Severity of Partner Violence." *Journal of Interpersonal Violence* 26, no. 8 (2011): 1503–1523.

Graham, K., M. Plant, and M. Plant. "Alcohol, Gender and Partner Aggression: A General Population Study of British Adults." *Addiction Research and Theory* 12, no. 4 (2004): 385–401.

Graham-Bermann, S. A., K. H. Howell, M. Lilly, and E. DeVoe. "Mediators and Moderators of Change in Adjustment Following Intervention for Children Exposed to Intimate Partner Violence." *Journal of Interpersonal Violence* 26, no. 9 (2011): 1815–1833.

Graham-Bermann, S. A., L. E. Miller-Graff, K. H. Howell, and A. Grogan-Kaylor. "An Efficacy Trial of an Intervention Program for Children Exposed to Intimate Partner Violence." *Child Psychiatry and Human Development* 406, no. 6 (2015): 928–239.

Green, B. L., C. Furrer, and C. McAllister. "How Do Relationships Support Parenting? Effects of Attachment Style, and Social Support on Parenting Behavior in an At-Risk Population." *American Journal of Community Psychology* 40, no. 1–2 (2007): 96–108.

Green, Rebecca. "Privacy and Domestic Violence in Court." 16 *Wm. & Mary J. Women & L.* 237 (2010).

Griffing, S., C. S. Lews, M. Chu, R. E. Sage, L. Madry, and B. J. Prim. "Exposure to Interpersonal Violence as a Predictor of PTSD Symptomatology in Domestic Violence Survivors." *Journal of Interpersonal Violence* 21, no. 7 (2006): 936–954.

Gross, Samuel R. "Expert Evidence." 1991 *Wis. L. Rev.* 1113 (1991).

Hall, W. Wendell. "Standards of Appellate Review in Civil Appeals." 21 *St. Mary's L. J.* 865 (1990)

Hans, J. D., M. L. Haselschwerdt, J. L. Hardesty, and L. M. Frey. "The Effects of Domestic Violence Allegations on Custody Evaluators' Recommendations." *Journal of Family Psychology* 28, no. 6 (2014): 957–966.

Hardesty, J. L., and G. H. Chung. "Intimate Partner Violence, Parental Divorce, and Child Custody: Directions for Intervention and Future Research." *Family Relations* 55, no. 2 (2006): 200–210.

Hart, S. D. "Preventing Violence: The Role of Risk Assessment and Management." In *Intimate Partner Violence Prevention and Intervention*, edited by A. C. Baldry and F. W. Winkel, 7–18. Hauppauge, NY: Nova Science Publishers, 2008.

Haselschwerdt, M. L., J. L. Hardesty, and J. D. Hans. "Custody Evaluators' Beliefs About Domestic Violence Allegations During Divorce: Feminist and Family Violence Perspectives." *Journal of Interpersonal Violence* 26, no. 8 (2011): 1694–1719.

Hayes, M. J. "Leaving Maryland Workers Behind: A Comparison of State Employee Leave Statutes." *University of Maryland Law Journal of Race, Religion, Gender, and Class* 9, no. 1 (2009): 19–31.

Hecht Schafran, Lynn. "Gender and Justice: Florida and the Nation." 42 *Fla. L. Rev.* 181 (1990).

Hecht Schafran, Lynn. "Overwhelming Evidence: Reports on Gender Bias in the Courts." *Trial* 26, no. 2 (1990): 28–35.

Hecht Schafran, L., and N. J. Wikler. *Gender Fairness in the Courts: Action in the New Millennium.* New York: Legal Momentum (Formerly NOW Legal Defense and Education Fund), 2001.

Hecht Schafran, L., and N. J. Wikler. *Operating a Task Force on Gender Bias in the Courts: A Manual for Action.* New York: Legal Momentum (Formerly NOW Legal Defense and Education Fund), 1986.

Heinze, M. C., and T. Grisso. "Review of Instruments Assessing Parenting Competencies Used in Child Custody Evaluations." *Behavioral Sciences and the Law* 14, no. 3 (1996): 293–313.

Henson, B. L. "Parenting Coordinator: Understanding This New Role." *The Colorado Lawyer* 35, no. 2 (2006): 31–36.

Herman, J. *Trauma and Recovery: The Aftermath of Violence—From Domestic Abuse to Political Terror.* New York: Basic Books, 1997.

Herman, S. P., J. E. Dunne, W. Ayers, V. Arnold, E. Bernedek, R. S. Benson, W. Bernett, G. A. Bernstein, E. Bryant, O. Bukstein, R. L. Gross, R. King, J. Kinlan, H. Leonard, W. Licamel, J. McClellan, and K. Shaw. "Practice Parameters for Child Custody Evaluation." *Journal of the American Academy of Child & Adolescent Psychiatry* 36, no. 10 (1997): 57S–68S.

Hetherington, E. M. "Coping with Family Transitions: Winners, Losers, and Survivors." *Child Development* 60, no. 1 (1989): 1–14.

Hetherington, E. M. "Intimate Pathways: Changing Patterns in Close Personal Relationships Across Time." *Family Relations* 52, no. 4 (2003): 318–331.

Hetherington, E. M. "An Overview of the Virginia Longitudinal Study of Divorce and Remarriage with a Focus on Early Adolescence." *Journal of Family Psychology* 7, no. 1 (1993): 39–56.

Hetherington, E. M., M. Cox, and R. Cox. "Divorced Fathers." *The Family Coordinator* (October 1976): 417–428.

Hetherington, E. M., M. Cox, and R. Cox. "Long-Term Effects of Divorce and Remarriage on the Adjustment of Children." *Journal of the American Academy of Child Psychiatry* 24, no. 5 (1985): 518–530.

Hetherington, E. M., and M. Stanley-Hagen. "The Adjustment of Children with Divorced Parents: A Risk and Resiliency Perspective." *Journal of Child Psychology and Psychiatry* 40, no. 1 (1999): 129–140.

Hetherton, J., and L. Beardsall. "Decisions and Attitudes Concerning Child Sexual Abuse: Does the Gender of the Perpetrator Make a Difference to Child Protection Professionals?" *Child Abuse and Neglect* 22, no. 12 (1998): 1265–1283.

Hirschel, D., E. Buzawa, A. Pattavina, and D. Faggiani. "Domestic Violence and Mandatory Arrest Laws: To What Extent Do They Influence Police Arrest Decisions?" *Journal of Criminal Law and Criminology* 98, no. 1 (2007): 255–298.

Holt, S., H. Buckley, and S. Whelan. "The Impact of Exposure to Domestic Violence on Children and Young People: A Review of the Literature." *Child Abuse and Neglect* 32, no. 8 (2008): 797–810.

Horowitz, David Paul. "Will the Gatekeeper Let Daubert In?" 78 *N. Y. ST. B.J.* 18 (2006).

Hoult, Jennifer. "Evidentiary Admissibility of Parental Alienation Syndrome: Science, Law, and Policy." 26 *Children's Leg. Rights J.* 1 (Spring 2006).

Hourani, L., J. Williams, R. Bray, and D. Kandel. "Gender Differences in the Expression of PTSD Symptoms Among Active Duty Military Personnel." *Journal of Anxiety Disorders* 29 (January 2015): 101–108.

Huber, P. *Galileo's Revenge: Junk Science in the Courtroom.* New York: Basic Books, 1991.

Humphreys, C., and R. K. Thiara. "Neither Justice Nor Protection: Women's Experiences of Post-Separation Violence." *Journal of Social Welfare and Family Law* 25, no. 3 (2003): 195–214.

Ivkovic, Sanja Kutnjak, and Valerie P. Hans. "Jurors' Evaluations of Expert Testimony: Judging the Messenger and the Message." 28 *Law & Soc. Inquiry* 441 (2003).

Jaffe, P. G., L. L. Baker, and A. J. Cunningham. *Protecting Children from Domestic Violence: Strategies for Community Intervention.* New York: Guilford Press, 2004.

Jaffe, P. G., and C. V. Crooks. "Understanding Women's Experiences Parenting in the Context of Domestic Violence: Implications for Community and Court-Related Service Providers." *Violence Against Women Online Resources* (February, 2005): 1–18.

Jaffe, P. G., J. Johnston, C. V. Crooks, and N. Bala. "Custody Disputes Involving Allegations of Domestic Violence: Toward a Differentiated Approach to Parenting Plans." *Family Court Review* 46, no. 3 (2008): 500–522.

Jaffe, P. G., N. K. D. Lemon, and S. E. Poisson. *Child Custody and Domestic Violence: A Call for Safety and Accountability.* New York: Sage Publications, 2003.

Johnson, M. P. "Conflict and Control: Gender Symmetry and Asymmetry." *Violence Against Women,* 12, no.11 (November 2006): 1003–1018.

Johnson, M. P. *A Typology of Domestic Violence: Intimate Terrorism, Violent Resistance, and Situational Couple Violence.* Boston: Northeastern University Press, 2008.

Johnston, J. R. "High-Conflict Divorce." *Children and Divorce* 4, no. 1 (1994): 165–182.

Johnston, J. R., and L. E. G. Campbell. "A Clinical Typology of Interparental Violence in Disputed-Custody Divorces." *American Journal of Orthopsychiatry* 63, no. 2 (1993): 190–199.

Johnston, J. R., and L. E. G. Campbell. *Impasses of Divorce.* New York: Free Press, 1988.

Johnston, J. R., and J. R. Goldman. "Outcomes of Family Counseling Interventions with Children Who Resist Visitation: An Addendum to Friedlander and Walters." *Family Court Review* 48, no. 1 (2010): 112–115.

Johnston, J. R., S. Lee, N. W. Olesen, and M. G. Walters. "Allegations and Substantiations of Abuse in Custody-Disputing Families." *Family Court Review* 43, no. 2 (2005): 283–294.

Johnston, J. R., V. Roseby, and K. Kuehnle. *In the Name of the Child: A Developmental Approach to Understanding and Helping Children of Conflicted and Violent Families,* 2nd ed. New York: Springer Publishing, 2009.

Johnston, J. R., and R. B. Straus. "Traumatized Children in Supervised Visitation: What Do They Need?" *Family Court Review* 37, no. 2 (1999): 135–158.

Jones, L., M. Hughes, and U. Unterstaller. "Post-Traumatic Stress Disorder (PTSD) in Victims of Domestic Violence." *Trauma, Violence, & Abuse* 2, no. 2 (2001): 99–119.

Juodis, M., A. Starzomski, S. Porter, and M. Woodworth. "A Comparison of Domestic and Non-domestic Homicides: Further Evidence for Distinct Dynamics and Heterogeneity of Domestic Violence Perpetrators." *Journal of Family Violence* 29, no. 3 (2014): 299–313.

Juodis, M., A. Starzomski, and M. Woodworth. "What Can Be Done About High-Risk Perpetrators of Domestic Violence?" *Journal of Family Violence* 29, no. 4 (2014): 381–390.

Kaminer, D., S. Seedat, and D. J. Stein. "Post-Traumatic Stress Disorder in Children." *World Psychiatry* 4, no. 2 (2005):121–125.

Karaaslan, O. "Comparison of Social Engagement of Children Having Disabilities with Their Mothers and Fathers." *Educational Sciences: Theory & Practice* 16, no. 5 (2016): 1649–1670.

Kashani, J. H., and W. D. Allan. *The Impact of Family Violence on Children and Adolescents.* New York: Sage Publications, 1998.

Katz, Alayne. "Junk Science v. Novel Scientific Evidence: Parental Alienation Syndrome, Getting It Wrong in Custody Cases." 24 *Pace L. Rev.* 239 (2003).

Keator, K., Lisa Callahan, H. Steadman, and R. Vesselinov. "The Impact of Treatment on the Public Safety Outcomes of Mental Health Court Participants." *American Behavioral Scientist* 57, no. 2 (2013): 231–243.

Keiley, M., P. S. Keller, and M. El-Sheikh "Effects of Physical and Verbal Aggression, Depression and Anxiety on Drinking Behavior of Married Partners: A Prospective and Retrospective Longitudinal Examination." *Journal of Aggressive Behavior* 35, no. 4 (2009): 296–312.

Keilin, W. G., and L. J. Bloom. "Child Custody Evaluation Practices: A Survey of Experienced Professionals." *Professional Psychology: Research and Practice* 17, no. 4 (1986): 338–346.

Kelly, J. B., and M. P. Johnson. "Differentiation Among Types of Intimate Partner Violence: Research Update and Implications for Interventions." *Family Court Review* 46, no. 3 (2008): 476–499.

Kendall-Tackett, K. *Treating the Lifetime Health Effects of Childhood Victimization,* 2nd ed. Kingston, NJ: Civic Research Institute, 2013.

Kernic, M. A., D. J. Monary-Ernsdorff, J. K. Koepsell, and V. L. Holt. "Children in the Crossfire: Child Custody Determinations Among Couples with a History of Intimate Partner Violence." *Violence Against Women* 11, no. 8 (2005): 991–1021.

Khan, F. I., T. L. Welch, and E. A. Zillmer. "MMPI–2 Profiles of Battered Women in Transition." *Journal of Personality Assessment* 60, no. 1 (1993): 100–111.

Kiecolt-Glaser, J., L. Fisher, P. Ogrocki, J. C. Stout, C. E. Speicher, and R. Glaser. "Marital Quality, Marital Disruption, and Immune Function." *Psychosomatic Medicine* 49, no. 1 (1987): 13–34.

Kimmel, M. S. *The Gendered Society.* New York: Oxford University Press, 2000.

Kimmel, M. S. "'Gender Symmetry' in Domestic Violence: A Substantive and Methodological Research Review." *Violence Against Women* 8, no. 11 (2002): 1332–1363.

King, M., and B. Batagol. "Enforcer, Manager, or Leader? The Judicial Role in Family Violence Courts." *International Journal of Law and Psychiatry* 33, no. 5/6 (2010): 406–416.

Kisthardt, M. K. "Re-thinking Alimony: The AAML's Consideration for Calculating Alimony, Spousal Support or Maintenance." *Journal of the American Academy of Matrimonial Lawyers* 21 (June 16, 2008): 61–85.

Kourlis, R. L., M. G. Taylor, A. M. Shepard, and M. Kline Pruett. "Courts and Communities Helping Families in Transition Arising from Separation and Divorce: Honoring Families Initiative White Paper." *Family Court Review* 51, no. 3 (2013): 351–376.

Koziol-McLain, J., C. J. Coates, and S. R. Lowenstein. "Predictive Validity of a Screen for Partner Violence Against Women." *American Journal of Preventive Medicine* 21, no. 2 (2001): 93–100.

Kroll, B., and A. Taylor. "Invisible Children? Parental Substance Abuse and Child Protection: Dilemmas for Practice." *Probation Journal* 47, no. 2 (2000): 91–100.

LaBotte, S., and N. Blaschak-Brown. "Standards for Supervised Visitation Practice." Supervised Visitation Network (July, 2006) http://www.afccnet.org/portals/0/public-documents/guidelines/supervised_visitation_nework–standardsfinal7–14–06.pdf

Lacey, M., S. Paolini, M. C. Hanlon, J. Melville, C. Galletly, and L. E. Campbell. "Parents With Serious Mental Illness: Differences in Internalised and Externalised Mental Illness Stigma and Gender Stigma Between Mothers and Fathers." *Psychiatry Research* 225, no. 3 (2015): 723–733.

Laing, L. "Secondary Victimization: Domestic Violence Survivors Navigating the Family Law System." *Violence Against Women* (August 23, 2016): 1–22.

Lambert, L. C., and J. M. Firestone. "Economic Context and Multiple Abuse Techniques." *Violence Against Women* 6, no. 1 (2000): 49–67.

Lansford, J. E. "Parental Divorce and Children's Adjustment." *Perspectives on Psychological Science* 4, no. 2 (2009): 140–152.

Lapp, K., and C. Watson. *Family Protection and Domestic Violence Intervention Act of 1994: Evaluation of the Mandatory Arrest Provisions*. Albany, NY: New York State Division of Criminal Justice Services, 2001.

Lee, Cheryl J. "Escaping the Lion's Den and Going Back for Your Hat: Why Domestic Violence Should be Considered in the Distribution of Marital Property upon Dissolution of Marriage." 23 *Pace L. Rev.* 273 (2002).

Lee, D. A., P. Scragg, and S. Turner. "The Role of Shame and Guilt in Traumatic Events: A Clinical Model of Shame-Based and Guilt-Based PTSD." *The British Journal of Medical Psychology* 74, no. Pt4 (2001): 451–466.

Lee, S. J. "Paternal and Household Characteristics Associated with Child Neglect and Child Protective Services Involvement." *Journal of Social Service Research* 39, no. 2 (2013): 171–197.

Lehmann, P., C. K. Simmons, and V. K. Pillai. "The Validation of the Checklist of Controlling Behaviors (CCB): Assessing Coercive Control in Abusive Relationships." *Violence Against Women* 18, no. 8 (2012): 913–933.

Lemon, Nancy K. "Statutes Creating Rebuttable Presumptions Against Custody to Batterers: How Effective Are They?" 28 *Wm. Mitchell L. Rev.* 2 (2001).

Leonard, K. E. "Alcohol and Intimate Partner Violence: When Can We Say that Heavy Drinking Is a Contributing Cause of Violence?" *Addiction* 100, no. 4 (2005): 422–425.

Leonard, K. E., and H. T. Blane. "Alcohol and Marital Aggression in a National Sample of Young Men." *Journal of Interpersonal Violence* 7, no. 1 (1992): 19–30.

Levinson, B. "Compensation for Domestic Violence Victims: Tort Remedies and Beyond." In *Lawyer's Manual of Domestic Violence,* 6th ed., edited by M. R. Rothwell Davis, D. A. Leidholdt, and C. A. Watson, 130–139. Supreme Court of the State of New York, Appellate Division, First Department, 2015.

Lewis, K. *Child Custody Evaluations by Social Workers*. Washington, DC: NASW Press, 2009.

Lewis, M. *Shame and Guilt in Neurosis*. New York: International Universities Press, 1992.

Libal, K., and D. Parekh. "Reframing Violence Against Women as a Human Rights Violation: Evan Stark's Coercive Control." *Violence Against Women* 15, no. 2 (2009): 1477–1489.

Lieberman, A. F. "Infants Remember: War Exposure, Trauma, and Attachment in Young Children and Their Mothers." *Journal of the American Academy of Child & Adolescent Psychiatry* 50, no. 7 (2011): 640–641.

Lieberman, A. F., and P. Van Horn. "Attachment, Trauma, and Domestic Violence: Implications for Child Custody." *Child and Adolescent Psychiatric Clinics of North America* 7, no. 2 (1998): 423–443.

Lippman, Jonathan. "Ensuring Victim Safety and Abuser Accountability: Reforms and Revisions in New York Courts' Response to Domestic Violence." 76 *Alb. L. Rev.* 1417 (2013).

Littwin, Angela. M. "Coerced Debt: The Role of Consumer Credit in Domestic Violence." 100 *Cal. L. Rev.* 951 (2012).

Lloyd, S., and N. Taluc. "The Effects of Male Violence on Female Employment." *Violence Against Women* 5, no. 4 (1999): 370–392.

Logan, T. K., L. Shannon, J. Cole, and R. Walker. "The Impact of Differential Patterns of Physical Violence and Stalking on Mental Health and Help-Seeking Among Women with Protective Orders." *Violence Against Women* 12, no. 9 (2006): 866–886.

Lonsway, Kimberly A., Leslie V. Freeman, Lilia M. Cortina, Vicki J. Magley, and Louise F. Fitzgerald. "Understanding the Judicial Role in Addressing Gender Bias: A View from the Eighth Circuit Federal Court System." 27 *Law & Soc. Inquiry* 205 (2002).

Luftman, V., L. Veltkamp, J. Clark, S. Lannacone, and H. Snooks. "Practice Guidelines in Child Custody Evaluations for Licensed Clinical Social Workers." *Clinical Social Work Journal* 33, no. 3 (2005): 327–357.

Maccoby, E. E., C. M. Buchanan, R.H. Mnookin, and S.M. Dornbusch, "Postdivorce Roles of Mothers and Fathers in the Lives of Their Children." *Journal of Family Psychology* 7, no. 1 (1993): 24–38.

Maccoby, E. E., C. E. Depner, and R. H. Mnookin. "Coparenting in the Second Year After Divorce." *Journal of Marriage and Family* 52 (February 1990): 141–155.

MacDowell, Elizabeth L. "When Courts Collide: Integrated Domestic Violence Courts and Court Pluralism." 20 *Tex. J. Women & L.* 95 (August 2011).

Macintosh, H. B., N. Godbout and N. Dubash. "Borderline Personality Disorder: Disorder of Trauma or Personality, a Review of the Empirical Literature." *Canadian Psychological Association* 56, no. 2 (2015): 227–241.

Maiuro, R. D., T. S. Hagar, H. Lin, and N. Olson. "Are Current State Standards for Domestic Violence Perpetrator Treatment Adequately Informed by Research? A Question of Questions." *Journal of Aggression, Maltreatment and Trauma* 5, no. 2 (2001): 21–44.

Mancoske, R. J., D. Standifer, and C. Cauley. "The Effectiveness of Brief Counseling Services for Battered Women." *Research on Social Work Practice* 4, no. 1 (1994): 53–63.

Margolin, G. "Effects of Domestic Violence on Children." In *Violence Against Children in the Family and Community*, edited by P. Trickett and C. Schellenbach, 57–101. Washington, DC: American Psychological Association, 1998.

Margura, S., and A. B. Laudet. "Parental Substance Abuse and Child Maltreatment: Review and Implications for Intervention." *Children and Youth Services Review* 18, no. 3 (1996): 193–220.

Marra, O. *Domestic Violence Death Review Committee Annual Report to the Chief Coroner*. Ontario: Office of the Chief Coroner, 2005.

Marsiglio, W., P. Amato, R. D. Day, and M. E. Lamb. "Scholarship on Fatherhood in the 1990s and Beyond." *Journal of Marriage and Family* 62, no. 4 (2000): 1173–1191.

Martin, L., W. G. Austin, L. Drozd, D. Gould-Saltman, H. D. Kirkpatrick, K. Kuehle, D. Kulak, D. McColley, A. Sheinvold, J. Siegel, and P. Stahl. *Model Standards of Practice for Child Custody Evaluations.* Madison, WI: Association of Family and Conciliation Courts (AFCC), 2006.

Martin, Lisa E. "Providing Equal Justice for the Domestic Violence Victim: Due Process and the Victim's Right to Counsel." 34 *Gonz. L. Rev.* 329 (1999).

Martin, S. E., and R. Bachman. "The Relationship of Alcohol to Injury in Assault Cases." *Recent Developments in Alcoholism* 13 (1997): 42–56.

Marvin, R., G. Cooper, K. Hoffman, and B. Powell. "The Circle of Security Project: Attachment– based Intervention with Caregiver-Pre-School Child Dads." *Journal of Attachment and Human Development* 4, no. 1 (2002): 107–124.

Mashburn, S. B. "Throwing the Baby Out with the Bathwater: Parenting Coordination and Pennsylvania's Decision to Eliminate its Use." *Journal of Dispute Resolution* 2015, no. 1 (2015): 191–206.

Maxwell, M. S., and K. Oehme. "Strategies to Improve Supervised Visitation Services in Domestic Violence Cases." *Violence Against Women Online Resources* (2001) http://citeseerx.ist.psu.edu/viewdoc/download?doi=10.1.1.208.7126&rep=rep1&type=pdf

McBride, K. *Child Sexual Abuse Investigations: A Joint Investigative Approach Combining the Expertise of Mental Health and Law Enforcement Professionals.* Ljubljana, Slovenia: College of Police and Security Studies, 1996. https://www.ncjrs.gov/policing/chi341.htm

McCord, J. "A Forty Year Perspective on Effects of Child Abuse and Neglect." *Child Abuse and Neglect* 7, no. 3 (1983): 265–270.

McIntosh, J., B. M. Smyth, and M. Kelaher. "Overnight Care Patterns and Psycho-emotional Development in Infants and Young Children." In *Post Separation Parenting Arrangements and Developmental Outcomes for Children*, edited by J. McIntosh, J. Smyth, B. Kelaher, Y. Wells, and C. Long, 85–169. Canberra: Report to the Australian Government Attorney General's Department, May 2010.

McIntosh, J. E. "Special Considerations for Infants and Toddlers in Separation/Divorce: Developmental Issues in the Family Law Context." In *Encyclopedia on Early Childhood Development*, edited by R. E. Tremblay, M. Boivin, and R. DeV. Peters, 1–6. Montreal: Centre of Excellence for Early Childhood Development, 2011.

McNiel, D. E., J. R. Chamberlain, C. M. Weaver, S. E. Hall, S.R. Fordwood, and R. L. Binder. "Impact of Clinical Training on Violence Risk Assessment." *American Journal of Psychiatry* 16, no. 2 (2008): 195–200.

McPherson-Sexton, S. A. "Normal Memory Versus Traumatic Memory Formation: Does Traumatic Stress Damage the Brain?" *Journal of Police Crisis Negotiations* 6, no. 2 (2006): 65– 78.

McQueeney, K. "Teaching Domestic Violence in the New Millennium: Intersectionality as a Framework for Social Change." *Violence Against Women* 22, no. 12 (2016): 1463–1475.

Medoff, D. "MMPI–2 Validity Scales in Child Custody Evaluations: Clinical Versus Statistical Significance." *Behavioral Sciences and the Law* 17, no. 4 (1999): 409–411.

Meier, Joan S. "Domestic Violence, Child Custody, and Child Protection: Understanding Judicial Resistance and Imagining the Solutions." 11 *Am. U. J. Gender Soc. Pol'y & L.* 657 (2003).

Meier, Joan S. "Getting Real About Abuse and Alienation: A Critique of Drozd and Olesen's Decision Tree." *Journal of Child Custody* 7, no. 4 (2010): 219–252.

Meier, Joan S. "Johnson's Differential Theory: Is It Really Empirically Supported?" *Journal of Child Custody* 12, no. 1 (2015): 4–24.

Menzano, K. L. "Parenting Coordination Eliminated in Pennsylvania." *The Legal Intelligencer* (July 9, 2013) http://www.hangley.com/news/parenting-coordination-eliminated-pennsylvania

Mercer, Kathryn L. "A Content Analysis of Judicial Decision-Making: How Judges Use the Primary Caretaker Standard to Make a Custody Determination." 5 *Wm. & Mary J. Women & L.* 1 (Winter 1998).

Meyer, David D. "The Constitutional Rights of Non-Custodial Parents." 34 *Hofstra L. Rev.* 1461 (2006).

Miller, S. L., and N. L. Smolter. "'Paper Abuse': When All Else Fails, Batterers Use Procedural Stalking." *Violence Against Women* 17, no. 5 (2011): 637–650.

Minnesota Supreme Court Task Force for Gender Fairness in the Courts. "Minnesota Supreme Court Task Force for Gender Fairness in the Courts, Final Report." 15 *Wm. Mitchell L. Rev.* 827 (1989).

Mirchandani, R. "Battered Women's Movement Ideals and Judge-Led Social Change in Domestic Violence Courts." *The Great Society* 13, no. 1 (2004): 32–37.

Moe Wan, A. "Battered Women in the Restraining Order Process: Observations on a Court Advocacy Program." *Violence Against Women* 6, no. 6 (2000): 606–632.

Montana Coalition Against Domestic and Sexual Violence. *MCADSV Court Watch Training Manual.* Washington, DC: US Department of Justice, Office of Justice Programs, 2007.

Moore, Samantha and Kathryn Ford. *Supervised Visitation: What Courts Should Know when Working with Supervised Visitation Programs.* New York: New York State Unified Court System, Center for Court Innovation, 2006.

Morrill, A. C., J. Dai, S. Dunn, I. Sung, and K. Smith. "Child Custody and Visitation Decisions when the Father Has Perpetrated Violence Against the Mother." *Violence Against Women* 11, no. 8 (2005): 1076–1107.

Morrison, F. "All Over Now? The Ongoing Relational Consequences of Domestic Abuse through Children's Contact Arrangement." *Child Abuse Review* 24, no. 4 (2015): 274–284.

Morrison, L. E., and J. P. Joy. "Secondary Traumatic Stress in the Emergency Department." *Journal of Advanced Nursing* 72, no. 11 (2016): 2894–2906.

Murphy, Jane C. & Robert Rubinson. "Domestic Violence and Mediation: Responding to the Challenges of Crafting Effective Screens." 39 *Fam. L.Q.* 53 (2005–2006)

National Association of Social Workers. *Code of Ethics: 55th Anniversary Edition.* Washington, DC: NASW Press, 2017.

Nielsen, Linda. "Shared Residential Custody: Review of the Research." 27 *Amer. J. Fam. L.* 123 (Spring 2013).

New York Task Force on Women. "Report of the New York Task Force on Women in the Courts." 15 *Fordham Urb. L.J.* 15 (1986).

Oberlander, L. B. "Ethical Responsibilities in Child Custody Evaluations: Implications for Evaluation Methodology." *Ethics and Behavior* 5, no. 4 (1995): 311–332.

O'Connell, M. E. "Child Custody Evaluations: Social Science and Public Policy, Mandated Custody Evaluations and the Limits of Judicial Power." *Family Court Review* 47, no. 2 (2009): 304–320.

Oehme, Karen and Kelly O'Rourke. "Protecting Victims and Their Children Through Supervised Visitation: A Study of Domestic Violence Injunctions." 3 *Faulkner L. Rev.* 261 (2011).

O'Sullivan, C. *Domestic Violence, Visitations and Custody Decisions in New York Family Courts, Final Report.* New York: Safe Horizon, 2002.

O'Sullivan, C., L. King, K. Levi-Russell, and E. Horowitz. *Supervised and Unsupervised Parental Access in Domestic Violence Cases: Court Orders and Consequences.* Washington, DC: National Institute of Justice, 2006.

Outlaw, M. "No One Type of Intimate Partner Abuse: Exploring Physical and Non-Physical Abuse Among Intimate Partners." *Journal of Family Violence* 24, no. 4 (2009): 263–272.

Owen, David G. "A Decade of Daubert." 80 *Denv. L. Rev.* 345 (2002).

Oyserman, D., C. T. Mowbray, P. A. Meares, and K. B. Firminger. "Parenting Among Mothers with a Serious Mental Illness." *American Journal of Orthopsychiatry* 70, no. 3 (2000): 296–315.

Pagelow, M. "The Effects of Domestic Violence on Children and Their Consequences for Custody and Visitation Agreements." *Conflict Resolution Quarterly* 7, no. 4 (1990): 347–363.

Park, S. "Working Towards Freedom from Abuse: Recognizing a 'Public Policy' Exception to Employment-at-Will for Domestic Violence Victims." *New York University Annual Survey of American Law* 59 (March 14, 2003): 121–162.

Parker, K.and W. Wang. *Modern Parenthood: Roles of Moms and Dads Converge as They Balance Work and Family.* Washington, DC: Pew Research Center, 2013.

Patel, S. H., and L. Hensley Choate. "Conducting Child Custody Evaluations: Best Practices for Mental Health Counselors who are Court-Appointed as Child Custody Evaluators." *Journal of Mental Health Counseling* 36, no. 1 (2014): 18–30.

Pat-Horenczyk, R., S. Cohen, Y. Ziv, M. Achituv, L. Asulin-Peretz, T. R. Blancard, M. Schiff, and D. Brom. "Emotion Regulation in Mothers and Young Children Faced with Trauma." *Infant Mental Health Journal* 36, no. 3 (2015): 337–348.

Pearlman, L., and P. Mac Ian. "Vicarious Traumatization: An Empirical Study of the Effects of Trauma Work on Trauma Therapists." *Journal of Professional Psychology: Research and Practice* 26, no. 6 (1995): 558–565.

Pearson, J., L. Davis, and N. Thoennes. "A New Look at an Old Issue: An Evaluation of the State Access and Visitation Grant Program." *Family Court Review* 43, no. 3 (2005): 372–386.

Peled, E. "Children of Battering Men: Living in Conflicts of Loyalties and Emotions." Paper presented at the 4th International Family Violence Research Conference, Durham, NH, July 1995.

Peled, E. "Parenting by Men Who Abuse Women: Issues and Dilemmas." *British Journal of Social Work* 30, no. 1 (2000): 25–36.

Peled, E., K. Gueta, and N. Sander-Almoznino. "The Experience of Mothers Exposed to the Abuse of Their Daughters by an Intimate Partner: 'There Is No Definition for It'." *Violence Against Women* 22, no. 13 (2016): 1577–1596.

Pence, E., and M. Paymar. *Education Groups for Men Who Batter: The Duluth Model.* New York: Springer Publishing, 1993.

Pepiton, M. B., B. R. Zelgowski, R. Geffner, and P. Pegolo. "Ethical Violations: What Can and Does Go Wrong in Child Custody Evaluations?" *Journal of Child Custody* 11, no. 2 (2014): 81– 100.

Phelps, B. P. "Helping Medical Students Help Survivors of Domestic Violence." *Journal of the American Medical Association* 283, no. 9 (2000): 1199.

Pico-Alfonso, M. A. "Psychological Intimate Partner Violence: The Major Predictor of Posttraumatic Stress Disorder in Abused Women." *Neuroscience and Bio-behavioral Reviews* 29, no. 1 (2005): 181–193.

Pico-Alfonso, M. A., M. Isabel Garcia-Linares, N. Celda-Navarro, C. Blasco-Ros, E. Echeburua, and M. Martinez. "The Impact of Physical, Psychological, and Sexual Intimate Male Partner Violence on Women's Mental Health: Depressive Symptoms, Posttraumatic Stress Disorder, State Anxiety, and Suicide." *Journal of Women's Health* 15, no. 5 (2006): 599–611.

Pierre-Louis, R. *New York City Domestic Violence Fatality Review Committee, 2014 Annual Report.* New York: Mayor's Office to Combat Domestic Violence, 2014.

Plummer, C. A., and J. A. Eastin. "System Intervention Problems in Child Sexual Abuse Investigations." *Journal of Interpersonal Violence* 22, no. 6 (2007): 775–787.

Pollet, S. L. "Economic Abuse: The Unseen Side of Domestic Violence." *NYSBA Journal* 83, no. 2 (2011): 40–44.

Portwood, S., and J. F. Heany. "Responding to Violence Against Women: Social Science Contributions to Legal Solutions." *International Journal of Law and Psychiatry* 30, no. 3 (2002): 237–247.

Powell, M. B., and S. Lancaster. "Guidelines for Interviewing Children During Child Custody Evaluations." *Australian Psychologist* 38, no. 1 (2003): 46–54.

Pruett, M. K., T. Y. Williams, G. Insabella, and T. D. Little. "Family and Legal Indicators of Child Adjustment to Divorce Among Families with Young Children." *Journal of Family Psychology* 17, no. 2 (2003): 169–180.

Ptacek, J. "Disorder in the Courts: Judicial Demeanor and Women's Experience Seeking Restraining Orders." PhD diss., Brandeis University, 1995.

Putnam, F. W. "Ten-Year Research Update Review: Child Sexual Abuse." *Journal of the American Academy of Child & Adolescent Psychiatry* 42, no. 3 (2003): 269–278.

Putnam, F. W., and P. K. Trickett. "Psychobiological Effects of Sexual Abuse: A Longitudinal Study." *Annals of the New York Academy of Science* 821 (June 21, 1997): 150–159.

Pynoos, R. S., A. K. Goenjian, and A. M. Steinberg. "Children and Disasters: A Developmental Approach to Posttraumatic Stress Disorder in Children and Adolescents." *Psychiatry and Clinical Neurosciences* 52, no. S1 (1998): S82–S91.

Quinnell, F. A., and J. N. Bow. "Psychological Tests Used in Child Custody Evaluations." *Behavioral Sciences and the Law* 19, no. 4 (2001): 491–501.

Raghavan, C., and S. J. Cohen. "Introduction." In *Domestic Violence: Methodologies in Dialogue*, edited by C. Raghavan and S. J. Cohen, vi–xi. Boston: Northeastern University Press, 2013.

Repitti, R. L., K. A. Mathews, and I. Waldron. "Employment and Women's Health: Effects of Paid Employment on Women's Mental and Physical Health." *American Psychologist* 44, no. 11 (1989): 1394–1401.

Resnick, J. "Asking About Gender in Courts." *Signs* 21 (Summer 1996): 952–960.

Risser, J., A. Messinger, D. Fry, L. Davidson, and P. Schewe. "Do Maternal and Paternal Mental Illness and Substance Abuse Predict Treatment Outcomes for Children Exposed to Violence." *Child Care in Practice* 19, no. 3 (2013): 221–236.

Roberts, K. A. "Women's Experience of Violence During Stalking by Former Romantic Partners." *Violence Against Women* 11, no. 1 (2005): 89–114.

Roddy, S. "Collaborative Practice: Survey of Emerging Case Law." *American Journal of Family Law* 30, no. 2 (2016): 110–111.

Ronner, Amy D. "Women Who Dance on the Professional Track: Custody and the Red Shoes." 23 *Harv. Women's L. J.* 179 (2000).

Roseby, V. "Use of Psychological Testing in a Child-Focused Approach to Child Custody Evaluations." *Family Law Quarterly* 29, no. 1 (1995): 97–110.

Rosen, L. N., and C. S. O'Sullivan. "Outcomes of Custody and Visitation Petitions when Fathers are Restrained by Protection Orders." *Violence Against Women* 11, no. 8 (2005): 1054–1075.

Rudiman, Stacia. "Part Three: Contingencies Constraining Judicial Discretion in Awarding Alimony: Domestic Violence as an Alimony Contingency: Recent Developments in California Law," 22 *J. Contemp. Legal Issues* 498 (2015).

Russell, D. E. "The Incidence and Prevalence of Intrafamilial and Extrafamilial Sexual Abuse." *Child Abuse and Neglect* 7, no. 2 (1983): 133–146.

Rutherford, Jane. "Duty in Divorce: Shared Income as a Path to Equality." 58 *Fordham L. Rev.* 539 (1990).

Sacco, V. F., and H. Johnson. *Patterns of Criminal Victimization in Canada*. Ottawa: Statistics Canada, 1990.

Sanders, C. K. "Economic Abuse in the Lives of Women Abused by an Intimate Partner: A Qualitative Study." *Violence Against Women* 21, no. 1 (2015): 3–29.

Saunders, D. "The Tendency to Arrest Victims of Domestic Violence: A Preliminary Analysis of Officer Characteristics." *Journal of Interpersonal Violence* 10 (June 1, 1995): 147–148.

Saunders, D., K. C. Faller, and R. Tolman. "Beliefs and Recommendations Regarding Child Custody and Visitation in Cases Involving Domestic Violence: A Comparison of Professionals in Different Roles." *Violence Against Women* 22, no. 6 (2015): 722–744.

Saunders, D., K. C. Faller, and R. Tolman. *Child Custody Evaluators' Beliefs About Domestic Abuse Allegations: Their Relationship to Evaluator Demographics, Background, Domestic Violence Knowledge and Custody-Visitation Recommendations*. Washington, DC: National Institute of Justice, 2011.

Scaia, M., and L. Connelly. "With Equal Regard: An Overview of How Ellen Pence Focused the Supervised Visitation Field on Battered Women and Children." *Violence Against Women* 16, no. 9 (2010): 1022–1030.

Schechter, S., and J. L. Edleson. *Effective Intervention in Domestic Violence and Child Maltreatment Cases: Guidelines for Policy and Practice* (also known as the *Greenbook*). Washington, DC: National Council of Juvenile and Family Court Judges, 1999.

Schepard, Andrew. "The Model Standards of Practice for Family and Divorce Mediation." In *Divorce and Family Mediation: Models, Techniques and Applications*, edited by Jay Folberg, Ann L. Milne, and Peter Salem, 516–541. New York: Guilford Publications, 2004.

Schindler, A., and S. Broning. "A Review on Attachment and Adolescent Substance Abuse: Empirical Evidence and Implications for Prevention and Treatment." *Substance Abuse* 36, no. 3 (2015): 304–313.

Schleuder, C., and V. Campagna. "Assessing Substance Abuse Questions in Child Custody Evaluations." *Family Court Review* 42, no. 2 (2004): 375–383.

Schwartz, C. D. "Unified Family Courts: A Saving Grace for Victims of Domestic Violence Living in Nations with Fragmented Court Systems." *Family Court Review* 42, no. 2 (2004): 304–320.

Schwartz, M. D. "Gender and Injury in Marital Assault." *Sociological Focus* 20, no. 1 (1987): 61–75.

Scott, M. E., F. Ballard, C. Sawyer, T. Ross, M. Burkhauser, S. Ericson, and E. Lilja. *The Parenting Coordination Project Implementation and Outcomes Study Report.* Washington, DC: Child Trends for the American Psychological Association Practice Directorate, 2010.

Sedlak, A. J., J. Mettenburg, M. Basena, I. Petta, K. McPherson, K. Greene, and S. Li. *Fourth National Incidence Study of Child Abuse and Neglect (NIS–4): Report to Congress.* Washington, DC: US Department of Health and Human Services, Administration for Children and Families, 2010.

Shepard, M. "Child-visiting and Domestic Abuse." *Child Welfare* 71, no. 4 (1992): 357–367.

Sherman, L. "The Influence of Criminology on Criminal Law: Evaluating for Misdemeanor Domestic Violence." *Journal of Criminal Law and Criminology* 83, no. 1 (1992): 1–45.

Shiono, P. H., and L. Sandham Quinn. "Epidemiology of Divorce, The Future of Children." *Children and Divorce* 4, no. 1 (1994): 15–28.

Shobe, K. K., and J. F. Kihlstrom. "Is Traumatic Memory Special?" *Current Directions in Psychological Science* 6, no. 3 (1997): 70–74.

Shuman, D. W. "What Should We Permit Mental Health Professionals to Say About the 'Best Interests of the Child?': An Essay on Common Sense, Daubert, and the Rules of Evidence." *Family Law Quarterly* 31, no. 3 (1997): 551–569.

Silvergleid, C. S., and E. S. Mankowski. "How Batterer Intervention Programs Work: Participant and Facilitator Accounts of Processes of Change." *Journal of Interpersonal Violence* 21, no. 1 (2006): 139–159.

Simonovic, D. "Global and Regional Standards on Violence Against Women: The Evolution and Synergy of the CEDAW and Istanbul Conventions." *Human Rights Quarterly* 36, no. 3 (2014): 590–606.

Simons, R. L., Les B. Whitbeck, Jay Beaman and Rand D. Conger. "The Impact of Mothers' Parenting, Involvement by Nonresidential Fathers, and Parental Conflict on the Adjustment of Adolescent Children." *Journal of Marriage and Family* 56 (May 1994): 356–374.

Slote, K. Y., C. Cuthbert, C. J. Mesh, M. G. Diggers, L. Bancroft, and J. G. Silverman. "Battered Mothers Speak Out: Participatory Human Rights Documentation as a Model for Research and Activism in the United States." *Violence Against Women* 11, no. 11 (2005): 1367–1395.

Smithburn, John Eric. "The Trial Court's Gatekeeper Role Under Frye, Daubert, and Kumho: A Special Look at Children's Cases." 4 *Whittier J. Child & Fam. Advoc.* 3 (Fall 2004).

St. Joan, Jacqueline. "Building Bridges, Building Walls: Collaboration Between Lawyers and Social Workers in a Domestic Violence Clinic and Issues of Client Confidentiality." 7 *Clinical L. Rev.* 403 (2001).

Staggs, S. L., S. M. Long, G. E. Mason, S. Krishnan, and S. Riger. "Intimate Partner Violence, Social Support, and Employment in the Post-Welfare Reform Era." *Journal of Interpersonal Violence* 22, no. 3 (2007): 345–367.

Stahl, P. M., and L. Martin. "An Historical Look at Child Custody Evaluations and the Influence of AFCC." *Family Court Review* 51, no. 1 (2013): 42–47.

Stark, E. "Commentary on Johnson's 'Conflict and Control: Gender Symmetry and Asymmetry in Domestic Violence.'" *Violence Against Women* 12, no. 11 (2006): 1019–1025.

Stark, E. *Coercive Control: How Men Entrap Women in Personal Life*. New York: Oxford University Press, 2007.

Stark, E. "Reframing Child Custody Decisions in the Context of Coercive Control." In *Domestic Violence, Abuse, and Child Custody: Legal Strategies and Policy Issues*, edited by M. Hannah and B. Goldstein, 11:1–11:31. Kingston, NJ: Civic Research Institute, 2010.

Stark, E. "Rethinking Custody Evaluation in Cases Involving Domestic Violence." *Journal of Child Custody* 6, no. 3 (2009): 287–321.

Stets, J. E. "Gender Differences in Reporting Marital Violence and Its Medical and Psychological Consequences." In *Physical Violence in American Families*, edited by M. A. Straus and R. J. Gelles, 151–165. New Brunswick, NJ: Transaction Publishers, 1990.

Stevens-Simon, C., and S. Reichert. "Sexual Abuse, Adolescent Pregnancy, and Child Abuse: A Developmental Approach to an Intergenerational Cycle." *Archives of Pediatrics and Adolescent Medicine* 148, no. 1 (1994): 23–27.

Stover, C. S., P. Van Horn, R. Turner, B. Cooper, and A. F. Lieberman. "The Effects of Father Visitation on Preschool-Aged Witnesses of Domestic Violence." *Journal of Interpersonal Violence* 18, no. 10 (2003): 1149–1166.

Straus, M. A. "Blaming the Messenger for the Bad News About Partner Violence by Women: The Methodological, Theoretical, and Value Basis of the Purported Invalidity of the Conflict Tactics Scales." *Behavioral Sciences and the Law* 30, no. 5 (2012): 538–556.

Straus, M. A., and R. J. Gelles. *Physical Violence in American Families—Codebook 7733*. Ann Arbor, MI: Institute for Social Research, 1980.

Straus, M. A., S. Hamby, S. Boney-McCoy, and D. Sugarman, "The Revised Conflict Tactics Scales (CTS2): Development and Preliminary Psychometric Data." *Journal of Family Issues* 17, no. 3 (1996): 283–316.

Straus, R. B. "Supervised Visitation and Family Violence." *Family Law Quarterly* 29, no. 2 (1995): 229–252.

Styron, T. H., M. K. Pruett, T. J. McMahon, and L. Davidson. "Fathers with Serious Mental Illness: A Neglected Group." *Psychiatric Rehabilitation Journal* 25, no. 3 (2002): 215–222.

Sung, H., and S. Belenko. "Failure After Success: Correlates of Recidivism Among Individuals Who Successfully Completed Coerced Drug Treatment." *Journal of Offender Rehabilitation* 42, no. 1 (2005): 75–97.

Swent, Jeannette F. "Gender Bias at the Heart of Justice: An Empirical Study of State Task Forces." 6 *S. Cal. Rev. L. & Women's Stud.* 1 (1996).

Swisher, Peter N. "The ALI Principles: A Farewell to Fault—But What Remedy for the Egregious Marital Misconduct of an Abusive Spouse?" 8 *Duke J. Gender L. & Pol'y* 213 (2001).

Testa, M., B. M. Quigley, and K. E. Leonard. "Does Alcohol Make a Difference? Within-participants Comparison of Incidents of Partner Violence." *Journal of Interpersonal Violence* 18, no. 7 (2003): 735–743.

Thoennes, N., and J. Pearson. "Supervised Visitation: A Profile of Providers." *Family Court Review* 37, no. 4 (1999): 460–477.

Tippins, T. M., and J. P. Wittman. "Empirical and Ethical Problems with Custody Recommendations: A Call for Clinical Humility and Judicial Vigilance." *Family Court Review* 43, no. 2 (2005): 193–222.

Tjaden, P., and N. Thoennes. *Full Report on the Prevalence, Incidence, and Consequences of Violence Against Women*. Washington, DC: National Institute of Justice, 2000.

Tollefson, D. R., E. Gross, and B. Lundahl. "Factors that Predict Attrition from a State-Sponsored Rural Batterer Treatment Program." *Journal of Aggression, Maltreatment and Trauma* 17, no. 4 (2008): 453–477.

Tower, L. E. "Domestic Violence Screening: Education and Institutional Support Correlates." *Journal of Social Work Education* 39, no. 3 (2003): 479–494.

Trocmé, N., and N. Bala. "False Allegations of Abuse and Neglect when Parents Separate." *Child Abuse and Neglect* 29, no. 12 (2005): 1333–1345.

Trocmé, N., B. MacLaurin, B. Fallon, J. Daciuk, D. Billingsley, M. Tourigny, M. Mayer, J. Wright, K. Barter, G. Burford, J. Hornick, R. Sullivan, and B. McKenzie. *Canadian Incidence Study of Reported Child Abuse and Neglect: Final Report*. Ottawa: Minister of Public Works and Government Services Canada, 2001.

United States Census Bureau. *Statistical Abstract of the United States: 1989*. Washington, DC: United States Census Bureau, 1989.

van Ijzendoum, M., and P. Kroonenberg. "Cross-cultural Patterns of Attachment: A Meta-Analysis of the Strange Situation." *Child Development* 59, no. 1 (1988): 147–156.

Ver Steegh, Nancy. "Yes, No, and Maybe: Informed Decision Making About Divorce Mediation in the Presence of Domestic Violence." 9 *Wm. & Mary J. Women & L.* 145 (June 2006).

Ver Steegh, N., and C. Dalton. "Report from the Wingspan Conference on Domestic Violence and Family Courts." *Family Court Review* 46, no. 3 (2008): 454–475.

Voices of Women Organizing Project. *Justice Denied: How Family Courts in New York City Endanger Battered Women and Children*. Brooklyn, NY: Battered Women's Resource Center, 2008.

Volpe, J. S. "Effects of Domestic Violence on Children and Adolescents: An Overview." 1996. The American Academy of Experts in Traumatic Stress. Accessed on March 22, 2017 http://www.aaets.org/article8.htm

Waksberg, J. "Representing Children on Appeal: Changed Circumstances, Changed Mind." *The Journal of Appellate Practice and Process* 12, no. 2 (2011): 313–329.

Waldman, E., and L. A. Ojelabi. "Mediators and Substantive Justice: A View from Rawls' Original Position." *Ohio State Journal on Dispute Resolution* 30, no. 3 (2016): 391–430.

Walker, E. A., A. Gelfand, W. Katon, M. Koss, M. Von Korff, D. Bernstein, and J. Russo. "Adult Health Status of Women with Histories of Childhood Abuse and Neglect." *The American Journal of Medicine* 107, no. 4 (1999): 332–339.

Walker, L. E. *The Battered Woman*. New York: Harper and Row, 1979.

Walker, L. E. *The Battered Woman Syndrome*. New York: Springer Publishing, 1984.

Walker, R., T. K. Logan, C. E. Jordan, and J. C. Campbell. "An Integrative Review of Separation in the Context of Victimization: Consequences and Implications for Women." *Trauma, Violence, & Abuse* 5, no. 2 (2004): 143–193.

Wallerstein, J. S., and J. B. Kelly. *Surviving the Breakup: How Children and Parents Cope with Divorce.* New York: Basic Books, 1980.

Wallerstein, J. S., J. M. Lewis, and S. Blakeslee. *The Unexpected Legacy of Divorce: A 25 Year Landmark Study.* New York: Hyperion, 2000.

Warrener, C., J. M. Koivunen, and J. L. Postmus. "Economic Self-Sufficiency Among Divorced Women: Impact of Depression, Abuse, and Efficacy." *Journal of Divorce & Remarriage* 54, no. 2 (2013): 163–175.

Weitzman, L. J. *The Divorce Revolution: The Unexpected Social and Economic Consequences for Women and Children in America.* New York: Free Press, 1985.

Widom, C. Spatz, K. G. Raphael, and K. A. DuMont. "The Case for Prospective Longitudinal Studies in Child Maltreatment Research: Commentary on Dube, Williamson, Thompson, Felitti, and Anda." *Child Abuse and Neglect* 28, no. 7 (2004): 715–722.

Winick, Bruce J., and David B. Wexler. "The Use of Therapeutic Jurisprudence in Law School Clinical Education: Transforming the Criminal Law Clinic." 13 *Clinical L. Rev.* 605 (2006).

Wolff, N. "Courting the Courts: Courts as Agents for Treatment and Justice." In *Community-Based Interventions for Criminal Offenders with Severe Mental Illness*, edited by W. H. Fisher, 43–198. Boston: JAI Press, 2003.

Wood, Cheri L. "The Parental Alienation Syndrome: A Dangerous Aura of Reliability." 27 *Loy. L.A. L. Rev.* 1367 (1994).

Woodhouse, J., and N. Dempsey. "Domestic Violence in England and Wales." *House of Commons Library, Briefing Paper 6337* (6 May 2016): 1–18.

World Health Organization. *The World Health Report 2002: Reducing Risks, Promoting Healthy Life.* Geneva: World Health Organization, 2002.

Wyatt, G. E. "The Sexual Abuse of Afro-American and White-American Women in Childhood." *Child Abuse and Neglect* 9, no. 4 (1985): 507–519.

Yeamans, R. "Urgent Need for Quality Control in Child Custody Psychological Evaluations." In *Domestic Violence, Abuse, and Child Custody: Legal Strategies and Policy Issues*, edited by M. Hannah and B. Goldstein, 21:1–21:21. Kingston, NJ: Civic Research Institute, 2010.

Zeoli, A. M., E. A. Rivera, C. M. Sullivan, and S. Kubiak. "Post-Separation Abuse of Women and Their Children: Boundary-Setting and Family Court Utilization Among Victimized Mothers." *Journal of Family Violence* 28, no. 6 (2013): 547–560.

Zorza, J. "New Typologies: A Reinvention or a Trivialization?" (Unpublished manuscript, undated), Microsoft Word file.

Zorza, J. "On Navigating Custody & Visitation Evaluations in Cases with Domestic Violence: A Judge's Guide." *Journal of Child Custody* 6, no. 3/4 (2011): 258–286.

INDEX

domestic violence as gendered crime against, 35, 91
gender bias toward
  in family courts, 198
as initiators of domestic violence, 42
international law protections for, 85–86
at risk of abuse years after separation, 45
Women and Men in the Courts
  NJEP for
    on gender bias, 74–75
Women at the Court House, 208

women shelter populations
  research on domestic violence concentrated on, 38–39
World Health Organization
  on abuse, 103

young children
  harmful effects of overnight visitations on, 21
  harmful effects of repeated separations on, 21